Reframing Resolution

Richard Saundry • Paul Latreille • Ian Ashman
Editors

Reframing Resolution

Innovation and Change in the Management
of Workplace Conflict

Editors
Richard Saundry
Plymouth Business School
Plymouth University
Plymouth, United Kingdom

Paul Latreille
Sheffield University Management School
Sheffield, United Kingdom

Ian Ashman
University of Central Lancashire
Lancashire Business School
Preston, United Kingdom

ISBN 978-1-137-51559-9   ISBN 978-1-137-51560-5   (eBook)
DOI 10.1057/978-1-137-51560-5

Library of Congress Control Number: 2016941471

Printed on acid-free paper

This Palgrave Macmillan imprint is published by Springer Nature
The registered company is Macmillan Publishers Ltd. London

Acknowledgements

The editors would like to thank all the contributors for their work in compiling this volume and also Sir Brendan Barber for writing the foreword. We would also like to acknowledge the support of the Advisory, Conciliation and Arbitration Service (Acas) in funding the empirical research which features in a number of Chapters. Furthermore we would like to acknowledge the funding of the Economic and Social Research Council for the seminar series 'Reframing Resolution – Managing Conflict and Resolving Individual Employment Disputes in the Contemporary Workplace' (Grant number: ES/J022276/1) which provided the foundation for this book.

Contents

Notes on Contributors

Ian Ashman is Director of the Institute for Research into Organisations, Work and Employment at the University of Central Lancashire. He has researched and published widely on various related subjects including downsizing, conflict, engagement, leadership and ethics. He is interested in the application of existentialism to these and similar topics.

Ariel Avgar is Associate Professor and Associate Dean at the School of Labor and Employment Relations at the University of Illinois at Urbana-Champaign. His research interests include organizational conflict management and dispute resolution and employment relations in the healthcare setting. He holds a PhD in Industrial Relations from the ILR School at Cornell University.

Greg Bamber is a Professor in the Department of Management, Monash University where he has served as: Director of Research & Discipline Leader: Human Resources & Employment Relations. He has more than a hundred academic publications, including in many refereed journals. He has also published numerous edited book chapters and several books.

Anthony Bennett is a freelance researcher and also a Director of RTB Consultancy. He formerly worked as Senior Lecturer in HRM at Sheffield Hallam University and the University of Central Lancashire. He is a practising mediator and has research interests in conflict management, equality and diversity, employee engagement and employee representation.

Virginia Branney is a part-time PhD student at the University of Central Lancashire. Since 1999, she has been an employment relations consultant and mediator. She is a member of the UK Employment Appeal Tribunal and also the Central Arbitration Committee. Prior to that, she was a national official for UNISON and the National Union of Public Employees.

Wonjoon Chung is a doctoral student in the School of Labor and Employment Relations, University of Illinois at Urbana-Champaign. His research interests include conflict in organizations, conflict management, and dispute resolution.

Gill Dix is Head of Strategy at the Advisory, Conciliation and Arbitration Service (Acas). She formerly held the role of Head of Research and Evaluation at Acas. Gill has a background in social and public policy research having worked in a number of public sector bodies, academia and the voluntary sector.

Liam Doherty is Managing Director of Ask HR Ltd, a private HR consultancy company and was formerly a Director of the Industrial Relations and Human Resources Division in IBEC, the national employers' organization in Ireland. He completed a PhD at The Queen's University, Belfast, which examined conflict management and dispute resolution systems in MNCs based in the Republic of Ireland.

John Forth is a principal research fellow and a member of the Employment Group at the National Institute of Economic and Social Research in London. His research is focused in three areas: the quality of employment relations; pay and rewards; and economic performance.

Jonny Gifford is CIPD Research Adviser for organizational behaviour. His interests include employee voice, social technology, workplace conflict and the application of behavioural science to HR. Previous research roles were at Roffey Park Institute and the Institute for Employment Studies.

Matthew Gould is a research fellow in the Centre for Employment Research at the University of Westminster, specializing in quantitative data analysis and mathematical models of behaviour. Matthew has worked on a variety of government commissioned projects and his work has been published in highly rated journals such as *Public Choice*.

Carol Jones is Principal Lecturer in Human Resource Management in the School of Management at the University of Central Lancashire, where she is also the Leader of the HRM Division. Her research interests include dispute resolution, the workplace impact of domestic violence and the impact of domestic violence and the role of trade union representatives.

Ryan Lamare is an assistant professor in the School of Labor and Employment Relations at the University of Illinois at Urbana-Champaign. His research interests include: labor and employment arbitration; ADR in the securities industry; the development of ADR systems in organizations; the role of unions in politics; employment relations and HR at multinational companies; and quantitative research methods. He has published extensively on these issues and serves on the editorial board at *Human Resource Management Journal*.

Paul Latreille is Professor of Management and Associate Dean for Learning and Teaching at Sheffield University Management School. His research in applied labour economics and employment relations focuses on workplace conflict, mediation/ADR and Employment Tribunals. He has published extensively for academic and policymaker/practitioner audiences, and has completed numerous externally-commissioned projects.

David B. Lipsky is the Anne Evans Estabrook Professor of Dispute Resolution in the School of Industrial and Labor Relations, and Director of the Scheinman Institute on Conflict Resolution at Cornell University. He served as the national president of the Labor and Employment Relations Association (formerly the Industrial Relations Research Association) in 2006. In his research and teaching activities he primarily focuses on negotiation, conflict resolution, and collective bargaining. David Lipsky served as Dean of the School of Industrial and Labor Relations at Cornell from 1988 until 1997.

Louise McArdle is Principal Lecturer and Leader of the Strategy and Enterprise Division in the School of Management at the University of Central Lancashire. She is also a member of the Institute for Research into Organisations, Work and Employment and has previously published in the areas of workplace flexibility, TQM and Fair Trade.

Eric J. Neuman is Associate Professor of Management at the Heider College of Business at Creighton University and earned his PhD from the University of Michigan. In addition to research on intragroup conflict, he has studied deregulation, corporate political activity, corporate foundations, and social network methodologies

William Roche is Professor of Industrial Relations and Human Resources at the School of Business, University College Dublin and Honorary Professor at the Management School, Queen's University, Belfast. He has published extensively in leading international peer-reviewed journals in industrial relations and human resource management. His recent books include *The Oxford Handbook of Conflict Management in Organizations,* Oxford University Press, 2014 (with Paul Teague and Alex Colvin).

Richard Saundry is Professor of HRM and Employment Relations at Plymouth University. His research interests are the management of workplace conflict and employee representation. He has published articles in a wide range of leading journals. He is a member of the editorial board of *Work, Employment and Society* and a Research and Policy Associate at Acas.

Paul Teague is Professor of Management at Queen's University, Belfast. He has written widely on the theme of the employment relations consequences of deeper European integration, social partnership and employment performance, workplace conflict management and human resources in the recession. He is co-editor with William Roche and Alex Colvin of *The Oxford Handbook of Conflict Management in Organizations,* which was published in 2014 by Oxford University Press.

Julian Teicher is Professor of Industrial Relations and the Director of Research in the Department of Management at Monash University and Director of the Australian Consortium for Research on Employment and Work. His research is in employment relations and public policy and management. He has published widely on topics including: conflict management, employee voice, privatisation, and e-governance.

Pete Thomas is a senior lecturer in the Department of Organisation Work and Technology at Lancaster University. His research interests centre on the place of discourse in organizations and applying Critical Discourse Analysis to investigate professionalization, mediation schemes and strategic management processes.

Peter Urwin is Director of the Centre for Employment Research, and Professor of Applied Economics at the University of Westminster. He has over 15 years' experience leading large-scale evaluations for government departments, including DWP, BIS, MoJ and MoD. Peter works in the areas of conflict resolution; education and employment economics; and equality and diversity.

Bernadine Van Gramberg is Professor and Dean of Swinburne Business School at Swinburne University of Technology. Bernadine's teaching, research and consulting are in the fields of workplace dispute resolution and public sector management.

Gemma Wibberley is a research associate at the Institute for Research into Organisations, Work and Employment, at the University of Central Lancashire. Her research interests include employees' experiences in the contemporary workplace, workplace conflict, and relationships with unions.

Abbreviations

Acas	Advisory, Conciliation and Arbitration Service (UK)
ACCI	Australian Chamber of Commerce and Industry
ACTU	Australian Council of Trade Unions
ADR	Alternative Dispute Resolution
BCC	British Chambers of Commerce
BIS	Department of Business, Innovation and Skills (UK)
CBI	Confederation of British Industry
CDA	Critical Discourse Analysis
CIPD	Chartered Institute of Personnel and Development
CMS	Conflict Management Systems
CPR	International Institute for Conflict Prevention and Resolution (CPR)
EC	Early conciliation
EIRO	European Industrial Relations Observatory
ET	Employment Tribunal (UK)
FMCS	US Federal Mediation and Conciliation Service
FTW	Fair Treatment at Work Survey Service
FWC	Fair Work Commission (Australia)
HSE	Health Service Executive (Republic of Ireland)
ICMS	Integrated Conflict Management System
ILO	International Labour Organization
LRC	Labour Relations Commission (Republic of Ireland)
MNC	Multi-national corporation
NHCT	National Health Service (UK)

NHS   National Health Service (UK)
PCC   Pre-claim Conciliation
PCT   Primary Care Trust
SACCMA   South African Commission for Conciliation, Mediation and
          Arbitration
SIPTU   Services, Industrial, Professional and Technical Union (Republic
          of Ireland)
STUC   Scottish Trades Union Congress
TEEU   Technical, Electrical & Engineering Union (Republic of Ireland)
TUC   Trades Union Congress (UK)
WERS   Workplace Employment Relations Study

List of Figures

List of Tables

1

Introduction

Ian Ashman, Paul Latreille, and Richard Saundry

Conflict at work is an important, and some would say, inevitable part of organizational life. However, the way in which it is expressed has undergone significant changes in recent years. In particular, we have seen a substantial reduction in the incidence of collective forms of industrial action, in most developed economies (Belanger and Edwards 2013). At the same time, increased attention has been given to individual manifestations of conflict, such as employee grievances or employment litigation, or more informal expressions such as absence and forms of workplace 'misbehaviour' (Ackroyd

I. Ashman
iROWE (Institute for Research into Organisations, Work and Employment),
University of Central Lancashire, Preston, UK
e-mail: iashman@uclan.ac.uk

P. Latreille
Sheffield University Management School, Sheffield, UK
e-mail: p.latreille@sheffield.ac.uk

R. Saundry
Plymouth Business School, Plymouth University, Plymouth, UK
e-mail: richard.saundry@plymouth.ac.uk

© The Editor(s) (if applicable) and The Author(s) 2016   **1**
R. Saundry et al. (eds.), *Reframing Resolution*,
DOI 10.1057/978-1-137-51560-5_1

and Thompson 1999; Saundry and Dix 2014). While a significant onus is often placed on the direct costs to the organization of individual employment disputes, the underlying conflict, which gives rise to such disputes, has major implications for the health and well-being of employees as well as threatening the psychological contract and limiting productivity (De Dreu 2008). Consequently, finding ways to manage and resolve workplace conflict is a key issue for employers, trade unions and policymakers.

This book introduces new empirical research from scholars brought together through a seminar series funded by the UK Economic and Social Research Council (ESRC) entitled 'Reframing Resolution – Managing Conflict and Resolving Individual Employment Disputes in the Contemporary Workplace' that concluded in September 2013. This in turn developed from a programme of research into conflict management in the UK funded by the Advisory, Conciliation and Arbitration Service (Acas) from which a number of the contributions in this volume are drawn.

For the most part, the evidence presented in the following chapters is located within the setting of the UK economy. However, the issues raised have relevance worldwide, and so to facilitate wider international contextualisation and comparison, as well as reflect international contributions to the seminar series itself, there are chapters focusing on experiences in the USA, Ireland and Australia. The aim of the book is to advance our understanding of contemporary theory and practice relating to the management of employment conflict and the extent to which innovative approaches are being developed and diffused. It seeks to contribute not only to academic debates but also to provide key insights for management and union practitioners responsible for day-to-day handling of conflict in the workplace.

Each chapter is self-contained and can be read independently of the other contributions. However, when taken as a whole, the content of this book presents a general argument that changes in the management and regulation of work have created a 'resolution gap' that current policy approaches and organizational strategies fail to acknowledge or address. For instance, the erosion of workplace representation, the changing nature of the human resource management function and the questionable people management abilities of many front-line managers are trends that are not confined to the UK, and so a particular emphasis of this book is to examine how organizations in the UK, USA, Ireland and

Australia are responding to such challenges in the development of new and innovative approaches to the management of conflict and dispute resolution. What follows is divided into four parts that take us from a careful delineation and conceptualization of workplace conflict, through an exploration of how conflict is experienced on the front lines of organizational activity and consideration of alternative dispute resolution theory and practice, to an examination of contemporary perspectives on conflict management.

The first part – *Surveying the Terrain* – begins with a chapter by Richard Saundry that seeks to overcome the lack of definitional clarity that has hampered our understanding of conflict management and dispute resolution over the years. There is a tendency in both academic and practitioner literature to conceive of conflict in generic and malleable ways. For many stakeholders conflict refers simply to the manifestations of discontent, which in turn shapes debates over the impact and importance of conflict as an organizational phenomenon. If, for instance, conflict is treated traditionally as synonymous with collective industrial disputes, then the decline in the incidence of industrial action across developed economies may be interpreted as reflecting either the decline of workplace unrest or the individualization of conflict (or both). Saundry counters such an assumption by arguing that the nature and extent of workplace conflict have altered relatively little, whereas the channels through which conflict is expressed and potentially resolved have changed considerably.

In Chap. 3, John Forth and Gill Dix draw on a range of large-scale survey data to examine the changing patterns of workplace conflict in the UK. In keeping with Saundry's assessment, they find little evidence of significant change in the incidence of employment disputes, but do suggest that despite the UK (in common with many countries) suffering the longest recession in living memory, there may be a progressive trend towards lower levels of conflict at work. Nevertheless, they also question the effectiveness of dispute resolution in UK organizations given the limited coverage of employee representation combined with questions over the ability of managers to tackle difficult human resource issues. Indeed, in Chap. 4 Jonny Gifford, Matthew Gould, Paul Latreille and Peter Urwin identify a disconnection between the perceptions of managers and their subordinates regarding their experiences of conflict and disputes. A key finding from their analysis of a representative survey of employees undertaken by the Chartered Institute of Personnel and Development is that those occupying managerial roles seem much more positive about the extent to which disputes have been resolved than those they manage, which has important implications for the handling of such problems.

The fourth and final chapter of Part 1 is a contribution from the USA by Ariel Avgar, Eric Neuman and Wonjoon Chung. They emphasize the importance of social structure and social capital as constructs that underpin and contextualize workplace conflict. They cite recent empirical research and earlier work by Avgar to argue that the strong social ties within small workgroups (organizations and teams) are likely to help resolve or suppress emergent conflict, and they find that the negative impact of internal disputes on group relationships are less likely where organizational leaders create social structures that anticipate successfully the likelihood and nature of inter- and intra-team conflict.

Having set the scene, Part 2 of this book sets out to examine how conflict and its resolution is experienced by personnel on the 'front line' of organizational product and service delivery. Chapter 6, from Carol Jones and Richard Saundry, goes straight to the heart of the matter by evaluating the evidence from a series of in-depth UK case studies that point to a crisis of confidence among operational line managers. The inherent contradictions for such managers seeking to, on the one hand, satisfy organizational performance demands, while on the other hand trying to maintain constructive relations with and between their subordinates are exacerbated by a fear of litigation or internal censure that leads them to avoid options for informal dispute resolution and to defer to formal procedure and their professional HR colleagues instead. Jones and Saundry's analysis points to the importance of a constructive relationship between line managers and HR practitioners. In particular, they argue that the prevailing attitude of HR professionals can over-emphasize the procedural aspects of conflict handling and that the increasing 'distance' between the HR function and operational managers makes creative and early dispute resolution less likely.

In Chap. 7 Gemma Wibberley and Richard Saundry draw on the same UK case studies to explore the relationship between employee voice and conflict management. Their assessment indicates that effective channels for employee voice are important in identifying and resolving workplace disputes between individuals, but they express reservations about the decline of employee representation in organizations and especially through recognized trade unions. There is some evidence that non-unionized employee representatives and employee engagement strategies in high-trust environments may help workers to voice their concerns pertaining to conflict and dispute, but that such alternatives do not replace sufficiently the absence of trade union representation. In the last Chap. 8 of Part 2, Ian Ashman examines a context specific site for organizational conflict – the downsizing or restructuring event. His own field study of 'downsizing envoys' – the people that deliver face-to-face the news of redundancy to victims – shows that whilst downsizing and restructuring is generally traumatic and rife with potential for conflict, it is by no means inevitable or predictable. He provides a compelling account of the challenges faced by 'envoys' and highlights the unexpected disputes and alliances that can occur among the various protagonists during downsizing exercises.

Part 3 of this book retains the empirically grounded approach to understanding conflict but shifts attention to dispute resolution. Mediation and other alternative dispute resolution practices are often seen as an antidote to some of the problems and challenges outlined in Parts 1 and 2. Mediation in particular, is argued to provide a successful and cost effective way of resolving conflict, as well as having a positive effect on the conflict-handling abilities of any parties who experience it first-hand. As such it may therefore offer an opportunity to counter the management skills deficit identified in Chap. 6. Some commentators and indeed policymakers have even suggested that mediation can transform the culture of conflict management. Ultimately, however, most mediation research has tended to adopt either a managerial focus, emphasizing the organizational experiences and impact of mediation, or one which highlights the role of mediators themselves, so the voice of disputants has largely been absent. In Chap. 9, Tony Bennett examines the mediation process from the disputant's perspective by drawing on a unique dataset of in-depth interviews with employees who have taken part in workplace mediation. He explores the trajectory of individual disputes and assesses participants' views of the effectiveness of mediation provision and the sustainability of the outcomes. The chapter not only sheds light on key issues such as workplace justice and the voluntary nature of mediation but also highlights lessons for organization in implementing mediation strategies. He finds that while mediation offers a positive and often cathartic opportunity to voice concerns, the more pragmatic focus on resolution often fails to address underlying concerns of justice.

Justice, and how it is seen to be done, is clearly a major concern for trade unions, which have often adopted a somewhat sceptical opinion of mediation, viewing it suspiciously as a managerial tool designed to undermine the ability of unions to enforce the 'rights' of the members through more conventional grievance processes. Perhaps surprisingly then, Virginia Branney, in Chap. 10, argues that whilst union representatives do place significant store in rights-based procedures, they nevertheless have a generally positive attitude to the use of mediation in specific contexts. Branney draws on her own recent survey of trade union representatives, the first such study of the attitudes of union activists and officers towards workplace mediation, and asks whether the wider use of mediation offers an opportunity to extend trade union influence over decision-making, or whether it may be a threat to their traditional representative role? She argues that mediation is not a replacement for more conventional grievance procedures but might provide a means through which unions can achieve improved outcomes for their members and at the same time demonstrate their effectiveness.

The next two chapters offer examples from outside the UK of how ADR techniques have been used in innovative ways. While much of this book emphasizes and examines trends towards the management of individual conflict, it is important not to neglect the collective dimension. To this end, in Chap. 11, Bill Roche looks at the growing field of the private facilitation of collective bargaining in Ireland during both dispute and non-dispute situations. Drawing on interviews with prominent and experienced privately-engaged facilitators and on detailed case studies, his discussion explores the nature and objectives of private facilitation, the influences on the use of private facilitators and the consequent outcomes. By contrast, Bernadine Van Gramberg, Julian Teicher and Greg Bamber, in Chap. 12, examine developments in the approach taken by the Australian Fair Work Commission (the national employment tribunal provider) in responding to the growing number of unrepresented parties appearing at tribunals. Using evidence from interviews with tribunal members, they explore and discuss apparent the shift towards using ADR methods in the context of the growing individualization of Australian employment relations.

To end Part 3, Louise McArdle and Pete Thomas offer, in Chap. 13, a critical account of the development of in-house mediation schemes by applying critical discourse analysis to a body of Acas-funded qualitative case study research data to explore the antagonistic relations in an organization and the role of articulation in the development of mediation. They focus on the importance of organizational context, and caution against the use of mediation as a panacea for workplace conflict. In some respects their conclusion is fairly consistent with more mainstream accounts which argue that mediation alone is unlikely to have any material impact on organizational approaches to conflict management. Their emphasis that the role of key actors (in their case particular managers and trade union officials) in the development of mediation schemes must be placed in context of the conjuncture of social and power relations and institutional structures that are found in organizations echoes aspects of the arguments presented by Ariel Avgar, Eric Neuman and Wonjoon Chung in Chap. 5.

To close the book, Part 4 provides an assessment of significant innovations in conflict handling across the USA, UK and Ireland. The idea of 'integrated conflict management systems' (ICMS) has gained increased traction in the USA in recent years, and Chap. 14, presented by David Lipsky, Ryan Lamare and Ariel Avgar, reviews the development of ICMS by drawing on their ground-breaking study of the conflict management practices of Fortune 1,000 corporations. Their evidence suggests that there has been a diffusion of innovative conflict resolution techniques among these 'blue-chip' organizations, and that there are signs of coherent and complementary bundles of rights and interest-based processes being adopted. They examine the factors and forces that have been driving such developments. Traditionally, it has been argued that ADR has been largely triggered by a desire to avoid unionization and, perhaps more importantly, by the high cost of employment litigation in the USA. However, Lipsky and his co-authors suggest that moves towards ICMS represent strategic managerial choices taken in response to competitive and regulatory pressures but also in pursuit of wider organizational goals.

Their conclusion is supported by Paul Latreille and Richard Saundry's detailed case study (Chap. 15) of the introduction of a more integrated and systemic approach to conflict resolution in a large health service provider in the UK. The case is notable because evidence of strategic approaches to conflict management in the UK is very rare. Here, mediation and a range of other interventions were developed, in part at least, as a response to growing problems of bullying and harassment in an environment characterized by pressures to meet targets and increase efficiency. However, it was crucially also seen as a proactive way of changing the culture of the organization, improving employee well-being and ultimately providing an environment in which patient care could be maximized. Nevertheless, as Louise McArdle and Pete Thomas suggest in Chap. 13, context may be critical, so in the case of the health service provider, the development of a more strategic approach was dependent on senior management to acknowledge both the inevitability of conflict and the importance of resolution. Moreover, the strategy was underpinned by the support of key stakeholders working in partnership.

The final chapter of Part 4, which draws on Liam Doherty and Paul Teague's research into non-union subsidiaries of overseas owned multinational corporations operating in Ireland, paints a contrasting picture from that of Paul Latreille and Richard Saundry's case. In the organizations that they examine, conflict is pushed to the margins and characterized as dissidence. They do, however, argue that this is not simply an avoidance of the issue but a deliberate attempt to develop organizational citizenship behaviour in which conflict is seen as pathological and that those involved in conflict are characterized as unhelpful dissenters.

Each of the chapters that follow, and which we have introduced above, provides an important contribution to both the evidence base and the debate over conflict management. Together they address a number of key questions which we will return to in our concluding commentary, including: How can we understand changes in the nature and pattern of conflict in the UK? What are the main barriers and challenges to the effective management of conflict? What is the potential of workplace mediation and the development of ADR? And to what extent are organizations adopting strategic and integrated approaches to managing workplace conflict?

References

Ackroyd, S., & Thompson, P. (1999). *Organizational misbehaviour*. London: Sage.

Belanger, J., & Edwards, P. (2013). Conflict and contestation in the contemporary world of work: Theory and perspectives. In G. Gall (Ed.), *New forms and expressions of conflict at work* (pp. 7–25). Basingstoke: Palgrave Macmillan.

De Dreu, C. (2008). The virtue and vice of workplace conflict: Food for (pessimistic) thought. *Journal of Organizational Behaviour, 29*, 5–18.

Saundry, R., & Dix, G. (2014). Conflict resolution in the UK. In W. Roche, P. Teague, & A. Colvin (Eds.), *The oxford handbook on conflict management in organizations*. Oxford: Oxford University Press.

Part I

Surveying the Terrain

2

Conceptualizing Workplace Conflict and Conflict Management

Richard Saundry

Introduction

As Paul Edwards has argued, 'conflict is one of the major underlying principles of relations between managers and workers' (1995: 434). A representative survey conducted by the CIPD in 2014 (and discussed in Chap. 4 of this book) found that 38% of people in the UK had experienced some form of conflict at work in the previous 12 months and 28% had 'ongoing difficult relationships' (CIPD 2015). Managing conflict is also clearly a central part of the day-to-day activities of employment relations practitioners. In the Workplace Employment Relations Study 2011, more than nine out of ten British HR practitioners reported spending time on disciplinary and grievance issues, a greater proportion than training, diversity, appraisals and pay. Similarly, discipline and grievance were the most common issues to which trade union representatives devoted attention (van Wanrooy et al. 2013).

R. Saundry (✉)
Plymouth Business School, Plymouth University, Plymouth, UK
e-mail: richard.saundry@plymouth.ac.uk

© The Editor(s) (if applicable) and The Author(s) 2016   **13**
R. Saundry et al. (eds.), *Reframing Resolution*,
DOI 10.1057/978-1-137-51560-5_2

One of the defining features of contemporary employment relations has been the rapid decline in the incidence of collective expressions of industrial conflict across developed economies. Academic research and analysis of conflict was traditionally preoccupied with collective industrial action; however, as this has become less frequent, academics have been relatively slow to turn their attention to individualised employment disputes, which, it could be argued, play a significantly greater role in the lives of workers and their organizations. Furthermore, both policy and academic debates over workplace conflict and its management are often plagued by a lack of conceptual precision. Perhaps most importantly, within academic literature the 'links between wider processes of conflict and overt disputes are rarely discussed' (Edwards 1995: 434).

Therefore, in this chapter we attempt to lay a basic conceptual foundation for the wide-ranging empirical analyses contained in this book. We start by defining conflict and drawing an important distinction between its manifestations, both informal and formal. We then explore the utility of existing theoretical frameworks before considering the dynamics of conflict formation and escalation. Finally, we examine how processes of dispute resolution and conflict management have been, and can be, understood.

Defining Conflict

A problem with contemporary debates over the management of conflict is a definitional malleability when discussing key concepts. As Belanger and Edwards (2013: 7) have pointed out, conflict can refer to 'underlying antagonisms or clashes of interests' and also 'concrete actions' such as strikes. However, Dix et al. (2009) draw a sharp and useful distinction between 'conflict' and 'disputes'. Conflict they argue, should be defined as '*discontent arising from a perceived clash of interests*'. Irrespective of the underlying causes, conflict can be triggered by a wide range of different factors but, as the definition above suggests, this 'discontent' is not always visible. Disputes, however, represent '*manifest expressions*' of that discontent. This is important because it also allows us to make a clear conceptual separation between 'conflict management' as an activity designed to address, accommodate and mediate discontent as opposed to 'dispute resolution' which describes attempts made to deal with manifest expressions of conflict.

Importantly, conflict can become manifest without necessarily escalating into a 'dispute' and can instead be expressed in a variety of informal and often covert ways. For example, individuals or groups of workers may choose not to voice concerns and/or may indirectly articulate them through absence, quitting or lower levels of performance. Furthermore, discontent can also be realised through petty theft (pilfering), mischief or misbehaviour, where rules are deliberately breached and even through industrial sabotage. Clark Kerr (1964) argued that expressions of conflict:

> ...are as unlimited as the ingenuity of man. The strike is the most common and visible expression. But conflict with the employer may also take the form of peaceful bargaining and grievance handling, of boycotts, of political action, of restriction of output, of sabotage, of absenteeism, and turnover, may take place on an individual as well as an organized basis and constitute alternatives to collective action (1964: 171)

Despite the increasing influence of unitaristic perspectives within both policy and organizational practice, conflict is rooted in the nature of the employment relationship. Although there are clearly areas in which the interests of workers and employees mesh with those of employers, the logic of production relations within capitalist economies infers a fundamental difference of interests, as Baldamus (1961) argued, '...*as wages are costs to the firm, and the deprivations inherent in effort mean "costs" to the employee, the interests of management and wage earner are diametrically opposed*'. In practice, this means that the balance of wage and effort (see Behrend 1957) is subject to a constant process of negotiation and re-negotiation (Edwards 1994) and it is here where workplace conflict is generated. This may involve discontent over pay but more commonly may revolve around managerial attempts to increase productivity and performance and a desire by workers to control the pace, intensity and autonomy of work.

In this context, it can be argued that, from a Marxist perspective, the key task of capitalist management is the continual control of the labour process in order to extract a maximum of surplus value by transforming labour power into work performance (Braverman 1974). Given the dynamics of exploitation and control, relationships between capital (management) and labour (workers) in the workplace are characterized by what Edwards (1986) termed 'structured antagonism'. Although management and employers need to control the labour process, they also require some level of co-operation from the workforce.

Accordingly, the outcome of this process is a range of responses from workers; they may give active consent to managerial demands, they might comply reluctantly or, in some circumstances, they resist. Moreover, the balance of control and co-operation will define the conditions for conflict to develop. Where employers seek to prioritize control by, for example, imposing strict workplace rules and rigid performance targets, low-trust relations (see Fox 1974) and conflict are more likely. Of course, in certain contexts, this may be of no great concern to employers as the costs of developing high levels of trust may outweigh any potential benefits in terms of productivity and profit.

It is also important to acknowledge that not all conflict at work originates from the employment relationship; Latreille and Saundry's case study of a large health organization (Chap. 14 of this book), found that a significant proportion of disputes originated from personal differences, which then spilled over into the workplace. Nonetheless, a violent argument between two colleagues may be entirely personal, but if held at work will be seen as having a detrimental impact on performance and consequently subject to organizational discipline. Therefore, what is often termed 'interpersonal conflict' does not take place outside the sphere of managerial control and in managing or adjudicating on such issues, management does not play an impartial role but acts in the interests of the organization.

The Dynamics of Conflict Formation: Informal Action and Resistance

It could be argued that conflict will occur where the implicit contract formed as a result of the effort bargain, described above, is broken or becomes unstable. From a radical perspective, this contract is in a state of perpetual instability as it is based on a relationship which is fundamentally unequal and in which the overriding emphasis is on cost minimization. However, the contract is also negotiated and renegotiated within a dynamic and complex context, which in turn is shaped by societal and organizational norms and also personal characteristics and orientations. For example, the response of individuals to a managerial instruction will rest on their resources and aspirations, which in turn will be shaped by the class, economic and social structure in which they live and work (Watson 1995). Whether a managerial request to an employee to work additional overtime results in conflict will depend on a range of factors including: their financial security; the impact of overtime on their home life; whether they trust and value their relationship with the manager; the extent to which they feel adequately recognized and rewarded by the company; perceptions of employment security or insecurity; access to representation and support; the broader climate of employment relations in the organization; and underlying attitudes to authority.

Where conflict does occur, it is often expressed in informal and unorganized ways. For example, a basic response to conflict is withdrawal, either of effort or self. Therefore conflict could be expressed in reduced motivation and therefore productivity on an individual level. Furthermore, workers could deliberately attempt to reduce the pace of work and so try to regain some control over the labour process. It could also be reflected in high levels of absence and ultimately turnover. Of course individuals may be absent due to sickness, while turnover may be a result of individual decisions which have nothing to do with underlying discontent. Nonetheless, the increasing use of rigid systems of absence management not only tends to escalate conflict (see Saundry and Wibberley 2014) but is also evidence that absenteeism can be a social as well as an individual expression of conflict (Edwards and Whitston 1989; Watson 1995).

For some commentators, workplace conflict is largely expressed through resistance. Moreover, as Thompson and McHugh (2009) argue there is a dialectical relationship between control and resistance – for example, rules and disciplinary processes are developed in order to control certain aspects of worker behaviour. The application of these rules can then lead to further conflict to which workers respond through organizational misbehaviour (Ackroyd and Thompson 1999). Employees may attempt to 'fiddle', 'pilfer' or 'steal' from their employer. It can be argued that by exaggerating expenses or taking home small items, workers are achieving a degree of distributional justice and readjusting the effort bargain (Williams and Adam-Smith 2010). Such misbehaviour could even extend to sabotage, which can take the form of physical destruction or in contemporary workplaces using social media to denigrate a product, the company and/or colleagues, an increasingly common occurrence in the UK (Broughton 2011). Humour is also one way in which workers can express (and respond to) discontent and a way of developing solidarity and challenging managerial control (Collinson 1992). Williams and Adam-Smith (2010), however, caution against such behaviours necessarily being interpreted as expressions of conflict. In helping workers deal with, and adapt to, the pressures of work they can act as a safety valve, which in essence helps to underpin rather than challenge managerial authority. For example, humour can also be used by management or within an organization to diffuse conflict, divert attention away from failure and deflect criticism (Barsoux 1993, cited in Watson 1995).

From Conflict to Disputes: Escalation and Mobilization

While the expressions of conflict discussed in the previous section are relatively 'unorganized', discontent can coalesce and escalate into concrete 'disputes' (Dix et al. 2009). At an individual level, these normally take one of two forms: disciplinary action taken by the employer or a grievance or complaint brought by an employee. What begin as individual disputes may take on a collective character as other workers identify a common cause with, and so provide support to, the affected worker. Alternatively, the source of discontent may itself be a collective issue, such as pay. In these circumstances, conflict can be expressed in an 'organized' way through strike or other industrial action. In this section we examine the characteristics of these different types of disputes.

Discipline: Correction and Control

The most common individual employment disputes revolve around the disciplinary decisions made by employers. Disciplinary action can take a number of forms – from informal verbal warnings and written warnings to suspension, demotion and ultimately dismissal. Such action is generally taken in response to misconduct, where an employee breaks a specific rule, or capability where the employer judges that the employee is unable to perform a role to the required standard.

The dominant view of workplace discipline and disciplinary action is that it is a means through which management can 'correct' employee behaviours which may impact negatively on organizational performance by applying 'fair' and 'just' procedures (Edwards and Whitston 1989). Disciplinary procedures are therefore institutions that aim to 'regularize and cope with potentially disintegrative conflicts of interest' (Watson 1995: 321). Alternatively, disciplinary action can be conceptualized as a management response to 'unorganized' employee expressions of conflict. From this perspective, disciplinary action is a function of the setting of rules and the exercise of managerial authority to exert control over the labour process and maintain order through 'punishment' (Jones 1961). The notion of order may be reflected in consistent evidence, which shows that disciplinary action is more likely to occur in larger workplaces and organizations. This could be a function of the impersonal nature of employment relations and the application of standardized rules and procedures. In contrast, in smaller workplaces, close relations between managers and staff can facilitate informal resolution through discussion (Forth et al. 2006).

In the UK, written disciplinary procedures are almost ubiquitous and can be found in nine out of ten workplaces (Wood et al. 2014). However, this is a relatively recent phenomenon. Up until 1970, disciplinary issues were subject to collective bargaining and a major source of industrial action. In terms of the preceding discussion, a decision to dismiss or discipline a fellow worker was generally defined in terms of collective interests. The spread of processes for dealing with disciplinary disputes was therefore seen as a way of removing such issues from the collective arena and bringing them within the ambit of managerial control. This points to the importance of national regulatory institutions in shaping patterns of conflict and resolution (Belanger and Edwards 2013). In the UK, the development of a regime of employment rights in the early 1970s, for example the introduction of a right for employees to challenge the fairness of a dismissal through legal action, triggered the spread and development of disciplinary procedures with elements of due process, such as appeal and representation (Edwards 1994). Similarly, Friedman and Lee (2010) found evidence that, in China, the development of legal rights for workers has made it more likely that conflict is expressed in an individual form.

In addition to the regulatory context, the nature and extent of disciplinary disputes is likely to be shaped by employer strategies in relation to conduct and performance and the response of trade unions and workers. In short, conflict will inevitably form around managerial attempts to both control the labour process and secure the consent of workers and employees (Hyman 1987). Furthermore, the way in which organizational actors seek to manage conflict will, in part, determine the incidence of individual employment disputes. For example, managers who adopt a 'problem solving' approach are more likely to resolve conflicts. Strong trade union organization is also associated with lower rates of disciplinary sanctions and dismissals, as a result of unions either restraining managerial prerogative or facilitating informal paths of resolution (Edwards 2000; Saundry et al. 2011).

Patterns of disciplinary action also reflect how individual workers respond to structures of managerial control, which will in turn be shaped by the external context. For example, if workers conform to organizational rules and norms, the incidence of discipline will be lower. It has been argued that this is one explanation for lower rates of disciplinary disputes in workplaces employing high proportions of women, older workers and those in more skilled occupational groups (Knight and Latreille 2000). Older workers and those in more senior positions, for example, may have more to lose by being subject to discipline or being dismissed. Alternatively, those in professional occupations and management grades may be able to contest managerial authority more effectively, so limiting the arbitrary use of discipline. In Britain, workplaces with higher proportions of 'non-white' employees have been found to have higher rates of disciplinary sanctions and dismissals. This is perhaps a function of discriminatory behaviour from managers but could also be explained by relatively low levels of knowledge of employment rights (Casebourne et al. 2006) , which may make it more difficult to contest disciplinary decisions.

Grievance Formation and Escalation

If workers challenge attempts by managers to exert control and discipline over the labour process, the result may be a formal grievance, whereby a complaint is made to someone of authority within the organization, often within the auspices of a structured procedure. Grievances from individual employees can centre on a wide range of issues. In the UK, the Workplace Employment Relations Study 2011 found that the most common cause, cited by almost 40 % of respondents, was 'unfair treatment' by a manager or supervisor – for instance, in relation to performance appraisals or perceived victimization. This compared to 'terms and conditions and pay' which was cited by just under one-third of respondents (van Wanrooy et al. 2013). In some senses, formal grievances represent a response to managerial attempts to impose greater control over the labour process leading to a 'spiral' of hostility and retaliation (Rapoport 1960).

Olson-Buchanan and Boswell (2008) have explored the dynamic processes through which an individual concludes that they has been mistreated and how they respond to that mistreatment. They argue that the nature or character of the mistreatment as perceived by the individual can shape their response. They suggest that mistreatment related to enactment of organizational policy is less likely to be 'internalized' and thus not seen as a personal attack by the employee. In contrast, perceived 'personalized mistreatment' can have a far more negative impact on their emotions, which can lead to greater 'job withdrawal' (Boswell and Olson-Buchanan 2004). Furthermore, the 'severity' or 'seriousness' of the perceived injustice (see also Todor and Owen 1991) will shape their response with harsher, socially unacceptable or intentional mistreatment more likely to lead to escalation.

Finally, if the employee feels that they have been denied procedural justice, if the complaint is not seen to have been fairly dealt with or there is a perception of ongoing mistreatment, there is likely to be a negative impact on the long-term performance and attitude of the employee. This may lead to a spiral of conflict in which the withdrawal of the employee is met with further disciplinary sanctions from management which deepens the sense of mistreatment. In contrast, if they perceive that they have achieved a positive resolution to their complaint then the individual is more likely to feel greater allegiance to the organization.

Lucy and Broughton (2011) (drawing on Korobkin 2006) identify five factors or processes that may shape the extent to which individual employees will seek to escalate a sense of grievance into a formal complaint. First, attribution bias is likely to restrict self-reflection and shift responsibility onto the other party. In short, disputants look for internal explanations of the other's behaviour, while rationalizing their own behaviour in objective terms (Irvine 2014). For example, a common finding in recent qualitative research into mediation revolves around disputes in which an employee accuses their manager of bullying behaviours, while the manager perceives the problem to rest with the attitude and performance of the employee (Saundry et al. 2013). Second, the way in which issues are framed may determine whether an issue is resolved at an early stage. Third, where individuals stand to lose a significant amount from a dispute they are more likely to adopt an adversarial approach.

The fourth factor identified by Lucy and Broughton is 'reactive devaluation' through which a party is less likely to accept a compromise because it comes from the individual or organization with whom the dispute originated. This therefore suggests the benefit of the involvement of third parties who are able to 'unfreeze' particular attitudes. The relatively high success rate of third party conciliation in the UK (Saundry and Dix 2014), workplace mediation (Latreille 2011) and also the constructive role seen to be played by union representatives (Saundry and Wibberley 2014) may suggest that this issue is influential in shaping dispute dynamics. Finally, Lucy and Broughton highlight the role of 'optimistic overconfidence' whereby either party may exaggerate the potential benefits of escalating a grievance, either in terms of improving their situation or winning legal compensation.

While an understanding of the psychology of grievance escalation is valuable, it is also important to place this within a broader context that takes into account the nature of workplace relations. For example, the existence of structures of employee representation and support is likely to influence the course of a grievance. Employee grievances, for instance, are more likely within unionized workplaces (Kersley et al. 2006), in which employees may well receive support in making formal complaints. There is also evidence to suggest that unrepresented workers are less likely to use formal grievance procedures (Pollert and Charlwood 2009). Moreover, in an adversarial employment relations climate, union representatives may use individual grievances as means through which broader collective issues are raised. Conversely, high trust relations within unionized environments can facilitate informal processes that help to resolve issues that threaten to escalate into formal disputes (Oxenbridge and Brown 2004; Saundry and Wibberley 2014). In these contexts, trade union representatives can play an important role in managing the expectations of members and guarding against 'optimistic overconfidence' (see Wibberley and Saundry in this volume).

Collective Disputes: Mobilizing Employee Discontent

Grievances can also escalate into collective industrial action, which has a number of different forms; groups of workers can take strike action where they withdraw their labour completely for a limited or an indefinite period. In addition, they can take industrial action, short of strike action, by refusing to work overtime, declining to complete certain parts of their normal duties or by strictly limiting their work to the terms of their employment contracts – sometimes known as 'working to rule'.

The question of whether and how conflict becomes manifest through collective disputes such as strikes is addressed to some degree by mobilization theory, developed by Charles Tilly (1978) and used by John Kelly (1998) to develop an account of the changing contours of workplace disputes. In short, mobilization theory suggests that five factors will shape the nature and extent of collective industrial action: interests, organization, mobilization, opportunity, and counter-mobilization.

The extent to which a particular issue is defined in terms of collective rather than individual interests is crucial – for example if an individual is experiencing bullying by management, this will probably become manifest in the form of an employee grievance but if this is part of a wider

24   R. Saundry

pattern of managerial behaviour, then there is the potential for collective action. However, workers must also have the capacity to take action and this in turn is dependent on the nature of union organization. Therefore, where union density is high, collective action is more likely. The sense of grievance must also be mobilized and this normally requires leadership from activists who are able to frame the issue in collective terms and convince workers of the potential benefits that could arise from any action. This is to some extent contingent on opportunity and whether the union has sufficient power to successfully carry out industrial action. Finally, action can be suppressed by the extent to which either the government or employer is prepared to counter-mobilize, for example by taking action against strikers, employing replacement workers or taking legal action against the union.

An analysis of these factors provides an explanation of why, in the UK, conflict is likely to escalate through individual rather than collective channels, as discussed in the following chapter of this book. Rapid industrial restructuring and the increased globalization of production have contributed to the decline of industries that had traditionally experienced relatively high levels of strikes and other industrial action (including coalmining, shipbuilding, and motor manufacturing). This has not only eroded the organizational capacity of unions but also the increased mobility of capital and the consequent threat of organizations relocating production has dramatically reduced union bargaining power and increased the potential risks of industrial action. In short, the capacity of trade unions to organize collective action in the face of conflict has been severely curtailed. This also means that workers may be less likely to see issues facing them or their colleagues in collective terms and union leaders and activists may face much greater difficulty in convincing workers that a collective dispute will yield a positive outcome. Furthermore, in the UK, this is exacerbated by restrictive legislation and the prospect of hostility from both State and employer.

Overall, the discussion above has demonstrated that while different types of disputes are clearly interrelated, a disciplinary decision can lead to an employee grievance and/or assume a collective character as workers mobilize through strike or other forms of industrial action. However, it is also important to consider their distinct characteristics. The extent to which conflict becomes transmitted as disciplinary action is a function of the degree to which worker behaviour contravenes rules and norms and the consequent managerial response. Furthermore, whereas a grievance is initiated by an employee, disciplinary action is fundamentally subject to managerial prerogative. This distinction is not simply theoretical but is crucial in understanding the way in which different types of disputes are resolved and therefore the efficacy of policy instruments designed to facilitate or encourage resolution. Whether conflict escalates into individual employment disputes, collective industrial action or is expressed through more informal action, it is likely to depend on a number of critical factors:

(i) *Political and legal context* – If the regulatory framework underpins employment rights and provides a clear route through which rights can be enforced, discontent is more likely to be converted into disputes. Whether this is in the form of individual grievances and litigation or expressed through industrial action will depend on the extent to which collective organization is supported or constrained by legislation and how this is balanced against individual employment protection.

(ii) *Organizational processes* – If there are accessible processes through which employees can raise concerns and managers can deal with issues of conduct and capability, discontent is likely to be expressed through formal grievances and disciplinary action. Where such processes are not present, conflict is more likely to be either expressed through informal and indirect channels such as quitting, absence and poor performance, or mobilized into collective action.

(iii) *Employee voice* – While formal processes may act as channels for employee voice, access to representation may be critical in mobilizing discontent and articulating this as an individual or collective grievance. At the same time, effective structures of representation may underpin informal processes of resolution, preventing the escalation of conflict.

(iv) *Personal characteristics and emotional contexts* – Emotional contexts can influence conflict escalation. Issues outside the workplace often shaped by economic circumstance may affect how individuals respond to conflict. Both manager and managed will rely on 'attributions' to make sense of the situation they find themselves in.

From Dispute Resolution to Conflict Management

In considering managerial attempts to resolve conflict, the academic literature has tended to be preoccupied with the relative efficiency of different dispute resolution processes and mechanisms. In the UK, this reflected a dominant pluralist paradigm which was built on the belief that the best way to manage employment relations was through a recognition of differences and structures through which those differences can be resolved. Therefore, governments of all political persuasions supported the idea of collective bargaining and encouraged the use of systematic procedural approaches to discipline and grievance. The role of state agencies such as the Advisory, Conciliation and Arbitration Service (Acas) and the use of conciliation in employment disputes were, and are, an essentially pluralist response to workplace conflict.

More recently, the focus has been on alternative methods of dispute resolution (ADR); however, much of the literature still locates mechanisms such as workplace mediation as a linear, technical process through which organizations are better able to resolve specific disputes. This managerial perspective has tended to focus on a narrow consideration of the benefits of dispute resolution. For example, proponents of mediation have long argued that it offers demonstrable advantages over slow, complex and adversarial grievance and disciplinary procedures, which tend to focus on rights as opposed to interests. In the UK, data suggest resolution rates (full or partial) of around 90% (or more) (Latreille 2011), mirroring US evidence that also points to high levels of participant satisfaction with both process and outcome (Bingham et al. 2009; Kochan et al. 2000). A radical critique of attempts to introduce alternative approaches to dispute resolution, such as mediation, would argue that these are merely ways in which management reinforces control over the labour process (see Colling 2004). Mediation, in particular, could be seen as means by which managerial oppression and mistreatment is recast as interpersonal conflict.

Commentators in the US have argued for a need to move away from using mediation and other forms of ADR to resolve disputes and towards 'integrated conflict management systems' (ICMS) (see Chap. 14). This, it is claimed, represents a new 'philosophy of organizational life' (Lynch 2001: 208) and a change in organizational 'mind-set' in regards to conflict management (Lipsky and Seeber 1998: 23). Accordingly, ICMS create a 'conflict competent culture' where all conflict may be safely raised and where persons will feel confident that their concerns will be heard, respected, and acted upon...' (Lynch 2001: 213) and where 'managers are expected to prevent, manage, contain and resolve all conflict at the earliest time and lowest level possible' (Lynch 2003: 212).

This therefore represents a clear shift from focussing on resolving disputes to developing approaches to manage discontent and conflict. Importantly, it reflects an acceptance of the inevitability of conflict and the importance of developing cultures in which employees feel able to challenge and raise any issues. In addition, it acknowledges the importance of providing employees with access to a rights-based process. Furthermore, it emphasizes the importance of locating conflict at the centre of organizational priorities and equipping managers with the capability to identify, address and resolve conflict at the earliest possible point (Lipsky and Avgar 2010; Lynch 2003).

The experience of the US suggests that integrated and innovative approaches are more likely to be found in 'high road' organizations which see conflict management as part of human resource strategy designed to maximize employee engagement and maintain competitiveness (Colvin 2014). In such organizations, therefore, the development of conflict management systems may be aligned and integrated with their existing strategy and culture (Lipsky and Avgar 2010). However, the link between the strategic management of conflict and employee engagement is, to date, notably absent from managerial discourses in Great Britain and Ireland. Instead, conflict management remains associated with the administration of disciplinary and grievance procedures and is consequently stereotyped as a low value and essentially transactional element of the management function. The fact that research points to an aversion among managers – and particularly senior managers – in UK organizations for accepting that conflict is even an issue might therefore militate against the development of more strategic approaches. This in turn highlights the importance of more detailed examination of the role that managers play in the diffusion of conflict management practices and systems in terms of both leadership and 'front-line' application.

Evidence also suggests that transforming the culture of conflict management is not straightforward and is critically related to the nature of managerial authority and the dynamics of workplace relations. Accordingly, the changes in the management of work which have increased pressures on managers to increase efficiency and improve performance have also created environments in which conflict is not only inevitable but an increasing feature of organizational life.

In some respects, the development of more strategic and systemic approaches to the management of conflict as opposed to reactive reliance on dispute resolution could be interpreted as a way of employers reasserting some degree of control over an increasingly unstable labour process. However, the most significant barrier to embedding a new culture of conflict management appears to be the attitude of managers themselves. Research points to an antipathy among managers in the UK and Ireland to the idea that conflict is an inevitable feature of organizational life (Teague and Doherty 2011). Indeed, a succession of studies have found the attitudes of line managers to represent a major barrier to the spread of ADR, viewing mediation as both an admission of failure and also a threat to their authority (Saundry and Wibberley 2014), reflecting what Lipsky and Avgar have characterized as the 'traditional approach to workplace conflict' (2010: 41).

Conclusion

Any evaluation of the significance of any resolution mechanism inevitably rests on the way in which the employment relationship, and specifically power and conflict, is conceptualized. For example, mediation can be located within unitary, pluralist and radical frames of reference. In the unitary view, mediation is a mechanism to cure the 'problem' of conflict, often through resolving interpersonal clashes and breakdowns in communication. From a pluralist perspective, mediation represents a classic institutional response – offering a process through which conflict can be regulated and contained. In contrast, a radical analysis would see mediation as a process affording 'bureaucratic control' (Edwards 1979) or what Hyman (1987: 40) refers to as a 'spurious' system of 'humanization and democratization' through which employees can be further co-opted by capital and the 'coercive' nature of work relations can be 'obscured'.

Existing policy debates undoubtedly see the adoption of ADR in unitary terms as a solution to the problem of 'pathological' conflict and its attendant costs, and exhibit a preoccupation with the efficiency of dispute resolution (see, for example, the review by Budd and Colvin 2008). This is problematic in a number of respects. It relies on a simplistic characterization of conventional grievance and disciplinary processes as formal and adversarial. This ignores the way in which formal procedure and informal processes often co-exist. Managers handle individual disputes in multi-faceted ways (Edwards and Whitston 1989) while union representatives not only challenge managerial authority but also often seek to negotiate informal resolutions for their members.

Accordingly, processes of dispute resolution cannot be divorced from the pattern of workplace relations (Colvin 2003). In the absence of strong unions or individuals with significant bargaining power, employers enjoy wide discretion as to how they 'resolve' individual employment disputes. Thus, procedures may be reduced to exercises in legal compliance, affording workers little chance to resolve problems or challenge perceived unfairness (Colling 2004; Pollert and Charlwood 2009). In contrast, effective structures of employee representation may provide a degree of procedural justice and also underpin informal resolution processes (Saundry et al. 2011). Therefore, outcomes of individual disputes are subject to processes of negotiation and renegotiation (Edwards and Whitston 1989) and conditioned by what Edwards (2000) calls the politics of the management of labour.

References

Ackroyd, S., & Thompson, P. (1999). *Organizational misbehaviour*. London: Sage.

Baldamus, W. (1961). *Efficiency and effort*. London: Tavistock.

Barsoux, J.-L. (1993). *Funny business: Humour, management and the business culture*. London: Cassell.

Behrend, H. (1957). The effort bargain. *International Labour Relations Review, 10*(4), 503–515.

Belanger, J., & Edwards, P. (2013). Conflict and contestation in the contemporary world of work: Theory and perspectives. In G. Gall (Ed.), *New forms and expressions of conflict at work* (pp. 7–25). Basingstoke: Palgrave Macmillan.

Bingham, L. B., Hallberlin, C., Walker, D., & Chung, W. (2009). Dispute system design and justice in employment dispute resolution: Mediation at the workplace. *Harvard Negotiation Law Review, 14*, 1–50.

Boswell, W. R., & Olson-Buchanan, J. B. (2004). Experiencing mistreatment at work: The role of grievance-filing, nature of mistreatment, and employee withdrawal. *Academy of Management Journal, 47*, 129–139.

Braverman, H. (1974). *Labour and monopoly capital*. New York: Monthly Review Press.

Broughton, A. (2011). Workplaces and social networking – The implications for employment relations. *Acas Research Papers, 11/11*.

Budd, J., & Colvin, A. (2008). Improved metrics for workplace dispute resolution procedures: Efficiency, equity, and voice. *Industrial Relations, 47*(3), 460–479.

Casebourne, J., Regan, J., Neathey, F., & Tuohy, S. (2006). *Employment rights at work—Survey of employees* (Employment Relations Research Series, Vol. 51). London: DTI.

CIPD (Chartered Institute of Personnel and Development). (2015). Getting under the skin of conflict: Tracing the experiences of employees, CIPD Survey Report.

Colling, T. (2004). No claim, no pain? The privatization of dispute resolution in Britain. *Economic and Industrial Democracy, 25*(4), 555–579.

Collinson, D. (1992). *Managing the shopfloor*. Berlin: de Gruyter.

Colvin, A. (2003). The dual transformation of workplace dispute resolution. *Industrial Relations, 42*(4), 712–735.

Colvin, A. (2014). Grievance procedures in non-union firms. In W. Roche, P. Teague, & A. Colvin (Eds.), *The Oxford handbook on conflict management in organizations*. Oxford: Oxford University Press.

Dix, G., Forth, J., & Sisson, K. (2009). Conflict at work: The changing pattern of disputes. In W. Brown, A. Bryson, J. Forth, & K. Whitfield (Eds.), *The evolution of the modern workplace*. Cambridge: Cambridge University Press.

Edwards, R. (1979). *Contested Terrain*. London: Heinemann.

Edwards, P. (1986). *Conflict at work*. Oxford: Blackwell.

Edwards, P. (1994). Discipline and the creation of order. In K. Sisson (Ed.), *Personnel management* (2nd ed., pp. 562–592). Oxford: Blackwell.

Edwards, P. (1995). Strikes and industrial conflict. In P. Edwards (Ed.), *Industrial relations: Theory and practice in Britain* (pp. 434–460). Oxford: Blackwell.

Edwards, P. (2000). Discipline: Towards trust and self-discipline? In S. Bach, & K. Sisson (Eds.), *Personnel management: A comprehensive guide to theory and practice in Britain* (3rd ed., pp. 317–339). Oxford: Blackwell.

Edwards, P., & Whitston, C. (1989). Industrial discipline, the control of attendance and the subordination of labour. *Work, Employment and Society, 3*(1), 1–28.

Forth, J., Bewley, H., & Bryson, A. (2006). *Small and medium-sized enterprises: Findings from the 2004 workplace employment relations survey*. London: Routledge.

Fox, A. (1974). *Beyond contract: Work, power and trust relations*. London: Faber.

Friedman, E., & Lee, C. (2010). Remaking the world of Chinese labour. *British Journal of Industrial Relations, 48*(3), 507–533.

Hyman, R. (1987). Strategy or structure? Capital, labour and control. *Work, Employment and Society, 1*(1), 25–55.

Irvine, C. (2014). Do you see what I'm dealing with here? Vicious circles in conflict. *Journal of Mediation and Applied Conflict Analysis, 1*(1), S.3.

Jones, D. L. (1961). *Arbitration and industrial discipline*. Ann Arbor: Bureau of Industrial Relations/University of Michigan.

Kelly, J. (1998). *Rethinking industrial relations: Mobilization, collectivism and long waves*. London: Routledge.

Kersley, B., Alpin, C., Forth, J., Bryson, A., Bewley, H., Dix, G., et al. (2006). *Inside the workplace: Findings from the 2004 workplace employment relations survey*. London: Routledge.

Kerr, C. (1964). *Labor and management in industrial society*. New York: Doubleday.

Knight, K., & Latreille, P. (2000). Discipline, dismissals and complaints to employment tribunals. *British Journal of Industrial Relations, 38*(4), 533–555.

Kochan, T., Lautsch, B., & Bendersky, C. (2000). An evaluation of the Massachusetts commission against discrimination alternative dispute resolution program. *Harvard Negotiation Law Review, 5*, 233–274.

Korobkin, R. (2006). Psychological impediments to mediation success: Theory and practice. *Ohio State Journal on Dispute Resolution, 21*(2), 281–327.

Latreille, P. (2011). Workplace mediation: A thematic review of the Acas/CIPD evidence, *Acas Research Paper*, 13/11.

Lipsky, D., & Avgar, A. (2010). The conflict over conflict management [Electronic version]. Dispute Resolution Journal 65(2–3), 38–43.

Lipsky, D., & Seeber, R. (1998). *The appropriate resolution of corporate disputes: A report on the growing use of ADR by U.S. corporations*. Ithaca: Institute on Conflict Resolution http://digitalcommons.ilr.cornell.edu/cgi/viewcontent. cgi?article=1003&context=icrpubs.

Lucy, D., & Broughton, A. (2011). Understanding the behaviour and decision making of employees in conflicts and disputes at work. *Employment Relations Research Series*, No. 119. London: BIS.

Lynch, J. F. (2001). Beyond ADR: A systems approach to conflict management. *Negotiation Journal, 17*(3), 207–216.

Lynch, J. (2003) *Are your organization's conflict management practices an integrated conflict management system?*. http://www.mediate.com//articles/systemsedit3.cfm. Accessed 15/4/13.

Olson-Buchanan, J., & Boswell, W. (2008). An integrative model of experiencing and responding to mistreatment at work. *Academy of Management Review, 33*(1), 76–96.

Oxenbridge, S., & Brown, W. (2004). Achieving a new equilibrium? The stability of co-operative employer–union relationships. *Industrial Relations Journal, 35*(5), 388–402.

Pollert, A., & Charlwood, A. (2009). The vulnerable worker in Britain and problems at work. *Work, Employment and Society, 23*(2), 343–362.

Rapoport, A. (1960). *Fights, Games, and Debates*. Ann Arbor: University of Michigan Press.

Saundry, R., Jones, C., & Antcliff, V. (2011). Discipline, representation and dispute resolution – Exploring the role of trade unions and employee companions in workplace discipline. *Industrial Relations Journal, 42*(2), 195–211.

Saundry, R., & Dix, G. (2014). Conflict resolution in the UK. In W. Roche, P. Teague, & A. Colvin (Eds.), *The Oxford handbook on conflict management in organizations*. Oxford: Oxford University Press.

Saundry, R., & Wibberley, G. (2014). Workplace dispute resolution and the management of individual conflict – A thematic analysis of five case studies. *Acas Research Papers*, 06/14.

Saundry, R., Bennett, T., & Wibberley, G. (2013). Workplace mediation: The participant experience. *Acas Research Papers*, 2/13.

Teague, P., & Doherty, L. (2011). Conflict management systems in non-union multinationals in the Republic of Ireland. *International Journal of Human Resource Management, 21*(1), 57–71.

Thompson, P., & McHugh, D. (2009). *Work organisations: A critical approach* (3rd ed.,). Basingstoke: Palgrave.

Tilly, C. (1978). *From mobilization to revolution*. Reading: Addison-Wesley.

Todor, W. D., & Owen, C. L. (1991). Deriving benefits from conflict resolution: A macrojustice approach. *Employee Responsibilities and Rights Journal, 4*(1), 37–49.

van Wanrooy, B., Bewley, H., Bryson, A., Forth, J., Freeth, S., Stokes, L., et al. (2013). *Employment relations in the shadow of recession – Findings from the 2011 workplace employment relations study*. London: Palgrave Macmillan.

Watson, T. (1995). *Sociology, work and industry* (3rd ed.,). London: Routledge.

Williams, S., & Adam-Smith, D. (2010). *Contemporary employment relations: A critical introduction* (2nd ed.,). Oxford: Oxford University Press.

Wood, S., Saundry, R., & Latreille, P. (2014). Analysis of the nature, extent and impact of grievance and disciplinary procedures and workplace mediation using WERS2011. *Acas Research Papers*, 10/14.

3

Exploring the Nature and Extent of Workplace Conflict

John Forth and Gill Dix

Introduction

Recent decades have witnessed some substantial changes in both the nature and the extent of workplace conflict in the UK. The number of collective disputes has declined significantly, but those that do take place are increasingly large in scale. In contrast, claims to employment tribunals have grown rapidly, with volumes heavily influenced in recent times by claims from groups of employees, rather than individuals. In spite of this changing picture, there do not appear to have been dramatic changes in the quality of employment relations inside the workplace, even though the UK has just experienced the longest recession in living memory. This suggests that the visible signs of conflict are shaped not only by the scale of underlying tensions but also by the available mechanisms for their expression (see Dix et al. 2009, for one discussion).

J. Forth
National Institute of Economic and Social Research (NIESR), London, UK
e-mail: j.forth@niesr.ac.uk

G. Dix
Advisory Conciliation and Arbitration Service (Acas), London, UK

© The Editor(s) (if applicable) and The Author(s) 2016
R. Saundry et al. (eds.), *Reframing Resolution*,
DOI 10.1057/978-1-137-51560-5_3

In this chapter, we examine these patterns of collective and individualized forms of conflict in some detail. We draw on official records of industrial action and Employment Tribunal applications and also report on survey data from workplace managers and employees. The latter provide information on the incidence of disputes inside the workplace, and evidence of the broader state of relations between managers and employees.

The chapter also examines the prevalence of different mechanisms for the resolution of workplace conflict. Recent decades have brought restrictions on employees' freedom to organize industrial action, and more recently, constraints on their ability to seek legal redress through the tribunal system. Instead, greater emphasis has been placed on the full use of workplace procedures for the resolution of individual disputes, and on recourse to conciliation and mediation as alternatives to escalation when early resolution proves elusive. The chapter will chart some of the broad changes in workplace policy and practice in these various respects.

The chapter focuses primarily on the experience of Britain over the past 15 years. Comment will occasionally be made on the longer sweep of history, but accounts of this longer time frame have already been provided elsewhere (e.g. Dix et al. 2009; Drinkwater and Ingram 2005). Some international comparisons will also be highlighted but, in the absence of a wide range of data on other countries' experiences, and in view of the difficulty of providing a proper contextualization of the patterns of conflict under different institutional, legal and social settings, our main focus will be on the British experience.

The chapter is organized into four main sections. First, we examine the changing incidence of collective expressions of conflict, looking in particular at the incidence of industrial action. Second, we examine the pattern of individual disputes, focusing in particular on trends in Employment Tribunal claims, where recent policy changes have had a considerable affect on volumes, but also looking at the incidence of disputes within the workplace. Third, we look beyond disputes to examine broader indicators of the climate of workplace employment relations, including trends in employees' evaluations of managerial behaviour. Fourth, we consider the wider context within which the employment relationship is conducted, covering issues such as the prevailing economic conditions, and changes in the prevalence of workplace disputes procedures and employee representation, as a means of exploring the broader range of factors influencing both the level and the expression of conflict at work. A short final section concludes.

Collective Disputes

We have already alluded to the significant decline in collective disputes in recent decades. Official statistics focus on the most public manifestation – strikes – counting the number of work stoppages, the total number of workers involved and the number of working days lost. The late 1980s and 1990s saw a dramatic fall in the number of stoppages, with each year between 1986 and 1994 successively witnessing the lowest number of officially recorded strikes since the Second World War. The number of stoppages has broadly stabilized since the mid-1990s (Fig. 3.1) and, although there are annual fluctuations, these are relatively minor when compared with historical levels.

The number of working days lost, which averaged around 300 for every 1,000 employees in employment during the 1980s, has stood below 100 per thousand employees in every year since 1989, and has been below 50 per thousand for all but four of those years. The UK is thus, overall, now experiencing a prolonged period of relative industrial peace. The spikes in

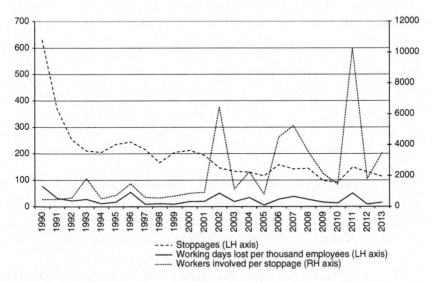

Fig. 3.1 Working days lost to stoppages, 1989–2013 (Source: Office for National Statistics (2014))
Source: Office for National Statistics (2014). Sources for numbers of stoppages, workers involved and working days lost: ONS Labour Disputes Annual Estimates 2013 (last published annual estimates). Downloaded from ONS web-site on 10/7/15

the series can mostly be attributed to short, large-scale strikes in the public sector – for example, those called in 2011–2012 in response to changes in pensions and ongoing pay freezes. In fact, the public sector now accounts for around four-fifths of all working days lost, despite accounting for only one-fifth of all employment (Office for National Statistics 2014), something which can be attributed to the enduring levels of union organization among public sector workers, tensions in the relationship with government as paymaster, and the large-scale nature of many public services. The final point is particularly notable, as there are few groups of private sector employees which have anything like the equivalent scope for widespread industrial unrest.

Official data also record the reasons for work stoppages, and show that the majority of days lost to work stoppages have pay issues at the heart of the dispute (Office for National Statistics 2014). In eight of the ten years from 2004–2013, pay issues accounted for at least three-fifths of all days lost. The exceptions were 2009 and 2010 – in the depths of the recent recession – when disputes around redundancies accounted for the lion's share (around 60 % in 2009 and around 85 % in 2010, compared with no more than 20 % in other years). This is not to imply that, outside of those 2 years, most strikes have necessarily been focused on the annual pay round: the figures cited above include large-scale disputes over pensions and smaller-scale stoppages over payment of wages. Acas data also show the heterogeneity of collective disputes, with requests being made for conciliation in disputes over union recognition, changes in working practices and disciplinary matters, among other things (Acas 2015a). The broad issue of pay still dominates the landscape of collective action, however.

When trying to gauge the prevalence of industrial action in the UK, it is natural to make comparisons with historic levels, but one can also look at the experience of other countries. Such comparisons are fraught with difficulty because of cross-national differences in the legal restrictions on industrial action, and variations in the practices of national statistical offices. However, the best estimates suggest that the number of working days lost per 1,000 employees in the UK is around half the average seen in the EU-15. On average, 24 days were lost annually per 1,000 employees in the UK over the period 2005–2009, compared with an average of 45 days in the EU-15.[1] Over this period, only Austria, Luxembourg, The Netherlands, Portugal and Sweden experienced lower rates than the UK. In contrast, the rate in France – one of the most strike-prone countries in Europe – was around five times higher than that seen in the UK.[2] The UK rate looks less favourable, however, when compared with Australia (16 days) and the USA (12 days).[3]

A complementary picture of industrial action in Britain can be obtained from the Workplace Employment Relations Study (WERS), which asks managers whether their workplace has experienced industrial action in the 12 months prior to the survey. WERS confirms the broad portrait above of a more strike-prone public sector (Table 3.1, row 2), but offers three advantages over official estimates of work stoppages. First, it collects data on non-strike action which, in some years, is shown to be at least as prevalent as strike action (Table 3.1, row 3). Second, it provides data on threats of industrial action and ballots (Table 3.1, rows 4 and 6), and so indicates the wider prevalence of threatened action as a feature of employment relations – particularly in the public sector. Third, the survey allows us to demonstrate that the lower propensity for industrial action in the private sector is not simply a consequence of lower levels of unionization.[4] In 2011, only 4 % of unionized workplaces in the private sector experienced industrial action, compared with 34 % of unionized workplaces in the public sector. This then points one's attention back to the particular dynamics of collective employment relations in the public sector.

As noted earlier, a particular feature of collective disputes in the public sector is the capacity for industrial action to disrupt key front-line public services such as health and education. This naturally gives unions a particular level of bargaining power, but it has also led to calls from some parties to restrict the situations in which public sector

---

[1] Author's calculations from Carley (2010) after excluding Norway.

[2] The discrepancy between the UK and France is largely due to the fact that the French public sector is particularly strike prone, with days lost in the private sector broadly on a par in the two countries (Milner 2015: 135).

[3] Figures for Australia and the USA are calculated for 2005–2009 from data published by the Australian Bureau of Statistics and US Bureau of Labor Statistics.

[4] Approximately one-in-ten private sector workplaces have recognized trade unions, compared with around nine-in-ten in the public sector.

Table 3.1 Industrial action by sector of ownership, 2004 and 2011

Percentage of workplaces

	All workplaces		Private sector		Public sector	
	2004	2011	2004	2011	2004	2011
Any industrial action	2	5	1	1	9	32
Strike action	1	4	0	1	6	29
Non-strike action	1	1	1	1	4	6
Threat of industrial action	4	4	3	2	11	22
Any industrial action taken or threatened	5	6	3	2	15	36
Any ballot	3	7	1	1	19	51
Any ballot or action threatened/taken	7	9	4	3	26	56

Source: Workplace Employment Relations Study
Base: all workplaces with 5 or more employees

industrial action may be considered lawful. At the time of writing, the government has introduced a bill that would require any successful ballot for industrial action to have a turnout of at least 50 %, and for ballots covering workers involved in certain public services to have at least 40 % of eligible voters deciding in favour (Cabinet Office 2015). The available evidence suggests that, if the proposed bill is passed, it will have a substantial effect on unions' ability to take lawful industrial action (Darlington and Dobson 2015). The landscape of industrial action changed markedly in the late 1980s and 1990s, and it may be about to change again.

Individual Disputes

Having considered collective disputes, we now turn to disputes that typically take place between an employer and an individual employee. As with collective disputes, we can look across a range of indicators, but we begin by looking at the most formal and public manifestation, which is for an employee to make a claim to an Employment Tribunal (ET) in cases where they feel that their employment rights have been infringed. Figure

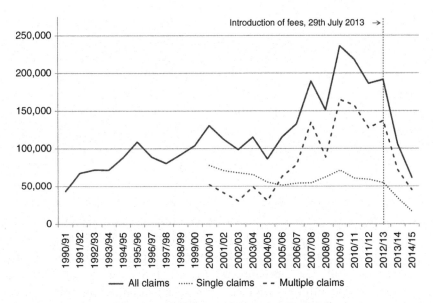

Fig. 3.2   Employment Tribunal claims, 1990/1991–2014/2015

Source: 1972–1979: Employment Gazette (1984); 1980–1998: Hawes (2000); 1998–2010: Employment Tribunal Service Annual Reports. 2012/13 and 2013/14 total and single/multi split for 2008–2013/14: Empt and EAT Tribunal stats for financial year 2013–14 (xls file): Table E1 Single/multi split for 2000/1–2007/8 estimated from stats provided by MoJ (15/7/15) that underlie Fig 1 in ET stats 2009–10 (in QoC ETStats folder).

Note: This series is an update from that quoted in Acas' "Conflict at work: The pattern of disputes in Britain since 1980" paper [ref 03/08]. This paper also provides a commentary to this series up to 2006 (pages 7–11)

3.2 shows that the total number of ET claims has grown substantially over the past two decades. A gradual rise was seen through the 1990s and early 2000s, with the total number of claims doubling between 1990/1991 and 2004/2005, but the increase since 2004/2005 has been much steeper, such that the number of claims doubled again in the second half of the 2000s.

Again, it is difficult to make international comparisons on this issue, because countries differ in terms of the range of individual rights that are available and the eligibility rules for applying to employment tribunals or labour courts. They also differ in their use of conciliation, mediation and arbitration as means of resolving disputes without recourse to a hearing (see Purcell 2010). However a recent five-country study covering the UK along with France, Italy,

Poland and Portugal concluded that, in all of these countries, there had been a rise in ET claims, occurring alongside a decline in strike action (CAMS 2009, 2010a, b). The UK's experience in recent decades is thus far from unique.

As the number of collective disputes has fallen in the UK, it has been tempting to look to the growth in the number of ET claims as giving expression to the types of conflict that would previously have been voiced through collective means. There may be some credence to this view, but the two are not direct substitutes for a number of reasons. First, industrial action typically takes place within the context of an ongoing employment relationship where there is a disagreement about what represents a 'fair' settlement in negotiations affecting the terms and conditions of a group of workers. The ET system, on the other hand, is designed to focus on actual or perceived infringements of employment rights, and claims are often issued in circumstances where the employment relationship has already come to an end. The mechanisms and basic rationales are thus different. Changes in the number of ET claims have also been influenced by factors relating to the law itself, including the progressive growth of individual rights (influencing the trend upwards), and the extension of the qualification period for unfair dismissal (influencing it downwards).[5] The level of employees' awareness of employment rights is also a determining factor affecting the propensity to claim. There is, nonetheless, some transmission between collective and individual means of dispute resolution, as trade unions have placed greater emphasis on the legal enforcement of individual rights (Colling 2012), including the use of the ET system as a mechanism for resolving issues covering groups of workers. Indeed much of the recent growth in the number of claims has been due to the growth in 'multiples', whereby a claim is lodged on behalf of a group of employees all working for the same employer; the number of single claims has been relatively flat in comparison (see Fig. 3.2). Such multiple claims – for instance those lodged with the support of a union in pursuance of a claim for equal pay – can reasonably be viewed as a form of collective action, even though it is too simplistic to view them as a direct substitute for industrial action.

Given these patterns, it is perhaps no coincidence that a substantial portion of the increase in the number of claims over the past decade relates

---

[5] The number of jurisdictions has risen from around 20 in the early 1980s to more than 60 at the present time (Dix and Barber 2015; Ministry of Justice 2015).

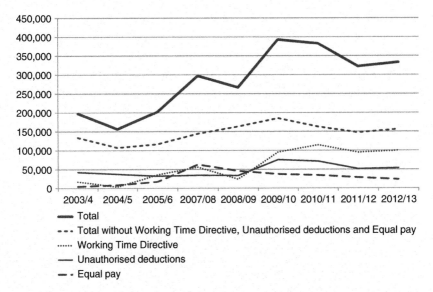

Fig. 3.3   Employment Tribunal receipts by jurisdiction, 2003/2004–2012/2013

to jurisdictions that are particularly influenced by 'multiples'. Around 75 % of the sharp increase between 2004/2005 and 2009/2010 was explained by rising numbers of claims about working time, unauthorized deductions from wages (including the National Minimum Wage) and equal pay (Fig. 3.3). If these three jurisdictions are excluded, then the total number of claims rose only marginally over the decade from 2003/2004 to 2012/2013.

The volume of ET claims has changed dramatically since 2013; however, with substantial changes being made to the rules governing applications. July 2013 saw the introduction of fees for claimants, motivated by government and business concerns about both the costs of the tribunal system and the perceived incidence of vexatious claims.[6] May 2014 then saw the introduction of Early Conciliation (EC), whereby all

---

[6] The fees currently stand at £160–£250 for registering a claim and £230–£950 for a claim to progress to a hearing. The amount depends on the type of case and may be remitted in full or in part if the claimant meets criteria for not being able to afford to pay. The tribunal can also order the fee to be repaid if the claim is successful.

potential tribunal claimants must notify Acas first of their intention to make a claim, at which point Acas offers to conciliate between the parties in order to prevent the need for a tribunal application. The introduction of EC follows an earlier initiative (introduced in April 2009) whereby Acas offered Pre-Claim Conciliation (PCC) to callers to its Helpline who were involved in potential ET claims; the critical difference is that EC is a mandatory stage (although engagement with conciliation is voluntary).

Looking at the trend of ET cases in recent years, it is tempting to credit PCC with the fall that occurred in single and multiple claims from 2009/2010 to 2010/2011 (Fig. 3.2), but that is hazardous because other factors were also at play (see Davey and Dix 2011, for a discussion). What is entirely unambiguous, however, is that the introduction of fees in July 2013 was immediately followed by a substantial reduction in the number of claims. The volume immediately fell from a steady average of around 5,000 lodged in each of the 18 months leading up to July 2013, to a steady average of around 1,700 lodged in each of the 12 months afterwards (Ministry of Justice 2015). This change, in particular, now makes it very difficult to use numbers of ET claims as any kind of barometer of workplace relations. Instead, one might now reasonably look to the number of EC notifications. These are not suggestive of any reduction in individual disputes in recent years – in fact they suggest an increase.[7] But of course, it is early days for EC, and indeed for fees. Going forward, it will be important to get a better understanding of how the new arrangements are changing the parties' decisions about whether to escalate a dispute, how they are changing the parties' experience of the process (particularly in respect of the adequacy of the outcome) and, more broadly, how they are changing the dynamics of dispute resolution inside the workplace.

---

[7] The introduction of EC restores the availability of a 'free' method for acquiring external intervention in a dispute (albeit from Acas conciliators rather than through free access to a tribunal). One might then seek to compare the total number of EC notifications under the current arrangements with the total number of ET cases filed in the 'pure tribunal' period before PCC. The latter are in fact larger, even though EC notifications from 'multiples' are only counted as one case. Around 84,000 EC notifications were made by employees between April 2014 and March 2015 (Acas 2015b); this compares with around 60,000 ET cases lodged between April 2012 and March 2013 (Ministry of Justice 2015).

Setting aside the statistics on ET claims and strikes, however, one can note that the vast majority of disputes at work do not manifest in tribunal claims (Casebourne et al. 2006), and the challenge is to develop a picture that incorporates less visible forms of conflict. We can turn again to WERS to begin to map this picture as the survey asks the main manager with responsibility for employment relations at the workplace a set of questions about the incidence of individual disputes, measured through the prevalence of grievances and disciplinary incidents (see Table 3.2).

The latest survey shows that one or more employees lodged a formal grievance in around one in six workplaces (17 %) in 2011; this figure is slightly higher in the public sector than in the private sector, but this is because workplaces tend to be larger in the public sector.[8] The number of formal grievances raised per 100 employees is similar across the two sectors (around 1.4 per 100 employees). Comparing with the situation in 2004, we find that there has been little change overall in the share of workplaces experiencing formal grievances. Disciplinary sanctions appear to have become a little less common, with the major change here being a fall in the percentage of private sector workplaces issuing sanctions short of dismissal. In contrast, the percentage of public sector workplaces using dismissal as a sanction rose slightly over the period. In aggregate, the number of disciplinary sanctions issued per 100 employees fell slightly from 5.1 per 100 employees in 2004 to 4.7 per 100 in 2011.[9]

These results thus help us to gauge the prevalence of workplace disputes without direct reference to the ET system. They serve to make two notable points. First, we do not see the sharp upturn here that we saw in the total volume of ET cases. This is then a further indication of how the overall picture on ETs has been skewed in recent years by the large number of multiple claims. Second, there appears to have been no sharp increase in the prevalence of workplace disputes in a period

---

[8] With a greater number of employees, there is a higher chance that at least one case will arise.

[9] WERS also indicates the reasons for grievances and disciplinary sanctions. The most common causes of grievances in 2011 were unfair treatment by managers (52 %), followed by bullying or harassment (30 %) and issues over pay or conditions (17 %). The most common causes of disciplinary sanctions were poor performance (59 %), poor timekeeping or absence (44 %) and theft or dishonesty (24 %).

Table 3.2 Individual workplace disputes by sector of ownership, 2004 and 2011

	All workplaces		Private sector		Public sector	
	2004	2011	2004	2011	2004	2011
Percentage of workplaces with a formal grievance	15	17	13	16	24	22
Number of formal grievances raised per 100 employees	–	1.4	–	1.4	–	1.3
Percentage of workplaces with any grievance	–	29	–	28	–	35
Percentage of workplaces issuing disciplinary sanctions	44	41	45	42	30	32
Percentage of workplaces issuing sanctions short of dismissal	42	36	43	37	30	30
Percentage of workplaces with disciplinary-related dismissals	21	19	22	20	8	12
Number of disciplinary sanctions issued per 100 employees	5.1	4.7	6.1	5.5	1.8	2.2
Percentage of workplaces with a claim made to an employment tribunal	6	4	5	4	6	7

Source: Workplace Employment Relations Study
Base: all workplaces with 5 or more employees
Note: All items refer to the incidence in the 12 months prior to the survey date. There is no comparable data on the rate of grievances or the incidence of informal grievances in 2004 (see Van Wanrooy et al. 2013: 152)
Note: Disciplinary sanctions comprise oral warnings, written warnings, suspensions, deductions from pay and internal transfers

that has seen the longest recession in living memory. That is not to deny the impact of the recession entirely: analysis of the 2011 WERS clearly shows that the incidences of grievances and disciplinary matters were both higher across workplaces that had experienced a larger shock from the economic downturn, when compared with equivalent workplaces that did not experience the shock (Van Wanrooy et al. 2013: 156). Some of the effect may also have dissipated by 2011.[10] But these caveats aside,

[10] As noted earlier, data on the causes of collective conflict indicate that redundancies accounted for at least 65 % of working days lost in 2009/2010 and 2010/2011, but for less than 5 % of working days lost in adjacent years.

there is little suggestion in Table 3.2 of any increases in the prevalence of formal workplace disputes.

The Climate of Employment Relations

The data presented in Tables 3.1 and 3.2 thus point towards a picture of relative stability in the incidence of workplace conflict over the past decade, at least in the private sector, which accounts for the majority of all employment in the economy. This impression is backed up by survey data on the climate of employment relations within the workplace.

One barometer is provided by the British Social Attitudes Survey, which, in 1999 and 2009, asked employees to rate the level of conflicts between managers and employees at their workplace. In 1999, some 8 % of employees reported 'Very strong conflicts' 38 % reported 'Strong conflicts' and 55 % reported either 'Not very strong conflicts' or 'No conflicts'. The 2009 survey registered a small improvement, with the figures standing at 3 %, 37 % and 60 % respectively.

A second measure comes, again, from WERS. Employees that have been surveyed in the last three WERS surveys have been asked to rate the relationship between managers and employees at their workplace, as a means of providing an overall impression of the quality of employment relations. Responses have been invited on a five-point scale from 'Very good' to 'Very poor': the results are shown in Table 3.3. The changes over the period 1998–2011 are not dramatic but there is nonetheless a clear

Table 3.3 The climate of employment relations, 1998, 2004 and 2011

Cell percentage			
	1998	2004	2011
Employees who consider that the relationship between managers and employees at the workplace is:			
'Good' or 'Very good'	55	60	63
'Neither good nor poor'	27	24	23
'Poor' or 'Very poor'	18	16	14

Source: Workplace Employment Relations Study
Base: all employees in workplaces with 10 or more employees

indication that relations have, on the whole, improved slightly over time. The percentage of employees who report that employment relations are poor has fallen slightly from 18 % in 1998 to 14 % in 2011, whilst the proportion reporting that relations are good has risen from 55 to 63 %. The larger part of this shift was seen in the period 1998–2004, with less change evident between 2004 and 2011.

Clearly, both of these sources indicate that conflictual or poor relations are still relatively widespread in the British economy, and this should undoubtedly be a cause for concern, both in terms of the effect on managers' and employees' wellbeing and in terms of workplace productivity. However, if one is interested in the general trend, there is at least some indication of small improvements in overall relations in recent years.

The Wider Context

In attempting to enumerate the prevalence and patterns of workplace conflict in recent years, the foregoing discussion has said relatively little about the broader context in which workplace relations are conducted. This is an important omission because disputes are partly a reaction to workplace events. It is, then, important to consider this broader context in order to come to a better understanding both of recent trends in workplace conflict, and how levels of conflict may evolve in the future.

The first thing to note is that, as far as the survey evidence suggests, the recession appears to have had a surprisingly muted impact on the labour market in Britain (see Van Wanrooy et al. 2013).[11] Clearly the downturn did lead to job losses, but the spike in redundancies was relatively short lived, and the overall decline in employment was nothing like that experienced in the recessions of the 1980s and 1990s, with employment levels unusually returning to their pre-recession level at least one year before national output did the same (see Forth and Bryson 2015). The more dramatic effect was seen on wages, with pay freezes being common and nominal wages being reduced in many instances (Elsby et al. 2013; Gregg et al. 2014). As noted earlier, there have been conflicts, most notably

---

[11] Britain is not unique in that respect (see Roche and Teague 2014).

in the public sector, where large disputes have been intrinsically linked with 'austerity'. However, the overall impression is one of workplaces and employees adapting to the changed economic conditions.

It is possible that this is a symptom of the decline in union organization in Britain, with workers less able to collectively challenge changes to terms and conditions. Indeed, evidence from WERS indicates that terms and conditions in unionized workplaces were at least as responsive to the changed economic conditions as those in non-union workplaces (Van Wanrooy et al. 2013: 176). But unions are also realistic and, with an eye on employment retention, may have accepted that some flexibility was necessary. Workers more generally may also have become more cautious, particularly with one eye on the labour market. A weak labour market reduces workers' outside options, and may serve to reduce the propensity to complain about worsening conditions which, alongside declining real wages, have also included higher workloads and higher levels of stress (Van Wanrooy et al. 2013; Green et al. 2013). Certainly, perceptions of job security fell through the recession, particularly in the public sector (Van Wanrooy et al. 2013; Gallie et al. 2013), and there is evidence that employers' power in the labour market has grown despite healthy employment levels (Manning 2015).

It is notable, however, that, in aggregate, employees' evaluations of their managers have not taken a sharp turn for the worse over this period. Comprehensive surveys of fair treatment at work show that there remain many instances in which employees judge their treatment to be unfair and find it difficult to obtain effective resolution of their claims (Fevre et al. 2009, 2012). Data from other surveys also indicate some increase over the past decade in the share of public sector workers who report fear of unfair treatment (Gallie et al. 2013), but the general experience of workers in the private sector appears, on the whole, to be have been more favourable (Forth 2013). Looking across the whole economy, employees have in fact become slightly less likely to give negative ratings of their managers' behavior in the workplace (see Table 3.4).[12]

---

[12] In the British Social Attitudes Survey, the percentage of employees agreeing that "management tries to get the better of employees" has fallen over time, from around 60 % in the period 1998–2003 to around 50 % in the period 2004–2010. The 2011 figure of 56 % may represent something of a reversal, but there is no data available beyond 2011 that can be used to corroborate this.

Table 3.4 Employees' evaluations of managers, 2004 and 2011

Cell percentage		
	2004	2011
Employees who 'Disagree' or 'Strongly disagree' that:		
Managers are sincere in attempting to understand employees' views	21	20
Managers deal with employees honestly	19	17
Managers can be relied upon to keep their promises	24	21
Managers treat employees fairly	20	19

Source: Workplace Employment Relations Study
Base: all employees in workplaces with 5 or more employees

A second, potentially important, element of the prevailing context for workplace relations is that arrangements for workplace dispute resolution have expanded considerably over the past decade or two, specifically in respect of individual disputes. A statutory three-step dismissal, disciplinary and grievance procedure was introduced in 2004 and encapsulated in the pre-existing Acas Statutory Code of Practice on Discipline and Grievance. It required the parties involved in disciplinary matters and employee grievances to go through three stages within the workplace: to set the matter out in writing, to hold a meeting to discuss the issue, and to allow for an appeal. The intention was to limit the proportion of cases that were escalated beyond the workplace. In 2009 the statutory three-step requirement was dropped and the Acas Code was revised to set out principles rather than prescription on how disputes should be handled. However, analysis of WERS suggests that the overall influence of these changes has been to encourage a systematization of workplace procedures. Between 2004 and 2011, the proportion of workplaces with a formal grievance procedure rose from 82 to 89 %, and the proportion of workplaces reporting the requirement to follow the 'three steps' rose from 37 to 46 % (Table 3.5). Similar rises were recorded in relation to procedures for handling disciplinary cases.

Another feature of the policy context around workplace dispute resolution has been the growing interest from policy makers and practitioners

Table 3.5 Workplace dispute resolution procedures, 2004 and 2011

Cell percentage		
	2004	2011
Collective disputes procedure	40	35
With provision for conciliation, arbitration or mediation	8	7
Formal grievance procedure	82	89
With provision for mediation by impartial third party	n/a	45
Formal discipline or dismissal procedure	84	89
With provision for mediation by impartial third party	n/a	45
Steps followed in handling of grievances[a]:		
Set out the concern in writing + Hold a meeting + Give opportunity to appeal	37	46
Steps followed in handling of disciplinary matters[a]:		
Set out the concern in writing + Hold a meeting + Give opportunity to appeal	69	81

Source: Workplace Employment Relations Study
Base: all employees in workplaces with 5 or more employees
Note: [a]The figures are for all workplaces (not merely those with formal procedures)

in the use of mediation (see Saundry et al. 2014). Table 3.5 shows that, in around half of those workplaces with formal procedures for grievance or disciplinary matters, the procedure makes some provision for mediation by an impartial third party. Further data from WERS show that, in 2011, mediation had been used in 13 % of workplaces that had experienced an individual disciplinary or grievance matter, although additional data would be needed in order to understand the situations in which it was, or was not, used.

The expansion of workplace dispute resolution procedures, as shown in Table 3.5, can be expected to compensate, in some way, for the relative scarcity of workplace employee representation in certain sectors of the economy. Union representatives, in particular, have traditionally been seen as a 'lubricant' within the workplace, helping to resolve workplace disputes and also potentially playing a role in managing the expectations of employees

(Edwards 2000). In the 2011 WERS, around four-fifths (78 %) of union representatives said they had spent time in the past year on grievances or disciplinary matters (Van Wanrooy et al. 2013: 155).[13] Yet only 40 % of all employees in 2011 had a union representative at their place of work (26 % in the private sector and 86 % in the public sector). These figures have changed little over the past 10–15 years, with the major decline in union representation being seen in the late 1980s and 1990s. Consequently, with the expansion of dispute resolution procedures, workplaces ought, in some senses, now to be better equipped to deal with workplace conflict.

The main caveat to that conclusion is that responsibility for the management of conflict at work appears to have increasingly been devolved from specialist human resource (HR) practitioners to line managers, who are less confident and less skilled in dealing with such issues (Jones and Saundry 2012; Saundry et al. 2014, 2015). The drivers for this devolution are argued to be twofold: firstly, the development of a more 'strategic' focus for HR; and secondly, an increasing tendency for outsourced models of HR management. It has been argued that one notable consequence is that difficult people management issues are more likely to be handled via formal procedures, which can result in the escalation of disputes rather than promoting their resolution in a culture of informality (*ibid.*).

Summary and Conclusions

The shape of workplace conflict in Britain is currently in a state of flux. Having been prevalent until the early 1990s, strikes and other forms of industrial action are now at historically low levels, and have been for a number of years. The exception, of course, lies in the public sector, where the dynamics of employment relations and the critical nature of many of the services delivered by public sector workers combine to make the strike threat a relatively common feature of negotiations around changes to rewards and working conditions. Over the same period, there has been a substantial growth in the volume of claims made to employment tribunals, but for over a decade this growth has largely been fuelled by multiple

---

[13] The corresponding figure for non-union reps was 44 %.

claims that are, in many ways, a form of collective action. In contrast, the volume of single claims has been relatively stable – at least until the dramatic fall caused by the introduction of fees – suggesting that the rise in total volumes is perhaps one indication of changes in trade unions' tactics rather than an accurate barometer of tensions or problems at work. Indeed, most measures of workplace disputes show little discernible change over the past decade or so. Those movements, which are apparent, tend, if anything, to point towards progressively lower levels of conflict at work.

This is particularly surprising given the backdrop of the longest recession in living memory. There have been disputes, of course, but the prolonged downturn has not lead to a large increase in volumes, despite extensive changes to terms and conditions. Instead, the available evidence suggests that many workers and workplaces have demonstrated a degree of acceptance. It is possible that employees have been dissuaded from resisting by the weakness of the labour market; but it is equally plausible that the depth and length of the recession served to persuade them of the need for substantial changes to terms and conditions. If either is true, then one may expect to see an upturn in disputes (at least those of a collective nature) as the economy begins to grow again and employees seek to recoup some of their recent losses in the context of a tightening labour market. The chances will be particularly high if wage growth in the private sector accelerates whilst wage growth in the public sector is still heavily restrained.

What is missing from this picture, however, is a comprehensive view of the scale of conflict within the employment relationship, particularly that which arises from unwanted behaviours. Most survey-based ratings of managerial behaviour suggest that the quality of social relations in the workplace is gradually improving over time. But few of the longitudinal measures that are available – and which have been reported in this chapter – provide an extensive degree of depth or detail. Our understanding would be considerably enhanced by repeated observations on the extent of fair treatment at work, as made by Fevre et al. (2009, 2012). However, such measures have tended to gain less attention within the policy narrative around conflict at work than measures of formal disputes which, as we have noted, are necessarily limited in their ability to chart changes in the quality of the employment relationship.

It is also important to monitor how the quality of workplace dispute resolution is changing. The last decade has seen a large expansion in the prevalence of workplace dispute resolution procedures, and a systematization of approaches to the handling of grievances or disciplinary matters. However, it has been strongly argued that, although this represents an improvement when compared with previous decades, particularly when viewed against the backdrop of a very partial coverage of workplace employee representation, there are still some considerable challenges involved in making workplace dispute resolution effective. One such challenge is to determine the extent to which workplaces' dispute resolution procedures have, in some senses, led to an over-formalization of the way conflict is handled at work. Procedures no doubt bring an important level of certainty to all parties about the framework for resolving conflict, but overreliance on them may have lead to a reduction in the emphasis on less formal approaches, in such a way as to reduce the chances of finding a restorative solution. A further challenge is how to instil a culture of conflict management in workplaces – one that forms part of the workplace agenda alongside other business priorities, and that promotes early and creative approaches to addressing difficulties or imbalances in power. These are among the major questions to be explored in subsequent chapters of the book.

References

Acas (2015a). *Annual report and accounts 2014–15*. London: HMSO.

Acas (2015b). *Early conciliation update 4: April 2014–March 2015*. London: Acas.

Askenazy, P., Bellmann, L., Bryson, A., & Moreno-Galbis, E. (Eds.). (Forthcoming). *Productivity puzzles across Europe*. Oxford: Oxford University Press.

Cabinet office (2015). *The Queens' speech 2015: lobby pack*. London: The Cabinet office.

CAMS (2009). *International workshop report – 18th September 2009: Social dialogue and the changing role of conciliation, arbitration and mediation services in Europe: A five country study*. London: CAMS Consortium.

CAMS (2010a). *Final report: Social dialogue and the changing role of conciliation, arbitration and mediation services in Europe: A five country study*. London: CAMS Consortium.

CAMS (2010b). *Summary findings: Social dialogue and the changing role of conciliation, arbitration and mediation services in Europe: A five country study*. London: CAMS Consortium.

Carley, M. (2010). Developments in industrial action 2005–2009. *European Observatory of Working Life*, Published online on 24th August 2010.

Casebourne, J., Regan, J., Neathey, F., & Tuohy, S. (2006). Employment rights at work: Survey of employees 2005. *Employment Relations Research Series No. 51*, London: Department of Trade and Industry.

Colling, T. (2012). Trade union roles in making employment rights effective. In L. Dickens (Ed.), *Making employment rights effective: Issues of enforcement and compliance* (pp. 183–204). Oxford: Hart Publishing.

Darlington, R., & Dobson, J. (2015). The Conservative Government's proposed strike ballot thresholds: The challenge to the trade unions. *Salford Business School Research Working Paper*, August.

Davey, B., & Dix, G. (2011). The dispute resolution regulations two years on: The Acas experience. *Acas Research Papers*, 07/11.

Dix, G., & Barber, B. (2015). The changing face of the world of work: Insights from Acas. *Employee Relations 37*(6), 670–682.

Dix, G., Forth, J., & Sisson, K. (2009). Conflict at work: The changing pattern of disputes. In W. Brown, A. Bryson, J. Forth, & K. Whitfield (Eds.), *The evolution of the modern workplace*. Cambridge: Cambridge University Press.

Drinkwater, S., & Ingram, P. (2005). Have industrial relations in the UK really improved? *Labour, 19*(2), 373–398.

Edwards, P. (2000). Discipline: Towards trust and self-discipline? In S. Bach, & K. Sisson (Eds.), *Personnel management: A comprehensive guide to theory and practice in Britain* (3rd ed.,). Oxford: Blackwell.

Elsby, M., Shin, D., & Solon, G. (2013). Wage adjustment in the Great Recession. *NBER Working Paper No. 19478*.

Fevre, R., Nichols, T., Prior, G., & Rutherford, I. (2009). Fair treatment at work report: Findings from the 2008 Survey. *Employment Relations Research Report No. 103*, London: Department for Business Innovation and Skills.

Fevre, R., Lewis, D., Robinson, A., & Jones, T. (2012). *Trouble at work*. London: Bloomsbury.

Forth, J. (2013). *Things looking up – But not if you work in the public sector*, Blog post on 13th December, last retrieved on 23rd September 2015 from: http://www.niesr.ac.uk/blog/things-looking-not-if-you-work-public-sector#.VgPwb9JViko

Forth and Bryson (2015). The UK productivity puzzle. *NIESR Discussion Paper No. 448*. Forthcoming in Askenazy, P., Bellmann, L., Bryson, A., & Moreno-Galbis, E. (Eds.). Productivity puzzles across Europe.Oxford: Oxford University Press.

Gallie, D., Felstead, A., Green, F., & Inanc, H. (2013). *Fear at work in Britain: First findings from the skills and employment survey 2012*. Cardiff: Cardiff University.

Green, F., Felstead, A., Gallie, D., & Inanc, H. (2013). *Job-related wellbeing in Britain: First findings from the skills and employment survey 2012*. Cardiff: Cardiff University.

Gregg, P., Machin, S., & Fernández-Salgado, M. (2014). Real wages and unemployment in the big squeeze. *Economic Journal, 124*(576), 408–432.

Jones, C., & Saundry, R. (2012). The practice of discipline: Evaluating the roles and relationship between managers and HR professionals. *Human Resource Management Journal, 22*(3), 252–266.

Manning, A. (2015). Shifting the balance of power: Workers, employers and wages over the next parliament. In G. Kelly, & C. D'Arcy (Eds.), *Securing a pay rise: The path back to shared wage growth* (pp. 47–52). London: The Resolution Foundation.

Milner, S. (2015). *Comparative employment relations: France, Germany and Britain*. London: Palgrave.

Ministry of Justice (2015). Employment tribunal receipts tables: Annex C. In *Tribunals and gender recognition certificate statistics quarterly: January to March 2015*. London: Ministry of Justice.

Office for National Statistics (2014). *Labour disputes – Annual article 2013*. London: Office for National Statistics.

Purcell, J. (2010). *Individual disputes in the workplace: Alternative disputes resolution*. Dublin: Eurofound.

Roche, B., & Teague, P. (2014). Do recessions transform work and employment? Evidence from Ireland. *British Journal of Industrial Relations, 52*(2), 261–285.

Saundry, R., Latreille, P., Dickens, L., Irvine, C., Teague, P., Urwin, P., & Wibberley, G. (2014). Reframing resolution – Managing conflict and resolving individual employment disputes in the contemporary workplace. *Acas Policy Series:* March.

Saundry, R., Wibberley, G., & Jones, C. (2015). The challenge of managing informally. *Employee Relations, 37*(4), 428–441.

Van Wanrooy, B., Bewley, H., Bryson, A., Forth, J., Stokes, L., & Wood, S. (2013). *Employment relations in the shadow of recession: Findings from the 2011 Workplace Employment Relations Study*. Basingstoke: Palgrave MacMillan.

4

Workplace Conflict: Who, Where, When, and Why?

Jonny Gifford, Matthew Gould, Paul Latreille, and Peter Urwin

Introduction

Over the last three decades there has been a radical shift in the regulatory framework dealing with formal manifestations of workplace conflict in the UK. Legal structures that supported collective industrial action have been weakened and replaced with a system that allows individuals to pursue

J. Gifford
Chartered Institute of Personnel and Development (CIPD), London, UK
e-mail: j.gifford@cipd.co.uk

M. Gould
Centre for Employment Research, University of Westminster, London, UK
e-mail: M.Gould2@westminster.ac.uk

P. Latreille (✉)
Sheffield University Management School, Sheffield, UK
e-mail: p.latreille@sheffield.ac.uk

P. Urwin
Centre for Employment Research, University of Westminster, London, UK
e-mail: urwinp@westminster.ac.uk

© The Editor(s) (if applicable) and The Author(s) 2016
R. Saundry et al. (eds.), *Reframing Resolution*,
DOI 10.1057/978-1-137-51560-5_4

57

enforcement of employment rights through litigation, via employment tribunals (ETs). Current debate often focuses on the costs of the ET system for the workers involved, in particular its implications for business performance and public expenditure (De Dreu 2008; OPP 2008; CIPD 2011; Gallie et al. 2013; Mangan 2013). Policymakers and academics consistently ask how we can best manage workplace conflict in order to prevent escalation to the ET process, and this area has accordingly seen various policy changes to rectify perceived problems following the publication of the Gibbons Review in 2007.

To move this debate forward, a large gap in the evidence base needs to be filled. Concentration on formal manifestations of conflict at the point of entry into the ET system means that, in any one year, we are considering the issues of only approximately 1 % of those in employment.[1] Within each UK workplace there is a continual process of conflict 'bubbling up'—some of which arises as part of the natural process of problem solving and decision-making—and this is either resolved informally or not. A minority of these conflicts escalate to more formal workplace-based resolution structures, and it is only when both these informal and formal workplace processes fail, that we potentially observe an ET case.

Whilst there is a reasonable understanding in the academic and policy literatures of the extent of formal mechanisms for handling workplace conflict and also the pattern of visible employment disputes (for instance, Knight and Latreille 2000; Saridakis et al. 2008; Wood et al. 2014), we know relatively little about the extent and nature of less formal manifestations of workplace conflict (but see Wood et al. 2014). This is particularly the case in smaller organizations and the majority of British workplaces in which there are no established mechanisms of employee representation, notwithstanding their prevalence at ETs (Saridakis et al. 2008).

It is too early to gauge the impact of recent policy developments, such as the introduction of fees and changes to the role of Acas in ETs, but Mike Emmott in a CIPD blog suggests 'there is some indication that early conciliation is opening up more opportunities for Acas to support

---

[1] Figures from *Understanding Society*, in Buscha, F., Latreille, P. and Urwin, P. (2013), *Charging Fees in Employment Tribunals*, commissioned by the Trades Union Congress.

employers in developing better employee relations'.[2] Organizations can benefit from development of effective conflict resolution practices and robust cultures in which it is easier to challenge and hold people to account without undue risk that it escalates into conflict and ultimately a formal dispute—the notion of 'conflict competence' (see Runde and Flanagan 2007). Existing research suggests that the two can be inter-related, with signs that the introduction of workplace mediation can contribute to a healthier organizational culture (Saundry and Wibberley 2012). Nonetheless, to achieve these aims, there is a need to understand the dynamics of workplace conflict more fully, including when it is low-level and not formalized.

Research into mediation has shed light on the workings of workplace conflict that does not reach employment tribunals. However, it is argued that mediation often enters the frame 'too late' (Latreille 2011; Wood et al. 2014; Saundry and Wibberley 2014), as it is seen as most effective when deployed at an earlier stage in the development of a dispute [before parties become entrenched in their positions]. It is often used to mitigate the fallout from a dispute (for example, by ending the employment relationship in a relatively peaceful way or avoiding an ET), rather than to repair or maintain relationships at an earlier stage (Lewis 2015). Thus, a fuller understanding of workplace conflict needs to look beyond that which is referred to mediation.

Lower-level problems at work are included in research conducted by Fevre et al. (2012), but this too differs from the current analysis in that it focuses squarely on problematic behaviour; in other words, how employees have been affected by perceived unfair treatment, such as unreasonable management, rather than on conflict and disputes. The main focus of this paper relates to 'individual' conflict in one-to-one relationships, although in some cases conflict between two colleagues may spread to, or even be inseparable from, conflict within a wider team. The key difference is that we are not concerned with 'collective' or 'industrial' disputes focused on the interests of wider groups of employees. Instead, we focus

---

[2] http://www.cipd.co.uk/blogs/cipdbloggers/b/policy_at_work/archive/2014/11/13/dispute-resolution-employment-tribunals-and-early-conciliation-a-brave-new-world-for-conflict-management.aspx

on problems located in specific relationships and the impact of these on individual employees.

The concept of relationship conflict describes interpersonal friction borne of annoyance or frustration (Jehn and Mannix 2001). This often relates to, but can be distinguished from, task or process conflict, the overlapping concepts rooted respectively in a clash of views on what should be done or in how it should be achieved (Behfar et al. 2011). Further, we distinguish between, on the one hand, *isolated disputes and incidents of conflict* and, on the other hand, *ongoing difficult relationships* that may include simmering tensions and less overt behaviour that is nonetheless felt to be disrespectful, threatening or otherwise unfair. We also include an analysis of the nature of the relationships in conflict, in particular the power dynamics due to whether they are management or colleague relationships.

The chapter contributes to this area of individual, relationship-based conflict through empirical analysis of data from a representative survey of 2,195 UK employees. The self-completion questionnaire covered a range of questions on the nature of workplace conflict experienced in the previous 12 months, the impacts it had, how individuals responded and how well it had been resolved to date.

Following this introduction, we give a short overview of the extent of conflict uncovered by the survey. We then present the results of multivariate analyses to look in turn at: in which types of organization and groups of employees conflict is most common; organizational and relationship factors related to how well conflict is resolved; the association between different approaches to resolving conflict and how fully it is resolved; and factors relating to the seriousness of the impact of conflict.

How Commonplace Is Workplace Conflict?

The survey found that 38 % of UK employees reported some form of interpersonal conflict at work in the last year. This includes 29 % reporting at least one case of an *isolated dispute or incident of conflict* and a similar proportion, 28 %, reporting at least one *ongoing difficult relationship*.

Relatively small numbers reported more than one case of either type (7 % and 5 % respectively).

The survey also asked employees about their perceptions of how common conflict is in their organizations. We find a general tendency to think it is not commonplace (48 %) but it is nonetheless significant that one in four employees (26 %) considers conflict *a common occurrence* in their organization. This should also be seen in the context of recent data, that identifies a rise in both workplace conflict (CIPD 2011) and fear of discrimination or victimization (Gallie et al. 2013; Saundry et al. 2014).

Some descriptive findings based on these data have already appeared in a CIPD (2015) survey report and in this chapter we present findings from a number of descriptive multivariate regression models, to identify the characteristics of firms and individuals that are most closely associated with conflict, its level of seriousness and its resolution, having controlled for a number of other potential differences/drivers.

Experiencing Conflict and Dispute

Table 4.1 sets out the results of a binomial logit regression equation, modelling those factors that are associated with the reporting of an 'isolated dispute or incident of conflict' in the previous 12 months (31 % of the estimation sample). We wish to attempt some form of multivariate analysis, as it provides clarity on the relative importance of key workplace and individual characteristics. For instance, in the CIPD (2015) survey report there is some suggestion that employees are more likely to report conflict if they work in public sector organizations, and also if they work in larger organizations. It is possible that a large component of the public/private difference is driven by the 'overlapping' issue of large firm/small firm difference—public sector employees are invariably working in 'large' firms. The use of a multivariate regression approach allows us some insight into whether these findings are driven by the public/private differential, or the large/small firm split, or possibly both.

Table 4.1 Binomial logit, modelling characteristics associated with reporting of 'Isolated dispute or incident of conflict' [=1]

	Coef.	Std. Err	t	P > t
Reference: Micro business (2–9 employees)				
Small (10–49 employees)	0.184	0.246	0.75	0.454
Medium (50–249)	0.184	0.234	0.78	0.433
Large (250+)	0.206	0.201	1.03	0.305
Ref: Private sector				
Public	0.181	0.146	1.24	0.215
Voluntary	0.854	0.259	3.29	0.001
Reference: Male				
Female	−0.158	0.126	−1.25	0.210
Reference: North				
Midlands	−0.201	0.200	−1.01	0.313
East	−0.010	0.224	−0.04	0.965
London	−0.053	0.217	−0.25	0.805
South	−0.248	0.169	−1.47	0.142
Wales	0.282	0.292	0.97	0.334
Scotland	0.006	0.216	0.03	0.978
Northern Ireland	−0.098	0.568	−0.17	0.863
Reference: Aged ≤24				
25–34	0.544	0.455	1.20	0.231
35–44	0.641	0.453	1.42	0.157
45–54	0.381	0.451	0.84	0.398
55+	0.174	0.453	0.38	0.701
Reference: Social class ABC1				
C2DE	0.250	0.135	1.85	0.064
Reference: Before tax pay is <£15,000				
£15,000–24,999	−0.023	0.171	−0.14	0.892
£25,000–34,999	0.020	0.192	0.10	0.917
£35,000–44,999	0.001	0.226	0.00	0.998
£45,000–59,999	−0.151	0.268	−0.56	0.572
£60,000 or more	0.219	0.248	0.88	0.376
Reference: Length of time with current employer is ≤ years				
>2 years	0.493	0.178	2.78	0.005
Constant	−1.788	0.500	−3.58	0.000

Considering the findings from Table 4.1, relating to an 'isolated dispute or incidence of conflict,' there is no statistically significant difference between the likelihood that this will be reported in firms of different sizes; none of the coefficient estimates are significantly different from zero.[3] There is no correlation between firm size and the extent to which individuals report an isolated dispute, but we do find that this form of conflict is more likely to be reported in voluntary organizations, when compared to private sector organizations (the reference category). In contrast, there is no significant public-private sector difference in reporting of this type of conflict.

There is similarly no apparent gender split that is significant, and the region of an individual's place of work does not seem to exert a separate impact on whether we observe isolated incidences of conflict being reported, although it is worth noting that being from the 'South' has an almost significant (at the 10 % level) negative impact, compared to being from the North. This may reflect recent economic history, where firms in the south have generally faced more favourable market conditions and we might expect such environments to be associated with lower levels of isolated conflict.

It is interesting that, relative to our youngest age group [of those aged 24 or less], those aged between 35 and 44 are significantly more likely to report an isolated dispute, whilst older age groups [aged 45+] are no more or less likely to report conflict, than their youngest colleagues. This suggests that the relationship between age and reporting of isolated conflict is 'non-linear,' as it seems most likely amongst those in the middle of the age distribution. *Skilled/ Semi-skilled/ Unskilled manual workers and Casual workers* (C2DE) are more likely to report isolated conflict, than those from *Higher/ Intermediate/ Junior managerial, administrative, professional or supervisory occupations* (ABC1), although this is a finding that is only weakly significant (at the 10 % level). There is no additional significance of earnings above and beyond the impact of social class. However, those with longer tenure (over 2 years with their current employer) are more likely to have experienced an isolated instance of conflict during the preceding 12 months.

Table 4.2 sets out the results of a standard binomial logit regression equation, modelling those factors that are associated with the reporting

---

[3] This chapter is for a non-specialist audience, so we attempt to avoid technical language. When we speak of a 'statistically insignificant' impact, we refer to the situation where we are unable to reject the null hypothesis of parameter insignificance. When we suggest a 'statistically significant' impact, we refer to the situation where we are able to reject the null hypothesis of parameter insignificance – in both cases we use language that is more accessible to non-technical readers.

Table 4.2 Binomial logit, modelling characteristics associated with reporting of 'ongoing difficult relationship' [=1]

	Coef.	Std. Err	t	P > t
Reference: Micro business (2–9 employees)				
Small (10–49 employees)	0.345	0.250	1.38	0.168
Medium (50–249)	0.430	0.238	1.81	0.070
Large (250+)	0.198	0.208	0.95	0.342
Ref: Private sector				
Public	0.308	0.147	2.10	0.036
Voluntary	0.703	0.261	2.69	0.007
Reference: Male				
Female	0.159	0.127	1.25	0.211
Reference: North				
Midlands	0.046	0.201	0.23	0.818
East	0.150	0.225	0.67	0.506
London	−0.008	0.219	−0.04	0.970
South	−0.129	0.172	−0.75	0.453
Wales	0.562	0.292	1.93	0.054
Scotland	−0.169	0.227	−0.74	0.457
Northern Ireland	0.400	0.548	0.73	0.466
Reference: Aged ≤24				
25–34	0.144	0.408	0.35	0.724
35–44	0.125	0.407	0.31	0.759
45–54	0.011	0.405	0.03	0.979
55+	−0.245	0.408	−0.60	0.547
Reference: Social class ABC1				
C2DE	0.149	0.138	1.08	0.280
Reference: Before tax pay is <£15,000				
£15,000–24,999	0.052	0.174	0.30	0.764
£25,000–34,999	0.167	0.195	0.86	0.392
£35,000–44,999	0.221	0.228	0.97	0.332
£45,000–59,999	0.158	0.267	0.59	0.555
£60,000 or more	0.264	0.255	1.03	0.301
Reference: Length of time with current employer is ≤2 years				
>2 years	0.426	0.177	2.41	0.016
Constant	−1.773	0.465	−3.82	0.000

of an 'ongoing difficult relationship.' Some 30 % of the estimation sample report such a relationship. We have some findings that are similar to those identified in Table 4.1, when we considered the factors associated with isolated disputes, but also some quite interesting differences. For instance, in Table 4.2 there is once again no significant impact of gender or pre-tax pay and we find little significant variation between regions. However, in contrast to our consideration of isolated disputes where the private/public split had no impact, we find that ongoing difficult relationships are significantly more likely (at the 5 % level) to be reported in public, as opposed to private, workplaces. A significant impact of the voluntary sector also remains, with reporting of ongoing difficult relationships much more likely in these sorts of workplaces. Part of the explanation for this finding, and particularly in the public sector, may be the impact of ongoing intensification of work arising from austerity measures by the coalition government; such pressure is likely to bring employees into conflict and exacerbate existing interpersonal strains and tensions (Latreille and Saundry 2015; CIPD 2012).

In contrast to Table 4.1, we also now find that those in medium-sized firms are significantly more likely to report ongoing difficult relationships when compared with those in micro-businesses. When considering the existence of ongoing difficult relationships, it would therefore seem that we have both a public–private split and a firm size effect. Also, while most of the regional dummies remain insignificant, it is interesting that those working in Wales are more likely than workers in the North to report an ongoing difficult relationship—a difference that is not apparent in any other region of the country.

Finally, in contrast to the findings of Tables 4.1 and 4.2 suggests no significant difference in the probability that an individual will report a difficult relationship amongst different age groups or when we consider those from different social backgrounds. In the CIPD survey report there is a suggestion that these two types of conflict are quite 'distinct' in people's minds, as there is relatively little overlap between the two, with most employees identifying either one or the other for specific people. For instance, focusing on conflict with colleagues in one's team, fewer than one in three respondents (28 %) report both an incident of conflict and an ongoing difficult relationship, with the clear majority reporting just the former (31 %) or the latter (41 %). The suggestion from Tables 4.1 and 4.2 is that there are different factors associated with the two types of conflict, and this lends some support to this suggestion.

Resolving Conflict and Disputes

Of the total respondents to the survey, 750 reported one or other of the two forms of conflict considered separately in the previous section. Table 4.3 focuses only on these respondents (n = 683 due to missing data on items used in the estimated model) and identifies the factors that are most closely associated with reporting that the issue has been 'fully' or

Table 4.3   Binomial logit, modelling characteristics associated with reporting of whether [most serious] dispute ['Fully' or 'Largely'] resolved [=1]

	Coef.	Std. Err	t	P > t
Reference: Micro business (2–9 employees)				
Small (10–49 employees)	–0.373	0.375	–1.00	0.320
Medium (50–249)	–0.073	0.353	–0.21	0.837
Large (250+)	–0.317	0.311	–1.02	0.309
Ref: Private sector				
Public	–0.207	0.218	–0.95	0.342
Voluntary	–0.274	0.361	–0.76	0.448
Reference: Line management relationship, 'Someone I report to'				
They report to me (directly or indirectly)	0.551	0.303	1.82	0.069
Colleague	0.311	0.216	1.44	0.150
Somebody external to organisation	0.879	0.263	3.35	0.001
Reference: Length of time with current employer is ≤2 years				
>2 years	–0.074	0.256	–0.29	0.774
Reference: Reporting of ongoing difficult relationship				
Reporting of isolated dispute	1.380	0.252	5.48	0.000
Reporting of both	0.069	0.218	0.32	0.751
Reference: Action taken to resolve is 'Do nothing'				
Informal action taken to resolve#	0.759	0.219	3.47	0.001
Mediation to resolve dispute	2.069	0.663	3.12	0.002
Formal approach to resolution##	1.645	0.381	4.32	0.000
Left the enterprise	–0.356	0.350	–1.02	0.309
Constant	–1.361	0.425	–3.20	0.001

Notes: # Informal action includes (i) informal discussion with the other person; (ii) discussion with my manager and/or HR; (iii) discussion with an employee representative or union official; (iv) discussion with someone outside of work (e.g. family, friend). ## Formal approach to resolution includes (i) formal grievance, discipline or complaints procedure; (ii) filed an Employment Tribunal claim; (iii) mediation 'largely' resolved.[4] Interestingly, fewer than four in ten (38 %) reported the conflict had generally been resolved, suggesting that significant numbers of workers are coping with unsatisfactory workplace relationships or unresolved incidents.[5]

As we can see from Table 4.3, whilst the previous analysis suggested that the reporting of conflict has a significant association with firm/workplace size, there is no difference in the reporting of *resolution* across firms of different sizes. Similarly, there are no significant differences in perceived resolution rates across firms in the public, private or voluntary sectors.

However, having controlled for these factors, it is clear from Table 4.3 that those reporting conflict with their boss are the least likely to suggest that it has been fully or largely resolved when compared to conflict that arises between colleagues of a similar grade or somebody outside the organization. The fact that those who are managers (i.e. 'they report to me') are significantly more likely to say that the dispute has been resolved, identifies an asymmetry in the perceptions of managers and their subordinates. Some form of conflict with a manager is less likely to be resolved satisfactorily in a reporting employee's eyes, but the manager is more likely to feel that it has been resolved.

An important feature of the data is that the type of dispute matters. As might be expected a priori, isolated incidents generally appear more amenable to resolution than those that involve ongoing difficult relationships. The latter are more long-standing and clearly represent problems that are more deep-seated and difficult to resolve. Crucially, there is also a clear indication from the data that doing so requires action to be taken in response to the situation.

One response is simply to leave the organization (an option exercised by around one in seven of those experiencing conflict—14 %

---

[4] The question of resolution necessitates a focus on a specific case of conflict. Thus, for the minority who reported more than one case of conflict in the previous year, each respondent was asked to identify 'the most serious problem (e.g. with the greatest consequences for those affected or the organization)' and to focus on this case for these questions.

[5] Specific figures are: 17 % of employees indicated that the conflict was 'fully resolved', 21 % 'largely but not fully resolved', 19 % 'partly resolved', 22 % 'mainly not resolved' and 20 % 'not at all resolved' ($n = 750$).

Table 4.4 Binomial logit, modelling characteristics associated with reporting of whether a dispute is associated with our 'Most Serious' category of impacts [=1]

	Coef.	Std. Err	t	P > t
Reference: Micro business (2–9 employees)				
Small (10–49 employees)	0.455	0.435	1.05	0.296
Medium (50–249)	0.517	0.419	1.24	0.217
Large (250+)	0.621	0.378	1.64	0.101
Ref: Private sector				
Public	0.025	0.221	0.11	0.911
Voluntary	−0.271	0.383	−0.71	0.479
Reference: Line management relationship, 'Someone I report to'				
They report to me (directly or indirectly)	0.131	0.301	0.43	0.664
Colleague	−0.019	0.218	−0.09	0.930
Somebody external to organisation	−1.131	0.346	−3.27	0.001
Reference: Length of time with current employer is ≤2 years				
>2 years	−0.669	0.257	−2.6	0.009
Reference: Reporting of ongoing difficult relationship				
Reporting of isolated dispute	−0.310	0.297	−1.04	0.296
Reporting of both	0.664	0.224	2.96	0.003
Constant	−1.652	0.484	−3.41	0.001

Notes: # Dispute has resulted in one or more of the following, as the most serious impact: (b) unworkable relationships; (c) sickness absence; (d) necessitated a change in job role; (e) meant that the individual resigned from the job; (f) resulted in formal disciplinary procedures; (g) dismissal or (h) a legal dispute

of the estimation sample in Table 4.4). Statistically this is no different in terms of resolution outcomes than taking no action (around a quarter of the estimation sample), and essentially constitutes an avoidance approach. Conversely, disputes were more likely to be reported by participants as fully, or at least partly, resolved following informal responses such as discussion with the other party; or with other organizational agents such as their manager, HR, an employee representative or union official; or indeed with someone outside of work (e.g. family, friend). Strikingly, around half of respondents experiencing conflict selected this as their most serious response to the issue (52 % of the estimation sample in Table 4.4).

Disputes were also more likely to be resolved for those pursuing mediation, as well as for more formal approaches to resolution including instigation of a grievance, discipline or complaints procedure or an ET claim. However, it should be noted that mediation was a very infrequent response (fewer than 2 % of those experiencing conflict)—in contrast to popular discourses around the willingness of workers to pursue formal processes—and so too were formal procedures (pursued by fewer than 7 % of those experiencing problems).

Table 4.4 next looks at the extent to which individuals who reported some form of conflict suffered the 'most serious' of impacts from the dispute. Here we are a little constrained by considerations of method, in the way we approach the issue. Of the 750 who report some form of dispute and/or ongoing difficult relationship, 65 % suggest one or more of the following as the most significant impact arising from the dispute:

The experience has been (a) stressful and their motivation or commitment has fallen; (b) it has resulted in unworkable relationships; or (c) sickness absence.

However, we then have 14 % of the 750 reporting that one or more of the following is the most serious consequence of the dispute:

It (d) necessitated a change in job role; (e) meant that the individual resigned from the job; (f) resulted in formal disciplinary procedures; (g) resulted in dismissal or (h) resulted in a legal dispute.

Unfortunately, if we estimate a model with (a) *through to* (h) recorded as 'serious,' then we will have only just over 20 % in our group who report none of the 'serious' impacts—in contrast, only considering (d) *to* (h) as 'most serious,' leaves us with 14 % in this category. Either approach is not particularly desirable, because we have such an imbalance between the size of our two dependent categories. Therefore, we adopt a [slightly more desirable] compromise, with (b) *through to* (h) constituting our 'most serious' category of impact, and those reporting stress and/or a drop in motivation or commitment, counted in the less serious category—leaving us with a category of 'most serious' that is 30 % of the total.

Once again, we find little impact for either firm size or our public/private/voluntary split. However, it is worth noting that individuals in our largest category of enterprise (250+) are almost statistically significantly more likely to report the most serious consequences, when compared to those in micro-businesses. Also, we find that those with longer tenure are significantly less likely to suffer serious impacts and the same is also true for those who report a dispute with somebody external to the organization. It is perhaps encouraging to note that line managers of those who are the subject of dispute are no less likely to report serious consequences of the dispute, compared to those who are line managed by the individual who was the subject of dispute. However, as we have already seen, there seems to be a difference in the perceived extent to which such disputes (serious or otherwise) have been satisfactorily resolved.

Table 4.4 also includes variables reflecting the nature of the dispute (ongoing problematic relationships; or one-off incidents; or both). Those who report *both* an ongoing difficult relationship and an isolated dispute are significantly more likely to report that this resulted in the most serious of consequences.

Finally, Table 4.5 reports on those factors associated with whether the route chosen to dispute resolution is either 'formal' or 'informal' (22 % and 78 % respectively). Formal approaches to resolution include 'formal grievance, discipline or complaints procedure' (reported in 9 % of cases; $n = 750$ in the whole sample); 'filed an Employment Tribunal claim' (<1 % of cases); and 'mediation' (2 % of cases). Informal responses include 'informal discussion with the other person' (26 % of cases); 'discussion with my manager and/or HR' (37 % of cases); 'discussion with an employee representative or union official' (8 % of cases); and 'discussion with someone outside of work such as a member of family or friend' (23 % of cases). While generally regarded as an informal method of dispute resolution, mediation is included in the former category given the highly structured (or even choreographed) approach as practised in the UK (Latreille 2011)—at least relative to more general, unscheduled and unstructured discussions with other actors.

Table 4.5 Binomial logit, modelling characteristics associated with whether it takes 'Formal' [=1] or 'Informal' [=0] action to resolve#

	Coef.	Std. Err	t	P > t
Reference: Micro business (2–9 employees)				
Small (10–49 employees)	−0.005	0.550	−0.01	0.993
Medium (50–249)	0.166	0.497	0.33	0.738
Large (250+)	0.230	0.448	0.51	0.607
Ref: Private sector				
Public	0.410	0.294	1.4	0.162
Voluntary	0.479	0.488	0.98	0.326
Reference: Male				
Female	−0.344	0.251	−1.37	0.171
Reference: North				
Midlands	0.180	0.406	0.44	0.657
East	0.040	0.446	0.09	0.928
London	−0.256	0.450	−0.57	0.569
South	0.231	0.348	0.66	0.506
Wales	−2.504	1.077	−2.32	0.020
Scotland	0.091	0.433	0.21	0.834
Northern Ireland	0.347	0.972	0.36	0.721
Reference: Aged ≤24				
25–34	1.015	0.907	1.12	0.263
35–44	0.854	0.904	0.94	0.345
45–54	1.113	0.909	1.22	0.221
55+	0.582	0.915	0.64	0.524
Reference: Social class ABC1				
C2DE	0.107	0.285	0.38	0.707
Reference: Before tax pay is <£15,000				
£15,000–24,999	0.647	0.361	1.79	0.073
£25,000–34,999	−0.071	0.407	−0.17	0.861
£35,000–44,999	0.082	0.472	0.17	0.862
£45,000–59,999	−0.097	0.588	−0.17	0.869
£60,000 or more	0.286	0.501	0.57	0.568
Reference: Length of time with current employer is ≤2 years				
>2 years	−0.899	0.344	−2.61	0.009
Reference: Reporting of ongoing difficult relationship				
Reporting of isolated dispute	0.229	0.364	0.63	0.529
Reporting of both	0.655	0.313	2.09	0.037
Reference: Dispute less serious				
Most serious category of dispute	1.090	0.249	4.38	0.000
Constant	−2.571	1.043	−2.46	0.014

Notes: # 'Formal' and 'informal' defined as in Figure 3, with mediation included in the former

Most of the standard demographics (organizational size, sector, region, age group, gender, social class and income) appear uncorrelated with the choice. Three exceptions are (i) the length of time an individual has worked for the organization, with those of longer tenure being less likely to pursue formal processes; (ii) those with before tax pay between £15,000 and £24,999, who are slightly more likely to pursue formal processes than those in the lowest pay band; and (iii) individuals in Wales, who are less likely to pursue formal action than those in the North of England.

Most of the key drivers of this choice appear to revolve around the dispute itself. Thus, whilst there is no difference in the choice of formal versus informal processes according to whether the problem relates to ongoing relationship problems or a specific incident/dispute, more formal approaches are significantly more likely where both are involved. Perhaps unsurprisingly, more formal measures are also more likely where the dispute is regarded as 'most serious' in its impact.

Emerging Conclusions

In the wake of the Gibbons Review of the UK system of dispute resolution (Gibbons 2007), public policy has emphasized the need for early and informal interventions to resolve disputes. This was particularly evident among small employers for whom the emphasis on formality and written communication was seen as 'counter-cultural' (Gibbons 2007). Consequently, the Employment Act 2008 abolished the statutory requirement to use statutory disputes procedures and provided for a shorter and less prescriptive Acas Code of Practice on Disciplinary and Grievance Procedures.

Despite this, evidence suggests a continued formalization of workplace procedures (Wood et al. 2014) alongside inflated perceptions by employers of the regulatory burden and consequent threat of employment litigation (Jordan et al. 2013). In order to avoid legal action, employers are often reluctant to adopt common sense, informal approaches, as this is seen as risky and leaves them less well-protected in the event of a claim (Jones and Saundry 2012). As a result, many employers adopt risk-averse strategies, arguing that the costs regime encourages weak, speculative claims that they are forced to settle to minimize expenditure on legal advice, representation and the cost of management time (British Chambers of Commerce 2011; CBI 2011). Similarly, they argue that the complexity of the legislative framework and fear of litigation discourages them from taking on new employees. This is partly what lies behind the drive to introduce fees in the face of 'frivolous' claims (see Mangan 2013).

This chapter goes some way to illuminate a starting point for the consideration of dispute and its resolution, whether or not it is formalized. One thing we need to keep in mind when considering a broader definition of conflict, is that it is quite possible that what constitutes a dispute is different in different settings. For instance, we need to remember that what constitutes conflict in the public sector, may be different to that in the private sector; and some of our results could be driven by a greater willingness, for instance amongst public sector employees, to report (what they consider to be) conflict. When considering only those types of conflict that are formalized, there tends to be less potential for this, as we are only picking up those disputes that 'fit' within certain jurisdictions. Also, we must remember that the multivariate analysis undertaken here does not isolate the causes of conflict, but rather those factors which are associated with higher or lower levels of conflict, and its resolution (i.e. they are correlates).

With these caveats in mind, we uncover some interesting differences in the correlates of conflict. Firstly, there seems to be some confirmation of a more general finding in the literature, which considers more formal manifestations of conflict in firms of different sizes. There is a raft of evidence that smaller firms have less formal procedures for managing conflict, and this reflects an approach to employment relations that (necessarily) tends to be less formal (see for instance, Urwin 2011; Urwin and Buscha 2012) when compared to larger firms. However, there is also evidence (for instance, Forth et al. 2006) that employment relations in small firms are less conflictual. For instance, 67 % of employees in the SME sector 'strongly agree' that managers treat them fairly, compared to just 53 % of those in large firms (Forth et al. 2006).

This may suggest that smaller workplaces or organizations provide more conducive environments in which managers can respond to employee concerns. Smaller businesses are less likely to levy serious sanctions such as dismissal than larger organizations (Forth et al. 2006). This may point to a greater willingness to resolve issues informally, something that is perhaps supported by the personal, sometimes familial and less formal nature of employment relations in small organizations in general (Edwards et al. 2004; Harris et al. 2008). We find that there is no firm-size effect when considering isolated disputes, but we do find that employees in medium-sized firms are more likely (though only at the 10 % level of significance) to report an ongoing difficult relationship. Similarly, whilst there seems no difference in the reporting of isolated disputes in public and private sector organizations, those in the public sector are significantly more likely to report a difficult relationship, when compared to those in the private sector. Overall, we have some support for the suggestion that it is not just in the formal manifestations of conflict that we see a small firm/large firm difference, but this is also evident when we consider the wider issue of ongoing difficult relationships (whether or not they are formalized). The extent to which these are subsequently resolved does not seem significantly different in larger and smaller organizations.

It is possible that the reporting of isolated disputes is picking up a greater proportion of incidents that arise as a result of the financial situation of the firm, or wider economic environment (when compared to the reporting of ongoing difficult relationships). However, one of the few significant patterns we have in this study when considering isolated disputes is the greater likelihood that these will be reported by employees who are often referred to as 'prime aged' (some are a little young to be referred to as 'middle-aged'). It would be unusual if this pattern were driven by issues of, for instance, downsizing, as it is still the case that younger workers tend to bear the brunt of labour force reductions (though they are also subsequently more likely to regain employment, when compared to older workers).

We also find that the likelihood of experiencing conflict decreases with tenure (specifically, as employment passes the two year mark). Whilst the 2008 Survey of Employment Tribunal Applications found that employment tribunals are more prevalent among longer-serving employees, with a median length of service of 3 years (Lucy and Broughton 2011), our finding is in line with the 2008 Fair Treatment at Work Survey (FTW), which found that problems in the workplace were more likely among newer employees with up to one year's length of service (Fevre et al. 2009). The key difference here relates to the seriousness of the conflict, with both the current survey and FTW focusing on a wider range of conflict, including lower-level disputes and a few cases that reach the point of a tribunal application. One likely explanation for this negative effect of tenure on experiences of workplace conflict is that, as employees get to know their organizations and colleagues better, they are better placed to navigate the dominant social structures; in particular, they know who to talk to and how to get issues resolved informally. It may also be that, as the employment relationship becomes more established, cases of conflict are more likely to be seen 'in the grand scheme of things' as relatively less important.

Our data also point strongly to the necessity of responding to conflict if it is to be resolved. One response—albeit essentially avoidance—is for an individual to leave the organization. This involves significant (transaction) costs for both the individual and employer, the latter especially in relation to recruitment and selection, but also where idiosyncratic skills/knowledge mean new recruits are less productive than experienced staff as they learn their role.

Finally, as we suggest in the analysis undertaken towards the end of this chapter, there is some indication that those who line-manage individuals are more likely to feel that a particular dispute has been satisfactorily resolved—but those who are subordinate in this relationship are less likely to feel that this is the case. This provides a clear lesson for some line managers, who perhaps need to be aware that their perceptions are not necessarily aligned with those of their subordinates. Thankfully, the extent to which any such disputes result in serious impacts seems not to differ significantly between line managers and those who are managed.

References

Behfar, K., Mannix, E., & Peterson, R. (2011). Conflict in small groups: The meaning and consequences of process conflict. *Small Group Research*, 42(2), 127–176.

British Chambers of Commerce (2011). *The workforce survey – Small businesses, October 2011*. London: British Chambers of Commerce.

CBI. (2011). *Settling the matter – Building a more effective and efficient tribunal system*, April.

CIPD. (2011). *Conflict management – Survey report*. London: CIPD.

CIPD. (2012). *Employee outlook: Spring 2012*. London: CIPD.

CIPD. (2015). *Getting under the skin of workplace conflict: Tracing the experiences of employees*. Survey report, April. London: CIPD.

De Dreu, C. (2008). The virtue and vice of workplace conflict: Food for (pessimistic) thought. *Journal of Organizational Behaviour, 29*, 5–18.

Edwards, P., Ram, M., & Black, J. (2004). Why does employment legislation not damage small firms? *Journal of Law and Society, 31*(2), 245–265.

Fevre, R., Nichols, T., Prior, G., & Rutherford, I. (2009). Fair treatment at work report: Findings from the 2008 Survey. *Employment Relations Research Series* No.103, Department for Business Enterprise and Regulatory Reform (BERR).

Fevre, R., Lewis, D., & Robinson, A. (2012). *Trouble at work*. London: Bloomsbury.

Forth, J., Bewley, H., & Bryson, A. (2006) *Small and medium sized enterprises: Findings from the 2004 Workplace Employment Relations Survey*. London: Department of Trade and Industry.

Gallie, D., Felstead, A., Green, F., & Inanc, H. (2013). *Fear at work in Britain – First findings from the skills and employment survey, 2012*. London: Centre for Learning and Life Chances in Knowledge Economies and Societies, Institute of Education.

Gibbons, M. (2007). *A review of employment dispute resolution in Great Britain*. London: DTI.

Harris, L., Tuckman, A., & Snook, J. (2008). Small firms and workplace disputes resolution. *Acas Research Papers*, 01/08.

Jehn, K., & Mannix, E. (2001). The dynamic nature of conflict: A longitudinal study of intragroup conflict and group performance. *Academy of Management Journal, 44*(2), 238–251.

Jones, C., & Saundry, R. (2012). The practice of discipline: Evaluating the roles and relationship between managers and HR professionals. *Human Resource Management Journal, 22*(3), 252–266.

Jordan, E., Thomas, A., Kitching, J., & Blackburn, R. (2013). Employment regulation – Part A: Employer perceptions and the impact of employment regulation. *Employment Relations Research Series*, 123, Department for Business, Innovation and Skills.

Knight, K. G., & Latreille, P. L. (2000). Discipline, dismissals and complaints to employment tribunals. *British Journal of Industrial Relations, 38*(4), 533–555.

Latreille, P. L. (2011). Workplace mediation: A thematic review of the Acas/CIPD evidence. *Acas Research Papers*, 13/11.

Latreille, P., & Saundry, R. (2015). Employment rights and industrial policy. In D. Bailey, K. Cowling, & P. Tomlinson (Eds.), *New perspectives on industrial policy for a modern Britain*. Oxford: Oxford University Press.

Lewis, C. (2015). *How to master workplace and employment mediation*. Haywards Heath: Bloomsbury.

Lucy, D., & Broughton, A. (2011). Understanding the behaviour and decision making of employees in conflicts and disputes at work. *Employment Relations Research Series* No. 119. Department for Business Enterprise and Regulatory Reform (BERR).

Mangan, D. (2013). Employment tribunal reforms to Boost the Economy. *Industrial Law Journal*, 42(4)), 409–421.

OPP (2008). *Fight, flight or face it – Celebrating the effective management of conflict at work*. Oxford: OPP.

Runde, C. E.,., & Flanagan, T. A. (2007). *Becoming a conflict competent leader*. San Francisco: Jossey-Bass.

Saridakis, G., Sen-Gupta, S., Edwards, P., & Storey, D. (2008). The impact of enterprise size on employment tribunal incidence and outcomes: Evidence from Britain. *British Journal of Industrial Relations*, 46(3), 469–499.

Saundry, R., & Wibberley, G. (2012). Mediation and early resolution – A case study in conflict management. *Acas Research Papers*, 12/12.

Saundry, R., Latreille, P., Dickens, L., Irvine, C., Teague, P., Urwin, P., & Wibberley, G. (2014). *Reframing resolution – Managing conflict and resolving individual employment disputes in the contemporary workplace*, Acas Policy Paper.

Saundry, R., & Wibberley, G. (2014). Workplace dispute resolution and the management of individual conflict —A thematic analysis of five case studies. *Acas Research Papers*, 06/14.

Urwin, P. (2011). *Self-employment, small firms and enterprise*. London: Institute of Economic Affairs.

Urwin, P., & Buscha, F. (2012). *Back to work: the role of small businesses in employment and enterprise*. Blackpool: Federation of Small Businesses.

Wood, S., Saundry, R., & Latreille, P. (2014). Analysis of the nature, extent and impact of grievance and disciplinary procedures and workplace mediation using WERS2011. *Acas Research Papers*, 10/14.

5

Social Structure and Conflict: A Relational Approach to the Study of Conflict and Its Management in Organizations

Ariel C. Avgar, Eric J. Neuman, and Wonjoon Chung

Introduction: The Reciprocal Relationship Between Conflict and Social Structure

Conflict and its management are central organizational phenomena affecting a wide array of outcomes ranging from individual attitudes and perceptions to group and firm-level performance (Amason 1996;

A.C. Avgar
School of Labor and Employment Relations, University of Illinois,
Urbana-Champaign, USA
e-mail: avgar@illinois.edu

E.J. Neuman
Department of Marketing & Management, Creighton University,
Omaha, USA
e-mail: EricNeuman@creighton.edu

W. Chung
School of Labor and Employment Relations, University of Illinois,
Urbana-Champaign, USA
e-mail: chung51@illinois.edu

© The Editor(s) (if applicable) and The Author(s) 2016
R. Saundry et al. (eds.), *Reframing Resolution*,
DOI 10.1057/978-1-137-51560-5_5

De Dreu 1997; De Dreu and van Vianen 2001; De Dreu and Weingart 2003; Jehn 1995, 1997; Lovelace et al. 2001; Schweiger and Sandberg 1989; Schwenk 1990). Over the past 30 years conflict scholars have amassed an impressive body of research documenting the effects that this construct can have on a host of organizational stakeholders and outcome measures, from employee wellbeing (De Dreu et al. 2004) to team effectiveness (De Dreu 1997; Jehn 1997). This research has also distinguished between different types of conflict. Most notably is a distinction made between relationship conflict, which centers on how well individuals get along, and task conflict, which centers on how individuals perform their work (Jehn 1995, 1997).

One of the central questions guiding much of this research has been the extent to which conflict serves as a functional or dysfunctional organizational force (see for example, De Dreu 1997; Jehn 1997). Can conflict provide teams and organizations with significant benefits alongside its associated challenges? If so, what types of conflict are most likely to do so? Scholars have long debated whether conflict is primarily a destructive or constructive construct (De Dreu 1997; Jehn 1997). While we think that this theme has provided a wealth of conceptual and empirical insights, the focus on, primarily, attitudinal and performance outcome measures, tends to reduce a complex construct to very simplistic and linear terms. Conflict, as we will maintain in this chapter, has a reciprocal relationship with the social structure in which it exists and is, therefore, likely to have a more nuanced effect on individuals, groups and organizations.

Conflict, at its core, is a relational phenomenon that both affects and is affected by the social context in which it is embedded. As such, conflict is inextricably linked to the social context in which it emerges (Nelson 1989). At its most basic level conflict is the product of dyadic tensions and disagreement, which can spillover and include larger relational configurations (Jehn et al. 2013). Even the most intricate and large scale organizational conflicts are comprised of this basic relational building block. Tensions and disagreements at the dyadic level are a powerful organizational force since they can dramatically alter the manner in which individuals in situations of conflict engage one another, interact, and exchange information and ideas. In so doing, conflict can redirect the actual paths of communications and interactions throughout an organization. Conflict, therefore, has the potential of affecting the relational landscape of a given organizational setting.

At the same time, the type of conflicts that arise within the boundaries of an organization are, in large part, also determined by the existing relational and structural patterns that are characteristic of the specific social setting (Nelson 1989). Relational network patterns and structures serve as the arteries through which conflict travels within the organization. In other words, conflict and its consequences are also shaped by the relational fabric present within the organization, the unit and the team. As such, determining the positive and negative outcomes associated with conflict may be far more difficult than some scholars assume for two reasons.

First, conflict is likely to have a pronounced effect on the quality of relational ties and dynamics in the workplace. Put simply, conflict alters the relational DNA of an organization by affecting the way in which individuals and consequently teams interact and communicate. To be clear, this is not to say that conflict is necessarily detrimental to social ties and dynamics within the organizations. As will be discussed below, conflict can, in certain situations, improve relational patterns. Rather, our argument is that conflict research needs to account not only for the effects that conflict has on attitudes, perceptions and various measures of performance, but also for how it influences social and relational factors.

Second, relational ties that exist among a group's members are also likely to affect the presence of conflict within the group (Labianca et al. 1998; Nelson 1989). Conflict seldom emerges spontaneously among a group of individuals; it arises in response to a perceived difference of interests. Interactions that occur among specific group members could be opportunities to discover such differences in interest, and for conflict to emerge, or they could be conduits for existing conflict to spread through each party's ties. We therefore argue that understanding a group's pattern of interactions is useful in learning how intragroup conflict can both emerge and develop.

Together, the preceding two points suggest that a group's conflict and its social structure have a reciprocal relationship: conflict affects social structure and social structure affects conflict. It is this argument that we advance in this chapter. In what follows, we review existing evidence on the link between conflict and different relational and social factors. We begin by documenting the relationship between conflict and organizational social capital and social networks. Next, we provide support for the argument that conflict is, among other things, the product of social factors and dynamics. We show, for example, that the network patterns within a team affect individual members' very ability to see or identify conflict. Second, we provide evidence regarding the relationship between the network configuration of conflict interactions and overall perceptions of conflict. Finally, we conclude with a discussion of the implications, practical and scholarly, that stem from this relational approach to understanding organizational conflict. We maintain that viewing conflict through this relational lens has a number of clear benefits as to how scholars understand conflict and how practitioners deal with and manage it.

Conflict and Its Effects on Organizations' Social Dynamics

In this section, we review evidence that examines how conflict can have a significant effect on social structure and relational patterns within an organization and its teams and groups. For the purposes of this chapter, we take a broad approach to the concept of social structure as it pertains to organizations and teams. Our use of the term 'social structure' will include both the actual pattern of relationships that exist in a team or organization (i.e. social networks) and the resources and opportunities that arise for actors within these relationships (i.e. social capital). The studies we review will consider both social capital and social network patterns. This research points to a clear link between conflict and conflict management in organizations and the patterns and quality of social ties. This is important since it strongly suggests that conflict serves as a vehicle through which organizational structure is shaped and reshaped. This evidence also highlights the nuanced relationship between conflict and social structure.

The Link Between Conflict and Social Capital

One way to demonstrate a link between conflict and social structure is to document a relationship between conflict and a central relational construct – social capital. Although defined in many different ways (Adler and Kwon 2002), social capital can generally be conceptualized as an asset that is embedded or inheres in social relations or networks (Coleman 1988; Leana and van Buren 1999; Nahapiet and Ghoshal 1998). Others have referred to social capital as the 'good will that is engendered by the fabric of social relations' (Adler and Kwon 2002). Like conflict, social capital has been shown to influence a host of organizational outcomes, from knowledge sharing and transfer to knowledge creation and innovation (Adler and Kwon 2002; Bouty 2000; Hansen 1999; Subramaniam and Youndt 2005). One way to think about social capital is as the relational glue that ensures intragroup and intergroup ties and overall cohesion. Social capital is, fundamentally, a relational construct influenced by the quality of relationships between individuals (Gittell 2000). Since social capital is viewed as a primarily positive organizational resource, much of the research examining its development has focused on the role that cooperative and consensus focused processes play in its creation and development (for a similar argument see Avgar 2010). What about non-cooperative dynamics? What about conflict? Can conflict affect the creation of this important organizational resource? Furthermore, can conflict have a positive effect on social capital?

Avgar (2010) sets forth the argument that conflict plays an important role in both enhancing and hindering the development of social capital. This argument is based, in large part, on the core characteristics of social capital. First, in contrast to other forms of capital, like human or physical, social capital is jointly and not individually owned (Nahapiet and Ghoshal 1998). In other words, no single organizational actor has sole ownership over this resource. Social capital, therefore, resides in the relational space between the actors in a given setting. Second, in addition to being jointly owned, social capital is built upon an inherent interdependence between those actors that own this resource (Burt 1992). Social capital represents the reciprocal good will between organizational actors and is, therefore, inherently dependent on the use of multiple parties. The very use of social capital requires, by definition, the cooperation and approval of all its owners.

Since social capital is both jointly owned and is a function of organizational actors' interdependence, it is likely that factors that influence the nature and quality of the relationship between the actors that own this resource will affect its creation and availability. Conflict, a construct that certainly affects the relationships between actors, is, therefore, likely to influence how much social capital is available in a given setting. Furthermore, it is likely that different types of conflict will have a different effect on organizational social capital. Conflict scholars have long distinguished between different types of conflict (Jehn 1997; Jehn and Mannix 2001). One of the most established typologies differentiates between relationship conflict that centers on how the parties get along, and task conflict that centers on how the parties execute work related tasks (Jehn and Bendersky 2003).

Building on this typology, conflict that is primarily related to the relationship between individuals is likely, according to this argument, to negatively affect social capital since it weakens and undermines the quality of the relationship between individuals, which, as noted above, stand at the heart of this relational construct (for a review of research regarding relationship conflict see De Wit et al. 2012). Relationship conflict has been shown to be destructive to a host of relational outcomes (Simon and Peterson 2000; Janssen et al. 1999; Jehn 1995; Wall and Nolan 1986) lending support for the argument that it will also undermine the creation of social capital. On the other hand, conflict that focuses primarily on disagreements regarding work-related tasks may actually increase social capital since it may serve to advance the way in which actors engage around the work at hand and does not necessarily weaken the parties' relationships (for a review of research regarding task conflict see De Wit et al. 2012). Task conflict has been shown to force parties to deliberate and communicate about how things are done and performed within the team (Lovelace et al. 2001; Pelled 1996). In contrast to relationship conflict, therefore, this type of conflict may have the capacity to improve and facilitate relational dynamics.

What role does conflict management play in affecting perceptions of social capital? In addition to examining the relationship between conflict and social capital, Avgar (2010) also assessed the role that different conflict management options play in affecting unit social capital. In particular, respondents were asked about the extent to which they used supervisors, peers or formal options, including an ombudsman, to address and resolve unit conflict. The author hypothesized that employee use of conflict management options to resolve unit conflict would have a positive direct effect on social capital. In addition to a proposed positive association between conflict management and social capital, it was argued that use of conflict management options would moderate the relationship between conflict and social capital. In other words, use of conflict management options was expected to mitigate the negative effects of conflict and to amplify the positive effects.

Avgar (2010) puts these overarching propositions to the test and examines the relationship between three types of conflict and unit level social capital in the healthcare setting. In particular, the author tested the relationship between task, relationship and patient care conflict, which captured the conflict that arises between employees associated with the delivery of care. The hypotheses set forth proposed a negative relationship between relationship conflict and social capital and a positive relationship between both task and patient care conflict and social capital. Analysis of survey data from 791 employees employed in a large teaching hospital provided partial support for these hypotheses. Relationship conflict was indeed negatively related to reported unit social capital. In other words, higher levels of reported relationship conflict were associated with lower levels of frontline employee-reported social capital. Task conflict, in contrast to the author's hypothesis, was also shown to be negatively related to social capital. Thus, both relational and task focused conflict appear to undermine unit social capital. Nevertheless, when looking at the relationship between patient care conflict, arguably a specific type of task conflict, and social capital, the author found a positive and significant relationship. Conflict that arose between healthcare professionals about how they deliver their care was associated with greater levels of reported social capital. This finding suggests that conflict about issues related to the core mission of the organization may serve to enhance relational connectedness.

Results from this study documented a positive relationship between the three conflict management options (supervisor, peer and formal dispute resolution) and reported unit social capital. Of the three options, however, only supervisor resolution moderated the relationship between conflict and social capital. Specifically, use of a supervisor to address relationship conflict was shown to mitigate the negative effects associated with high levels of this type of conflict. Use of supervisors to help address task conflict was shown to amplify the benefits associated with low levels of this type of conflict. In other words, use of supervisors to help address conflict was shown to have an indirect effect on social capital, but operated differently for task and relationship conflict.

These findings have three important implications for this chapter's over-all argument. First, they provide support for the claim that conflict has the potential to influence the very social setting in which it emerges. Social capital, which is a function of the relational dynamics between its owners, appears to be influenced by reported conflict. Second, this evidence also suggests that conflict's effect on social capital can vary by conflict type. While task and relationship conflict appear to decrease reported social capi-tal, conflict specific to the core mission of the organization – patient care – seems to have the potential to increase reported social capital. Conflict can, therefore, both hinder and enhance a crucial relational construct. Finally, the manner in which organizations and units address conflict also affects the reported levels of social capital. Proactive resolution of conflict appears to have a positive and direct and indirect effect on social capital, thereby providing yet additional support for the importance of this organizational activity. Conflict is an inevitable part of organizational life, but its negative effects on unit relational strength is not. Organizations can implement, foster and support practices and processes designed to address workplace conflict that, among other things, can limit the conflict's damage to social capital. Interestingly, supervisor-assisted resolution, which tends to be somewhat ignored in the dispute resolution literature, was shown to play a central role in mitigating the negative consequences of conflict.

The Link Between Conflict and Social Networks

Another way to assess the extent to which conflict shapes social structure is by examining its effects on network patterns and ties. One way to think about networks is as the social infrastructure through which relational properties, like social capital, flow (Walker et al. 1997). As such, the development of an array of network ties within and outside a given group or team can be essential for effectiveness and performance (Cross and Cummings 2004). For example, network research has demonstrated that teams with more extensive bridging or external ties outperform teams with fewer bridging ties (Sparrowe, Liden et al. 2001). Since teams vary in their network patterns in general and their bridging ties in particular, scholars have attempted to better understand the factors that influence tie formation (Madhavan et al. 2004; Ozcan and Eisenhardt 2009).

Much of the scholarship on antecedents to the formation of bridging ties has focused on individual level factors (Neuman and Avgar 2014). Interestingly, the role of conflict as an antecedent to tie formation, especially as it relates to bridging ties, has been relatively absent from this discussion (for exceptions see Labianca et al. 1998; Nelson 1989). Does conflict alter the ways in which individuals connect to those inside and outside of their work groups? What role does conflict play in explaining different tie formation patterns? If conflict changes the nature of the relationships within and outside teams and influences member perceptions of their social reality, it is likely to influence the way in which team members connect to their peers (Labianca et al. 1998).

Neuman and Avgar (2014) conceptualized and empirically tested the link between team conflict and the formation of bridging ties. Conflict, they maintain, will shape the pattern of team member ties with internal and external team members. Specifically, the authors develop the argument that different types of conflict (task and relationship) will have a different effect on the documented tie formation patterns. As with the study of conflict and social capital discussed above, Neuman and Avgar examined the effects of both relationship and task conflict and maintain that given the nature of the differences between both types of conflict, they will affect bridging tie formation in different ways.

Specifically, the authors set forth the argument that relationship conflict, which undermines the quality of interpersonal relationships between team members, is likely to push individuals to form ties with members of other teams. Among the many established negative consequences associated with relationship conflict is the hampering of decision-making quality and information processing abilities (Jehn and Mannix 2001). Relationship conflict is, therefore, associated with reduction in team members' interactions. The absence of positive, satisfying and fulfilling ties inside one's team will, according to the authors, incentivize team members to pursue relational ties with members of other teams.

Task conflict, on the other hand, requires increased engagement and connection on the part of team members since it calls for work-related deliberations and debates and will therefore decrease the number of external ties formed. In fact, task conflict has been shown to increase decision-making quality and increases the quantity and quality of interactions (Baron 1991; Fiol 1994; Janssen et al. 1999; Putnam 1994; Schweiger et al. 1986; Schweiger et al. 1989; Simons and Peterson 2000). Unlike relationship conflict which challenges a team's relational foundation, task conflict is likely to lead to the strengthening of internal ties, thereby decreasing the need or ability to form external ties. Neuman and Avgar maintain that the increase in interactions associated with task conflict not only decreases the need to form external ties but likely limits the resources, cognitive and time related, to form additional external ties.

The authors tested these hypotheses using data from a Fortune 100 financial services firm headquartered in the Midwest. Specifically, they were granted access to study a prestigious 11-week internship program conducted, in large part, in interdisciplinary project teams. The 51 participants were surveyed six times during the duration of the internship program, allowing us to collect rich data both on the patterns of conflict within each team and the network tie formation patterns. Analysis of this survey data provides strong support for the overarching argument that conflict affects social structure. First, team members who perceived greater levels of relationship conflict were more likely to form ties with members of other teams. Relationship conflict, therefore, appears to push members to form social ties outside their team. In addition, team members who reported higher levels of task conflict were less likely to form ties with members of other teams. Task conflict appears to, therefore, pull members closer into the team.

These findings have important implications for this chapter's primary inquiry and add further support for the link between conflict and social structure. The relational dynamics inside a team, expressed through conflict, shape the patterns of connections made by team members. This relationship, however, is nuanced and is contingent on the type of conflict being experienced. This evidence provides a closer and more micro look at how conflict might alter an organization's social structure suggesting that at the most foundational level conflict changes individual tie formation patterns. In the aggregate these changes are likely to have a profound effect on an organization's network configuration. These results also point to the complex relationship between conflict and social structure. As noted above, relationship conflict has been almost exclusively deemed to be a detrimental construct with a host of negative consequences for individuals, teams and organizations. When it comes to bridging ties, which are often seen as an essential source of new information and ideas, it appears as though this 'maligned' form of conflict may, under certain conditions, have silver lining in that it increases the likelihood that members will form ties outside their team. This increase in external ties can translate into greater team social capital. Adding social structure as a lens through which to study and understand conflict is likely to shed light on new and unexpected relationships between these phenomena.

The Effects of Social Structure on Conflict

The second piece of the argument advanced in this chapter is that alongside social structure being affected by conflict, conflict is affected by social structure. Conflict represents the manifestation of tensions and disagreements between at least two individuals and often spread across a given workplace setting (Jehn et al. 2013). Given the role that social structure plays in shaping interaction and communication patterns, it seems likely that it will also influence the manner in which these tensions and disagreement get expressed and played out in organizations.

Social Networks and Conflict

Although limited, there is a body of seminal research that supports this proposed relationship between social structure and conflict. For example, Nelson (1989) provided early evidence regarding the link between social networks and conflict in an organizational setting. Nelson hypothesized that organizations in which groups developed more frequent and strong external ties would experience low levels of conflict. Frequent and strong intragroup conflict, on the other hand, should be associated with higher levels of organizational conflict according to Nelson. In other words, variation in the presence of conflict within organizations was, according to Nelson, a function of the strength and frequency of both internal and external ties with each of these ties affecting the development of conflict differently. Using data from 20 organizations Nelson found general support for the argument that organizational conflict is a product of social networks. He noticed that, in general, strong ties (both internal and external) appear to be associated with low conflict organizations. Nevertheless, analysis of data from these organizations pointed to a more complex reality. One of the key differences between high and low conflict organizations, Nelson found, was not just the frequency or strength of social ties. Rather, the absence of a dominant group with strong ties to other groups was associated with high levels of conflict. In other words, organizational conflict appears, according to these findings, to be related to the characteristics of the ties within and between groups and, perhaps more importantly, the structural configuration of these ties. As such, this study provides important support for the proposition that structure matters when it comes to explaining variation in organizational conflict.

Labianca et al. (1998) also studied the relationship between social networks and perceptions of conflict. Interestingly, the authors moved beyond merely examining the social network structure. Rather, they also included an assessment of the substantive nature of the ties between organizational members. Specifically, they distinguished between friendship ties and ties that were associated with negative relationships. They hypothesized that the number of friendship ties with members of other groups will be negatively associated with perceptions of intergroup conflict while the number of negative relationship ties will be positively related to such perceptions. Furthermore, the authors also proposed that perceptions of intergroup conflict was also a function of indirect relationships, or the type of ties that an individual's friends have with others. Thus, Labianca et al. (1998) hypothesized that the number of friendship ties with individuals who have negative relationships with peers in other teams will be positively associated with perceptions of intergroup conflict while the number of ties with individuals that have friendships with peers from other teams will be negatively associated with conflict perceptions. Using data collected in a university health center the authors found partial support for their hypotheses. Friendship ties were not significantly related to perceptions of conflict, but negative relationships were. Nevertheless, friendship ties with others that had both positive and negative relationships with peers from other teams were significantly related to perceptions of conflict in the expected direction. This study provides important evidence for the role that social networks and the substantive nature of individual ties play in affecting how team members perceive conflict. Thus, it is not just the structure of social relationships that matter, but also the nature of those relationships that helps explain variation in how conflict is perceived inside organizations.

Social Networks and Conflict Accuracy

Labianca et al. (1998) provided support for the relationship between the pattern and substantive nature of networks and employee perceptions of conflict. Recently, Avgar and Neuman (2015) introduced the concept of team member conflict accuracy, or the ability of individuals to accurately identify conflict between peers. In doing so the authors move beyond the question of general perceptions of conflict and explore the extent to which network and relational factors help explain variation in individuals' ability to accurately detect conflict when it is present and not to imagine it when it is not present. Much of the existing conflict research operates under the assumption that individuals are accurate in their ability to detect conflict between peers.

Recent scholarship has acknowledged variation in team members' perceptions of conflict (Jehn et al. 2010). Members of the same team may hold different views of how much conflict they perceive within a team. Furthermore, this variation is likely to affect performance outcomes. While this attention to conflict variation is important in terms of constructing a more realistic understanding of conflict, this research has focused on differences in the level of overall group conflict observed by individual members and not whether conflict is accurately identified to begin with. In addition, this emerging research on variation in conflict perceptions does not, for the most part, assess antecedents to variation in conflict perceptions and seeks to understand the consequences associated with the level of team conflict consensus. The question of variation in team member conflict accuracy is, fundamentally, a social structure question. Is the nature of social ties between two team members easily recognizable and identifiable by other team members? If so, do relational and structural factors help to explain why individuals differ in their ability to accurately identify conflict?

Avgar and Neuman (2015) address these questions by studying conflict patterns between team members in 26 teams in a state scientific agency. Among the factors that were hypothesized to influence how accurately team members detected conflict between peers, two are relevant for the argument developed in this chapter. First, building on the findings of Labianca et al. (1998), the authors proposed that conflict with members of the dyad being assessed would decrease an individual's ability to accurately identify conflict between the two peers. In other words, a negative relational tie with a team member was expected to hinder an individual's conflict accuracy.

Second, Avgar and Neuman hypothesized that an individual's structural position within a team's network will also affect their conflict accuracy. In particular, they maintain that the more central a team member is within a social network the better one will be at accurately observing conflict when it is present and not imagining it when it is not. This hypothesis is based on the argument that where one 'sits' within a team's network likely influences the vantage point through which relational information is attained (for a similar argument see Burt 1992). Individuals who are more central to their network are likely, according to this argument, to have a better handle on the nature of relationships between team members (Freeman 1979; Perry-Smith and Shalley 2003). The authors examine centrality in two types of networks: workflow and socializing. Workflow centrality captures an individual's position with a network as it relates to executing work tasks. Socializing centrality, on the other hand, captures an individual's positon within a network as it pertains to non-work-related interactions.

Data analysis from the 26 scientific teams provides general support for the link between network and relational factors and conflict accuracy. First, the authors found that team members' conflict with members of an evaluated dyad had a significant effect on conflict accuracy for both relationship and task conflict. Being in a state of conflict with peers was, therefore, shown to reduce one's ability to accurately detect conflict between others. With regards to centrality, they found that a team member's workflow centrality increased conflict accuracy for task conflict supporting the argument that having a more central position in a network can shape the way one sees conflict. Socializing centrality, on the other hand, was not significantly related to conflict accuracy suggesting that not all network types are equal in shaping promoting or hindering conflict accuracy.

Taken together, this evidence adds another important building block to the link between social structure and conflict. It also raises some interesting questions regarding the assumptions much of the conflict research has made about the how accurate individuals are about the conflict that surrounds them in organizations. These findings indicate that seeing conflict should not be taken for granted and, central to this chapter, that it likely varies as a function of the nature and pattern of ties connecting team members.

Conflict Network Patterns and Perceptions of Team Conflict

As noted above, the dominant measure for team and group conflict used in much of the organizational behavior focused studies of conflict does not assess tensions or disagreements between specific team members (Jehn et al. 2013; Neuman and Avgar 2014). Rather, this measure captures member overall perceptions about the climate of conflict in the team or group (Neuman and Avgar 2014). While this measure has thus provided a wealth of insights regarding conflict in teams, it cannot address who specifically in the team is in conflict with one another; that is, it cannot account for the network pattern of conflict ties. Given the aforementioned evidence of the relationship between network patterns and team level conflict, it seems reasonable to assume that one of the determinants of the overall team-level measure of conflict is the configuration of conflictual ties in a given setting. In other words, the structural pattern of conflict in a team is likely an antecedent to the individual and aggregated perceptions of team level of conflict. Put differently, two teams might have the same number of members that are in conflict, but the overall perceptions regarding how much conflict exists may differ as a result of different structural patterns of conflict.

Neuman and Avgar (2014) examine the role that the structural patterns of conflict play in explaining perceptions of team conflict. Their objective in doing so was to more carefully unpack the network factors that are likely driving team member perceptions of conflict. First, do more dyadic conflict ties translate into higher levels of reported overall conflict? If so, are these perceptions affected by the actual portrait of conflict in teams? Do individual and aggregated perceptions vary when the configuration of conflict ties take on a different form? In order to address these questions the authors used data collected from 39 teams in the two state scientific agencies referenced above.

Using this individual and team level data, Neuman and Avgar tested three hypotheses. First, they proposed that teams with more dyadic ties that reported conflict would also experience greater team level perceptions of conflict. In other words, greater dyadic conflict density would be associated with higher levels of team conflict. The existing evidence on the factors that drive team level conflict points to the need for additional empirical evidence on this relationship between network patterns of actual conflict and team level perceptions. As such, there is limited evidence as to whether increased conflict density leads to increased perceptions of team conflict. For example, research has not addressed the question of whether a team member's own dyadic conflict ties has a stronger influence on overall perceptions of conflict than other team member's dyadic conflict. Thus, in addition to testing the relationship between dyadic conflict density and perceptions of conflict, the authors also distinguish between the perceiver's own dyadic conflict and other's dyadic conflict. If a team member's own dyadic conflict has a stronger effect on perceptions of team level conflict it will provide additional support for the argument that relational and social factors have important implications for the way in which conflict is perceived.

In addition, and central to this chapter, examining the direct relationship between density of dyadic conflict and team level perceptions provides a foundation for testing indirect network effects. In other words, are there network patterns that moderate the relationship between dyadic conflict density and team level perceptions of conflict? Neuman and Avgar maintain that the answer to this question is yes. Dyadic conflict density is an important predictor of team level conflict, but it is influenced by the specific configuration of these ties. The translation of dyadic conflict into perceptions of team conflict, they argue, differs as a function of network structures. The second and third hypotheses, therefore, propose a moderating effect of the network shape of these conflict ties. The authors hypothesize that the centralization and cliquishness of dyadic conflict will affect perceptions of team level conflict. Conflict centralization captures the extent to which conflict ties are concentrated around a small number of team members. The extent to which conflict is patterned in such a way will significantly alter the way in which dyadic conflict translates into perceptions of team conflict. Conflict cliquishness refers to the extent to which dyadic conflict is concentrated within subgroups. Here too, Neuman and Avgar argue that the level of cliquishness will matter in terms of the strength of the effect that dyadic conflict has on perceptions of team level conflict.

Findings from this study provide strong support for the proposed relationship between the network structure of conflict and perceptions of team conflict. First, the authors find that dyadic conflict density has a significant effect on perceptions of team level conflict. Interestingly, the link between conflict density and team-level conflict is more pronounced for relationship conflict than it is for task conflict. In other words, each relationship conflict tie appears to have a stronger effect on perceptions of team level relationship conflict than does each task conflict tie on perceptions of team level task conflict. They also find that the perceiver's own dyadic conflict is more strongly related to overall perceptions of team conflict than is what the perceiver reports about the dyadic conflict of others. This suggests that one's own embeddedness in the social structure has a significant effect on perceptions of team level conflict. Second, findings suggest that not only does the raw number of conflict ties affect one's perceptions of team level conflict but the configuration of the ties matters, too, as both centralization and cliquishness of dyadic conflict moderate the relationship between density and perceptions of team conflict. Specifically, both centralization and cliquishness weaken the association between dyadic conflict density and perceptions of team conflict. These findings suggest that when dyadic conflict is confined to a small number of individuals (centralized) or to specific subgroups (cliquish), its effects on general perceptions is more limited. Network patterns of centralization and cliquishness seem to buffer team members from the reverberations of dyadic conflict.

Taken together, these findings also provide additional evidence for the proposed link between social structure and conflict. In this case, we demonstrate that the social structure of conflict is an important predictor of how conflict is perceived within the team. Given that perceptions of conflict have been shown to affect a very wide array of important team and individual outcomes, this evidence makes an important contribution to a more fine-grained understanding what is actually driving these perceptions.

Conclusions

Conflict is an inextricable feature of organizational life with the capacity to affect a host of important individual, group and organizational outcomes. Conflict scholars have spent the last three decades documenting many of the consequences associated with conflict and distinguishing between different types of conflict. While this impressive body of scholarship has significantly advanced what is known about conflict, there is one domain that has received considerably less scholarly attention. Despite the intuitive reciprocal link between conflict, a relational phenomenon, and social structure, there has been relatively little attention given to the way in which they affect each other. This chapter has advanced the argument that, in order to fully understand the way in which conflict plays out in organizations, it must be explicitly studied in relation to the social context in which it is embedded. Furthermore, we reviewed recent research that provides initial evidence for the relationship between conflict and social structure and social structure and conflict. Conflict appears to affect unit social capital and inter-team network tie formation. At the same time, key dimensions of conflict are, according to this review, the product of network factors and patterns. Thus, individuals' ability to accurately identify conflict is affected by the network related factors. In addition, the review points to the relationship between the network patterns of dyadic conflict and overall perceptions of team conflict. This research provides a first step in what, we believe, should be a long and fruitful scholarly journey.

The research reviewed in this chapter has clear implications for both scholarship and practice. From a scholarship perspective, the established link between conflict and social structure points to a need for additional research. Interestingly, both the study of conflict and the study of social networks have seen an impressive growth over the past decades. Each of these fields of study has contributed tremendous insights to the manner in which organizations and teams operate. Nevertheless, integration of insights across these domains is still in its infancy. We believe that the integration of these insights is likely to prove extremely fruitful. As noted above, we also believe that this integration will likely lead to a more complex and nuanced understanding of workplace conflict. For example, this integration would shed new light on the antecedents to conflict. The question of where conflict comes from has, in many ways, alluded scholars. As noted above, much of the focus has been on the role that conflict plays as an independent variable with far less attention given to the variables that predict or explain it. A better understanding of how social structure affects conflict would paint a much richer portrait of the way in which conflict is shaped and reshaped. This scholarly integration would also extend knowledge regarding the consequences that conflict has in the workplace. Social structure represents a new and intriguing lens, one that moves beyond attitudes and perceptions, through which to assess the implications that conflict has for organizations.

Future studies would, of course, go beyond the research reviewed above. For example, it should build on the many different network patterns and dimensions documented in the literature. Future research should also examine the mechanisms, or mediating variables, through which conflict and social structure affect one another. How does conflict shape social structure? How does social structure shape conflict? In addition, future research should also examine the manner in which contextual factors shape the direct relationship between the two constructs. To what extent do variables such as organizational and team climate, leadership and conflict management styles moderate the relationship between conflict and social structure?

The argument advanced in this chapter also has clear implications for practice. In particular, the relationship between conflict and social structure has implications for the management of conflict in organizations. First, if conflict is, among other things, a manifestation of specific network patterns and dynamics then its management is inextricably linked to the way teams and groups are structured. Organizations seeking to better anticipate and address intra- and inter-team conflict would be well served to recognize the ways in which decisions about how to structure groups and teams, designed to advance various performance outcomes, can also have dramatic consequences for the types and levels of conflict experienced. In other words, one of the considerations that should guide organizations in making structural decisions is how these will influence the emergence of conflict.

Second, if conflict has the capacity to shape structure and relational patterns between individuals in ways that may or may not be consistent with those deliberately designed by the organization, then it adds yet another motivation for organizations to be proactive in how they manage it. Organizations are often reluctant to put in place sophisticated conflict management procedures. Evidence reviewed in this chapter suggests that this lack of attention to conflict will likely come at the expense of intra-organizational relational strength. Organizations with a more developed conflict management infrastructure may be better positioned to minimize this conflict-related cost. Understanding the reciprocal relationship between conflict and social structure can, therefore, provide organizations and their leaders with an additional tool with which to manage relational dynamics in the workplace and their consequences for different stakeholders.

References

Adler, P. S., & Kwon, S. W. (2002). Social capital: Prospects for a new concept. *Academy of Management Review, 27*, 17–40.

Amason, A. C. (1996). Distinguishing the effects of functional and dysfunctional conflict on strategic decision making: Resolving a paradox for top management teams. *Academy of Management Journal, 39*, 123–148.

Avgar, A. C. (2010). Negotiated capital: Conflict, its management, and workplace social capital. *International Journal of Conflict Management, 21*, 236–259.

Avgar, A. C., & Neuman, E. J. (2015). Seeing conflict: A study of conflict accuracy in work teams. *Negotiations and Conflict Management Research, 8*, 65–84.

Baron, R. A. (1991). Positive effects of conflict: A cognitive perspective. *Employee Responsibilities and Rights Journal, 4*, 25–36.

Bouty, I. (2000). Interpersonal and interaction influences on informal resource exchanges between R and D researchers across organizational boundaries. *Academy of Management Journal, 43*, 50–65.

Burt, R. S. (1992). *Structural holes: The social structure of competition.* Cambridge, MA: Harvard University Press.

Coleman, J. S. (1988). Social capital in the creation of human capital. *American Journal of Sociology, 94*, S95–S120.

Cross, R., & Cummings, J. N. (2004). Tie and network correlates of individual performance in knowledge-intensive work. *Academy of Management Journal, 47*, 928–937.

De Dreu, C. K. W. (1997). Productive conflict: The importance of conflict management and conflict issues. In C. K. W. De Dreu, & E. van de Vliert (Eds.), *Using conflict in organizations.* London: Sage Publications.

De Dreu, C. K. W., & van Vianen, A. E. M. (2001). Managing relationship conflict and the effectiveness of organizational teams. *Journal of Organizational Behavior, 22*, 309–328.

De Dreu, C. K. W., & Weingart, L. R. (2003). Task versus relationship conflict, team performance, and team member satisfaction: A meta-analysis. *Journal of Applied Psychology, 88*, 741–749.

De Dreu, C. K. W., van Dierendonck, D., & Dijkstra, M. T. M. (2004). Conflict at work and individual well-being. *International Journal of Conflict Management, 15*, 6–26.

De Wit, F. R. C., Greer, L. L., & Jehn, K. A. (2012). The paradox of intragroup conflict: A meta-analysis. *Journal of Applied Psychology, 97*, 360–390.

Fiol, C. M. (1994). Consensus, diversity, and learning in organizations. *Organization Science, 5*, 403–420.

Freeman, L. C. (1979). Centrality in social networks conceptual clarification. *Social Networks, 1*, 215–239.

Gittell, J. H. (2000). Organizing work to support relational Coordination. *International Journal of Human Resource Management, 11*, 517–539.

Hansen, B. E. (1999). Threshold effects in non-dynamic panels: Estimation, testing, and inference. *Journal of Econometrics, 93*, 345–368.

Janssen, O., van De Vliert, E., & Veenstra, C. (1999). How task and person conflict shape the role of positive interdependence in management teams. *Journal of Management, 25*, 117–141.

Jehn, K. A. (1995). A multi-method examination of the benefits and detriments of intragroup conflict. *Administrative Science Quarterly, 40*, 256–282.

Jehn, K. A. (1997). Affective and cognitive conflict in work groups: Increasing performance through value-based intragroup conflict. In C. K. W. De Dreu, & E. van de Vliert (Eds.), *Using conflict in organizations.* London: Sage Publications.

Jehn, K. A., & Bendersky, C. (2003). Intragroup conflict in organizations: A contingency perspective on the conflict-outcome relationship. In R. M. Kramer, & B. Staw (Eds.), *Research in organizational behavior*. Greenwich, CT: JAI Press.

Jehn, K. A., & Mannix, E. A. (2001). The dynamic nature of conflict: A longitudinal study of intragroup conflict and group performance. *Academy of Management Journal, 44*, 238–251.

Jehn, K. A., Rispens, S., & Thatcher, S. (2010). The effects of conflict asymmetry on workgroup and individual outcomes. *Academy of Management Journal, 53*, 596–616.

Jehn, K. A., Rispens, S., Jonsen, K., & Greer, L. (2013). Conflict contagion: A temporal perspective on the development of conflict within teams. *International Journal of Conflict Management, 24*, 352–373.

Labianca, G., Brass, D. J., & Gray, B. (1998). Social networks and perceptions of intergroup conflict: The role of negative relationships and third parties. *Academy of Management Journal, 41*, 55–67.

Leana, C. R., & van Buren, H. J. (1999). Organizational social capital and employment practices. *Academy of Management Review, 24*, 538–555.

Lovelace, K., Shapiro, D. L., & Weingart, L. R. (2001). Maximizing cross-functional new product teams' innovativeness and constraint adherence: A conflict communications perspective. *Academy of Management Journal, 44*, 779–793.

Madhavan, R., Gnyawali, D. R., & He, J. (2004). Two's company, three's a crowd? triads in cooperative-competitive networks. *Academy of Management Journal, 47*, 918–927.

Nahapiet, J., & Ghoshal, S. (1998). Social capital, intellectual capital, and the organizational advantage. *Academy of Management Review, 23*, 242–266.

Nelson, R. E. (1989). The strength of strong ties: Social networks and intergroup conflict in organizations. *Academy of Management Journal, 32*, 377–401.

Neuman, E. J., & Avgar, A. C. (2014). Uncovering the drivers of individual perceptions of team level conflict: A comparison between dyadic and team-level measures. Working paper, University of Illinois.

Ozcan, P., & Eisenhardt, K. M. (2009). Origin of alliance portfolios: Entrepreneurs, network strategies, and firm performance. *Academy of Management Journal, 52*, 246–279.

Pelled, L. H. (1996). Demographic diversity, conflict, and work group outcomes: An intervening process theory. *Organization Science, 7*, 615–631.

Perry-Smith, J. E., & Shalley, C. E. (2003). The social side of creativity: A static and dynamic social network perspective. *Academy of Management Review, 28*, 89–106.

Putnam, L. L. (1994). Productive conflict: Negotiation as implicit coordination. *International Journal of Conflict Management, 5*, 284–298.

Schweiger, D. M., & Sandberg, W. R. (1989). The utilization of individual capabilities in group approaches to strategic decision-making. *Strategic Management Journal, 10*, 31–43.

Schweiger, D., Sandberg, W., & Ragin, J. (1986). Group approaches for improving strategic decision making: A comparative analysis of dialectical inquiry, devil's advocacy, and consensus approaches to strategic decision making. *Academy of Management Journal, 29*, 57–71.

Schweiger, D., Sandberg, W.J., & Rechner, P. (1989). Experiential effects of dialectical inquiry, devil's advocacy, and consensus approaches to strategic decision making. *Academy of Management Journal, 32*, 745–772.

Schwenk, C. R. (1990). Conflict in organizational decision making: An exploratory study of its effects in for-profit and not-for-profit organizations. *Management Science, 36*, 436–448.

Simons, T. L., & Peterson, R. S. (2000). Task conflict and relationship conflict in top management teams: The pivotal role of intragroup trust. *Journal of Applied Psychology, 85*, 102–111.

Sparrowe, R. T., Liden, R. C., Wayne, S. J., & Kraimer, M. L. (2001). Social networks and the performance of individuals and groups. *Academy of Management Journal, 44*, 316–325.

Subramaniam, M., & Youndt, M. A. (2005). The influence of intellectual capital on the types of innovative capabilities. *Academy of Management Journal, 48*, 450–463.

Walker, G., Kogut, B., & Shan, W. (1997). Social capital, structural holes and the formation of an industry network. *Organization Science, 8*, 109–125.

Wall, V. D., & Nolan, L. L. (1986). Perceptions of inequity, satisfaction, and conflict in task-oriented groups. *Human Relations, 39*, 1033–1051.

Part II

Managing Conflict on the Front-line

6

A Crisis of Confidence? Front-line Managers and the Complexities of Conflict

Carol Jones and Richard Saundry

Introduction and Background

Although there has been a progressive devolution of the responsibility for people management from human resource professionals to line managers, the handling of individual employment disputes has remained a jointly regulated activity (Hall and Torrington 1998a; Kersley et al. 2006; Hales 2005; Whittaker and Marchington 2003). 'Regulation' has taken the form of increasingly detailed policy and procedures with limits on the degree of autonomy that line managers have and the decisions that they can take (Kersley et al. 2006; Hales 2005). Historically, line managers are perceived to have favoured 'informal' approaches and the 'flexibility' to be able to make decisions that

C. Jones
Institute for Research into Organisations, Work and Employment (iROWE), School of Management, University of Central Lancashire, Preston, UK
e-mail: cjones7@uclan.ac.uk

R. Saundry (✉)
Plymouth Business School, Plymouth University, Plymouth, UK
e-mail: richard.saundry@plymouth.ac.uk

© The Editor(s) (if applicable) and The Author(s) 2016
R. Saundry et al. (eds.), *Reframing Resolution*,
DOI 10.1057/978-1-137-51560-5_6

reflect contextual and cultural factors at work unit level (Rollinson 1992, 2000; Dunn and Wilkinson 2002; Franklin and Pagan 2006). Line managers thus tend to have developed different styles for handling discipline and grievance that reflect their own preferences, beliefs and objectives (Hook et al. 1996; Earnshaw et al. 2000). The potential for this to result in procedural irregularities that may trigger litigation and the consequent financial and reputational damage to the organization has been a powerful driver of formalization in the way that workplace conflict is handled and managed (Earnshaw et al. 2000; Harris et al. 2002). Further, there is a related concern to ensure consistency in the treatment of employees across the organization, as inconsistency has been found to be damaging to employee morale, trust and commitment (Cole 2008; Hall and Torrington 1998b).

In this context, HR professionals, in their role as procedural and legal 'experts' have tended to emphasize process compliance as a prime objective in conflict handling. It could be argued that formalization, and the related drive for standardization, has enabled HR departments to control managerial actions at local level to some extent, but it does not necessarily either prevent arbitrary behaviour on the part of managers, nor does it ensure that the process of being disciplined is experienced as 'objective' and non-judgemental (Cooke 2006). There are also tensions around HR professionals 'policing' the actions of line managers (Renwick 2003) and the extent that HR interventions are regarded as both time-consuming and as bureaucratic encumbrances (Guest and King 2004).

There have also been ongoing concerns about the general lack of training line managers receive (Cunningham and Hyman 1999; Hunter and Renwick 2009; Harris et al. 2002: 222–4). As Rollinson (2000: 748) has commented, 'having procedures is one thing, and knowing how to apply them can be another'. That being said, there is also a general acceptance of the need for formal procedures and an understanding of the role they play in underpinning managerial authority as they set out standards both of expected behaviour and of the procedure an employee would experience if they transgressed (Goodman et al. 1998: 544). Managers can, therefore, also welcome tight procedures since they provide a justification for managerial action (Cooke 2006: 698) and to some degree protect them if a case if brought (Cole 2008; Harris et al. 2002). The role the HR function plays in clarifying rules, procedures and legislation has also tended to be welcomed by line managers (Cunningham and Hyman 1999).

In the UK, since 2007 there has been a shift in emphasis at policy level towards promoting the early resolution of disputes through informal processes of discussion and negotiation. Organizations have been encouraged to avoid unnecessary procedural formality and to give managers the scope and discretion to deal flexibly with difficult issues. However, whether managers in the UK have the confidence or the competence to take up this challenge is a moot point. The view of the HR profession was that 'managers are neither willing nor capable of taking this on effectively' (CIPD 2008: 8) and this also shaped government perceptions with the conclusion that, 'many more problems could be prevented from escalating into disputes if line managers were better able to manage conflict' (BIS 2011:17). In a survey of its members in 2007, the CIPD found that 30 % of HR practitioners agreed that their line managers were good at resolving disputes informally; 3 % agreed they were excellent; and over half said they were average and nearly one-fifth said they were poor (CIPD 2007a:12).

The lack of confidence felt by front-line managers has several dimensions. A significant factor is the perception that managers are risk averse in relation to managing conflict and prefer the security of tight procedural compliance. According to a CIPD survey in 2008, 'managers shy away from tackling disputes in case they do or say something that might be held against them during formal proceedings' (2008: 18). Research has found that managers are indeed concerned about the legal implications of their actions (Edwards 2000; Harris et al. 2002; Latreille 2011; Jones and Saundry 2012). This concern is also fuelled by HR professionals' own caution about informality, as a recent report by the CIPD makes clear: 'many HR managers lack confidence in developing informal approaches to managing conflict and continue to be nervous about departing from grievance procedures' (2015: 3).

Managers are not normally recruited on the basis of their people management skills (Townsend 2013). This is an important point in assessing the responses of line managers regarding early resolution and more informal approaches. The written policy and procedure represents 'a form of codified HR knowledge for line managers' (Hunter and Renwick 2009: 407) and as such is largely prescriptive and compliance oriented. Training for managers has tended to focus on the application of this procedure (CIPD 2007a) and therefore runs the danger of the wary and conservative approach that seems to characterize many organizational responses to conflict and dispute management.

Early resolution or intervention utilizing more informal solutions relies on 'tacit' knowledge of people management, allowing for and dependent upon managerial discretion. However, to be effective, it is also needs to be underpinned, by specific experiential learning in handling conflict – something many managers do not have the opportunity to acquire (Teague and Roche 2012) or to practice. Indeed, the CIPD has recently noted that 'conflict management' and 'managing difficult conversations' are the two most challenging parts of a line manager's role (CIPD 2013: 7). In addition, Renwick and Gennard (2001) argue that HR professionals themselves need a wide range of skills and expertise to enable them to handle discipline and grievance issues thoroughly. Although there is more recent evidence to suggest that some employers are taking this need for training more seriously, it is also recognized that the costs and constraints on managers' time continue to be factors that can impede progress (CIPD 2015).

In stressing the importance of consistency and the risks of procedural irregularity, it could be argued that HR professionals have, to a degree, created a dependency relationship for line managers. Indeed, by 2007 two-fifths of HR professionals' time was spent on operational activities, of which the most time-consuming and common was supporting line managers (CIPD 2007b: 19). However, HR has increasingly moved to a 'business partner' model (Caldwell 2003; Pritchard 2010) so there is less likely to be on-site HR support and advice is often now delivered via phone or the Internet, focusing on what are perceived to be routine or operational matters. Although this more 'arms-length' approach may force line managers to be more self-reliant, if it is not underpinned by the appropriate training it is unlikely to engender confidence in relation to handling conflict informally (Whittaker and Marchington 2003; Keegan et al. 2011).

Early studies of devolution highlight that it was often difficult for line managers to balance the time needed to deal effectively with people management with their often extensive operational responsibilities (McGovern et al. 1997). More recently, the role of line managers has expanded to become heavily focused on performance management (Hales 2005, 2006/2007) and the management of 'poor performance' in particular (Dunn and Wilkinson 2002; Newsome et al. 2013). It is common for organizations to have policies related to absence and

capability that are intended to support managing pe'
which often have a connection to disciplinary action o'
cases involving accusations of bullying and harassmer
Wibberley 2014). This is likely to increase the pressure v..
ers and further exacerbate the concern that if these activities are nv.
monitored or stressed as objectives, they might not be taken as seriously
as more immediate 'business' related priorities (Hales 2005). Further,
senior managers are not necessarily sending a clear message about the
significance of effective dispute resolution as they tend to expect managers to focus on short-term operational targets (Teague and Roche
2012; Hutchinson and Purcell 2010) and do not recognize the time
and skill needed to deal with performance issues and the conflict this
can generate (Hyde et al. 2013). In this context, line managers can see
people management as a 'discretionary' activity when it does not form
part of the way in which their performance is assessed or where its
importance is not reinforced by HR and/or senior managers (Purcell
and Hutchinson 2007).

The aim of this chapter is to examine in detail how a sample of line
managers experience handling conflict situations and to explore both the
contextual factors that might make this challenging as well as those that
facilitate the successful management of conflict, particularly in relation to
the early and informal resolution that is now at the heart of public policy.
The rest of the chapter is organized as follows. First, we will outline the
methodology on which the research is based and then we will explore the
context in which managers have operated and the factors which might
contribute to the claim that they lack confidence in handling conflict. We
will then move on to assess the situations in which managers are able to act
with confidence and the support that might be necessary for this to occur.

Research Design

Five organizational case studies undertaken between 2009 and 2011 (see
Table 6.1) were conceived as stand-alone projects; however, the methods
used and the similarity of the key research questions in each case allow
for cross comparison. The organizations in the sample were selected for

able 6.1 Breakdown of sample

Organization	Industrial and sector type	Sector	Employment	Employee representation
A	Health	Public	2–3,000	Unions recognized – high density
B	Services	Private	5–7,000	Unions recognized – high density
C	Public administration	Public	8–10,000	Unions recognized – high density
D	Services	Private	Over 50,000	Non-unionized – active staff association
E	Social services	Non-profit	4–5,000	Unions recognized – low density

two reasons. In organizations A, C and D more innovative approaches to conflict management were being utilized, including in-house mediation. Organizations B and E were in sectors of particular interest as they had been overlooked in terms of previous research. Across the sample there was a representation of organizations in different sectors and with varying patterns of employee representation. They varied in size but they all employed more than 1,000 staff and would be considered large organizations. In order to preserve anonymity and confidentiality only broad details are given of the sample.

The data collection within each organization concentrated on three main elements:

1. Policy documents dealing with individual employment disputes and relevant collective agreements were examined
2. In-depth interviews were conducted with key stakeholders, including HR practitioners, operational managers and employee representatives
3. Where available, statistical data regarding employment, workforce demographics and pattern of individual employment disputes was reviewed

Across the five organizations a total of 131 interviews were conducted, comprising 53 HR practitioners ranging from advisor to director level, 61 line and operational managers, and 17 employee representatives.

Findings

Understanding the 'Crisis' of Confidence

Across the sample, procedures used for handling individual employment disputes had traditionally been lengthy and detailed. This often included additional levels of appeal, precise guidance on how the investigations should be conducted and expectations of the roles that HR and operational managers would be expected to play. In public sector organizations, the approach was adversarial and semi-judicial, with issues explored through the examination and cross-examination of witnesses. However, respondents generally agreed that complex procedures were not conducive to the early and effective resolution of conflict. Instead, they encouraged zero-sum approaches to conflict which benefitted neither party:

> There are plenty of people in management and trade unions who'll say "Well according to section five paragraph three of the procedure you've haven't followed this. You haven't shown the letters in time so we'll scrap the whole process." And that's what becomes a win/lose type of approach and I don't think it's ever paid dividends for anyone that I've had experience of representing. (Trade union representative – Organization C)

Importantly, operational and line managers were particularly critical of the application of procedure which they argued tended to develop an unstoppable momentum and made 'off the record' discussion and informal resolution extremely difficult:

> Our [disciplinary procedure] is almost too formal. You have to follow the format once you get to that and there's nothing that enables me to nip it in the bud...Once it starts it's like a ball that rolls and there are things you have to do and letters you have to send and there isn't anything to take it offline with a chat in a room... (Operational manager – Organization D)

Therefore, in line with previous research (see, for example, Dunn and Wilkinson 2002), operational and line managers within the sample expressed a preference for more flexible approaches that reflected the contexts within which they worked and the needs of the organization. One might have expected managers to embrace the opportunity to take control over conflict management provided by the devolution of HR matters and also the policy emphasis on informal resolution. However, according to HR practitioners, most line and operational managers had not taken this chance and found discussing issues of conduct or capability with team members extremely challenging:

> They find it really difficult to feedback about poor behaviour. I mean it's a really big thing and they really get themselves worked up about it and I think it is because they work so closely and they know each colleague on a very personal level. (HR manager – Organization C)

As the quote above suggests, managers found such 'difficult conversations' particularly problematic when they had close personal relationships with their subordinates. For example, in Organization E, staff worked together in small teams in residential units for young adults. HR practitioners in this case complained that because teams were 'very close-knit' there was insufficient 'distance' between managers and staff who were sometimes 'too friendly'. Consequently, the lines of authority between manager and employee became blurred and managers were reluctant to address conflict.

The evidence also highlighted concerns of line and operational managers that raising issues of conduct and capability with individual staff could have wider implications for team performance. For example, taking action against team members could have a negative impact on morale and in some cases trigger retaliatory grievances from the staff concerned. Moreover, managers voiced worries that any escalation of the issue into formal process and procedure could involve them in unwanted and time-consuming 'bureaucracy'. Therefore, as has been noted by other researchers (Cole 2008), managers may decide to let '*staff get away with certain behaviours*' because it was not '*worth all the time and hassle*' (Operational manager – Organization C).

The lack of confidence discussed above was also compounded by uncertainty among line and operational managers over whether attempts to manage conflict would be supported by senior management. For instance, in one not-for-profit organization a team had three managers in the previous 18 months and each of them was moved when employees complained about attempts to address problems:

> We've moved the manager out, where I think, really, we should have turned round and looked at it and said, 'It's not the manager's problem, it's actually the team's problem and we need to disband the team rather than changing the manager all the time. (HR practitioner – Organization E)

In such situations, managers were unlikely to address problems with capability or conduct knowing that if they were challenged, their judgement would not be backed. This lack of support extended to a dearth of investment in training and perhaps more importantly a refusal to acknowledge the importance of providing managers with the time and space to manage conflict. Instead, line and operational managers commonly complained that their superiors were only interested in fulfilling short-term operational goals. For example, in Organization D, a very large private sector employer, a departmental manager argued that he did not have time to resolve underlying conflict within his team because he was under constant pressure from senior managers to maintain levels of stock:

> I think the pressure on the department managers at the moment is so heavy because we're trying to achieve so much. If one dealt with a couple of issues, just take 5 minutes out of your day, stop filling shelves so hard and deal with your long-term absence, you would either get this person back into work or they'd leave, and we'd have somebody else in the store.

In short, for many line and operational managers the safest and simplest course of action was simply to 'sweep' issues 'under the carpet' – if there was no formal action, managers would not become enmeshed in complex and bureaucratic process and there was no possibility of a procedural breach.

However, avoidance was becoming more difficult as managers were also subject to demands to manage performance in a more assertive manner, which could create tensions and challenges, particularly when there appeared to be a disjuncture with previous practice:

Managers have a job to do and quite often people don't like the feedback. They will come in and say that my manager is bullying me, or harassing me, when, actually, there's no evidence to suggest they are…they're feeding back about how they've done something, and they don't like what's being said to them. (Operational manager – Organization D)

In the face of such challenges, HR practitioners argued that line and operational managers were in fact more comfortable with prescriptive approaches to handling workplace conflict. Two main reasons were given for this: first, procedures provided a set of rules that they could follow and second, procedures helped to legitimize and depersonalize decision making, shielding managers from criticism from either other managers or the individuals involved in the dispute. An HR practitioner from Organization D explained that managers in her organization demanded clearly defined rules or standards which if breached led to predetermined outcomes. If their actions were questioned, they could then respond that they had '*just followed things in line with procedure, in line with policy*'.

In addition, HR respondents claimed that this lack of confidence meant that rather than taking greater responsibility for addressing and managing difficult issues, managers were still dependent on HR advice and intervention. Indeed, interviews with managers seemed to support this as the following comments illustrate:

It's so important that you've somebody that you can knock on their door and they don't mind you asking questions – maybe three or four times the same thing. You know you've got to feel able to talk to your HR and you've got to feel that they support you. (Operational manager – Organization B)

The majority of cases that I deal with… I'm dealing with a manager who's never dealt with something like this before. So it's not something that they've come across and therefore they spend a lot more time with us, I guess, trying to make sure that they get the right guidance, advice and support through the process. (HR manager – Organization B)

But closer scrutiny of the data suggests that this lack of confidence and dependence on HR, was a function, at least in part, of the failure of organizations to place sufficient weight on the importance of conflict management and also the emphasis placed by HR practitioners on procedural and legal compliance. Although HR practitioners in the sample stressed the importance of early and informal resolution, their main preoccupation was to minimize risk, either of reputational damage, or litigation. In this respect, the fear of legal challenge or internal criticism was used to ensure that operational managers were compliant and consistent in applying procedure:

> So we've said, "sex discrimination, race, disability"...and they're petrified about talking to people about things that might not be comfortable... rather than say, "look, let me explain it to you", they'll say, "put it in writing, let HR deal with it". Unfortunately, we've moved away from just knowing people, knowing our teams, knowing how to manage them as people and we're now trying to get back to that a bit more...[But] there's a big fear factor around the [managers] that they may have to go to court, they may have to be up in the dock. (HR practitioner – Organization D)

This fear created an incentive for line and operational managers to retreat behind a protection blanket of rigid procedural adherence. The potential threat of litigation was a powerful restriction on the confidence of managers to pursue informal solutions. For example, one operational manager from Organization B argued that there was some 'concern' among his colleagues that mistakes could lead to employees taking a claim to an employment tribunal and winning 'a pot full of money'. As has been argued elsewhere (Saundry and Dix 2014) litigation in the UK is relatively rare and compensation levels tend to be relatively modest. However, within the case study organizations, there was a clear perception that deviating from procedure or pursing more creative informal resolutions was fraught with danger:

> Every manager in this organization will know of a grievance that went horribly wrong and that ended up in an employment tribunal...there's a lot of fear if they dabble in some sort of informal approach they might get it wrong and then the complaint will turn against them. (Mediator – Organization C)

The lack of trust and confidence that many HR practitioners had in the managers that they advised had also led them to formalize informal aspects of conflict handling. For examples, managers were routinely encouraged to document conversations with staff and to follow up discussions about performance or capability in writing or by issuing what one organization had termed 'improvement notes'. While the intention was to help managers by providing them with a clear process to follow and to ensure consistency and fairness, there was a danger that this simply encouraged managers to deal with conflict in a routinized manner, defined by the organization's HR function.

The nature of the relationship between HR and line and operational managers was also shaped by the growing distance between HR and the line. Changes to the location, size and focus of the HR function in many organizations had seen practitioners withdraw from direct involvement in day-to-day conflict management. Centralization (and often rationalization) of HR resources meant that much HR advice was provided remotely or 'flown-in', whereby HR practitioners would visit a site only if there was a problem. Furthermore there was a growing reliance on advice through telephone or email. HR practitioners in these organizations argued that these changes would force line and operational managers to take responsibility for conflict handling:

> If you're involved in everything how are you developing the skills of the line managers? How are they becoming accountable for their staff? HR aren't… we can support and facilitate but you're the one who's working with that individual all day in and day out. (HR practitioner – Organization B)

In some respects, HR practitioners appeared to treat managers as children who would only learn if they were left to fend for themselves. In reality, however, the increasing remoteness of HR support advice undermined high-trust relationships between HR and managers and consequently hampered informal resolution. The informal day-to-day contact between line managers and HR practitioners that built trust was, therefore, difficult to find. In addition, line managers were more dependent on written guidance, which while designed to provide a degree of consistency again reduced the room for creative resolution.

Overall, our findings suggested that line managers were under increasing pressure to manage performance in order to try and increase efficiency or reduce staff absence. However, there was little recognition of the time and skills required to resolve the conflict that this could give rise to. It was apparent from the interviews that training was insufficient to prepare line managers to handle conflict with confidence. Moreover, there was little evidence within the sample that organizations were willing to invest necessary resources by freeing up managers to give them the specific training in conflict management that might both improve their confidence and reduce their dependency on procedurally focused approaches and on HR. This was summed up by one operational manager working in a large public sector organization (Organization C) who described the problems facing managers working in a highly unionized organization:

I think the difficulty in resolving issues when they're on a formal footing is that the union teams are very adept at how to handle a grievance or a disciplinary scenario. They know all the formal processes and they're operating with them on a daily basis, whereas for managers encountering those scenarios you might get, if you're lucky, a sort of half-day training course on handling a grievance or a disciplinary and you might if you're lucky see ten screens of a PowerPoint presentation that give you the salient points. (Operational manager – Organization C)

Engendering Confidence

Despite the 'crisis of confidence' discussed in the previous section, our findings also pointed to a number of contextual factors that both supported informal resolution and enhanced the ability of all stakeholders (including line managers) to adopt such an approach (Jones and Saundry 2012; Saundry and Wibberley 2014). The first of these was the development of high trust relationships between the parties, most particularly between HR professionals and union representatives and between HR professionals and line managers. High levels of trust gave these actors the confidence to enter into discussions outside formal process and procedure and to look for more nuanced resolutions to difficult issues. In some cases, this was not simply reactive (i.e. in response to a specific case) but proactive, with union representatives and HR practitioners holding regular meetings to identify areas of conflict and develop joint approaches to resolve it:

> I have an off-the-record meeting with the site manager and HR once a month and the basis of that is that we don't want to be airing our dirty laundry in public really. Can we get it sorted before any meetings? That suits me because if it's getting stuff sorted I don't care what way it's done, really. But it's through these meetings that you build your relationships anyway. (Trade union representative – Organization B)

There is considerable evidence that such constructive employer–union relations facilitate informal resolutions and can reduce the use of disciplinary sanctions (Oxenbridge and Brown 2004; Saundry et al. 2008, 2011). However, in our sample, all parties had to be receptive to this and willing to take this approach. Not all union representatives (or indeed all HR officers or operations managers) had sufficient trust in other parties to feel secure in initiating or responding to 'off-the-record' discussions.

The second factor that could provide managerial confidence in pursuing informal approaches to conflict resolution was a positive employee relations climate. This was illustrated by the contrasting situations in two organizations. In Organization A, a 'grievance culture' had developed whereby trade unions responded to employer antipathy to their role by adopting an adversarial stance in representing their members. HR practitioners commented that union representatives did not feel that they had a great deal of voice and were often not treated with respect by senior operational managers. As a result, they would encourage their members to register formal complaints through the organization's grievance procedure.

Trade union representatives felt that any concessions or admissions made in informal discussions would be used against them and so used their detailed knowledge of procedure to as a way of exerting pressure on management:

> I think it was always a case of we didn't trust management. We would never enter into any kind of informal discussion because we were mindful that at some point in the future that would be used against us so we were always very formal…. (Union representative – Organization A)

Conversely in Organization B, a private sector services organization, the attitudes of both management and unions were underpinned by a commitment to partnership working. While there were positive relationships between HR practitioners and trade unions, senior operational managers also recognized the value of engaging with key union representatives and maintaining open channels of communication and discussion. A senior manager had made gaining the trust of local union representatives a priority in his first days in the role:

> When I came into the operational role the most important thing was to engage the union and for them to understand that actually I'm not this ogre of a manager who's just going to run all over you and make life hard for your staff and it's taken me a long time to get that trust and understanding. What I always do, which is key, is if you're making any changes just tell the union and when someone comes knocking on [their] door they'll say, we know about it, we haven't got a problem with it. (Operational manager – Organization B)

The attitude and behaviour of front line managers will shape employment relations; however, developing good relationships with trade union representatives itself demands confidence, time and experience and is likely to be more difficult for junior managers, particularly where the wider organizational context and/or the approach of senior management is negative.

The third dimension necessary to develop confidence was the recognition of the importance of conflict management skills and consequent investment in skills development. This was most apparent in Organization C where a number of managers, HR practitioners and union representatives had received specific conflict resolution training. The benefit was articulated by an operational manager:

> The training gave issues a vocabulary and a set of techniques and it also professionalized it in that it took out the emotional response to it and turned it into an approach and a set of actions that gave you time to breathe and gave you time to get out of the two people involved some ways forward and in that sense it was absolutely marvellous. (Operational manager – Organization C)

Another operational manager in the same organization was clear that the training raised their confidence in seeking informal and early resolution. Importantly, they argued that having the 'technique' to be able to address problems 'as soon as they come up, to try and get the people to sit down and talk about issues' was the most effective 'defence' against criticism, retaliatory grievances and litigation. Significantly, this joint approach to training had also provided the basis for building more positive relationships between unions and management and countered what had previously been an adversarial environment.

Furthermore, respondents argued that one of the most effective methods to develop improved skills and confidence was coaching by HR practitioners or more experienced operations managers. Here, HR practitioners would talk managers through specific cases, reviewing meetings and decisions and accompanying them where necessary, but with a view to the manager becoming more independent in the long run. However, these practices seemed to be more common where HR practitioners were 'on-site' and therefore came into day-to-day contact with managers. This runs counter to the argument expressed by some HR practitioners in the previous section that only by removing day-to-day contact could managers be weaned off their dependence on HR.

Finally, and perhaps most importantly, early and informal resolution was more likely to be found where senior management recognized the importance of effective conflict management and supported junior managers by providing them with time and space to address and resolve issues through discussion and negotiation and also by giving them the confidence that their judgement would be backed. Thus the leadership offered by senior managers could have a decisive effect on how their managers responded to workplace conflict. An HR practitioner in Organization E explained this as follows:

> I just see the two managers dealing with their services completely differently. In [region] they've got motivation, they've got support from [regional director] and they're just different managers; they are fundamentally different managers…they are allowed, dare I say, to fail. They are allowed to, you know, take those risks. (HR practitioner – Organization E)

Conclusions

The perception that conflict is managed poorly has been ascribed to a lack of capability, confidence and willingness on the part of managers. The research presented here confirms that managers are cautious about departing from more procedural approaches and are concerned about litigation. However, it is also clear that certain contextual factors within organizations both shape this situation and contribute to the extent to which managers are more willing to risk pursuing informal routes to conflict resolution. Not least of these is the fact that managing conflict requires skills that managers have often not had the opportunity to acquire, either through training or experience.

The increasing tendency to have HR support located off-site or reliant on telephone or intranet interactions can also remove the opportunity a manager might otherwise have had to informally discuss a case with HR colleagues with whom they had built up a professional relationship. This, coupled with their knowledge that, in unionized environments, the union representative is likely to be better trained and to have had more experience in handling dispute resolution, can also lead to a more cautious and procedurally driven approach on the part of managers.

Faced with competing demands on their time, it is unsurprising that many managers prefer the apparent certainty of a procedure that can be followed. However, the attitude of HR practitioners must bear some responsibility for this. Despite rhetorical support for the idea of informal resolution, there remains an overriding emphasis on consistency and compliance. This is illustrated by the use of prescriptive approaches to what were previously informal processes, such as performance management. This is rationalized in terms of a lack of managerial competence but only serves to reinforce the concerns of line and operational managers about the consequences of procedural irregularity and encourage a simplistic and rigid approach to conflict.

It is apparent from the research evidence presented here that where organizations invest in specific and detailed conflict resolution training, managers, HR and the trade union representatives can benefit from this and the employee relations climate in an organization can be improved as a result. Both coaching and mediation training appear to be positive factors in developing both skills and confidence in this respect. It is also clear that high trust relationships, developed over time between managers, HR professionals and union representatives are most likely to support proactive and creative conflict resolution.

References

BIS (Department of Business, Innovation and Skills). (2011). *Resolving workplace disputes: A consultation.* http://www.bis.gov.uk/assets/biscore/employment-matters/docs/r/11-511-resolving-workplace-disputes-consultation.pdf

Caldwell, R. (2003). The changing roles of personnel managers: Old ambiguities, new uncertainties. *Journal of Management Studies, 40*(4), 983–1004.

CIPD (2007a). *Managing conflict at work.* London: CIPD.

CIPD (2007b). *The changing HR function.* London: CIPD.

CIPD (2008). *Workplace mediation – How employers do it?* London: CIPD.

CIPD (2013). *Real-life leaders: Closing the knowing-doing gap.* London: CIPD.

CIPD (2015). *Conflict management: A shift in direction.* London: CIPD.

Cole, N. (2008). Consistency in employee discipline: An empirical exploration. *Personnel Review, 37*(5), 109–117.

Cooke, H. (2006). Examining the disciplinary process in nursing: A case study approach. *Work, Employment and Society, 20*(4), 687–707.

Cunningham, I., & Hyman, J. (1999). Devolving human resource responsibilities to the line. Beginning of the end or a new beginning for personnel? *Personnel Review, 28*(1/2), 9–27.

Dunn, C., & Wilkinson, A. (2002). Wish you were here: Managing absence. *Personnel Review, 31*(2), 228–246.

Earnshaw, J., Marchington, M., & Goodman, J. (2000). Unfair to whom? Discipline and dismissal in small establishments. *Industrial Relations Journal, 31*(1), 62–73.

Edwards, P. (2000). Discipline: Towards trust and self-discipline? In S. Bach, & K. Sisson (Eds.), *Personnel management: A comprehensive guide to theory and practice in Britain* (3rd ed., pp. 317–339). Oxford: Blackwell.

Franklin, A., & Pagan, J. (2006). Organization culture as an explanation for employee discipline practices. *Review of Public Personnel Administration, 26*(1), 52–73.

Goodman, J., Earnshaw, J., Marchington, M., & Harrison, R. (1998). Unfair dismissal cases, disciplinary procedures, recruitment methods and management style. Case study evidence from three industrial sectors. *Employee Relations, 20*(6), 536–550.

Guest, D., & King, Z. (2004). Power, innovation and problem-solving: The personnel managers' three steps to Heaven? *Journal of Management Studies, 41*(3), 401–423.

Hales, C. (2005). Rooted in supervision, branching into management: Continuity and change in the role of first-line manager. *Journal of Management Studies, 42*(3), 471–506.

Hales, C. (2006/2007). Moving down the line? The shifting boundary between middle and first line management. *Journal of General Management* 32(2), 31–55.

Hall, L., & Torrington, D. (1998a). *The human resource function. The dynamics of change and development*. London: Pitman.

Hall, L., & Torrington, D. (1998b). Letting go or holding on – The devolution of operational personnel activities. *Human Resource Management Journal, 8*(1), 41–55.

Harris, L., Doughty, D., & Kirk, S. (2002). The devolution of HR responsibilities – Perspectives from the UK's public sector. *Journal of European Industrial Training, 26*(5), 218–229.

Hook, C., Rollinson, D., Foot, M., & Handley, J. (1996). Supervisor and manager styles in handling discipline and grievance: Part one – Comparing styles in handling discipline and grievance. *Personnel Review, 25*(3), 20–34.

Hunter, W., & Renwick, D. (2009). Involving British line managers in HRM in a small non-profit organization. *Employee Relations, 31*(4), 398–411.

Hutchinson, S., & Purcell, J. (2010). Managing ward managers for roles in HRM in the NHS: Overworked and under-resourced. *Human Resource Management Journal, 20*(4), 357–374.

Hyde, P., Granter, E., Hassard, J., McCann, L., & Morris, J. (2013). *Roles and behaviours of middle and junior managers: Managing new organizational forms of healthcare. Final report*, NIHR Service Delivery and Organization programme.

Jones, C., & Saundry, R. (2012). The practice of discipline: Evaluating the roles and relationship between managers and HR professionals. *Human Resource Management Journal, 22*(3), 252–266.

Keegan, A., Huemann, M., & Turner, R. (2011). Beyond the line: Exploring the HRM responsibilities of line managers, project managers and the HRM department in four project-oriented companies in The Netherlands, Austria, the UK and the USA. *The International Journal of Human Resource Management, 23*(15), 3085–3104.

Kersley, B., Alpin, C., Forth, J., Bryson, A., Bewley, H., Dix, G., et al. (2006). *Inside the workplace: Findings from the 2004 workplace employment relations survey.* London: Routledge.

Latreille, P. L. (2011). Workplace mediation: A thematic review of the Acas/CIPD evidence. *Acas Research Papers,* 13/11.

McGovern, P., Gratton, L., Hope-Hailey, V., Stiles, P., & Truss, C. (1997). Human resource management on the line? *Human Resource Management Journal,* 7(4), 12–29.

Newsome, K., Thompson, P., & Commander, J. (2013). "You monitor performance at every hour": Labour and the management of performance in the supermarket supply chain. *New Technology, Work and Employment,* 28(1), 1–15.

Oxenbridge, S., & Brown, W. (2004). Achieving a new equilibrium? The stability of co-operative employer-union relationships. *Industrial Relations Journal,* 35(5), 388–402.

Pritchard, K. (2010). Becoming an HR strategic partner: Tales of transition. *Human Resource Management Journal,* 20(2), 175–188.

Purcell, J., & Hutchinson, S. (2007). Front-line managers as agents in the HRM-performance causal chain: Theory, analysis and evidence. *Human Resource Management Journal,* 17, 3–20.

Renwick, D. (2003). Line manager involvement in HRM: An inside view. *Employee Relations,* 25(3), 262–280.

Renwick, D., & Gennard, J. (2001). Grievance and discipline. In T. Redman, & A. Wilkinson (Eds.), *Contemporary human resource management: Texts and cases* (pp. 168–192). London: Prentice Hall.

Rollinson, D. (1992). Individual issues in industrial relations: An examination of discipline, and an agenda for research. *Personnel Review,* 21(1), 46–57.

Rollinson, D. (2000). Supervisor and manager approaches to handling discipline and grievance: A follow-up study. *Personnel Review,* 29(6), 743–768.

Saundry, R., & Dix, G. (2014). Conflict resolution in the UK. In W. Roche, P. Teague, & A. Colvin (Eds.), *The Oxford handbook on conflict management in organizations.* Oxford: Oxford University Press.

Saundry, R., & Wibberley, G. (2014). Workplace dispute resolution and the management of individual conflict – A thematic analysis of five case studies. *Acas Research Papers,* 06/14.

Saundry, R., Antcliff, V., & Jones, C. (2008). Accompaniment and representation in workplace discipline and grievance. *Acas Research Papers,* 06/08.

Saundry, R., Jones, C., & Antcliff, V. (2011). Discipline, representation and dispute resolution – Exploring the role of companions in workplace discipline. *Industrial Relations Journal,* 42(5), 195–211.

Teague, P., & Roche, W. (2012). Line managers and the management of workplace conflict: Evidence from Ireland. *Human Resource Management Journal*, *22*(3), 235–251.

Townsend, K. (2013). To what extent do line managers play a role in modern industrial relations? *Asia Pacific Journal of Human Resources*, *51*(4), 421–436.

Whittaker, S., & Marchington, M. (2003). Devolving HR responsibility to the line. Threat, opportunity or partnership? *Employee Relations*, *25*(3), 245–261.

7

From Representation Gap to Resolution Gap: Exploring the Role of Employee Voice in Conflict Management

Gemma Wibberley and Richard Saundry

Introduction

This chapter explores the role of employee voice in the resolution of the management of conflict and the resolution of individual employment disputes. It is taken from a broader study of conflict management in the UK, based on five organizational case studies funded by the Advisory, Conciliation and Arbitration Service (Acas). Since the publication of the Gibbons Review into the UK's system of employment dispute resolution in 2007, substantial policy attention has been paid to the ways in which organizations deal with individual workplace conflict. However, the role of employee voice in supporting (or challenging) organizations in the

G. Wibberley
iROWE (Institute for Research into Organisations, Work and Employment),
University of Central Lancashire, Preston, UK
e-mail: gwibberley@uclan.ac.uk

R. Saundry (✉)
Plymouth Business School, Plymouth University, Plymouth, UK
e-mail: richard.saundry@plymouth.ac.uk

© The Editor(s) (if applicable) and The Author(s) 2016   **127**
R. Saundry et al. (eds.), *Reframing Resolution*,
DOI 10.1057/978-1-137-51560-5_7

management of conflict has been a notable omission from this debate. Therefore this chapter seeks to begin to fill this gap and offer a greater understanding of the function that employee voice plays.

Typically, employee voice is understood as two-way communication between workers and managers, either 'directly' with no intermediary or 'indirectly' via an employee representative (union or non-union) (Rollinson and Dundon 2007). Direct voice includes activities such as one-to-one meetings with managers and team briefings given by managers to discuss workplace issues with groups of employees. Indirect voice has been traditionally provided through trade union representatives; however, this has been dramatically undermined by declining union density and the erosion of workplace labour organization. Importantly, this 'representation gap' has not been filled by alternative non-union forms of indirect representation, which is found in just 7 % of British workplaces (van Wanrooy et al. 2013). Instead, for most employers, voice is increasingly viewed through the prism of employee engagement, although whether this provides new channels through which conflict can be resolved has been questioned (Colvin 2013).

In this chapter we begin by briefly examining the changing context of dispute resolution in the UK and then we explore the extant literature regarding the development of patterns of employee voice within UK workplaces and how this relates to the management and resolution of conflict. Findings from five detailed organizational case studies are then presented and discussed. Our analysis suggests that structures of employee representation, underpinned by high-trust relationships between key actors, facilitate the informal and early resolution of workplace conflict. However, the growing representation gap in UK workplaces and the consequent reliance on direct voice is progressively eroding the capacity of organizations to manage conflict effectively.

Voice, Engagement and Conflict

In recent years, policymakers and practitioners have given increased attention to the prevention and resolution of individual employment disputes (Gibbons 2007; BIS 2011; CIPD 2011). This has been largely driven by concerns raised by employers over the costs of managing workplace conflict and the consequent impact on organizational performance (British Chambers of Commerce 2010; CBI 2011). In response, the UK government has sought to reduce regulation, encourage more flexible and informal approaches to disputes and has also promoted the use of alternative dispute resolution (ADR) processes, such as workplace mediation.

The focus of reform has been on reducing the legal risks associated with terminating the employment and also on resolving disputes outside the workplace (Saundry et al. 2014). For example, the government has, for the first time, introduced a system of fees that employees must pay before their case can be brought before an employment tribunal.[1] Employers argue that this will deter weak and speculative claims, while other commentators, and particularly trade unions, argue that many employees will simply be 'priced out of justice' (TUC 2014: 2) In addition, a process of 'Early Conciliation' has been established under which, before a legal claim is registered, the Advisory, Conciliation and Arbitration Service (Acas) must be notified and an attempt made to reach a settlement. The introduction of these measures has been accompanied by a dramatic fall in the volume of employment tribunal applications.

Unfortunately, this debate has tended to focus on the end of the employment relationship and litigation rather than on the processes through which conflict emerges and is managed within the workplace. Although research has clearly shown that in most large organizations, these processes are shaped by the relations between line managers, HR practitioners and employee representatives (Jones and Saundry 2012), the role of employee voice in developing effective approaches to conflict management and resolution has been largely ignored by policy makers.

Bryson et al. (2006: 279) explain that formal mechanisms of employee voice generally 'involve two-way forms of communication between employers and employees' through which organizations try to obtain important information and secure improved productivity and performance by providing employees a 'meaningful say' at work. This can be indirect, via a third party such as a trade union or staff association or direct, between individuals or groups of employees and management. Employee voice can be heard through multiple and sometimes contradictory channels. At a basic level, it represents an opportunity for staff to make managers aware of their opinions on workplace issues (Dundon

---

[1] Employment tribunals are public bodies that have the authority to adjudicate on claims made under UK legislation in relation to unfair dismissal, discrimination and other employment related jurisdictions.

and Rollinson 2004) and this in turn can, depending on the response of managers, shape decision making processes (Wagner 1994). Indeed, if the voices of employees and workers are not taken into account in the decisions that impact on their working lives, this may lead to discontent and conflict (IPA and Tomorrow's Company 2012).

Voice can be beneficial for both employers and employees by increasing employee tenure and satisfaction (Avery et al. 2011) as well as reducing the costs of unresolved or formal grievances (Charlwood and Pollert 2014). Direct voice is seen as particularly important in positively shaping the relationship between managers and their subordinates and Donaghey et al. (2011) argue that benefits fall predominantly to managers who can acquire useful information that, for instance, may help to improve organizational efficiency.

Despite these perceived advantages, many firms choose not to have any formal voice channels and it has been suggested that employers will only establish such channels if measurable cost efficiencies and other organizational gains can be demonstrated (Bryson et al. 2006; Marginson et al. 2010). Where existing voice channels are perceived to challenge managerial prerogative, employers will often shut them down and attempt to dilute their influence by refusing to use them as a means for 'negotiation and consultation' and focusing only on one-way downward communication to their employees (Cathcart 2013; Townsend 2013; Wakeling 2014).

Furthermore, the mere existence of voice structures does not necessarily mean they will be used by employees. For workers to express their voice, they need to have trust in those with whom they want to communicate so that they feel secure in making their views known and confident that they will be treated fairly and listened to and also that their voice will be heard and acted upon (Gollan 2007; Donaghey et al. 2011; Farndale et al. 2011; Wilkinson and Fay 2011). In this way, the effectiveness of mechanisms for employee voice is also dependent on the quality of employment relations and the attitude of the employer to involving members of the organization in decision making.

In terms of managing workplace conflict, voice is facilitated through both direct and indirect channels. At a basic level, employees can raise concerns directly with their line manager who can in turn seek to resolve any issues that she might have with the employee. Interestingly, in a recent survey of conflict conducted by the CIPD (2015), over one-third of respondents said that they would respond to conflict at work by discussing the issue with a manager or HR. Where organizations ensure that employees meet regularly with their managers to discuss workplace issues, they are more likely to be able to resolve problems at work and this in turn reduces turnover and improves organizational performance. Therefore, the response of managers is critical in generating trust and also developing channels of direct voice through which conflict can be resolved (Charlwood and Pollert 2014).

However, the power imbalance between manager and employee may inhibit this (Timur et al. 2012; Charlwood and Pollert 2014), particularly as conflict at work is most common between line managers and their subordinates (CIPD 2015). In addition, it places a greater emphasis on the conflict resolution skills of the line manager. While Pyman et al. (2010) suggest that effective direct voice typically exists in organizations with other good HR practices, there is mounting evidence, reviewed by Jones and Saundry in Chap. 6, of a fundamental deficit in managerial confidence and competence in responding to conflict. They argue that managers are not only ill-equipped to have 'difficult conversations' with their staff but that such opportunities for direct voice are crowded out by operational goals and imperatives.

Formal grievance procedures can also be seen as providing a source of direct of 'employee voice' in offering a way in which employees can raise concerns with their employer (Batt et al. 2002). Formal procedures may also help maintain standards of equity and natural justice and act as a bulwark against draconian managerial action (Sanders 2008). However, employees may be deterred from making formal complaints by concerns over possible employer reprisals (Boroff and Lewin 1997; Lucy and Broughton 2011; Marsden 2011). For example, Pollert and Charlwood's (2008) study of low paid and unrepresented workers found that they were unlikely to use formal grievance procedures if they came into conflict with their employer.

In this context, it is not surprising that the CIPD survey mentioned above found that only eight per cent of respondents that they would use a formal procedure to respond to conflict. In contrast, 25 % of respondents reported that they just let the issue 'go', 12 % looked for a new job and 23 % turned to someone outside the workplace for advice (CIPD 2015).

This suggests that for a significant proportion of workers, direct voice does not offer an accessible route through which concerns can be aired and problems resolved (Lucy and Broughton 2011).

One solution to this problem is the use of indirect voice through which representatives can rebalance the employment relationship and provide some protection to employees in conflict situations. Representation in employee grievances and disciplinary cases has traditionally been a central function of trade unions. Workplaces in which trade unions are recognized and union density is high tend to have lower rates of disciplinary sanctions and dismissals (Antcliff and Saundry 2009). The data is less clear in regard to employee grievances; however, employees are more likely to utilize formal procedures in unionized settings (Kersley et al. 2006).

However, union voice has been substantially eroded in recent years as membership and density have fallen steadily and workplace structures of representation have weakened. In 1984, there were an estimated 335,000 trade union representatives in British workplaces. However, by 2004 this number had fallen by more than 60 % to just 128,000 (Charlwood and Forth, 2009). According to the 2011 Workplace Employment Relations Study (WERS2011), workers in only 7 % of workplaces had access to an on-site union representative (van Wanrooy et al. 2013). This decline has placed greater significance on the role of non-unionized employee representatives (NERs). These are employees who are enabled and directed by their company to support their colleagues. There are a variety of motives for employers to invest in the development of such representative structures including: compliance with regulation; union avoidance; and a desire to increase employee involvement in decision making and secure greater levels of engagement (Gollan 2007; Timur et al. 2012, Campolieti et al. 2013). However, despite these drivers there is little evidence that non-union representatives have filled the gap left by trade union decline (Charlwood and Terry 2007; Van Wanrooy et al. 2013).

There are also concerns about the extent to which non-union representatives provide an effective counterweight to employers. Research has suggested that non-union representatives are constrained by: dependence on the employer for both their existence and their resources; inability to levy realistic sanctions against the employer; lack of training and experience;

and also the fact that they have fewer of the rights and protections enjoyed by their unionized counterparts (Gollan 2007; Charlwood and Pollert 2014). Campolieti et al. (2013) found that in North America NERs are becoming substitutes for trade unions, rather than 'complementary', as a decreasing proportion of workers want to unionize.

Furthermore, while there is evidence of isolated attempts to develop roles for non-union employee representatives within dispute resolution, they are rarely trained to represent staff in disciplinary and grievance matters and WERS2011 found that less than half spent any time on discipline and grievance issues (Podro et al. 2007; van Wanrooy et al. 2013). Charlwood and Terry's (2007) analysis of WERS2004 also found that workplaces with non-union representatives (and no trade union presence) were likely to have higher dismissal rates.

Therefore, there has been a profound change in the pattern of employee voice in UK workplaces, and a shift away from indirect representative mechanisms and towards direct communication (Bryson et al. 2013). Employers see a greater emphasis on direct voice as helping to build organizational commitment, smoothing change processes and improving performance (Bryson et al. 2013). It could also be argued that direct voice addresses workplace conflict in a proactive way by minimizing discontent rather than simply reacting when conflict escalates (Luchak 2003). As Clarke (2013) notes, data from WERS2011 shows that the majority of employees feel that they are better placed to represent themselves, rather than seeking the services of union representatives.

It could be argued that rather than looking to resolve disputes though representation, a focus on enabling employee engagement, through direct voice (MacLeod and Clarke 2009) is a more effective way of responding to the challenge of workplace conflict. However, whether engagement can be separated from employers' attitudes to indirect representation and dispute resolution is highly questionable. High levels of trust is an important antecedent of engagement (Alfes et al. 2013; Rees et al. 2013) and as John Purcell (2012) has suggested, this is also linked to notions of organizational justice. At the same time MacLeod and Clarke (2009) acknowledge that another key enabler of engagement, organizational integrity, is influenced by relationships between employees and their immediate managers. Consequently, it could be argued that the way in which managers respond to, and deal with, conflict, together with the nature of their relationships with employee representatives will have an impact on levels of employee engagement.

In the rest of this chapter we examine the way in which the changing pattern of employee voice discussed above has shaped the way in which organizations respond to, and deal with, workplace conflict. In particular, we explore the implications of the apparent diminution of structures of representation and ask whether a reliance on direct voice can provide a basis for the effective management of conflict and resolution of individual employment disputes?

Methodology

This chapter draws on data from five organizational case studies undertaken between 2009 and 2011. While each of the studies were conducted as a standalone project, the methods used and the key research questions addressed were broadly similar allowing cross comparison. The organizations also represented different properties in terms of industrial activity, sector and nature of employee representation. They also differed in terms of size; however, they would all be considered large organizations employing more than 1,000 staff. Broad details are contained in Table 7.1,

Table 7.1 Characteristics of case study organizations

Organization	Industry	Sector	Employees	Employee representation
A	Health	Public	2–3,000	Unions recognized – high density
B	Services	Private	5–7,000	Unions recognized – high density
C	Public administration	Public	8–10,000	Unions recognized – high density
D	Services	Private	Over 50,000	Non-unionized – active staff association
E	Social services	Non-profit	4–5,000	Unions recognized – low density

although specific features are not identified in order to preserve anonymity and confidentiality.

Within each organization, research normally consisted of three main elements: examination of policy documentation for dealing with individual employment disputes and relevant collective agreements; in-depth interviews with key informants including HR practitioners, operational managers and employee representatives; and exploration of available statistical data regarding employment, workforce demographics and pattern of individual employment disputes.

In total, 131 interviews were conducted, comprising 104 hours of interview data. In broad terms the sample across the five cases could be broken down as follows: 53 HR practitioners ranging from HR adviser to HR director level; 61 line and operational managers; and 17 employee representatives. Importantly, case studies were not focused on how individual cases were conducted but on the formal and informal processes that constitute the management of conflict within the organization. Accordingly, details of individual cases were not requested. In addition interviews were neither sought nor conducted with individuals who were involved with individual employment disputes. In all but one case (Organization E) membership of either trade unions and/or staff association was relatively high, therefore, we would suggest that the views of employee representatives interviewed would provide an indication of the broad views of employees within the organization. Of course, we must be cautious in drawing broad conclusions from the data which is drawn from five separate case studies all of which have been conducted in large organizations, with employee representation either from trade unions or trained colleagues.

Findings

Through these case studies the chapter will now explore how different forms of employee voice influenced the way in which conflict was managed and individual employment disputes were resolved. We first examine the use of employee engagement strategies to minimize the incidence of workplace conflict, before exploring the way in which line managers sought to identify and resolve difficult issues. Finally, we present evidence of the role played by employee representatives in facilitating informal processes of resolution.

Minimizing Conflict Through Engagement?

Management respondents claimed that effective employee engagement strategies could minimize conflict by improving commitment and motivation of staff, as envisaged by Macleod and Clarke (2009). They argued that engagement, the incidence of conflict, and management responses to it were intertwined:

> It has to start with the recognition that you can't be successful unless you've got people who are engaged come in, come in on time, and you treat fairly; firmly but aware of the boundaries. So there are lots of things that actually make up the ability to have a good department...our engagement score is the highest across the Group, but that for an operation area it's been consistently up over 85, 86 per cent. Couple that with low absence, low turnover, you kind of get people who want to be there, who want to deliver and your costs kind of get reduced so there's an equilibrium. (Operational manager – Organization B)

Importantly, there was a link between the way that employees were treated and employee engagement. In essence, dealing with any problems fairly and equitably was more likely to secure the engagement of staff which would mean that problems with conduct and capability were less likely to occur.

In the same organization, respondents highlighted the role of staff forums and actions set up in response to the annual staff survey. These included one senior manager establishing an online facility where staff could pose questions and raise concerns and a similar initiative in which staff were able to log any problems or issues on a central noticeboard which would then be addressed by managers. Interestingly, Organization B was highly unionized and engagement mechanisms ran alongside robust structures of representation with union respondents seeing no conflict between these 'twin-tracks'.

Without such channels, there was a danger that low levels of grievances may mask underlying conflict. A senior manager in Organization E argued that although his organization received very few formal complaints this was mainly because 'people just keep stuff to themselves'. Multiple reasons are proposed for employee silence: fear (Gollan 2007); concerns that raising concerns may appear disloyal (Boroff and Lewin 1997); and lack of capability on the part of both staff and managers (Lucy and Broughton 2011). In Organization E which provided social care, staff worked in small residential teams which provided an environment in which both staff and managers tended to avoid conflict.

A number of respondents argued that 'grievance cultures' had developed in parts of the organizations in which they worked, due to the fact that employees did not feel that they were being listened to or did not have access to channels to voice their concerns. This provided fertile conditions in which discontent could grow. For example, an HR practitioner described work at a site at which in the past there had been '*three of four grievances every week*'. He explained that staff felt the only way that management would take notice of their concerns was if a formal complaint was made through the grievance procedure (Batt et al. 2002):

> The process gets them an audience...because we didn't have the [staff] survey, we didn't have the engagement...if I was on the shop floor and I wanted to raise something, maybe the grievance process was the best way to go about it.

In this case, senior managers argued that the development of engagement mechanisms such as a staff survey provided a vital channel for the expression of discontent, which in turn reduced the incidence of grievances. However, it was also clear from the sample that this could not be separated from the impact of collective representation. In three of the cases, the development of a 'grievance culture' was linked by respondents to a breakdown in trust between union representatives and management. The reasons for this were various but a common feature was a sense on the part of union representatives that they were being excluded from consultative and decision-making processes. In addition, broader concerns over the handling of restructuring and changes to working practices created a negative atmosphere within which formal grievance procedures became a way of challenging managerial authority. Therefore, problems with collective aspects of employment relations could spill over into the way that organizational actors dealt with individual disputes. For managers within such an environment, there was a perception that the union were acting in a confrontational and adversarial manner:

> It tended to go from nought to a hundred on the Richter scale of disputes very, very quickly…I would be, for example, called up by the union to be told that a member of staff was taking out a grievance…there's been no kind of heads up in advance of that, or any discussion or any attempt to resolve the matter; it was simply a case of moving straight in to a formal process. (Operational manager – Organization A)

Irrespective of outcomes, this tended to encourage parties to adopt defensive postures to disputes, and led to profound mistrust, fuelling conflict in the future. Therefore, although securing employee engagement may limit the incidence of conflict, this is itself shaped by the way that managers handle conflict when it escalates.

Direct Voice: The Importance of an 'Open Door'

Respondents in all organizations emphasized the importance of resolving issues as 'close to the ground' as possible; identifying problems at an early stage and then 'nipping them in the bud'. The key to this was the ability of line managers to spot emerging problems by maintaining regular communication with their staff, often through an 'open door' policy. However, this was not only dependent on line managers having the time and inclination to keep in regular contact with their staff but also creating an environment in which staff felt confident to voice their concerns (Donaghey et al. 2011):

> I think the site has a pretty open culture. We encourage people to air their views, we encourage people to bring forward their ideas and opinions…we tend to encourage people to put them on the table and have an adult conversation. (Operational manager – Organization B)

This informal contact was backed up to some extent by formal performance management mechanisms. In one organization, all staff had regular one-to-one meetings with their line managers which were logged and recorded. Both management and union respondents saw this as maintaining important channels of communication, and also providing a place in which employees and managers could raise and try to resolve concerns.

Nonetheless, there was a danger that employee appraisals were reduced to 'box ticking' exercises. This suggests that the existence of a channel does not necessarily translate into actual voice (Farndale et al. 2011). In the case studies it did not appear that there were insidious reasons for silencing employees. Instead, for managers, high workloads and extreme pressure to meet operational targets tended to squeeze out informal communication while more formalized performance management was seen as a 'chore'. As a result, warning signs of conflict could be missed or simply ignored:

> I think one of our biggest faults of performance management is that it comes to the end of year review and then people are then just told that they're not good enough but there's been nothing through the year, there's been no sort of coaching, there's been no inkling of it…. (HR practitioner – Organization D)

All organizations within our sample emphasized the importance of managers communicating with their staff. However, even where managers are convinced that their 'door is always open', it may be difficult for employees to raise issues with managers, fearing possible ramifications (Marsden 2011). To a certain extent more formalized systems of communications such as one-to-ones, review meetings and appraisals potentially provided a more structured and transparent way of managers giving an opportunity to employees to air their views.

While this undoubtedly provided an element of 'direct' voice, it was constrained by the nature of the relationship and the fact that any discussion took place in the context of the employee's performance. Informal processes of resolution should not need to extend beyond manager and employee, nevertheless, the authority and the power relationship that exists between them makes this problematic (Charlwood and Pollert 2014). Where the employee has no access to representation they may have insufficient trust in management to explore an alternative to formal procedure. In our sample, it appeared that conflict often remained hidden and either unnoticed or ignored by managers until it escalated into a formal grievance. The receipt of a written complaint could therefore be the first indication of a problem. An HR practitioner explained that:

> often it doesn't actually come to anyone's attention until somebody gets a call in [HR] because there's a grievance being raised by five people against one colleague and everyone is a bit like, 'God what are we going to do with this (HR practitioner – Organization D)

Indirect Voice: The Key to Conflict Resolution

The most consistent finding across the sample was the central importance of employee representation (both union and non-union) in underpinning effective conflict resolution (Timur et al. 2012). Representatives provided an 'ear to the ground' and therefore not only were issues more likely to be identified but there was a greater chance that the root causes of conflict could be revealed and addressed. Organization D, which did not recognize trade unions, had trained a network of representatives, elected by staff, to represent their colleagues in disciplinary and grievance issues. For managers, these non-union representatives provided an early warning system of developing conflict:

> [Representatives] are the eyes and ears on the floor…and they're the ones that talk to the [staff], so if there is some kind of rumbling…we're expecting them to be picking that up and then going to the relevant [manager] and discussing that, and then going from there. (Operational manager – Organization D)

Some of the difficulties faced by managers in resolving conflict at an early stage were overcome through informal discussions between employee representatives and HR practitioners, who were able to broker resolutions away from the emotion of the situation and sometimes the entrenched attitudes of manager and employee(s). The vast majority of union representatives that we interviewed had a clear preference for informal resolution wherever possible:

> I'm not fussed about how we get to a resolution of things...if I can phone HR, or a manager, and say 'Can we talk about this before we go into a formal meeting?'...then I'll do that. (Union representative – Organization A)

However, the simple presence of employee representatives was not necessarily enough. Positive and trusting relationships between representatives, HR practitioners and managers were crucial for constructive informal contact (Jones and Saundry 2012).

> It's having that open culture where people open up and have those discussions and say things like, 'I'm a bit worried about somebody's behaviour... (Trade union representative – Organization A)

Where these relationships were absent, it was unlikely that representatives would share information with management as they would be concerned that this could be used against them. Instead they would often seek to escalate the issue by encouraging the employee to take formal action. Individual disputes became a battleground in which representatives attempted to 'win' the case rather than seek a resolution to the issue.

But, where high-trust relations between employee representatives and managers existed, informal contact was commonplace. At the outset of a grievance or disciplinary action, it was normal for the employee representative to be informed. This could be just a courtesy but sometimes provided an early opportunity to establish the context of the problem and explore options as to how the case could progress:

> They [union representatives] will be involved right from the very beginning. They'll often know about the grievance before we do and you know, they'll often come to see us and say you've got this grievance, what are your intentions, basically? 'What are you going to do?' (HR practitioner – Organization B)

Importantly, the intervention of employee representatives helped to ensure that any mitigating factors were identified at an early stage as employees were more likely to discuss sensitive issues with their representatives as opposed to their managers. In addition an important part of the representatives' role was to ensure that employees properly understood the implications of the case.

> In fact, often, it would be me, or my colleagues, that will say to an individual, you do understand that this could mean...'God, you mean I could lose my job?'...it's sometimes about getting the person they're comfortable representing, to actually say, well, you know, we've done this.... You need to be straight with people. (Employee representative – Organization D)

In this way, employee representatives could try to minimize a sanction and the longer term implications for the employee. For example, where employees were facing dismissal, it was not uncommon for representatives to negotiate for their member to resign their post. These findings challenge Luchak's (2003) suggestion that indirect voice is 'reactive' and does not propose win–win solutions to resolve disputes.

Our research also showed that informal processes did not end with the start of formal proceedings. Even in disciplinary cases, informal discussions and contact often shadowed the formal procedure. For example, it was common for employee representatives and managers to discuss possible agreements and resolutions during breaks or adjournments in formal hearings. Furthermore, managers often worked with employee representatives to uncover the reasons for an employee's misbehaviour or poor performance. However, this was largely dependent on the presence of employee representatives and on the existence of constructive employment relations.

A key theme of these case studies was the importance of employee representation in underpinning informal processes of resolution. However, the current debate over workplace dispute resolution takes place in a context in which most workers have no access to workplace representation of any type (van Wanrooy et al. 2013). Employee representation is therefore crucial as it provides an intermediary who lies outside the relationship between manager and employee and can act on staff's behalf without any fear of the consequences:

In a unionized environment such as ours, it can help in some ways to diffuse some of these situations…in non-unionized environments I've worked in the past, it's either you like what your manager says or you've got a grievance issue. (HR practitioner – Organization B)

Conclusion

Concerns over employment dispute resolution lie at the centre of contemporary debates over public policy and organizational practice. However, these debates have tended to focus on perceived burdens imposed by employment regulation and the threat of litigation rather than on the way in which key organizational actors interact to resolve conflict *inside the workplace*. In particular, the role of employee voice and particularly indirect channels of employee representation have been largely ignored.

The central finding from our research is that employee representation plays a vital role in facilitating early and informal processes of conflict resolution. While it might be expected that employees or representatives themselves may take this view, it was notable that within our interviews, the vast majority of management respondents also expressed this opinion. While there were some cases in which they were able to discuss and resolve issues in an informal way with their staff, managers accepted that this was not always easy, and that employees may be more likely to talk openly and honestly to an employee representative. Furthermore, they may also be more likely to listen to the advice from a representative who could play an important role in managing expectations and explaining the implications of their situation. By working with employee representatives, managers and HR practitioners were able to identify conflict at an early stage, avoid the necessity for the application of formal procedures and even within formal situations they were often able to negotiate a way forward.

However, the precise impact of representation turned on the nature of employment relations within the organization and in particular the existence of high-trust relationships between representatives, managers and

HR practitioners. Where there was reciprocity and trust, managers and representatives had the confidence to go outside the process, to exchange their views and explore possible solutions. Where this was not the case, parties would cling to procedure for fear that any 'off the record' discussion would be used against them at a later date. Trust was, in part, related to broader collective issues and it is important to acknowledge that some of the organizational changes noted above could place a strain on these relationships, but it was also centred on the extent to which employee representatives felt that they had a genuine voice within the organization.

More worryingly, these relationships and consequent structures of informal resolution are under significant pressure. Perhaps most obviously, the erosion of union organization has not been compensated by a parallel growth in non-union mechanisms of indirect voice. This representation gap threatens to undermine the social processes of discussion and negotiation which form the basis of conflict resolution. It might be argued that direct voice and related mechanisms designed to secure employee engagement could be the answer to this apparent problem. Certainly, our findings suggest that engagement strategies which provide a direct channel for employee voice have the potential to create more open workplace cultures in which conflict is less likely to emerge and escalate.

But a reliance on direct voice inevitably makes the relationship between the manager and employee the locus of conflict resolution. This is problematic given the acknowledged problem of low levels of confidence and competence among line and operational managers in UK workplaces (see Chap. 6). Furthermore, even where managers have the necessary skills to address and seek to resolve difficult issues, many employees will find it difficult to raise issues directly with their managers, due to the inherent power imbalance within the employment relationship. In contrast, representatives can act as a conduit for negotiation and remove the parties from the emotion and intensity of the situation.

These findings have important implications for policy and practice: first, they suggest that encouraging the development of effective structures of representation should be a critical consideration for policymakers. Second, direct voice alone cannot compensate for the loss of representative voice mechanisms, rather they provide complementary channels through which difficult issues can be addressed and resolved. Finally, employee engagement should not be seen as a replacement or alternative to employee representation; instead, developing effective conflict resolution processes, underpinned by high-trust relationships between key organizational actors can play a key role in developing workplace justice, trust and consequently securing employee engagement.

References

Alfes, K., Shantz, A., Truss, C., & Soane, E. (2013). The link between perceived human resource management practices, engagement and employee behaviour: A moderated mediation model. *The International Journal of Human Resource Management, 24*(2), 330–351.

Antcliff, V., & Saundry, R. (2009). Accompaniment, workplace representation and disciplinary outcomes in British workplaces – Just a formality? *British Journal of Industrial Relations, 47*(1), 100–121.

Avery, D., McKay, P., Wilson, D., Volpone, S., & Killham, E. (2011). Does voice go flat? How tenure diminishes the impact of voice. *Human Resource Management, 50*(1), 147–158.

Batt, R., Colvin, A., & Keefe, J. (2002). Employee voice, human resource practices, and quit rates: Evidence from the telecommunications industry. *Industrial and Labor Relations Review, 55*(4), 573–594.

BIS (2011). *Resolving workplace disputes: A consultation*. London: BIS.

Boroff, K., & Lewin, D. (1997). Loyalty, voice, and intent to exit a union firm: A conceptual and empirical analysis. *Industrial and Labor Relations Review, 51*, 50–63.

British Chambers of Commerce (2010). *Employment regulation: Up to the job?* London: British Chambers of Commerce.

Bryson, A., Gomez, R., & Willman, P. (2006). Voice at work: What do employers want? A symposium summary. *Socio-Economic Review, 4*, 279–282.

Bryson, A., Willman, P., Gomez, R., & Kretschmer, T. (2013). The comparative advantage of non-union voice in Britain, 1980–2004. *Industrial Relations: A Journal of Economy and Society, 52*(s1), 194–220.

Campolieti, M., Gomez, R., & Gunderson, M. (2013). Does non-union employee representation act as a complement or substitute to union voice? Evidence from Canada and the United States. *Industrial Relations: A Journal of Economy and Society, 52*(s1), 378–396.

Cathcart, A. (2013). Directing democracy: Competing interests and contested terrain in the John Lewis Partnership. *Journal of Industrial Relations, 55*(4), 601–620.

CBI (2011). *Settling the matter – Building a more effective and efficient tribunal system*, April.

Charlwood, A., & Forth, J. (2009). Employee representation. In W. Brown, A. Bryson, J. Forth, & K. Whitfield (Eds.), *The evolution of the modern workplace* (pp. 74–96). Cambridge: Cambridge University Press.

Charlwood, A., & Pollert, A. (2014). Informal employment dispute resolution among low-wage non-union workers: Does managerially initiated workplace voice enhance equity and efficiency? *British Journal of Industrial Relations, 52*(2), 359–386.

Charlwood, A., & Terry, M. (2007). 21st-century models of employee representation: Structures, processes and outcomes. *Industrial Relations Journal, 38*(4), 320–337.

CIPD (2011). *Conflict management – Survey report*. London: CIPD.

CIPD (2015). *Getting under the skin of workplace conflict – A survey of employee experiences of interpersonal conflict at work*. London: CIPD.

Clarke, N. (2013). *The future of trade unionism: What does WERS tell us?* http://www.ipa-involve.com/news/the-future-of-trade-unionism-what-does-wers-tell us/?utm_source=Adestra&utm_medium=email&utm_term=. Accessed 1 November 2014.

Colvin, A. (2013). Participation versus procedures in non-union dispute resolution. *Industrial Relations: A Journal of Economy and Society, 52*(s1), 259–283.

Donaghey, J., Cullinane, N., Dundon, T., & Wilkinson, A. (2011). Reconceptualising employee silence: Problems and prognosis. *Work, Employment and Society, 25*(1), 51–67.

Dundon, T., & Rollinson, D. (2004). *Employment relations in non-union firms*. London: Routledge.

Farndale, E., Van Ruiten, J., Kelliher, C., & Hope-Hailey, V. (2011). The influence of perceived employee voice on organizational commitment: An exchange perspective. *Human Resource Management, 50*(1), 113–129.

Gibbons, M. (2007). *A review of employment dispute resolution in Great Britain*. London: DTI.

Gollan, P. (2007). *Employee representation in non-union firms*. London: Sage Publications.

IPA and Tomorrow's Company. (2012). *Releasing voice for sustainable business success*. http://www.ipa-involve.com/resources/publications/releasing-voice-for-sustainable-business-success/. Accessed 20 November 2014.

Jones, C., & Saundry, R. (2012). The practice of discipline: Evaluating the roles and relationship between managers and HR professionals. *Human Resource Management Journal, 22*(3), 252–266.

Kersley, B., Alpin, C., Forth, J., Bryson, A., Bewley, H., Dix, G., et al. (2006). *Inside the workplace: Findings from the 2004 workplace employment relations survey.* London: Routledge.

Luchak, A. (2003). What kind of voice do loyal employees use? *British Journal of Industrial Relations, 41*(1), 115–134.

Lucy, D., & Broughton, A. (2011). *Understanding the behaviour and decision making of employees in conflicts and disputes at work,* Employment Relations Research Series no. 119, BIS, Institute for Employment Studies.

MacLeod, D., & Clarke, N. (2009). *Engaging for success: Enhancing performance through employee engagement.* London: Department of Business, Innovation and Skills.

Marginson, P., Edwards, P., Edwards, T., Ferner, A., & Tregaskis, O. (2010). Employee representation and consultative voice in multinational companies operating in Britain. *British Journal of Industrial Relations, 48*(1), 151–180.

Marsden, D. (2011). Individual voice in employment relationships: A comparison under different forms of workplace representation, *CEP Discussion Paper,* No 1070.

Podro, S., Suff, R., & Purcell, J. (2007). Employee representatives: Challenges and changes in the workplace. In *Acas policy discussion papers.* London: Acas.

Pollert, A., & Charlwood, A. (2008). Who experiences problems at work, what problems do they experience, what do they do about them and what happens as a result?. *Working Paper 11 – The Unorganised Worker: Problems at Work, Routes to Support and Views on Representation,* Centre for Employment Studies Research (Bristol Business School).

Purcell, J. (2012). The limits and possibilities of employee engagement. *Warwick papers in industrial relations,* Number 96. University of Warwick: Industrial Relations Research Unit.

Pyman, A., Holland, P., Teicher, J., & Cooper, B. K. (2010). Industrial relations climate, employee voice and managerial attitudes to unions: An Australian study. *British Journal of Industrial Relations, 48*(2), 460–480.

Rees, C., Alfes, K., & Gatenby, M. (2013). Employee voice and engagement: Connections and consequences. *The International Journal of Human Resource Management, 24*(14), 2780–2798.

Rollinson, D., & Dundon, T. (2007). *Understanding employment relations.* London: McGraw-Hill.

Sanders, A. (2008). Better dispute resolution in Part 1 of the employment act 2008? *Industrial Law Journal, 38*, 30–49.

Saundry, R., Latreille, P., Dickens, L., Irvine, C., Teague, P., Urwin, P., & Wibberley, G. (2014). Reframing resolution – Managing conflict and resolving individual employment disputes in the contemporary workplace, *Acas Policy Series*.

Timur, T., Taras, D., & Ponak, A. (2012). 'Shopping for voice': Do pre-existing non-union representation plans matter when employees unionize? *British Journal of Industrial Relations, 50*(2), 214–238.

Townsend, K. (2013). To what extent do line managers play a role in modern industrial relations? *Asia Pacific Journal of Human Resources, 51*, 421–436.

TUC (2014). *At what price justice? The impact of employment tribunal fees.* London: TUC.

van Wanrooy, B., Bewley, H., Bryson, A., Forth, J., Freeth, S., Stokes, L., et al. (2013). *Employment relations in the shadow of recession – Findings from the 2011 workplace employment relations study.* London: Palgrave Macmillan.

Wagner, J. A. (1994). Participation's effects on performance and satisfaction: A reconsideration of research evidence. *Academy of Management Review, 19*(2), 312–330.

Wakeling, A. (2014). Does social media strengthen or dilute employee voice? In *Employment relations comment.* London: Acas.

Wilkinson, A., & Fay, C. (2011). New times for employee voice? *Human Resource Management, 50*, 65–74.

8

Downsizing: Managing Redundancy and Restructuring

Ian Ashman

Introduction and Background

Employee downsizing is a term used widely to describe processes that result in the elimination of jobs from an organization and that are often accompanied by the dismissal of the job incumbents. A typical definition is 'a planned set of organizational policies and practices aimed at workforce reduction with the goal of improving firm performance' (Datta et al. 2010: 282). Downsizing is often treated as synonymous with terms such as redundancy or layoff but, while frequently including those processes, it can be achieved through a wide variety of alternative or accompanying restructuring activities including outsourcing, redeployment, natural wastage, recruitment freezes, short-time working, sabbaticals and pay freezes or cuts (CIPD 2015).

I. Ashman (✉)
iROWE (Institute for Research into Organisations, Work and Employment),
University of Central Lancashire, Preston, UK
e-mail: iashman@uclan.ac.uk

© The Editor(s) (if applicable) and The Author(s) 2016   **149**
R. Saundry et al. (eds.), *Reframing Resolution*,
DOI 10.1057/978-1-137-51560-5_8

Employees have been discharged from their place of work by various means ever since the first attempts to organize human activity collectively, so downsizing is not new; however, it is only in the last few decades that it has become recognized as a legitimate and ubiquitous organizational strategy (Gandolfi and Littler 2012) and it has been described by Cascio (2013:51) as 'a defining characteristic of modern life in organizations'. It is apparent that downsizing is now to be found operating under all conceivable political and economic systems in every part of the world and it is as common in the public sector, in the UK at least, as it is in the private sector. Perhaps more surprisingly it has become clear that downsizing is a strategy not only associated with addressing market contraction and organizational decline but also a strategy associated with efficiency driven changes in organizations that may be thriving (Freeman and Cameron 1993).

The legitimation of downsizing strategy seems to be all pervasive and attitudes towards its implementation have changed noticeably over the last few decades. Whereas, once the announcement of closures, job reductions and restructures would frequently lead to industrial conflict and direct action between employers and collective labour interests today it seems that the approach of trade unions generally is not to confront employee downsizing strategies head-on but to simply minimize compulsory job losses by influencing the downsizing policies, processes, practices and criteria that impact upon their membership. Certainly, from a UK perspective, the days of mass disputes against organizational restructuring, retrenchment and closure, such as the UK miners' strikes or the News International Wapping dispute in the 1980s, seem consigned to the industrial relations of yesteryear, in part because of structural factors such as globalization and technological innovation but also because of the changing attitudes of labour and its representing organizations.

The shift by trade unions from adversarial industrial relations to partnership and cooperation based on notions of 'mutual gain', risk mitigation and arresting membership decline (Martínez-Lucio and Stuart 2005) is unquestionably an important foundation of this effect and a number of studies have sought to examine the consequences of this emerging approach. Rodriguez-Ruis (2015) explores the trade union response to downsizing at Telefonica the giant Spanish telecommunications company and, in particular, asks why the unions were so accommodating of the strategy at a time (during 2011) when the company was highly profitable? He concludes that:

> When responding to organizational restructuring [the union] had to choose between challenging corporate decisions or ensuring an orderly departure and beneficial arrangements for the workforce. (Rodriguez-Ruis 2015:96)

Ultimately, they chose the latter – a 'soft compromise' in the face of a variety of pressures including the perceived legitimacy of downsizing and restructuring as a 'common sense' managerial discourse, an unfavourable political climate and a local media hostile to proactive trade union agendas.

MacKenzie (2009) discovered a similar response to restructuring from trade unions in the Irish telecommunications industry where the Communication Workers Union accepted an increase in subcontracting by Eircom in return for potentially favourable but, nonetheless, fragile commitments such as the company subcontracting to 'union friendly' external suppliers and, therefore, extending union membership beyond the firm. Downsizing is undoubtedly a complex organizational strategy that is almost always detrimental for the majority of employees (victims and survivors) but how collective labour interests can and should respond to downsizing is equally complicated. In the UK, under the adverse economic conditions of the global financial crisis, when car manufacturer Toyota announced retrenchment affecting 4,500 employees the Unite union opted to accept a ten per cent reduction in working hours and wages for its members rather than countenance redundancies or take direct action against the cuts. A Unite representative said:

> The agreement we have reached with Toyota will ensure none of our members' benefits are eroded and that these skilled workers will remain in place and at work ready for when the upturn comes. (BBC 2009)

Many other car manufacturers negotiated similar agreements with trade unions at around the same time.

It has been noted in this book and elsewhere (Saundry et al. 2014) that the agency of most organizational conflict and dispute has shifted from the collective to the individual and the attitudes of trade unions to downsizing along with the empirical evidence that will be presented in this chapter seem to bear that out. As we will see shortly, trade union representatives can be unexpected but important allies of the agents of downsizing in organizations.

There is an enormous amount of literature, originating mostly in North America, that examines the phenomena of downsizing but the focus is generally on the causes and consequences of downsizing with relatively little attention being given to the management of associated policies, processes and practices. In an important review of the causes and effects of employee downsizing Datta and his colleagues (2010:285) present a model that illustrates the situation (adapted in Fig. 8.1). They identify and examine dozens of recent studies that fit within the four corner boxes of the model but they acknowledge that there is precious little research that fits into the highlighted middle box – the management of downsizing – and that this absence has a limiting influence on our understanding of the various causal streams. They make the point that:

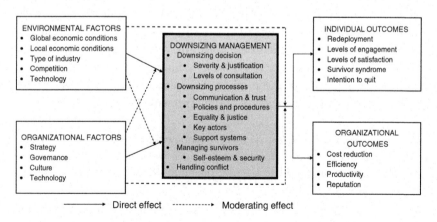

Fig. 8.1 A model of employee downsizing

It is axiomatic that change is hard, and this is especially true of change involving reductions in jobs and people. [...] From an organizational change perspective, both "process" and "contextual" factors likely influence the extent to which downsizing yields positive or negative outcomes. (Datta et al. 2010:341)

It is unsurprising, therefore, that research exploring downsizing and conflict directly is very hard to find. It can be taken for granted that the list of factors appearing in the 'downsizing management' box in Fig. 8.1 represent fertile grounds for conflict between groups and individuals and to issues such as trust, justice, support, esteem and insecurity and we can add factors falling into the categories of performance, citizenship, work/home life overspill and negative behaviours (Hargrove et al. 2012).

Taking account of the relative paucity of research exploring issues of conflict in the context of downsizing this chapter will undertake an exploration of the potential manifestations of conflict rather than attempt to conduct a systematic analysis of incidences of conflict during downsizing events. It will do so by reflecting on evidence drawn from an Acas sponsored study of the people undertaking a role that elsewhere has been somewhat harshly referred to as 'executioner' (Wright and Barling 1998; Gandolfi 2009) or 'grim reaper' (Clair and Dufresne 2004) but here is referred to as 'downsizing envoy' (Ashman 2012a, b, c, 2013). Envoys are defined as 'the people whose role it is to deliver face to face the news of downsizing decisions' (Ashman 2012a:5) and the term is applied to better reflect the primary endeavour of the task, which generally involves tact, diplomacy and the maintenance of constructive and cooperative relationships among victims and survivors rather than simply and coldly dismissing employees.

The study in question was conducted in 2011 and 2012 (Ashman 2012a, b) and entailed in-depth interviews with fifty downsizing envoys, drawn from nine public sector organizations and eight private sector organizations along with two independent consultants – thirty are HR professionals (including the consultants) and twenty from other management functions. Given the absence of an identifiable research population, envoys were sampled by making appeals through existing networks in the north of England. They were drawn from across organizational hierarchies and so for both HR and non-HR categories there is a mix of management levels, although not all of the HR participants had line management responsibilities. The interviews were structured loosely around the recollection of downsizing events, which enabled respondents to identify and evaluate the key issues and experiences for themselves. On average each interview lasted around seventy minutes and the depth of auto-exploration that this afforded each envoy is an important feature of the data gathered.

Perhaps the only thing that can be said with any degree of certainty is that the situations around which conflict arises in downsizing events and the manner in which conflict becomes manifest are not predictable. There are many stakeholders with interests connected to the outcomes of downsizing programmes but to keep things relatively simple we can identify five key groups: the downsizers (the executive that decides the strategy); the envoys (the employees that deliver the message); the employee representatives (often trade unionists that act as intermediaries between the other parties); the victims (the employees that lose their jobs); and the survivors (the employees that keep their jobs).

Conflict is rarely as simple as a dispute between the downsizers and the victims because it is hard to anticipate how groups or individuals will react under particular circumstances. Understandably, for instance, employees that are relatively independent, mobile and sought after often view redundancy as a positive opportunity to move on (perhaps with a healthy monetary cushion), whereas those that have family commitments, are tied to an area and are not so marketable are more likely to see it as deeply worrying and upsetting.

Matters are complicated more generally, as is the case with this Acas research, by the fact that employees are often told that they are 'at risk' of redundancy at the start of a statutory consultation period, which makes them simultaneously potential victims and potential survivors, and in addition they may also be acting as envoys or representatives so the categories are not exclusive or discrete. We will consider the dynamic of conflict between the various stakeholders in due course, but in the first instance a case study will help to illustrate the potential unpredictability of conflict during a downsizing event.

Unanticipated Conflict and Unexpected Alliances: A Brief Case Study

Smith and Jones (a pseudonym) is a company with headquarters in the north of England, a number of production sites throughout England and Ireland and around 1,400 employees. Sue and Jane were at the time the only HR professionals working for the Company so they were asked to act as 'downsizing envoys' and organize the closure of one of the production sites, which would eventually involve redeploying forty of the 140 employees at the site to a new purpose built facility only a mile away, making eighty employees redundant and shedding the remainder by other means. Sue said:

> I was faced with my first site closure and my first redundancy programme. I was very inexperienced and had to feel my way through it. We needed to get rid of only eighty people, which actually made it even harder than losing the whole site of 140 because selecting eighty people out of the site was very, very difficult … [The employees] all seem to be related somehow – fathers, sons, brothers and cousins – you were putting whole families out of work.

Jane reflected on the potential for internecine conflict and added:

> In some ways it's easier in situations where everyone is going because nobody can feel bitter against anybody else – they are all in the same boat together.

At the time Jane was the junior colleague and had no experience of downsizing either but Sue, in particular, did not want to betray her inexperience to the company directors as she felt it was a task that she and Jane should and could do, and she didn't want consultants brought in to deny them the opportunity to demonstrate their mettle. In reality the 'opportunity' proved immensely challenging and rife with tension and hostility.

Much of the conflict seemed to arise as a consequence of cultural differences rather than the downsizing directly. The plant to be closed was located in the part of a city with a large ethnic community that meant that the entire workforce was male and all but a few employees were of Asian origin – many did not have English as a first language. Being young white females had significant implications for Sue and Jane although initially they were unaware of them. Sue noted that there had been problems at the site previously:

> Culturally it was very difficult [for instance] they revere age and seniority and, you know, for example, a young supervisor scoring an older operative was causing issues. They often didn't recognize things from outside of their culture but luckily the general manager was of Asian descent and he was really good at getting our point across to the workforce in their own language and in a way that they would appreciate.

However, when the closure was first announced by the general manager to the workforce, with Sue and Jane in attendance, what had previously seemed like good fortune may have exacerbated a sense of hostility as Sue recalls:

> That first meeting was very difficult because [the employees] were looking at me, the general manager was talking, but they were looking at me and I realized at that point that it wasn't going to be how I thought … I went into it thinking that I was going to be a support function – not that I was going to be heading things. Even though I wasn't the one speaking it felt like I was leading the event and that was really weird. I assumed that I would stand behind and that employees would see me as an ally that they would go to for help and that it would all be wonderful and fluffy, but it wasn't at all. [To the workforce] I was personally responsible for the whole process from start to finish and I was left in no doubt about that.

After the initial announcement there were subsequent meetings with groups and individuals that because of the lack of understanding and trust were no easier for Sue – the level of conflict was palpable:

> I thought I was going to get attacked, honestly it was quite frightening, in fact the whole process face-to-face was quite frightening for me. I was a white woman in an Asian man's world and that was difficult.

According to Jane:

> [The employees] were irate – in fact, irate doesn't really cover it!

The timescale was tight but the site closure was carefully trailed and comprehensive procedures for consultation, notification, redeployment and redundancy selection and appeal were put in place along with outside job search and counselling support. Nevertheless, this was a workforce that gave more weight to informal personal interactions than formal procedures and so even on the penultimate day of site operations there were still many employees that did not believe the closure would really happen. Sue and Jane arranged one-to-one meetings for all redundant staff in order that they would depart with as positive a frame of mind as possible. Sue explained:

> We delivered the final message on the Thursday that 'tomorrow is your last day'. In our naivety we thought it was going to be – 'here's your letter, you know what is in it, thank you very much and if there is anything we can do to help let us know as we'll be here to wave you off tomorrow'. I can't describe the situation of what was supposed to be individual meetings – people were banging the door down. It felt very threatening. When one person came on about twenty others tried to enter the small office at the same time. In the end we had to get the general manager to sit in with us because it was so aggressive.

The general manager's position in all this is intriguing because, throughout the downsizing process, his job was under threat also and yet, fortunately for Sue and Jane, he chose to support them in their task at the risk of alienating himself from his workforce. Another unexpected ally was the site trade union representative, also an employee at the facility, which Sue described as being:

> A really good guy that we got on very well with. He was really helpful even though he was also losing his job – he was supportive and protective. [If he hadn't been?] Oh my God!

On the other hand, officials from the trade union's regional office were a source of disappointment to Sue and Jane as they felt that the officials were not representing their members effectively because they did not attend any announcements, consultations or one-to-one meetings and seemed to lack knowledge or experience of downsizing events. They appeared to be standing on the side lines and encouraging hostilities from a distance rather than advising their members effectively.

Sue and Jane conducted a number of downsizing programmes subsequently and each one had their particular antagonisms but none matched the intensity of their first experience.

Downsizing Decision Makers and Conflict

A small number of the envoys interviewed for the Acas research were at a level in their organization where they could also be considered as downsizing decision makers and their perspective and experiences proved informative. The more typical scenario, however, as described in the case study above, was for executive decision makers to declare a downsizing strategy with associated targets then step aside and leave it to middle managers and first line supervisors to implement, justify and deliver it. Kets de Vries and Balazs (1997) have argued that executive 'executioners' often suffer psychologically and fear karmic retribution for their decisions but, if that is the case, it is generally experienced at some distance from the other stakeholders that are affected.

Nevertheless, a site of conflict that may be unique to the decision makers is dealing with the influence of extra-organizational agencies, such as politicians and the media. For instance, a senior executive at a large manufacturing company explained how local politicians were critical of the company's downsizing strategy that was detrimental to their constituents, but which he felt was unavoidable given the economic climate and was being handled very responsibly by the organization. He said:

> Politicians come and vilify me. I'm trying to do my best for everybody and the way that they react is irresponsible. They've seen the overall dynamic of the business case but when they sit at a local level they won't acknowledge that and they will fight tooth and nail. It makes it difficult because they put hope in people's hearts – "we can make this go away" – whereas, they can't.

A senior HR colleague in the same organization explained how media interest compromised preparations:

> Speculation appeared in the press and on the TV that there was going to be this major redundancy ... The company had to respond and was basically forced almost into making the redundancy [announcement] earlier than it would have liked ... I think it really placed us on the back foot.

An executive with a public sector local authority also had to deal with conflicting political interests that created great difficulties for her and her staff trying to manage cuts to funding. From her perspective the politicians had a very direct influence on where downsizing would occur. So, often decisions were made for political expediency rather than towards strategic ends and it would be left to her and her colleagues to justify closures and redundancies whether they agreed with them or not. Furthermore, there were instances where politicians would brief against one another and leak confidential information to the media. The effect was that the Authority was forced into a number of U-turns on downsizing decisions and that employees on occasions would read about alleged redundancies in the newspapers before they had been confirmed by the Authority or could be communicated in a controlled and formal manner. Inevitably, feelings of insecurity, anger and distrust of management was heightened across affected departments and beyond. Conflict between individuals and groups that were ostensibly 'in the same boat' was being fanned by outside forces. A manager at the Authority summed circumstances up by saying:

> The organization can do everything in its power to try to help their managers and the victims, but all that gets blown out of the water by politics.

Downsizing Envoys and Conflict

The case study set out earlier reflects an extreme situation that confronted two downsizing 'envoys' but fortunately it is some distance from being a typical experience. In fact, despite most envoys describing the role as the most emotional and traumatic work-related experience they had ever had to deal with, the majority found that the face to face interactions with potential victims were relatively free of conflict. Instances of aggression and hostility certainly did arise but they were the exception rather than the rule. Many envoys claimed that it was the stoic, passive or visibly upset victims that were harder to cope with from an emotional point of view compared with those that expressed anger. There was tacit recognition that the anger was not personal or directed at the envoy and simply acted as a form of catharsis for the victim and that it was part of the envoy role to empathize and allow the release to take place. As one envoy put it:

> Yeah, tears and despair, I think for me, are much worse than anger. I can deal with anger. You just let people talk and kind of let them vent their way through it. But the minute that switches from anger to crying or, well, you know, that's really tough.

No other envoys from the research sample reported feeling threatened in any way similar to the experience of Sue and Jane in the case example. One experienced HR manager was frustrated that the 'at risk' employees did not seem to want to actively confront the downsizing rationale:

> You weren't being challenged in terms of the business need, the logic why redundancies were needed ... 'Come on, fight me!' Make me work hard to convince you that that's the case.

In some circumstances another unexpected setting for conflict was between the envoys themselves. A typical scenario is for a HR manager and an appropriate line manager to act as dual envoys in face to face meetings with at risk employees where the line manager is intended to be the familiar reassuring presence that delivers the difficult message and the HR manager is there for technical advice. In a number of public sector organizations there was clear evidence of tensions across what were intended to be complementary envoy roles. HR envoys complained that line managers were unwilling to take ownership of the downsizing events and treated meetings with potential victims as good cop/bad cop routines with the HR envoy cast in the role of bad cop. Ironically, some line managers felt they could not take ownership because their HR colleague was there to police them rather than support them in a difficult and unfamiliar task. One HR manager did not shy away from admitting as much:

> I do not let them go off script at all, and if they do, they get a boot under the table.

The reasons for this surprising antagonism are complicated and may in part be a consequence of personality clashes but it surely reflects the different priorities of the envoys, with HR managers focussed on adhering to procedures in order to avoid legal challenges and line managers wanting to ease the exit of colleagues and maintain cordial relationships with the survivors in their work environment. What is harder to explain is why the phenomenon occurred only in the public sector – in private sector organizations the relationship between HR and non-HR functions appeared to be much more constructive and harmonious.

Downsizing, Trade Union Representatives and Conflict

All but one of the organizations covered by the Acas envoys research recognized trade union representation for at least some of their employees and although it might be thought that consultations and negotiations between unions and employers would create conflict there was relatively little evidence of it. That is not to say that antagonism never arose (for instance, one union that cooperated with a previous downsizing programme felt 'stabbed in the back' when another event followed at the same organization soon after) but both sides often recognized that the difficulties being experienced came from economic pressures that were beyond their control. One HR director acknowledged the somewhat invidious position that trade union officials can find themselves in when negotiating downsizing:

> We try to come to a mutual solution to problems. When it's a redundancy situation, whatever we agree about, it's very difficult for [the unions] because they can't condone job losses that will affect their members. So, even if it came to agreeing selection criteria... they won't be able to say 'yes,

we agree it'. They'd have to say 'yes, we've commented on it', but they can't agree it because it means they're condoning job losses.

At the collective level the relative absence of conflict may also be a consequence of the 'mutual gain' agenda being adopted by unions, but at the individual level (drawing admittedly only on evidence provided by envoys) it seemed to stem from a shared sense of purpose. Downsizing envoys when dealing with trade union representatives, despite ostensibly representing conflicting interests, were more likely to encounter cooperation and empathy than hostility and generally the feelings were reciprocated. Even where there were incidences of confrontation there was an accompanying recognition from envoys that employee representatives were often in a difficult situation. One envoy's experience is instructive:

> The unions got on the stage and said "we'll fight them on the beaches". Personally, I didn't expect it and I had a really good relationship with the work's convener so I kind of went after him afterwards and said what was all that about? [I was] genuinely quite upset by what he'd done. I had a really good conversation with him and I understood why he'd done it and actually I was quite grateful because … he needed to show [his membership] that he had a level of authority, number one and number two that he would represent them and could take all of them with him. What would have been worse, is if they hadn't have had any faith in him and he'd have been disempowered.

In fact, the main source of frustration from the envoy perspective, as was mentioned at the end of the case study, occurred where trade unions seemed unwilling or unable to represent effectively the interests of an 'at risk' group of employees.

Downsizing Victims, Survivors and Conflict

It is tempting to think of the victims and survivors of downsizing programmes as distinct categories but in the initial phases at least, as was intimated earlier, they are not and do not become differentiated until after the process is over. Almost all of the envoys spoken to for the Acas research found themselves 'at risk' during the downsizing events they were involved with, and ultimately they all survived, but they spoke eloquently of the feelings they experienced at a time of considerable challenge. The reactions of 'at risk' employees is perhaps the most difficult thing to predict in what we already know to be an unpredictable situation and evidence of conflict can become manifest in a number of ways. At an extreme level there may have been a case of sabotage with one envoy working for a food manufacturer reporting how, during a round of redundancies, razorblades were discovered in some cakes on the production line. The culprit was never identified but it was suspected to be a parting gesture from an angry victim. A number of envoys spoke of how disgruntled employees would resort to using social media to vent their feelings. A HR manager said:

> We had examples of sabotage with people taking ridiculous pictures in the factory, and various disgusting things, then putting them on Facebook – it's as if they were thinking "oh, it's a laugh and they're going to sack us anyway".

Downsizing is often selective and has the habit of placing colleagues in competition with one another for a reduced number of positions as one envoy remarked:

> Although there's an element of we're all going through this together, there's also, I guess, an element of competitiveness and you've got to sit and you've still got to do your day job, thinking for the next three months I've no idea whether I'm going to have a job or not.

The issue of how employees are identified for compulsory redundancy is evidently a vexed one regardless of advice offered by organizations such as the CIPD (2015) and Acas (2014) to rely on objective and demonstrable measures for selection. Data from the 2011 Workplace Employee Relations Study (WERS) shows that 9 % of all grievances were associated with matters related to selection for redundancy with evidence of the figure increasing (van Wanrooy et al. 2013). Dissatisfaction with the processes and procedures invoked to manage downsizing is likely to have a significant effect on how successfully an organization moves forwards post-retrenchment as it will influence morale and may lead to resentment that harbours conflict for the future. Similarly, 'survivor syndrome' is now viewed as a recognized condition among some employees that remain after downsizing and which is characterized by a mixture of emotions including guilt (perhaps as a consequence of competing and succeeding where former workmates failed), anger, insecurity and disengagement. Unsurprisingly, these emotions can lead to increased levels of resistance, distrust and ultimately conflict (Cutcher-Gershenfeld 1991; Cascio 1993; Macky 2004).

An interesting feature of this competitive environment is the antagonism apparent between front line and back office (or support) staff in the public sector. Public service providers in sectors such as health, education and the emergency services establish a noticeable distinction between those employees that deliver the service to the public and those that support them in that delivery. At times of privation, as Bach (2011) has noted, it is the support functions that bear a disproportionate brunt of the cuts as one envoy recognized:

> They've been working here on their restructuring and it's turned out it's 140 jobs. Let's have a look and see who's impacted. A big percentage of them are people like me, the non-uniform staff as we're called, or support staff; very few uniformed. You know that galls me because we're half the cost. You know? So it's going to take more of us to make up that change.

The Acas envoys research certainly confirmed the perception of imbalance and there was evidence of conflict at a collective and individual level between the two categories that it is reasonable to assume may spill over into important working relationships during post-downsizing renewal. Envoys reported that front line employees were often inconsiderate and unsympathetic to the plight of their support colleagues although one envoy acknowledged that the senior management in her organization were aware of the situation:

I had an impression that the [front line staff] were just like "oh well, whatever..." and didn't really understand the impact that [downsizing] has on people who are [support] staff ... The senior [official] actually turned round to the [front line staff] – anyone who's basically whinging – and just said "your colleagues have been made redundant and you're moaning about having to work 'til 8 o'clock tonight" ... and he sent a clear message.

The distinction can be made between front line and support staff in many private sector organizations but it is generally not as defined as it is in the public sector and perhaps as a consequence the Acas envoys study found no evidence of this sort of tension among the private sector participants.

Conclusion

The discussion and evidence presented in this chapter indicates that conflict is an inherent aspect of downsizing strategy, policy and practice and that it has the potential to affect all of the various parties involved in a multitude of ways. It also suggests, however, that the nature and experience of conflict is far from predictable and that, despite the obvious competing interests of certain stakeholders, hostility is not inevitable and that cooperation may transpire in unexpected ways. The anticipation and handling of conflict is likely to be an important factor in successful downsizing that will influence the effectiveness of procedures, the experiences of the people required to deliver them, the extent to which victims leave with dignity and the climate in which the survivors take the organizations forwards. On that basis it seems evident that more research is needed into the management of the human side of downsizing to complement the existing body of material that examines the causes and consequences of a now ubiquitous phenomenon.

References

Acas. (2014). *Handling large-scale redundancies*. London: Acas. Available at http://www.acas.org.uk/media/pdf/b/2/Handling-large-scale-collective-redundancies-advisory-booklet.pdf.

Ashman, I. (2012a). *"The nature of bad news infects the teller": The experiences of envoys in the face to face delivery of downsizing initiatives in the UK public sector* (Acas Research Paper 03/12). Available at http://www.acas.org.uk/media/pdf/b/f/0312_Downsizing_envoys_Ashman.pdf. Accessed Aug 2015.

Ashman, I. (2012b). *Downsizing envoys: a public/private sector comparison* (Acas Research Paper 11/12). Available at http://www.acas.org.uk/media/pdf/7/1/Downsizing-envoys-a-public-private-sector-comparison-accessible-version.pdf. Accessed Aug 2015.

Ashman, I. (2012c, August). A new role emerges in downsizing: special envoys. *People Management*, 32–35.

Ashman, I. (2013). The face-to-face delivery of downsizing decisions in UK public sector organizations: the envoy role. *Public Management Review*, *17*(1), 108–128.

Bach, S. (2011). *A new era of public service employment relations? The challenges ahead.* Acas workplace relations discussion paper. Available at http://www.acas.org.uk/media/pdf/m/c/Future-workplace-relations-series-publicservice-accessible-version-august-2011.pdf. Accessed Aug 2015.

BBC. (2009). *Toyota cuts working hours and pay.* Available at http://news.bbc.co.uk/1/hi/business/7936397.stm. Accessed Aug 2015.

Cascio, W. F. (1993). Downsizing: What do we know? What have we learned? *Academy of Management Executive*, *7*(1), 95–104.

Cascio, W. F. (2013). How does downsizing come about? In C. L. Cooper, A. Pandey, & J. C. Quick (Eds.), *Downsizing: Is less still more?*. Cambridge: Cambridge University Press.

CIPD. (2015). Redundancy. *Factsheet.* Available at http://www.cipd.co.uk/hr-resources/factsheets/redundancy.aspx. Accessed Aug 2015.

Clair, J. A., & Dufresne, R. L. (2004). Playing the grim reaper: How employees experience carrying out a downsizing. *Human Relations*, *57*(12), 1597–1625.

Cutcher-Gershenfeld, J. (1991). The impact on economic performance of a transformation in workplace relations. *Industrial and Labor Relations Review*, *44*(2), 241–260.

Datta, D. K., Guthrie, J. P., Basuil, D., & Pandey, A. (2010). Causes and effects of employment downsizing: A review and synthesis. *Journal of Management*, *36*, 281–348.

Gandolfi, F. (2009). Executing downsizing: The experience of executioners. *Contemporary Management Research*, *5*(2), 185–200.

Gandolfi, F., & Littler, C. (2012). Downsizing is dead; long live the downsizing phenomenon: conceptualization and the phases of cost-cutting. *Journal of Management and Organization, 18*(3), 334–345.

Freeman, S., & Cameron, K. (1993). Organizational downsizing: a convergence and reorientation framework. *Organization Science, 4*(1), 10–29.

Hargrove, M. B., Cooper, C. L., & Campbell Quick, J. (2012). The stress outcomes of downsizing. In C. L. Cooper, A. Pandey, & J. Campbell Quick (Eds.), *Downsizing: Is less still more?* Cambridge: Cambridge University Press.

Kets de Vries, M., & Balazs, K. (1997). The downside of downsizing. *Human Relations, 50*(1), 11–50.

MacKenzie, R. (2009). Union responses to restructuring and the growth of contingent labour in the Irish telecommunications sector. *Economic and Industrial Democracy, 30*(4), 539–563.

Macky, K. (2004). Organisational downsizing and redundancies: the New Zealand worker's experience. *Journal of Employment Relations, 29*(1), 63–87.

Martínez-Lucio, M., & Stuart, M. (2005). 'Partnership' and new industrial relations in a risk society: an age of shotgun weddings and marriages of convenience? *Work, Employment and Society, 19*(4), 797–817.

Rodriguez-Ruiz, O. (2015). Unions' response to corporate restructuring in Telefónica: locked into collective bargaining? *Employee Relations, 37*(1), 83–101.

Saundry, R., Latreille, P., Dickens, L., Irvine, C., Teague, P., Urwin, P., & Wibberley, G. (2014). Reframing resolution – Managing conflict and resolving individual employment disputes in the contemporary workplace. Acas Discussion Paper. Available at http://www.acas.org.uk/media/pdf/6/9/reframing_policy_paper_FINAL.pdf. Accessed Aug 2015.

van Wanrooy, B., Bewley, H., Bryson, A., Forth, J., Freeth, S., Stokes, L., et al. (2013). *Employment relations in the shadow of recession: Findings from the 2011 workplace employment relations study*. Basingstoke: Palgrave.

Wright, B., & Barling, J. (1998). The executioners' song: Listening to downsizers reflect on their experience. *Canadian Journal of Administrative Sciences, 15*(4), 339–355.

Part III

Workplace Mediation and Alternative Dispute Resolution

9

Experiencing Mediation from the Disputants' Perspective

Anthony Bennett

Introduction

There is growing evidence in the UK that organizations and individuals are increasingly turning to mediation as a means of conflict resolution in the workplace. Research suggests, in particular, that mediation can often help to resolve issues that would otherwise escalate into lengthy and costly disputes (Latreille 2011; Latreille et al. 2012; Saundry 2012). Studies also reveal that the use of mediation in an organization can have a positive impact on conflict handling abilities and also the overall employment relations climate (Bennett 2014; Saundry and Wibberley 2014). Furthermore, in the context of the individualization of the employment relationship and the erosion of representative structures (see Chap. 7), it has been argued that mediation offers a degree of equality for the employee that is largely absent in other dispute resolution processes (CIPD 2011; Latreille 2011; Bennett 2013).

Advocates of mediation argue that it avoids the need to adopt a more formal and often confrontational route, characterized by rights-based

A. Bennett (✉)
Tony Bennett, ROSTON HR Consultancy, Rochdale, UK
e-mail: rtbconsultancy@outlook.com

© The Editor(s) (if applicable) and The Author(s) 2016   **171**
R. Saundry et al. (eds.), *Reframing Resolution*,
DOI 10.1057/978-1-137-51560-5_9

grievance and disciplinary procedures. Its aim is not to apportion blame to either of the parties but rather, through discussion and greater understanding of each other's views, to rebuild the relationship into the future (Acas/CIPD 2013).[1] In contrast, critics claim that mediation is simply another way of cementing employer control over the labour process and insulating organizations against the reputational and other damage associated with managerial mistreatment (Colling 2004; Latreille and Saundry 2014).

Methodologically, the investigative lens to date has focused on the effectiveness of mediation as seen by managers, mediators and mediation providers, with the views and experiences of the disputants remaining largely unreported. The aim of the research discussed in this chapter was, in part, to address this deficit in our understanding. To that end, twenty-five individuals were interviewed, from a variety of occupations and organizations, to examine their views of the purpose of mediation and their experience of the process and its outcomes. The chapter opens with a review of the current literature. There then follows a short overview of the methods adopted for the research. The findings of the research are then considered. We close with a critical reflection on the key themes highlighted in the chapter.

Literature Review

Mediation is not a new concept. It has its origins in the resolution of family and community disputes (Aubrey-Johnson and Curtis 2012). The use of mediation is well established in the USA with 86 % of Fortune 1000 corporations reporting in 2011 that they used mediation in employment-related disputes (Lipsky et al. 2012). Its longstanding use and success within the American Postal Service is also an impressive example of a large scale industrial strategy for the resolution of individual employment disputes in a key sector (Bingham and Pitts 2002).

Elsewhere, the evidence is very patchy, with mediation widely used in Australia and New Zealand and some signs that its use has grown

---

[1] Acas provides information, advice, training, conciliation and other services for employers and employees in the UK to help prevent or resolve workplace problems; CIPD is the chartered institute in the UK for members of the human resources and development profession.

across a number of EU states (Latreille and Saundry 2014). In the UK, until recently, mediation was rarely applied to employment issues within the workplace. The publication of the Gibbons Review (2007), commissioned by the UK government to review the system of workplace dispute resolution placed workplace mediation at the centre of debates over dispute resolution. Furthermore, the consequent revision of the Code of Practice on Disciplinary and Grievance Procedures[2] issued by the Advisory, Conciliation and Arbitration Service (Acas) in 2009, suggested that organizations should consider using mediation if employers and employees were unable to resolve disputes.

There is some evidence to suggest that this stimulated interest in workplace mediation in the UK (Rahim et al. 2011). However, the extent of its adoption is unclear. Recent surveys conducted by the CIPD paint a very mixed picture with almost one-quarter of employers reporting having used an internally trained mediator to resolve an employment dispute and 9 % having called on an external mediator. In addition, just 1.5 % of employees who had experienced conflict had participated in mediation, most of which was provided by the employer (CIPD 2015a, b). Wood et al.'s (2014) analysis of the 2011 Workplace Employment Relations Study found that mediation by an impartial third party had been used by 17 % workplaces (in the previous 12 months) that had experienced a formal individual grievance. Where mediation is used, it also tends to be limited to large, public sector organizations (Saundry et al. 2014; Wood et al. 2014). Furthermore, while there is growing evidence of US corporations adopting 'conflict management systems' of which mediation is a key part (Lipsky et al. 2012), Saundry and Wibberley (2014) have found little evidence of this in the UK. Organizations may use mediation but rarely is this part of any broader strategic approach to workplace conflict.

Nonetheless, the case for mediation remains persuasive. Proponents argue that it allows disputants to consider what they can obtain from

---

[2] The Code of Practice provides basic practical guidance to employers, employees and their representatives and sets out principles for handling disciplinary and grievance situations in the workplace. It is not binding as such in law. However, if a dispute reaches an employment tribunal, it is expected that the employer will have managed their dispute resolution process in accordance with the Code.

a possible solution by concentrating on common ground rather than their differences. Because the process is facilitated by a neutral mediator who is charged with balancing asymmetries of power and creating a non-threatening environment, it is claimed that disputants are more likely to listen to the other person's viewpoint and understand how their behaviour is affecting the other party. It can also be argued that the parties are more likely to commit to a solution if they have been involved in finding that solution, rather than feeling that it has been imposed upon them. The confidential nature of mediation is also purported to be another important benefit of the process giving participants the confidence that anything that they say will not be put on record or be used against them at a later stage (Acas/CIPD 2013).

In contrast, more sceptical commentators have claimed that rather than empowering employees, mediation can offer a means of controlling dissent and asserting control (Colling 2004). By using mediation, in certain cases, the responsibility for unfair treatment can be shifted to the employee and the employer can evade the responsibility for changing practices and holding managers to account. Keashly and Nowell (2011) point out that because mediation focuses on the future, it has no means of addressing or 'punishing' past behaviour. Therefore, some writers have questioned whether mediation is appropriate in addressing sensitive and power-based disputes such as bullying and harassment (Dolder 2004; Branch et al. 2009).

In practice, it is notable that the decision to utilize mediation in the workplace can depend on the type of dispute, the stage of the dispute and, crucially, what type of resolution is being sought. As Shapiro and Brett rightly stress, 'the type of outcome obtained from a dispute resolution procedure (e.g. a win, lose or compromise) may influence processes underlying judgements of procedural justice [by participants]' (1993:1170). Crucially, mediation can be used at any point in the course of a dispute, but research suggests that chances of success are increased by early use (Bennett 2013). This said, generalized rules are not particularly helpful and each case should be treated on its merits. Fundamentally, mediation is most likely to be appropriate where both parties are prepared to attempt to rebuild and maintain that relationship (Acas/CIPD 2013).

The deployment of mediation can also vary among and within sectors depending on the context and organizational approaches to conflict resolution (see Saundry and Wibberley 2012, 2014). Bennett (2014) highlights the key issue of sectoral differences in his study of the utilization of mediation in higher education in the UK. Significantly, this research revealed that mediators saw a key strength of mediation as being its ability to address inequality and 'power imbalance' between disputants. Moreover, it found that the nature of conflict management was shaped by the particular nature of organizational culture and workforce composition of the sector.

To date, the voice of mediation participants in the literature has tended to be limited to quantitative assessments of their satisfaction with the process. For instance, in relation to the USPS Redress programme for mediation, Bingham captured the experiences of participants through a detailed exit survey which revealed that participants were consistently highly satisfied with key areas of the mediation and in particular, the respect they were accorded and the opportunity they were given to present their views (2004:157). In the UK, Acas (2012, 2013) have conducted annual surveys of the commissioners of their mediation service, and the participants in those mediations. Acas reports focus solely on the efficacy of an externally facilitated mediation intervention but also point to a relatively high level of success with around two-thirds of respondents (in 2013) reporting that the dispute had been at least partly resolved. In addition, just over half of participants said that they would take part in mediation again and eight in ten participants were either 'very satisfied' or 'fairly satisfied' overall with the mediation process.

While such findings are valuable in quantifying participant satisfaction, they are not able to explore the experiences of participants in the context of the disputes in which they have become involved. In this study, by using in-depth interviews with disputants we are able to shed light on: the nature of, and background to, the disputes that give rise to the mediation; the nuanced interactions between the parties and mediator; and importantly the role that power plays in shaping the process and outcomes. In addition, as many of the interviews took place more than 12 months after the mediation took place, this research was able to assess the sustainability of mediation settlements.

Methodology

The sample for the research was drawn from a number of sources. The majority of respondents had experienced Acas mediation and, subsequently, agreed to share their views. The remainder of the sample was made up of clients of two private providers, and two organizations with in-house schemes. Overall, the sample comprised of 25 subjects. Given that the sample was self-selecting, it cannot claim to be representative of the population of mediation participants. Therefore, we must be extremely cautious about drawing broad generalizations from the data. In particular, it might be suggested that those willing to discuss their experiences of mediation may be more likely to have strong feelings of either satisfaction or dissatisfaction. It is also important to note that, in most instances, the views of participants reflected only one side of a dispute. As the research team was dependent on self-referrals, there was no means by which other disputants could be contacted. The findings therefore need to be considered with this in mind.

In-depth, semi-structured interviews were carried out with participants that lasted between 30 and 90 min. Overall, 22 h of interview data were collected. The interviews allowed the disputant to explain their experiences in-depth. However, where possible, interviewers ensured that a number of key issues were covered including: the context of the dispute, previous experiences of mediation, the basis of the dispute, motivation to participate, who suggested mediation, their expectations, the support provided, degree of satisfaction with the process, nature and sustainability of the outcome, and the impact on their attitudes to conflictual issues and practice in handling conflict.

Utilizing template analysis (King 2004), the data was analysed by comparing responses to the key themes and questions outlined above. These themes were then refined and new themes were added as issues emerged from exploration of the data. The interviews were then re-examined to assess the extent of evidence with respect to these new themes.

Findings

Context and Cases

The majority of the disputes within the sample had taken place in large, state-owned organizations, with access to HR expertise, reflecting the conventional profile of mediation users (Wood et al. 2014). Sixty per cent of cases were mediated by Acas, with six cases managed within in-house mediation schemes and four by a private mediation provider. It is of note that some organizations that had in-house mediators still chose to use external providers, in the main due to the seniority of the staff involved in the dispute. The majority of respondents were female and were also in managerial positions when interviewed. Furthermore, 21 of the 25 cases involved one party who had authority over the other.

A quarter of the cases centred on personality clashes, differences in management style or conflict over operational strategy. Respondents typically linked the escalation of conflict to their own attitudes or, more commonly, those of the other party. For example, one respondent accepted that the dispute they were involved in was linked to the fact that they 'tended to be very forthright' while the other party 'tends to take things very personally'. Another respondent criticized for not being approachable, argued that what he considered to be normal behaviour was seen as being detached by the other party:

> I walk past in the corridor, or whatever, and I won't say anything because I've got my head in my bag or I'm on my phone but she doesn't see me on my phone...

Critically, all the cases of this type involved staff of a level of seniority that meant that the dispute either had an impact on key operational and strategic decisions or had a detrimental effect on others working in their teams. It is important to note that there were very few cases in the sample in which mediation had been used to resolve disputes between junior staff.

Managers and HR were often reluctant to use formal procedures or disciplinary action and hence mediation was seen as the only way to deal with apparently intractable issues. There were also four instances of alleged discrimination or harassment, which seemed to be unrelated to performance. Here, respondents reported that the other party had a history of such behaviour within the organization but formal complaints procedures and processes were either not thought to be appropriate or had failed to produce a conclusive result.

Mediation is often seen as suitable for interpersonal disputes or employee grievances but less appropriate for disciplinary issues, particularly those where there has allegedly been an infringement of employment rights (Acas/CPD 2013). In reality, the majority of cases involved a complex mix of grievance and potential disciplinary issues, and most had their roots in a manager seeking to raise performance issues with the other party. Often, the background to the dispute was the introduction of some change in the structure of work or responsibility of the other party, thus leading to the dispute. Furthermore, managers often argued that although they were powerless to alter the underlying organizational context, they had to manage the consequences of rapid change. Consequently they became the focus for discontent:

> A lot of the problems that I was dealing with when people submitted their grievance, it was more to do with them as individuals....The organization was going through a very, very turbulent amount of change....They [the other party] need to change, they didn't want to change and they see me [as the problem].

In such situations, whilst staff might not so readily acquiesce to change, managers, often under pressure to improve efficiency and quality, apply more stringent policies in terms of performance, absence and capability. This can lead to staff perceiving such action as unfair and, in some instances, as bullying. In our sample, the experiences of those respondents in subordinate positions also suggested that poor people management skills were an important ingredient in the escalation of conflict (Latreille 2011). Managers, perhaps not surprisingly, appeared to react badly to accusations of bullying. They often felt that the complaint was a personal attack and paradoxically in some cases was a rejection of the 'help' that they believed they were giving the other party. As a result, both parties felt aggrieved, deepening the gulf between them and attributing the blame for the dispute on the other party as opposed to their own actions.

Perceptions of Mediation

Generally, respondents had little prior knowledge of mediation and how it fitted in to the more conventional dispute resolution procedures in their organization. A few had some experience of mediation outside the workplace, such as family or community mediation. Otherwise mediation was simply assumed to be an 'informal discussion' or facilitation conducted by HR or a senior manager. Surprisingly, even where an in-house service existed, interviewees had little knowledge of its overall purpose.

Some of the respondents within our sample, certainly at the start of the process, welcomed the opportunity for resolution and the chance to discuss their concerns with a third party outside the immediate organizational environment. One manager typical of this group reported that:

> I felt that mediation might just be what we both needed…to talk openly about what was going on and maybe come out feeling much better and be able to take things forward. So after thinking about it I thought 'well, I'd welcome that'. I think I'd welcome anything other than, you know, the grievance and the long processes of going through what went on in the end anyway.

However, the majority of interviewees, particularly managers, were reluctant about entering mediation. For some managers, agreeing to mediation was an admission of failure which reflected badly on their conflict handling ability (Saundry and Wibberley 2014). In others, in which there had been allegations of bullying or mistreatment, participation in mediation represented an admission of guilt. At a more practical level, most of the line managers within our sample had little expectation that mediation would deal with what they saw as the underlying problem – the performance and/or capability of the other disputant. This was partly related to the stage at which mediation occurred but also with the suitability of the process for examining managerial evaluations of capability or conduct. As one manager commented:

My concern was could mediation resolve this, when actually the issue was a performance issue? Okay, that wasn't what she was raising, she was raising that I was bullying her ...but I couldn't see how we could separate the two, so kind of, have mediation around our relationship and how she felt I was bullying her, while trying to keep the performance issue out of it.

Interestingly, managers against whom complaints had been made approached mediation with the intention of using the process to challenge what for them were unfair and unfounded 'charges' made against them that had seriously affected their working relationship with the perceived victim. Therefore it appeared that respondents in this situation did not view the process as one in order to seek a resolution but simply to explain and justify their actions. Moreover, managers tended to rationalize their involvement in mediation by claiming that while they did not expect to benefit from the process they were prepared to enter into mediation 'if it would help' the other disputant.

It was perhaps not surprising that victims of alleged bullying were sceptical about the potential for mediation to change the behaviour of the other party. A senior manager who had himself been the subject of bullying behaviour from a colleague, concluded that:

I think that a bully rarely identifies that they are a bully so, they want to get through the process as quickly as possible, they tick the boxes [by agreeing to mediation] and continue life as normal.

In these cases, mediation was generally seen as the 'least worst' option available in the circumstances or because other organizational channels had failed to deliver a satisfactory outcome for the complainant (see Saundry and Wibberley 2012). Unsurprisingly, attribution of responsibility was a major issue for interviewees in such cases. Those respondents who felt that they were victims of discrimination or bullying feared that participation in the mediation could infer that they were also in some way to blame for the dispute. This echoed a real concern voiced by some commentators that re-interpreting discrimination or bullying as a personality clash deflects the culpability to resolve the real issues away from management and onto the victim (Dolder 2004; Keashly and Nowell 2011).

Crucially, the data questioned the extent to which participation in mediation was voluntary. Consistently, the managers interviewed for the study appeared reluctant participants. This is not to say that they were forced into mediation but that they felt that their co-operation was expected by their superiors and HR. Or that refusal would reflect poorly if the matter escalated to a formal grievance or an employment tribunal. The following manager's response was typical:

> It was put to me very nicely, and it, it wasn't insisted upon. I think it was just from my own point of view, in that it would go on file that I wasn't willing to undergo mediation. Although that was understandable, I just felt that it would work against me somehow. So, I sort of felt pressured.

This also had an impact on outcomes with most respondents agreeing that if parties did not enter the process willingly, an eventual and sustainable resolution was much less probable. Failure was particularly likely if one or both of the parties adopted a confrontational attitude to mediation. For example, a number of respondents reported that, the difficulties in reaching a resolution were signalled at an early point in the mediation process by the negative body language or verbal hostility of the other party.

The Process

In most cases, the decision to refer a dispute to mediation came from either senior managers or HR. In a few cases, mediation was requested by the disputants or followed interventions from occupational health, trade unions or professional bodies. Importantly, mediation was rarely suggested at the early stages of a dispute. Rather, contrary to recommended best practice (Acas/CIPD 2013), it occurred after other procedures had failed and where there was a potential for litigation. The objective was to simply get the parties working together again. As one typical senior manager explained:

> …[the organization] don't expect these two to be bosom buddies ever but they just need them to be able to conduct themselves [in] ….a professional manner that allows one to draw on the expertise of the other and vice versa.

In the majority of cases mediation was used as a last resort. Even when procedures had not been enacted, disputes had typically gone on for some time and had become increasingly intractable. This led to two main problems. Firstly, by the time that mediation occurred, the parties had developed extremely entrenched views of the issues. In one case, mediation had only taken place nine months after a complaint was made. As a senior manager reflected:

> I think perhaps we might have got to mediation sooner, in which case... perhaps feelings might not have become quite so entrenched....I think we hopefully might have had a better outcome.

As another senior manager explained with reference to their dispute, it was difficult to reach a resolution as mediation had occurred only after formal complaints of bullying had been made:

> I think it would have been great to do, or to try and do, mediation ahead of formal complaints of bullying...you've almost, set your...stall out at that stage haven't you, from both sides...So he's said 'you're bullying me', I've said 'no I haven't' and it's quite difficult to recover from that regardless of how successful the mediation is.

Interestingly, in organizations which operated an in-house mediation scheme, there was some evidence that referrals were made at an earlier point. This could be explained by a greater awareness of mediation and its purpose where such a service was in place. In addition, internal mediation can be organized more quickly and does not involve a direct financial cost.

Importantly, the vast majority of respondents valued the role played by the mediator. They were seen as impartial and effective in allowing both parties to explain their positions. Even where the situation between the participants was very difficult, most respondents felt that mediators did all they could to diffuse the situation and encourage the disputants to reflect on their own contribution to the dispute, irrespective of the outcome. One disputant who had been a mediation 'sceptic' explained his experiences as follows:

I guess if was being honest I'm not sure that I understood the power of it as an intervention and nor did I necessarily appreciate the positioning that the facilitators have in getting individuals to think about their contribution towards a solution.

The Complexity of Mediation Outcomes

The variety and complexity of outcomes of the mediations covered in the study highlighted how difficult it can be to measure its success. Although a majority of cases had been concluded with some sort of agreement, the settlement was still in place at the time of the research in less than one third. In one case, although the mediation had been quite traumatic, the relationship, between a senior practitioner and her line manager, had improved considerably. They were, as she explains, now able to work together in a constructive way:

> I can honestly say, if we had not have had that mediation, we would not be in this position. It was entirely because of the mediation from Acas, and I don't believe that that would, even if they'd have tried to have done it in house, I don't believe that it would have worked.

Conversely, in other cases, the mediation had ended without an agreement. Where this happened, it was apparent that either the issues were too intractable to make a resolution possible or one or both of the parties had no interest in reaching any kind of settlement. One such participant felt that in her case, mediation was doomed to failure as neither party was willing to compromise. Reflecting on the mediator, she concluded that:

> ...however good her mediation skills are, she was not going to budge [name] or me, because we both think we're right. [name] thinks she's right for telling me those comments...she thinks it's being taken out of context...she thinks that what she'd said is right and I think what she's done is not nice.

Furthermore, in cases in which the dispute centred on some managerial decision, as opposed to the behaviour of the parties, there appeared to be less scope for movement and hence resolution. Although most mediations concluded with an agreement, it was clear that many respondents questioned the sustainability of the settlement. Indeed in some instances, parties admitted to reaching an agreement in mediation in the full knowledge that matters had not been resolved. This was particularly apparent where performance issues were involved. For example, one manager felt uncomfortable talking about the return to work of a member of staff during mediation. They felt that this was not going to be possible due to outstanding concerns over the individual's capability. In such cases there was a pervasive view that while mediation had resolved the initial complaint and in that sense led to resolution, it had still not addressed the fundamental problem. For example, an operational manager explained that she had come into conflict with a member of her team to whom she had given a poor performance appraisal rating:

> I think what came out of [mediation] is that we both agreed that we had a reasonably good working relationship and we both agreed that everything else was working well apart from the fact that she did not like her appraisal rating....So I think something came out of the mediation. [However later]....in terms of the working relationship it kind of went downhill because she came back, when we came back we had to prepare for this new restructure, so the tensions built up because she now said because her appraisal rating wasn't very good it had impact on her and she might lose her job so she was more and more withdrawn.

The fears of the manager were realized – there was little improvement in the situation and the other individual subsequently left the organization. Therefore, if the 'solution' did not fully address the issues for the 'aggrieved', this could lead to further tensions in the relationship. For instance, if that party felt that the mediator was simply aiming to 'call an end to hostilities'. In some cases this problem was exacerbated by organizations that, in trying to persuade participants to enter into mediation, exaggerated or misinterpreted what mediation could achieve.

Given these reservations and mixed outcomes, it is important to note that the vast majority of interviewees felt that their participation in mediation had been beneficial. In some cases in which there was no fundamental change in attitude or behaviour, mediation still provided a breathing space in conflict and a way of finding a pragmatic solution so that the parties could continue to work together. As one respondent explained:

> ...if I was in the same position again, I would go for mediation but not necessarily because I think it's the be all and end all, but actually because it was a constructive process...if you're working with people, you've got to try everything you can to make that relationship at least bearable.

Even where there was no settlement, taking part in mediation had also provided some disputants with a voice. In particular it provided disputants in subordinate positions to 'have their say' in a relatively safe environment. In this sense the involvement of an impartial mediator gave the process a semblance of equity which more conventional, managerially controlled disciplinary and grievance processes did not have. Thus, even for those participants who claimed to be victims of bullying and discrimination, access to mediation could be empowering. One respondent explained this as follows:

> I think it's helpful because it gets your mindset in the right place...because she had been bullying me and making me feel very uncomfortable at work, I had to turn the situation round...I've tried my best to make this situation better, I've done all I can, it's up to her now and if she can't, um, see that then it's her problem and I can't own her problem. I feel more empowered...I know that I can move forward...

Perhaps significantly, it was generally those in subordinate positions who found mediation to be more 'empowering'. In contrast, managers who were the subject of complaints of unfair treatment felt that mediation did not provide an opportunity to scrutinize such allegations. As a consequence, they did not feel that mediation delivered a just outcome. In the following example, a very senior member of staff within a public sector organization explained that mediation was not what he was expecting:

> because what hurt me most was the fact that...such a fundamentally serious criticism had been made dishonestly, not a single shred of evidence... and it hurt me badly. And it was the fact that someone can do so much harm and get off scot free which was the ultimate injustice to me, and what made me seriously upset.'

At the same time, most of the respondents who had brought complaints against line managers were sceptical as to whether their manager's behaviour had fundamentally changed. For one respondent mediation was 'a waste of time' because 'it didn't do anything to him [the manager]'. This respondent argued that his manager was simply 'jumping through the hoops that he felt he had to jump through because HR told him he had to do this'. Indeed, a number of respondents were concerned that managers saw mediation either as a soft option, or something they had to do, and had no intention of adhering to any consequential agreements.

Discussion and Conclusion

Interest continues to grow in workplace mediation in the UK, and we are well served by research on its efficacy and limitations as informed by the views of the commissioners and deliverers of the service (Latreille 2011; Bennett 2013; Saundry and Wibberley 2014). In contrast, there has been limited research into the perspectives of disputants themselves, and also the nature and sustainability of mediation outcomes. Given the confidential and sensitive nature of the issues and process, this is perhaps not that surprising. The research discussed in this chapter, while faced with the same obstacles, has been a tentative step towards redressing this gap in our knowledge. There are, therefore, a number of key findings worthy of discussion.

Firstly, the research offers some real insight into the outcomes of mediation. In contrast to the more optimistic reports of its effectiveness cited above (Bingham 2004; Bennett 2013), we found that while most mediated disputes in this study led to an agreement between the parties, a number broke down relatively quickly. The lack of sustainability of mediation settlements can partly be explained by the reluctance of many of the parties to enter into mediation. While mediation is generally positioned as a voluntary process, it was common for participants, particularly managers, to feel that they had little other choice. Consequently, there was a tendency for some participants to 'go through the motions'. This was exacerbated by the clear finding that most mediations were only introduced at a late stage in the dispute and was seen by many disputants as 'the last resort' (Saundry and Wibberley 2014). By this point attitudes were often entrenched making the chances of a lasting resolution much more improbable.

Secondly, the results raise the whole question of how we define 'success'. Indeed, to expect deep underlying conflicts to be resolved through mediation is often unrealistic. In some cases finding a pragmatic way of individuals being able to work together or at least stay in the organization may be the best that can be achieved (see Hoffman 2012). Furthermore, mediation that does not result in agreement may still have a positive impact for at least one of the parties. A number of respondents, welcomed and benefitted from the opportunity to voice their concerns and exert some control over a difficult issue, even if they were under no illusions that the behaviour of the other party was unlikely to change.

Thirdly, this raises the role of mediation in challenging managers' behaviour. In disputes between managers and managed, it was the former who felt more uncomfortable with the process. Supporting the findings of Saundry and Wibberley (2014), the greatest resistance to mediation is likely to come from managers, particularly, in relation to performance related issues, which made up the majority of disputes in the sample. Managers not only felt under pressure to agree to mediation but also that simply participating was an admission of either their guilt or that they lacked the necessary skills to manage people. This casts doubt on arguments that mediation is a way in which management are able to essentially reassert their grip over the employment relationship and reinforce their authority (Colling 2004; Keashly and Nowell 2011). Instead, it would appear to provide a channel through which employees are able to challenge to some degree managerial prerogative over key issues such as performance. There was little evidence that differences in power or status restricted employees from raising their concerns during the process. This does not mean that mediation provides an 'equal' playing field between managers and workers. Nonetheless, this research suggests that mediation can offer something more than just 'procedural justice' (Shapiro and Brett 1993).

Finally, although mediation may provide a relatively safe environment in which workers can challenge the behaviours of their colleagues and the authority of their immediate managers, its impact on wider outcomes and the potential to offer 'distributive justice' was less clear. For example, managers accused of unfair treatment felt that the process provided little opportunity to decide whether such allegations were merited. At the same time, employees who felt that they had been unfairly treated by managers or colleagues were generally sceptical as to whether mediation would result in any lasting change. Instead, the overriding focus of mediation was to achieve a pragmatic success – getting people back to work if not restoring and repairing the employment relationship.

To criticize mediation for its pragmatism is perhaps unfair – ultimately, mediators are limited by the context in which they work and the broader approach of the organization to workplace conflict. The attitude of the organizations in our sample is reflected in the finding that mediation tended to be used as a last resort when all other attempts at resolution had failed. Therefore, it was seen as a 'bolt-on' mechanism to rid the organization of unwelcome problems rather than part of a wider commitment to address the underlying causes of workplace conflict.

Overall, while this research identifies that mediation can benefit both participants and the organizations in which they work, it also highlights the impact on disputants and points to the complexity of the issues that mediators confront and the ambiguity of consequent outcomes. It suggests that organizations need to consider the experiences and expectations of participants in deciding how and when mediation is used and how it relates to wider employment relations processes. Furthermore, this study demonstrates the need for more detailed research into the longer term sustainability and consequences of mediated settlements but also into the role of mediation within broader processes of conflict management.

References

Acas. (2012). Individual mediation: Feedback from participants and commissioners. *Acas Research Papers*, 16/12.

Acas. (2013). Individual mediation: Feedback from participants and commissioners. *Acas Research Papers*, 7/13.

Acas/CIPD. (2013). *Mediation: An approach to resolving workplace issues*. London: Acas.

Aubrey-Johnson, K., & Curtis, H. (2012). *Making mediation work for you: A practical handbook*. London: Legal Action Group.

Bennett, T. (2013). Workplace mediation and the empowerment of disputants: Rhetoric or reality? *Industrial Relations Journal*, 44(2), 189–209.

Bennett, T. (2014). The role of workplace mediation: a critical assessment. *Personnel Review*, 43(5), 764–779.

Bingham, L. (2004). Employment dispute resolution: The case for mediation. *Conflict Resolution Quarterly*, 22(1–2), 145–174.

Bingham, L., & Pitts, D. (2002). Highlight of mediation at work: Studies of the national REDRESS evaluation project. *Negotiation Journal*, 18(2), 135–146.

Branch, S., Ramsay, S., & Barker, M. (2009). Workplace bullying. In T. Redman, & A. Wilkinson (Eds.), *Contemporary human resource management* (3rd ed.,). Harlow: FT Prentice Hall.

CIPD. (2011). *Workplace mediation: How employers do it*. London: CIPD Publications.

CIPD. (2015a). *Conflict management: a shift in direction?* London: CIPD.

CIPD. (2015b). *Getting under the skin of workplace conflict – A survey of employee experiences of interpersonal conflict at work*. London: CIPD.

Colling, T. (2004). No claim, no pain? The privatization of dispute resolution in Britain. *Economic and Industrial Democracy*, 25(4), 555–579.

Dolder, C. (2004). The contribution of mediation to workplace justice. *Industrial Law Journal*, 33(4), 320–342.

Gibbons, M. (2007). *Better dispute resolution: A review of employment dispute resolution in Great Britain*. London: Department of Trade and Industry.

Hoffman, E. (2012). *Co-operative Workplace Dispute Resolution*. Farnham: Gower.

Keashly, L., & Nowell, B. (2011). Conflict, conflict resolution and bullying. In S. Einarsen, H. Hoel, D. Zapf, & C. Cooper (Eds.), *Bullying and harassment in the workplace: Development in theory, research and practice*. Boca Raton: CRC Press, Taylor and Francis Group.

King, N. (2004). Template analysis. In G. Cassell, & G. Symon (Eds.), *Essential guide to qualitative methods in qrganizational research*. London: Sage.

Latreille, P. (2011). Mediation: A thematic review of Acas/CIPD evidence. *Acas Research Papers*, 13/11.

Latreille, P., & Saundry, R. (2014). Mediation. In W. Roche, P. Teague, & A. Colvin (Eds.), *The Oxford handbook on conflict management*. Oxford: Oxford University Press.

Latreille, P., Buscha, F., & Conte, A. (2012). Are you experienced? SME use of and attitudes towards workplace mediation. *International Journal of Human Resource Management, 23*(2), 590–606.

Lipsky, D. B., Avgar, A. C., Lamare, J. R., & Gupta, A. (2012). The antecedents of workplace conflict *management* systems in U.S. corporations: evidence from a new survey of Fortune 1000 companies. Mimeo.

Rahim, N., Brown, A., & Graham, J. (2011). Evaluation of the Acas code of practice on disciplinary and grievance procedures. *Acas Research Papers*, 06/11.

Saundry, R. (2012). Conflict resolution and mediation at Bradford MDC: A case study. *Acas Research Papers*, 8/12.

Saundry, R., & Wibberley, G. (2012). Managing individual conflict in the private sector: A case study. *Acas Research Papers*, 05/12.

Saundry, R., & Wibberley, G. (2014). Workplace dispute resolution and the management of individual conflict – A thematic analysis of five case studies. *Acas Research Papers*, 6/14.

Saundry, R., Latreille, P., Dickens, L., Irvine, C., Teague, P., Urwin, P., & Wibberley, G. (2014). Reframing resolution – Managing conflict and resolving individual employment disputes in the contemporary workplace. *Acas Policy Series*.

Shapiro, D., & Brett, J. (1993). Comparing three processes underlying judgments of procedural justice: A field study of mediation and arbitration. *Journal of Personality and Social Psychology, 65*(6), 1167–1177.

Wood, S., Saundry, R., & Latreille, P. (2014). Analysis of the nature, extent and impact of grievance and disciplinary procedures and workplace mediation using WERS2011. *Acas Research Papers*, 10/14.

10

Workplace Mediation and UK Trade Unions: The Missing Link?

Virginia Branney

Introduction

Dealing with individual union members' problems at work is one of British trade union representatives' core activities (van Wanrooy et al. 2013; Charlwood and Angrave 2014). This important but unglamorous work has commanded less attention from scholars in the field of UK employment relations than the collective activities of union officials. Of course, no dispute involving an individual worker can be completely divorced from the context of the employment relationship, and employers' processes to manage individuals' disputes (such as grievance procedures and mediation) can be seen as devices to individualize conflict and 'de-fang' its potential to invoke collective resistance. In practice, union representatives appreciate that most people join unions for support and help if they have a problem at work and new recruits bring added demands for one-to-one assistance. From this perspective, it can be mutually beneficial to cooperate with employers' moves to manage workplace conflict more effectively or at least

V. Branney (✉)
University of Central Lancashire, Preston, UK

© The Editor(s) (if applicable) and The Author(s) 2016
R. Saundry et al. (eds.), *Reframing Resolution*,
DOI 10.1057/978-1-137-51560-5_10

improve the efficiency of their dispute resolution procedures. This chapter discusses the response of UK unions to the adoption of workplace mediation by employers. It draws on the results of a survey of UK trade union representatives, *Dealing with Individual Union Members' Disputes at the Workplace*, undertaken by the author in 2014. The findings cast light on UK union representatives' experiences of, and attitudes towards, workplace mediation – a subject that has not been previously explored in depth.[1]

The chapter begins by explaining how workplace mediation was defined for the purposes of the survey and comments on its incidence in the UK. It then outlines TUC and Scottish TUC policy on workplace mediation as a precursor to the main discussion of the survey findings on union involvement and representatives' attitudes towards workplace mediation. The role of workplace mediation in relation to organizational justice is briefly considered. The penultimate section draws on the survey responses to make some observations about union involvement in workplace mediation from a conflict management perspective. It then debates to what extent involvement with workplace mediation might be a 'missing link' in terms of union renewal. It is recognized that the subject neglects workers who fall through the cracks of employment protection legislation and particularly those working in non-union workplaces.

What Is Workplace Mediation: Where Is It Found?

Applying a dictionary definition, 'mediation' is what union representatives do whenever they act as a 'go-between' to facilitate the resolution of work-related conflict or disputes. However, for the purposes of this study, survey respondents were asked to discount their own role as mediators and also their experiences of Acas conciliation,[2] given the focus of the study on mediation as a management process for dealing with individual (as opposed

---

[1] In addition to the survey, the author's study comprises interviews with national officials from a range of unions that have representation in sectors where workplace mediation is used and case studies of a small number of 'high user' unions.

[2] Acas (the Advisory, Conciliation and Arbitration Service) is a non-departmental public body of the UK government. It provides dispute resolution services in Great Britain including conciliation of individual employment rights disputes, most commonly in cases involving a potential employment tribunal claim. The Labour Relations Agency is the equivalent body in Northern Ireland.

to collective) disputes in the workplace where the employment relationship has not ended. The survey defined workplace mediation as 'a way of dealing with conflict between individuals in the workplace using a third party (the mediator) to assist them to resolve their differences themselves'. (This was supplemented with information for respondents on what *not* to include as workplace mediation.) The aim was to capture union representatives' experiences of employers' internal mediation provision and their use of external mediators. Internal provision could include arrangements where a manager (or management representative) not directly involved in the dispute acts as the mediator; or formal procedures where the employer has an in-house mediation scheme with a team or pool of mediators selected from its own staff who may be volunteers, managers, HR personnel or staff in specialist roles (such as occupational health), or in-house schemes where the pool of mediators comprises union and management representatives. External provision refers to situations where the employer brings in external mediators from (for example) employment consultancies, mediation suppliers and Acas (CIPD 2011:12) – Acas provides a chargeable service for individual workplace mediation unrelated to its conciliation function.

How widespread is the use of workplace mediation by UK employers? The indications from the first findings of the 2011 Workplace Employment Relations Study (WERS) were that 'just seven per cent of all workplaces recorded having used it in the last 12 months.... However in workplaces that had experienced workplace grievances (i.e. issues potentially amenable to mediation) 17 % had turned to mediation while 14 % of workplaces that had dealt with disciplinary cases had used mediation' (Wood et al. 2014:21).

More recently, a Chartered Institute of Personnel and Development (CIPD) survey found that 24 % of organizations had used 'internal mediation by a trained member of staff' in the last 12 months and nine per cent had used 'external mediation' to deal with workplace issues and 'across the board, public sector organizations...report making more use of every method of managing conflict than those in ... the private or voluntary sectors...in some cases, such as mediation, the difference is substantial' (CIPD 2015:11). The use of externally provided mediation was 'significantly higher in the public sector (at 17 per cent) and in public administration (21 per cent)' (CIPD 2015:2–3). In contrast, Wood et al. (2014:22–23) reported that 'no difference was found between the proportions of workplaces that used mediation between the public and private sector' (eight per cent and seven per cent respectively in the last 12 months). A plausible explanation for the divergent findings on the use of workplace mediation is that WERS respondents are more likely to have understood 'mediation' to include Acas conciliation. While it is not possible to be definitive about the extent of its use, particularly by sector, it is apparent that workplace mediation has established a niche in the UK.

What motivates employers to take up workplace mediation? Saundry and Latreille (2014:195) conclude that 'increased interest in the use of mediation...has largely been driven by employing organizations searching for more efficient and effective ways to resolve workplace disputes'. Mediation is claimed to be quicker, cheaper and less adversarial than formal investigative and multi-stage grievance procedures and to be less damaging to working relationships.

TUC and Scottish TUC Policy

The TUC has stated its position on workplace mediation in responses to government consultations and most fully in a guide for trade union representatives published in conjunction with Acas (TUC and Acas 2010). In 2009, the Scottish TUC congress carried a resolution on 'individual employment disputes and mediation' moved by the University and College Union (Scotland) stating that 'collective action...will generally be the best way to resolve problems arising in the workplace. However, where members have to (or choose to) pursue matters individually, they may use internal procedures such as grievance or may seek union advice on legal claims. A further option is mediation...' The resolution set out the basis for union support and guidance as follows:

> Congress believes that mediation schemes should only be introduced after negotiation involving the recognized unions at the design stage. Mediation should be available to individual employees where appropriate and should only ever proceed on the basis of informed consent. Union reps should have training so as to be able to advise members of the pros and cons and

ensure that adequate safeguards are in place. Negotiators should ensure that members entering mediation do not thereby lose the right to pursue their concerns through formal procedure, in the event that mediation fails (STUC 2009, pp.48–49).

The safeguards set out in the resolution were reflected in joint TUC and Acas guidance for trade union representatives published the following year. The foreword by the TUC General Secretary and the Chair of Acas stated: 'Mediation is not offered as a panacea, and there are some types of conflict where it will not be suitable. However, when used appropriately, it can offer a way to avoid the potentially destructive effects of drawn-out conflict…. It is not…a replacement for trade union representation, and nor should it undermine the valuable role of trade union representatives. It is, rather, a complementary process' (TUC and Acas 2010:1). The guide listed situations to which 'mediation is particularly well suited' and 'situations where mediation may not be suited' and included a 'mediation checklist' for trade union representatives.

In its response to the government consultation *Resolving workplace disputes* (BIS and Tribunals Service 2011) the TUC recognized that some employers had already or would be likely to set up in-house schemes:

It is essential that mediators act in an impartial manner and are seen to be independent of management. In some instances this can be achieved through the use of in-house mediators with both employees and managers being trained. (TUC 2011:12).

The two largest UK unions took a different view. In its response, Unite stated:

The Union can see no advantages to in-house mediation. There are, however, obvious disadvantages. In particular, it is difficult to see how an "in-house" mediator could be seen as independent by an employee. Further, an "in-house" mediator employed by the employer would have an inevitable conflict-of-interest whenever seeking to resolve a dispute which was, in reality, between the employer and an employee and not simply between employees. (Unite 2011:6).

UNISON went further:

> Any mediation scheme could not use in-house staff – this would be seen by individuals and their unions as just another branch of the organization's HR department, lacking the necessary impartiality. (UNISON 2011:3).

By the time of the *Resolving workplace disputes* consultation, at local, regional or sector level, union branches and officials had encountered workplace mediation in one form or another in a number of NHS trusts, local authorities, universities and colleges, police services, civil service departments and agencies, third sector organizations and (to a lesser extent) private sector companies. Against that backdrop, the next section considers the survey responses from union representatives.

Workplace Mediation and UK Union Involvement

Workplace Mediation in Unionized Organizations

Workplace mediation is a 'management process' (Banks and Saundry 2011:10); however, as a relatively new dispute resolution method, in organized workplaces unions can be in a powerful position to scupper it, by advising their members not to participate. On the other hand, union representatives can encourage take-up by assisting members to choose the best 'forum to fit the fuss' (Sander and Goldberg 1994), which, for example, in disputes about relationships rather than rights may be mediation. Clearly employers have an incentive to gain union cooperation. Aside from that, unionized UK organizations have traditionally involved unions in matters to do with dispute resolution to varying degrees. In some cases, joint initiatives and partnership agreements have spawned workplace mediation schemes, as in the NHS (Acas and Social Partnership Forum 2009). In the Royal Mail, the 2014 *Agenda for Growth* national agreement provides for in-house and external mediation of collective disputes; also in 2014, the employer and unions (Communication Workers' Union and Unite) appointed external mediators to offer an informal resolution process for bullying and harassment issues (Royal Mail 2014). In 2012, a cross-government Civil Service Mediation Service was set up to link with existing departmental mediation teams and to extend workplace mediation to all departments. In local government and higher education, while the national employers have praised and promoted workplace mediation, it is left to individual employers to take it up (as a significant number have done). The initiative usually comes from the employer; however, individual union officials have acted as powerful advocates for, and champions of, workplace mediation either pro-actively (Bleiman 2008) or as converts (Saundry et al. 2011).

No UK union appears to have a national policy of outright opposition to workplace mediation as a matter of principle, although workplace representatives in particular may reject it if they suspect the employer's motives. But even where there is a relationship of trust between the union and employer, obviously union representatives will have concerns about safeguarding the interests of individual members and the collective standing of the union, as was reflected in the responses to the author's survey. Before turning to the findings, the next section outlines the survey methodology.

Survey Methodology

Aimed at UK trade union representatives, the survey, *Dealing with Individual Union Members' Disputes at the Workplace*, was available online for anonymous completion, via a link from the TUC employment rights web page between August and October 2014. The survey instrument (a questionnaire) comprised 38 closed questions and two free-text questions where respondents could add comments on workplace mediation and using grievance procedures. Eighty-three respondents commented on workplace mediation (discounting eight unusable responses). Although the comments comprise a small subset of the total sample, the additional data provide insights into union representatives' experiences and views – the quotes cited in this chapter are drawn from these anonymous comments.

On workplace mediation, respondents were asked whether their union had formal policy on it; their sources of information about it; sectors and industries where workplace mediation is being used; types of complaints being mediated; the nature and extent of their involvement with workplace mediation; in what ways they transmitted their experience of workplace mediation to other union representatives and to employers; and their views on the impact of its use on relations between the union and management. The survey also sought union representatives' views about grievance procedures. The survey instrument (an online questionnaire) did not include questions about how union representatives experienced the process of workplace mediation – this will be explored through case studies.

As the respondents comprised a non-representative sample, the findings cannot be generalized to the population of UK union representatives. Of 528 responses, 89 % were from workplace representatives (mainly stewards, convenors and branch officials). Eight per cent of the respondents were regional officials and three per cent were national officials employed by unions. Responses were received from representatives of 39 unions, all but four being affiliated to the Trades Union Congress (TUC). Around 230 respondents had had some form of involvement with workplace mediation at some time. This was not extensive – the majority (181 respondents) had been involved in or associated with one to five mediations in the past two years. In this sample, representatives had encountered workplace mediation mainly in local government, health and (mostly tertiary) education, finance and business services and central government and/or its agencies.

Introducing Workplace Mediation: Union Involvement

In regard to workplace mediation, 97 respondents said their involvement to date had been 'being consulted by the employer about using it in the organization'. Sixty-one respondents said 'negotiating with the employer about introducing or using it in the organization'. Only 22 respondents said 'being on a management-union group overseeing the introduction/use of workplace mediation'. As mediation forms part of employers' dispute resolution procedures, it is not surprising that unions are not co-owners (and would not necessarily want to be); however, these responses suggest that particularly at workplace level, unions are not as involved in employers' decisions to adopt workplace mediation and scheme design as recommended by the TUC and STUC. (There are exceptions, for example in Royal Mail, where at national level, the unions and management have co-designed mediation provision). Latreille (2011:38) also found that 'a number of...organizations with formal schemes...had made a point of consulting or otherwise involving them [recognized unions] in the design of the scheme'.

It seems that very few union representatives act alongside management (typically HR) as coordinators of in-house schemes or gatekeepers deciding which cases are suitable (or not) for mediation. The process of deciding which dispute resolution procedure is appropriate is a pivotal point in the trajectory of an individual dispute. It might be expected that employers would not want to relinquish power in this respect, although there can be mutual benefits when they do (Saundry et al. 2011). Anecdotally, it seems that joint appointment of external mediators is a rarity – the Royal Mail being an exception.

Workplace Mediation: Voluntary or Compulsory?

Voluntary participation is a core tenet of the facilitative model of mediation which is the most commonly practised by UK workplace mediators. However, there can be compulsion to *attempt* mediation either formally (procedural compulsion) or informally (pressure to participate). In answer to the question 'in your experience, in organizations using workplace mediation, how do the mediations come about', 41 respondents said 'under the organization's procedures, it's compulsory to attempt mediation at a certain stage (or stages)' while 125 respondents said 'the organization's complaint/grievance procedure mentions workplace mediation as a possible option', indicating (in this sample) that procedural compulsion is not exceptional. However, some of the comments suggested the picture is not always clear-cut: 'Some employers try to enforce mediation which does not work' (Royal College of Nursing full-time official). It may not always be clear to employees and representatives when and under what circumstances a grievance or bullying complaint (for example) is to be dealt with in the formal machinery or be put forward for mediation (by managers especially) as this comment indicated: 'Clearer guidance on the voluntary aspect of mediation [needed] and not a pre-requisite to resolution' (UNISON branch official). Compulsion was seen as being counter-productive: 'Mediation is a good process but only if all parties agree to it; if it is a forced process, then any benefits will be lost' (Public Commercial Services (PCS) steward).

Another source of data about 'negative pressure' is provided by Acas. Responses from participants in mediations commissioned from Acas who gave feedback (based on averaged figures for 2010–13) show that five per cent felt they had no choice; 18 % felt pressure such that it would have been difficult to say no; and a third said they had been encouraged but could have declined if they wanted to. Less than half (44 %) felt fully able to make their own decision. The data do not distinguish feedback from managers and subordinates; however, negative pressure to participate came overwhelmingly from the employer (Acas 2011, 2012, 2013).

These findings and the survey respondents' comments highlight the need for unions to have an effective voice in the 'reform' of grievance and related procedures and the design of mediation processes. Union representatives also have an important role in assisting members to make informed decisions about whether to try mediation and to resist negative pressure to participate.

Workplace Mediation: The Role of Union Representatives

The most prevalent form of involvement with workplace mediation reported by survey respondents was 'advising a union member (or members) about whether to take part in a mediation' (184 responses). 'Going with a member to a meeting with the mediator (where the other party was not present)' was selected by 101 respondents; and 103 respondents selected 'attending a meeting with the mediator/s where your member and the other party were present'. Since documentary evidence (for example, Saundry et al. 2013) indicates that UK in-house mediation schemes disallow or discourage representatives from attending joint sessions (that is, when both (or all) disputants meet with the mediator), on the face of it, this is a surprising result and is likely to include situations where a manager not directly involved in the dispute or (for example) an HR officer acts as an 'honest broker' – a process which may not or may not be labelled as 'mediation' but is understood as such by all parties.

It is part of the ideology of non-evaluative models of workplace mediation that resolution lies in the hands of the disputants and there appears to be a consensus in the HR profession and mediation industry – shared by the TUC – that (with some exceptions) representation in *joint* sessions is unnecessary and possibly unhelpful. The CIPD advises that 'Restricting mediation meetings to the parties themselves can allow more open and honest discussion' (CIPD and Acas 2013:28) while the TUC goes further: 'Mediation is most successful where no representatives are present. Experience has shown that it is the individuals involved who are best able to explain how they feel. An open and frank discussion of the issues, which is controlled by the mediator to ensure fairness and appropriate behaviour, can be the key to sorting out the conflict' (TUC and Acas 2010:11). Apparently, as a rule, an employee should only need the support of (for example) a union representative at the initial one-to-one meeting with the mediator: 'Allowing representation/accompaniment at the separate meeting may allay fears that an individual has and enable them to see that they do not need that person in the joint meeting' (CIPD and Acas 2013:28); and in a similar vein, 'The initial one-to-one meetings can be an opportunity for the individual to build up a rapport with the mediator, with their representative present, and feel more secure about continuing with the mediation on their own' (TUC and Acas 2010:12).

The CIPD warns that 'one of the pitfalls involved in using representatives is that it may lead to the formalization of the process' (CIPD and Acas 2013:28). 'Moreover, there can be a tendency for representatives to shift the emphasis from joint problem-solving to negotiating for the best deal for their candidate to the detriment of the other party, instead of parties finding their own solution that will benefit both sides. Having said this, the mediator is there to ensure that this does not happen.' (CIPD and Acas 2013:29). The TUC guide states: 'Where a party wishes to have the support of their trade union representative this must be agreed by all the parties in the mediation. This can result in the other side also deciding to bring a representative. Where it is agreed, the role of the representative is as an advisor and supporter and not as a formal representative…' (TUC and Acas 2010:11).

As to the views of participants, based on feedback to Acas in regard to workplace mediations conducted by its officers in 2012–13, it was noted that:

> Almost all participants (97 per cent) indicated that they had not been accompanied during the mediation process and of these the majority (63 per cent) were content with this arrangement…21 per cent indicated they would have preferred to have been accompanied with 16 per cent reporting that they "don't know". (Acas 2013:6).

There were very few specific comments on accompaniment in mediation from survey respondents. To give an example: '…Formal mediation in my workplace is confidential and union reps do not attend. Informal mediation can involve union reps' (UNISON steward). The practice of not permitting disputants to be accompanied in joint sessions does not seem to be a contentious issue. This may be because mediation is largely a voluntary process and if it fails, the employee retains their right to pursue a grievance. Also, union representatives are nevertheless involved in advising members about whether to participate or possibly as in-house mediators. But it may be that there are more employees being accompanied in joint mediation sessions than has been supposed, even allowing for survey respondents including informal discussions with both disputants present where a manager and/or union representative facilitates a resolution. (In the author's experience, disputants are sometimes accompanied in entrenched, 'high stake' disputes that are externally mediated.) If, in fact, accompaniment in joint sessions is rare, the Acas data suggest that a significant proportion of participants would have valued being accompanied.

A small number of respondents have been involved in workplace mediation as in-house scheme mediators. Sixteen reported 'being part of an in-house team or pool of workplace mediators drawn from representatives of management and the unions' and 7 respondents were 'part of an in-house team or pool…selected from employees who volunteered'. Judging by the comments, this did not seem to have caused issues for them about conflict of interest although one respondent commented 'many members are suspicious of management's motives and if it [mediation] does not go well, trade unionists themselves can come under suspicion....You need to tread carefully' (UNISON steward). On the other hand, knowing that mediators include employees who are also union representatives can help allay members' fears that mediation could be a management stitch-up (Saundry et al. 2011; TUC and Acas 2010). These comments echo the 'divergent views' found by Latreille (2011:41) among mediation managers and union representatives as to whether employee/union representatives should act as mediators.

Workplace Mediation: Criticisms and Praise

The majority of comments from survey respondents on workplace mediation were reflections on the conditions necessary for its appropriate and effective use including careful selection of cases for mediation, right timing (early on in the dispute), voluntary participation, the need for parties' commitment to the process, the importance of mediator competence and impartiality, joint management–union training on mediation, the need for formal procedures as back-up if there is no resolution, and recognition that mediation is not a panacea and is unlikely to be appropriate for discrimination and serious harassment cases which call for formal action by management. A couple of comments highlighted the suitability of mediation in conflicts between co-workers (particularly where both disputants are union members) and between managerial staff. Some respondents felt that mediation worked best between peers or co-workers; others doubted its suitability for disputes between managers and subordinates. There were a related set of comments about implementation issues including lack of guidance for managers, poor administration, selection of inappropriate cases for mediation in lieu of using the disciplinary procedure, and reluctance or resistance on the part of managers to participate.

Adverse comments concerned the way in which mediation had been implemented by employers (poor guidance for managers, poor administration, and inappropriate case referrals – especially disciplinary cases), and the quality and impartiality of the mediator. Most of the latter appeared to be directed at in-house mediators who were said to lack experience and skills, and whose close links with management called into question their impartiality. The most trenchant criticisms (made by a small number of respondents) were that the 'employer tries to use mediation as another control level, to keep the union out, and keep their grievance statistics down' (UNISON branch official); and it was used 'as a tool to dissuade staff from progressing bullying complaints' (University and College Union full-time official). In a similar vein, 'HR attempt to force or harass the aggrieved into mediation, rather than take the manager to task or discipline them for glaringly obvious abuses of power or position…' (Unite steward). A roughly equivalent number of comments praised the process – it encouraged open communication, provided a safe environment and helped repair relationships.

A broader picture of respondents' views can be obtained from the responses to the question 'overall, based on your experience, how likely would you be to recommend the wider use of workplace mediation', 44.4 % said they would be 'likely' to recommend its wider use and 23.3 % said they would be 'very likely' to. Just under a quarter said they would be 'neither likely or unlikely' to recommend its wider use. A much smaller proportion gave a negative response – 6.1 % said they would be 'unlikely' to recommend its wider use and 2.5 % said they were 'not at all likely' to. While the data is not representative, it suggests that most union representatives are likely to be open to the use of workplace mediation; whether that translates into positive support depends largely on representatives' experiences of how management seek to use it.

Enhancing Workplace Justice

What role might workplace mediation play in relation to organizational justice? When mediation is used by employers to divert complaints against managers and shelter them from formal sanctions (as was mentioned by some respondents), workplace justice is obviously diminished. Lack of impartiality on the part of the mediator and failure to enforce ground rules in mediation meetings offend both procedural and interpersonal justice. However, positive comments from the survey respondents illustrate aspects of interactional justice in mediation. Applying the 'six-factor model' of organizational justice (Nabatchi et al. 2007) interactional justice encompasses interaction between the mediator and disputants and the interpersonal interaction between the disputants themselves. In contrast with formal dispute resolution procedures, disputants (especially subordinates) are more likely to be able to speak for themselves in a supposedly confidential and safe environment. In seeking to explore disputants' interests rather than rights and wrongs, mediation has the potential to get to the (emotional) heart of the matter in a way that highly formalized procedures usually cannot. Distributive justice in mediation is a vexed question but it is arguable that a fraught employment relationship stands a better chance of being preserved through mediation than drawn out formal complaints procedures which are stressful and leave the disputants' dysfunctional relationship in limbo, if not in tatters.

Interestingly, respondents' opinions were mixed on whether taking grievances through formal procedures escalates or worsens conflict between the disputants: 32.4 % of respondents disagreed and ten per cent strongly disagreed; 19.1 % of respondents agreed; and 2.7 % strongly agreed. One third of respondents neither agreed nor disagreed (possibly because it might depend on the circumstances of the case). Of course, union representatives are once removed from the conflict and their experience of it is different from that of the disputants. Nevertheless, a number of respondents said that mediation was not appropriate in all cases, it was not a panacea, and the formal route must remain an option for the employee where mediation fails to resolve the problem. Crucially, grievance and related procedures were seen as giving voice to employees – when managers would not listen or chose to ignore complaints or not take them seriously, the grievance procedure was needed. (Sometimes the threat of 'going formal' was enough to prompt a response.) There were 84.1 % of respondents in agreement that grievances procedures are an important mechanism for obtaining workplace justice for members (35.2 % strongly agreed and 48.9 % agreed). Four per cent disagreed and 1.7 % disagreed strongly (9.9 % of respondents neither agreed nor disagreed and 1.1 % did not know or were not sure.) These findings suggest that mediation may enhance organizational justice in some respects but, from a union perspective, it is not a substitute for established dispute resolution processes. Workplace mediation would be seen as undermining organizational justice (and very likely meet union resistance) if employees did not have access to a grievance procedure where mediation was inappropriate or unsuccessful.

Workplace Mediation and Unions: Missing Links?

Mediation, Unions and Conflict Management

Although not representative, the survey responses suggest that UK unions are likely to be more supportive of (albeit conditionally) and less hostile towards workplace mediation than some employers and mediation advocates might assume. From a conflict management perspective, respondents preferred to deal with disputes informally and the drawbacks of taking complaints through grievance procedures were mentioned. It was observed that some disputes concerning individuals are more suited to workplace mediation than formal grievance or other complaint procedures. The main exceptions mentioned were discrimination complaints, serious cases of bullying and disciplinary cases. Union support for workplace mediation is more likely to be forthcoming when representatives are involved from the outset, and at least fully consulted over its introduction and how it will operate in the organization. Unions will want mediators to be properly trained, qualified and as impartial as is possible. Joint training of management and union representatives has been shown to be particularly important in demystifying mediation and overcoming suspicion of management motives (Saundry et al. 2011); and equipping union representatives for what appears to be their primary role – assisting members to decide whether mediation is in their best interests.

The survey responses are consistent with other findings that workplace mediation tends to be used (with some exceptions) in UK workplaces where industrial relations are good even though there may be high levels of individual conflict in the form of formal grievances and other employee complaints. When asked to think about the employer who uses workplace mediation the most, the majority of respondents (67.7 %) said the relationship between the union and management was good overall – moderately good (34.6 %); very good (24.6 %); extremely good (8.5 %). Just under a third of respondents said the relationship between the union and management was either fair (17.3 %) or poor (14.9 %), broken down as follows: moderately poor (9.2 %); very poor (3.8 %); extremely poor (1.9 %). However, in this sample of respondents, thinking of the same employer, the use of workplace mediation had not made a dramatic difference to relations between the union and management (bearing in mind most respondents thought they were good to begin with): 46.4 % said 'relations are much the same as before the use of workplace mediation'. Just over a third said they were better: slightly better (26 %), much better (9.4 %). Far fewer respondents 3.4 %, said relations were slightly worse; 1.5 % said much worse; and 13.2 % answered 'don't know/not sure'. Mediation is unlikely to be adopted where relationships are highly adversarial unless management wants the situation to change; and while workplace mediation can have quite a dramatic impact on employment relations in an organization, on its own, its use has limited capacity to transform the culture of conflict management in organizations (Saundry and Wibberley 2014). Workplace mediation schemes and training are also vulnerable to cuts and restructuring in public sector organizations, and the loss of influential supporters among management and union representatives.

Workplace Mediation and Union Renewal

Workplace mediation can be seen as antithetic to union renewal. Put simply, it diverts scarce union resources to servicing individual members to no collective purpose. It individualizes workplace conflict and encourages collusion on the part of unions, weakening the prospects for building collective resistance against exploitative labour processes in the workplace. Arguably, workplace mediation is a worse alternative for union members than established dispute resolution procedures: there is an inbuilt power imbalance where the disputants are a manager and subordinate that cannot be eliminated or substantially mitigated by an impartial mediator; the so-called empowerment of subordinates in mediation is ephemeral; and there is no right of accompaniment. Strict confidentiality prevents failure and success from being aired widely, so poor management practices and systemic problems remain hidden and unaddressed and the union does not benefit from any 'inspirational' or 'radiating effects' (Colling 2009) of successes that may be achieved by employees in mediation. Reframing conflict at work between individuals as (for example) 'personality clashes' inhibits its potential to be seen as oppressive and stifles the employee's sense of injustice – the crucial building block for union mobilization (Kelly 1998).

On the other hand, in general, mediated cases take up fewer resources than formal grievances, giving over-stretched workplace representatives more time for organizing activities. Interestingly, just under two-thirds of the survey respondents did not agree that representing members with grievances took up too much time, although there was extensive comment on the downside of formal grievances for representatives and members. Burnout and stress were mentioned, and it was recognized that the grievance process and outcomes were often unsatisfactory where deeply conflictual interpersonal relationships lay at the heart of complaints. Given the pressures on union resources, Colling (2012:199) observes that 'there is clear potential for grievances to go undetected and for representation through to formal litigation to be rationed by scarce resources'. Even in organized workplaces, members may not report issues to a union representative (for various reasons) and, across UK workplaces, the profile of employees who go on to register employment tribunal claims differs from those who report problems at work (Lucy and Broughton 2011). Analysis of the 2008 Fair Treatment at Work Survey by Fevre et al. (2009:119) found that one of the most frequent single reasons for 'resolution' of the most serious problem experienced by (employee) respondents was 'nothing happened or went on as before' (14 %).

Space precludes discussion of gaps in UK evidence and the complexities of (for example) a gender-based or intersectional analysis of employees' experience of dispute resolution procedures so it remains an open question as to under what circumstances workplace mediation might be seen as an alternative or better option; and what part union representation might play in that. There may also be cases that have a rights-based element but individuals might prefer to attempt to resolve them in mediation where relational issues, confidentiality and privacy are important to the complainant (in discussing the impact of a disability or ill health on an individual, or issues relating to sexuality or gender identity, for example). Clearly there is a need for union advice and support in such cases to safeguard mediation being used by the employer to evade legal obligations or short-circuit disciplinary/dismissal procedures. With discrimination-related complaints (for example), this presupposes that union representatives are knowledgeable about the relevant law and that (like mediators) they can relate to the worldview of complainants with backgrounds different from their own. Unions representing managers and professionals in senior roles also recognize that their members may value the privacy and confidentiality of mediation. Resorting to formal procedures could be perceived (by them and the employer) as being unprofessional or potentially damaging to their careers. A survey respondent observed that (in regard to less senior staff) depending on 'the culture of the organization' – taking grievances could be a 'career killer [or]…seen as legitimate channels for discovering disparities of treatment' (University and College Union branch official).

The evidence is that UK workplace mediation is used largely in cases framed as relationship breakdown, dysfunctional working relationships, and bullying and unreasonable treatment, as opposed to rights-based cases (Latreille 2011; CIPD 2008). This was supported by the responses to the author's survey. However, taking 'personality clashes' as an example, Gwartney-Gibbs (1994, p.9) argues that 'personality conflicts are a constellation of disputable issues, interpersonal treatment and feelings'. She observes that 'how tasks should be done… and interpersonal treatment … [are] domains [that] frequently intertwine and become emotional' (Gwartney-Gibbs 1994, p.6). So does the use of mediation undermine the mobilization potential of these disputes? A pragmatic answer is that in contrast to disputes over individuals' terms and conditions, it is very difficult to collectivize these types of grievances when a systemic issue is not obvious and where complainants feel justice will be done if (for example) they get a personal apology and a promise that the offending behaviour will stop. But union involvement in mediation (including, ideally, gate keeping and accompaniment) could help representatives to detect patterns or repeated occurrences of poor management, discriminatory practice and systemic failures – issues which can be taken up collectively. Admittedly, on its own mediation (akin to legal action relating to single claims) has precious little inspirational effect in terms of mobilization. It could be argued to have limited 'radiating effects [which] extend from the specific case to change behaviour among employers or membership constituencies' (Colling 2012:198).

The confidentiality of mediation (which can also apply to formal grievance outcomes) inhibits but does not preclude the sharing of anonymized feedback and commissioners' monitoring data provided that there are sufficient numbers of cases for this to be feasible. Of course, union representatives who attend mediation sessions will have first-hand knowledge of what has transpired. At the least this is a learning experience and being no strangers to keeping confidences, union representatives are likely to be adept at absorbing and applying lessons learnt. In this respect, of the mediation users, 124 survey respondents reported giving feedback of their experiences of workplace mediation to other union representatives. 80 said they had given feedback of their experience in that organization to the employer (for example to HR). Bearing in mind that respondents could select all options that applied, 59 respondents had suggested changes to that organization's employment/HR policies or practices; 63 said they suggested changes to management or staff training; 50 respondents had proposed changes to procedures for dealing with grievances of complaints in that organization; and 65 respondents had suggested changes to the way workplace mediation operated in that organization. Confidentiality does not seem to be a barrier to these UK union representatives acting on their experiences of workplace mediation in more diverse and proactive ways than has been previously documented.

Conclusion

The survey responses indicate that, in the main, the position taken by union representatives (at least in this sample) who have encountered workplace mediation is one of qualified support. Their experience of it has not been overwhelmingly positive and the potential for its misuse is clearly recognized. On the other hand, used for appropriate cases (with competent and impartial mediators), mediation could be a better option than going through formal grievance procedures, enhancing workplace justice. However, if mediation was not freely chosen by disputants or it failed, the right to pursue a formal grievance was seen as essential. Although this was not articulated, employees have rights in relation to grievance procedures (to be accompanied, to appeal decisions) that they do not in mediation and in that sense it offered an inferior form of justice. Importantly, lodging grievances was seen as registering the member's (and union's) concern so that it could not be ignored.

Judging from this sample of respondents, it appears that most employers have sought union cooperation (to varying degrees) in introducing workplace mediation although the extent of union involvement falls short of the gold standard represented by TUC and STUC policy. Old habits die hard, so it is probably still quite revolutionary for an employer to offer, and for the union to accept, a role as joint scheme coordinator and gate keeper, though this could bring benefits for both parties (Saundry et al. 2011). Given its importance in relation to workplace justice, the question of accompaniment/representation also deserves more attention – and revisiting – by unions as well as employers, professional HR bodies and workplace mediation providers.

It remains to be seen if the use of workplace mediation will explode in the UK – it has been a slow burn so far – and positive support from the State for its take-up is now in short supply. If anything, recent moves by government (such as the introduction of tribunal fees) and planned legislation (the Trade Union Bill 2015) are disincentives for employers to reform workplace dispute resolution procedures. In the struggle for renewal, whatever the extent of their 'coercive power', unions have to be seen to be relevant to employees (members and non-members) and to enhance their 'legitimacy power' – the power that derives from employers' acceptance of the legitimacy of unions' representation and bargaining roles (Simms and Charlwood 2010). Union involvement in improving workplace dispute resolution procedures can boost the legitimacy power of unions (Saundry et al. 2011). Individuals will always have problems at work that do not have ready collective solutions. For some complaints, employees will prefer mediation over impersonal, adversarial dispute resolution mechanisms and often want support from the union.

Issues raised in mediation that have collective implications can migrate to the collective bargaining arena. Servicing members in regard to mediation need not undermine the collective strength of the union – it could provide a 'missing link'.

References

Acas. (2011). Acas mediation 2010/11: Responses from participants and commissioners. *Acas Research Papers*, 12/11.

Acas. (2012). Acas individual mediation 2011–12: Responses from participants and commissioners. *Acas Research Papers*, 16/12.

Acas. (2013). Acas individual mediation: Feedback from participants and commissioners. *Acas Research Papers*, 07/13.

Acas and Social Partnership Forum. (2009). *Using partnership to introduce mediation to resolve workplace disputes*. www.socialpartnershipforum.org. Assessed 25 Oct 2010.

Banks, L., & Saundry, R. (2011). *Mediation – A panacea for the ills of workplace dispute resolution? A comprehensive review of the literature examining workplace mediation*. iROWE, University of Central Lancashire. http://www.uclan.ac.uk/research/environment/groups/assets/irowe_mediation_research_paper.docx. Accessed 1 Aug 2013.

BIS, & Tribunals Service. (2011). *Resolving workplace disputes: A consultation. January 2011*. London: BIS.

Bleiman, D. (2008). *Should I try mediation? A discussion paper for trade union members*. Georgia State University Digital Archive @ GSU Paper 16: 1 1–23 CNCR-Hewlett Foundation Seed Grant White Papers. http://digitalarchive.gsu.edu/colpub_seedgrant/16. Accessed 27 Feb 2012.

Charlwood, A., & Angrave, D. (2014). Worker representation in Great Britain 2004–2011: An analysis based on the Workplace Employment Relations Study. *Acas Research Papers*, 03/14.

CIPD. (2008). *Survey report. Workplace mediation: How employers do it*. London: CIPD.

CIPD. (2011). *Conflict management: Survey report March 2011*. London: CIPD.

CIPD. (2015). *Conflict management: A shift in direction? Research Report March 2015*. London: CIPD.

CIPD, & Acas. (2013). *A guide. February 2013. Mediation: An approach to resolving workplace issues*. London: CIPD.

Colling, T. (2009). *Court in a trap? Legal mobilization by trade unions in the United Kingdom.* Warwick Papers in Industrial Relations, Number 91.

Colling, T. (2012). Trade union roles in making employment rights effective. In L. Dickens (Ed.), *Making employment rights effective: Issues of enforcement.* Oxford: Hart Publishing.

Fevre, R., Nichols, T., Prior, G., & Rutherford, I. (2009). *The fair treatment at work report. Findings from the 2008 survey.* London: BIS.

Gwartney-Gibbs, P. (1994). Gender differences in clerical workers' disputes over tasks, interpersonal treatment and emotion. http://www.bethroy.org/uploads/Gwartney.pdf. Accessed 9 Aug 2015.

Kelly, J. (1998). *Rethinking industrial relations. Mobilization, collectivism and long waves.* London: Routledge.

Latreille, P. (2011) *Mediation: A Thematic Review of the Acas/CIPD Evidence,* ACAS Research Paper. Ref: 13/11.

Lucy, D., & Broughton, A. (2011). *Understanding the behaviour and decision making of employees in conflicts and disputes at work, Employment Relations Research Series No. 119.* London: BIS.

Nabatchi, T., Bingham, L. B., & Good, D. H. (2007). Organizational justice and workplace mediation: a six-factor model. *International Journal of Conflict Management, 18*(2), 148–176.

Royal Mail. (2014, February 19). Royal Mail and its trade unions sign contract to employ external mediators. *News and Press Releases.* http://www.royalmailgroup.com/royal-mail-and-its-unions-sign-contract-employment. Accessed 6 Apr 2014.

Sander, F., & Goldberg, S. (1994). Fitting the forum to the fuss: A user-friendly guide to selecting an ADR procedure. *Negotiation Journal, 10,* 49–68.

Saundry, R., & Latreille, P. (2014). Workplace mediation. In W. Roche, P. Teague, & A. Colvin (Eds.), *The Oxford handbook of conflict management in organizations.* Oxford: Oxford University Press.

Saundry, R., & Wibberley, G. (2014). Workplace dispute resolution and the management of individual conflict – A thematic analysis of 5 case studies. *Acas Research Papers,* 06/14.

Saundry, R., McArdle, L., & Thomas, P. (2011). Transforming conflict management in the public sector? Mediation, trade unions and partnerships in a primary care trust. *Acas Research Papers,* 01/11.

Saundry, R., Bennett, T., & Wibberley, G. (2013). Workplace mediation: the participant experience. *Acas Research Papers,* 02/13.

Scottish TUC. (2009). *Annual congress 2009 decisions booklet.* http://www.stuc.org.uk/files/Congress%202009/DECISIONS%20ANNUAL%20CONGRESS%202009.pdf. Accessed 8 Aug 2015.

Simms, M., & Charlwood, A. (2010). Trade Unions: Power and influence in a changed context. In T. Colling, & M. Terry (Eds.), *Industrial relations: Theory and practice* (3rd ed.,). Chichester: John Wiley and Sons.

Trades Union Congress. (2011). *Resolving workplace disputes. TUC response to government consultation.* http://www.ier.org.uk/sites/ier.org.uk/files/Sarah%20 Veale%20Resolving%20Workplace%20Disputes%20TUC%20 Response%20-%20FULL.pdf. Accessed 11 Aug 2015.

Trades Union Congress, & Acas. (2010). *Mediation: A guide for trade union representatives.* http://www.tuc.org.uk; www.acas.org.uk. Accessed 13 Apr 2013.

UNISON. (2011). *Department for Business, Innovation and Skills – Consultation April 2011 "Resolving workplace disputes" UNISON – Response.* UNISON: London.

Unite. (2011). *Unite response to resolving workplace disputes consultation 2011.* http://centrallobby.politicshome.com/fileadmin/epolitix/stakeholders/Unite_response_to_Resolving_Workplace_Disputes.pdf. Accessed 12 Nov 2012.

van Wanrooy, B., Bewley, H., Bryson, A., Forth, J., Freeth, S., Stokes, L., & Wood, S. (2013). *The 2011 workplace employment relations study: First findings.* https://www.gov.uk/government/publications/the-2011-workplace-employment-relations-study-wers. Accessed 1 Aug 2013.

Wood, S., Saundry, R., & Latreille, P. (2014). Analysis of the nature, extent and impact of grievance and disciplinary procedures and workplace mediation using WERS 2011. *Acas Research Papers*, 10/14.

11

Turning Third-Party Intervention on Its Head: Assisted Bargaining and the Prevention of Workplace Conflict in Ireland

William K. Roche

Introduction

In conventional dispute resolution procedures, assistance by third parties, whether they be public dispute resolution agencies or privately-engaged facilitators, usually arises several steps into the procedure when deadlock has arisen. This has long been viewed as a key principle of voluntary collective bargaining in which the parties are expected to take primary responsibility for their mutual dealings and for striving to reach settlements in negotiations or disputes before seeking assistance from third parties (Steadman 2003). The 'classic triad' of dispute resolution activities, conciliation, mediation (often taken to mean a more directive style of conciliation in which proposals may be put to the parties by the third party) and arbitration, pivot around this principle (EIRO 2006; Valdes Dal-Re 2003; Welz and Kauppinen 2005).

One significant strand of innovation in conflict management in Anglo-American countries involves turning this principle on its head by involving

W.K. Roche (✉)
College of Business, University College Dublin, Dublin Republic of Ireland
e-mail: bill.roche@ucd.ie

© The Editor(s) (if applicable) and The Author(s) 2016   **215**
R. Saundry et al. (eds.), *Reframing Resolution*,
DOI 10.1057/978-1-137-51560-5_11

third parties at or close to the outset of negotiations, with a view to avoiding deadlock and encouraging agreement. State dispute resolution agencies and private facilitators now sometimes provide facilitation of this type. This mode of conflict resolution or prevention has not been examined in detail in the international literature. The purpose of this chapter is to provide a detailed analysis of assisted bargaining as conducted by the main state agency for dispute resolution in Ireland, the Labour Relations Commission (LRC).

The International Conduct of Assisted Bargaining

In the UK, Acas conducts 'assisted bargaining' and describes the process as early assistance to the parties involved in collective industrial relations issues, with a view to preventing a dispute arising. In assisted bargaining the outcomes of negotiations remain in the hands of the parties, the role of Acas being to facilitate the parties in arriving at mutually acceptable solutions. In such circumstances an Acas facilitator might chair negotiations. Assisted bargaining tends to occur in cases where there is a history of disputes (Acas 2009:4). A review of 25 years of Acas's activities portrayed assisted bargaining or 'advisory mediation' as a process that was normally concerned with less urgent longer-term issues and thus more likely to be seen as 'more preventive or strategic than dispute mediation' (Goodman 2000:38). It was observed that the distinction between assisted bargaining and conciliation was not clear-cut. In some instances initiatives such as the creation and chairing by Acas of 'joint working parties' to handle longer-term strategic issues might be an extension of conciliation, especially if undertaken against the background of a potential dispute or as part of a conciliation settlement (Goodman 2000:38). In practice, there was 'some flexible blurring of activities' at the interface between conciliation and advisory mediation or assisted bargaining (Goodman 2000:32).

The International Labour Organization (ILO) identifies 'facilitated negotiation or assisted bargaining' as a form of ADR that is less commonly used internationally than other ADR practices. The ILO defines the process as the use of independent third parties that facilitate a negotiation process before any dispute has arisen. The facilitator uses chairing and mediation skills and, with the permission of the parties involved, can hold private meetings with each as part of the facilitation process. The process is sometimes preceded by negotiation skills training and a pre-negotiation meeting (Steadman 2003). In the specific case of public service dispute resolution, the ILO advocates 'active facilitation' in the pre-bargaining phase of negotiations that might involve multiple unions, with possibly conflicting bargaining priorities (Thompson 2010:25). Facilitated negotiations are also presented as a form of positive dispute prevention rather than reactive dispute resolution, where pre-emptive steps can be undertaken by the facilitator to shape bargaining dynamics from the outset (Thompson 2010:31).

The ILO observes that assisted bargaining can be facilitated by independent professionals or by state agencies involved in conflict resolution. Another agency providing assisted bargaining is the South African Commission for Conciliation, Mediation and Arbitration (SACCMA) The SACCMA is available to assist parties involved in restructuring negotiations at the outset of their mutual engagement and can provide a route to gaining agreement on a protocol for engagement. The facilitator also chairs negotiations (Thompson 2010:31).

Collective bargaining that has not (yet) become bogged down in disputes or conflict is also facilitated by the US Federal Mediation and Conciliation Service. The FMCS can assist employers and unions by providing mediation from the outset when contracts are open for renegotiation and also by convening and facilitating dialogue and negotiations involving public service employers and unions (as well as other parties) (FMCS 2012; Thompson 2010:32). 'Proactive labour-management facilitation' by the FMCS is equated mainly with the provision of joint training for partnership initiatives (Cohen 2010).

The well understood problem of distinguishing in practice between different forms of dispute resolution, blurred interfaces between modes of third-party involvement and the fact that 'diversity prevails over homogeneity' in different dispute resolution systems, makes it difficult to portray trends in the field, particularly in Europe, where the problem of definition or categorization of different dispute resolution processes is compounded by different legal systems and traditions (Valdes Dal-Re 2003:14; Welz and Kauppinen 2005). Some commentators hold that developments like more intense international

competition, new forms of work organization and greater involvement by unions in company decision-making are leading to a growing reliance on the 'classic triad' of dispute resolution activities over
the judicial determination of disputes (Valdes Dal-Re 2003) Brown
(2014) has noted that in the Anglo-American world collective bargaining has increasingly come to emphasize co-operation over confrontation and dispute resolution agencies have been devoting more
resources to promoting better industrial relations.

Consistent with this view, it has been observed that in the US
'interest-based bargaining' has gained widespread use in the private and
public sectors, with the result that mediators or facilitators have had to
become skilled in facilitating this process, as well as in conciliating in
more traditional adversarial or positional bargaining (Kochan and Zack
2013:171). Following the advent of the Great Recession, the FMCS's
role as proactive facilitator broadened into a 'new model for managing
labour-management conflicts' (Cohen 2011). This new model includes
the provision of joint training, as before, but extends into a series of
additional modes of mediation. These include convening seminars on
good practice in joint problem-solving and early contract (re)negotiation;
facilitating partnership structures and arrangements; being available to
parties in instances where intense conflicts were anticipated or had arisen;
and early involvement in areas of the public sector, such as education,
where reform programmes are being implemented to provide both training and facilitation to support interest-based bargaining (Cohen 2011).

While facilitation and assisted bargaining have attracted interest and
commentary, especially as distinctive mediation processes that may be
becoming more common in response to developments in the economic
and business environment, few empirical studies of assisted bargaining
exist internationally. The rest of this chapter presents an analysis of
assisted bargaining in the Irish Labour Relations Commission. It highlights the circumstances in which employers and unions seek this type
of third-party mediation, the core features of assisted bargaining and
how it differs from conventional collective mediation or conciliation,
and the objectives of the parties and outcomes of the process.

The LRC, Facilitation and Assisted Bargaining

The Labour Relations Commission is Ireland's principal agency for conflict resolution, responsible for resolving disputes involving individual employees or small groups and collective disputes involving trade unions. The LRC's jurisdiction with respect to collective dispute resolution and prevention spans the private sector, state-owned commercial firms and areas of the public service.[1]

The LRC brokers agreements between employers and unions through conventional conciliation and through a process that it calls 'facilitation', which includes assisted bargaining as understood in the literature. This chapter examines the role of the LRC in assisted bargaining, supported by the views and experiences of facilitators and by case studies of instances of assisted bargaining. Drawing on eight interviews with industrial relations officers with experience of assisted bargaining and on case studies, it begins with an overview of the LRC's broader facilitation function and then examines the specific third-party processes involved in assisted bargaining.

Facilitation

Within the LRC, support to employers and unions at the outset of the process of negotiation is provided as part of a more general set of activities known as 'facilitation'. The LRC has engaged in some 30–40 instances of facilitation each year in recent years. The overall incidence of facilitated bargaining remains modest in the context of a case-load of over 1,000 referrals to conciliation in 2011, although, as will become clear, facilitation has grown in incidence, sometimes involves large employers and significant areas, such as the health service, and may involve complex change and reorganization programmes.

---

[1] In 2015 the LRC will merge with other state agencies responsible for mediation and adjudication in employment rights disputes and for policing the enforcement of employment standards to form a new agency, the Workplace Relations Commission. The LRC conciliation and facilitation services will continue within the new agency.

Facilitation was described by a senior LRC officer as 'extra procedural' in nature: that is employer and unions avail of this form of assistance where either one or both do not wish to engage with standard dispute procedures, because they are predicated on union recognition, or involve steps or stages culminating in LRC conciliation, Labour Court hearings, or equivalent procedural stages that arise in public service organizations. In the standard Irish dispute resolution process, the Labour Court typically becomes involved in investigating industrial disputes following failure by the parties to reach settlement through conciliation at the LRC.

Extra-procedural support through facilitation is offered by the LRC to parties dealing with a broad spectrum of issues. At one end of the spectrum are instances where facilitation involves exploring ways of dealing with complex and sensitive disputes, such as where liability falls for funding redundancy payments or where employers refuse to concede union recognition. Where firms oppose recognition they may 'stand over their reluctance to engage with unions by engaging through the mediator with the union' – even if sometimes they demur from meeting a facilitator in the same building, or even in the same city or town.

The other end of the spectrum is marked by circumstances where the parties have exhausted all steps in a dispute procedure and are nevertheless assisted to resolve remaining differences beyond the reach of the formal agreed procedure. Employers and unions in the public service also sometimes avail of assistance outside of formal procedures, where they are reluctant to enter a process involving dispute resolution stages that culminate in arbitration.

Extra-procedural support is also provided within this spectrum of issues. In some circumstances conventional conciliation at the LRC, in the words of one facilitator, 'transmogrifies' into facilitation when it emerges that the immediate issue in dispute, for example plans to make people redundant, reflect deeper underlying problems that might benefit from facilitated engagement around multiple issues. In other instances, facilitation arises directly from requests by employers and unions for assistance at the outset of negotiations around complex multi-stranded change programmes, or dealing with difficult issues. Such instances are domain of assisted bargaining, as understood in the literature.

As practised by the LRC, facilitation then represents a flexible, multi-purpose mode of dispute resolution and sometimes of dispute prevention.

Drawing on the spectrum of circumstances in which the LRC has become involved, Box 11.1 categorizes the different modes of facilitation practised by the LRC.

> **Box 11.1 Modes of Facilitation**
>
> *Exploration and Informal Diplomacy:* Facilitation is non-directive and mainly involves exploratory sounding or talks and possibly cautious and tentative dealings with parties, particularly employers. The standard operating procedures of conciliation are suspended in favour of informal offers of assistance to one or both parties. Facilitation may be conducted mainly by phone or email. The parties may have no direct dealings with each other and fail to agree to meet simultaneously in the same building, or even to engage with the facilitator in the same location. Proposals for settlements are understood to emanate from the facilitator.
>
> *Brokerage in the Shadow of Adjudication:* Facilitation mainly involves directive conciliation and is conducted in the shadow of a recommendation by the Labour Court or decision by a Rights Commissioner, or by suspending adjudication pending direct engagement between the parties. Mandate to seek solution to dispute takes account of the position of adjudication bodies.
>
> *Assisted Bargaining:* Facilitation is non-directive, oriented to a longer time horizon and conducted outside the context of a dispute. Bargaining agendas are often complex or technical in nature and the parties to bargaining commonly seek the assistance of an independent third party to facilitate settlement.

Assisted Bargaining

This section considers in more detail the features of facilitation when practised in circumstances where no current dispute exists and where the parties to facilitation have opted to address significant issues outside of standard dispute resolution procedures (see Box 11.1).

Antecedent and Core Features of Assisted Bargaining

In the LRC the practice of assisted bargaining stretches back to the 1990s. The LRC's first Director of Conciliation traced the advent of this kind of intervention to several significant disputes during that decade (McGee 2013). In the manufacturing firm, Waterford Crystal, and the state-owned public utilities, ESB (electricity generation and distribution), Aer Lingus (airlines) and Irish Rail (rail transport) – all affected by major changes in commercial conditions – one or more LRC officers were assigned to work with management and unions over periods of up to 4 months. These early instances of assisted bargaining had a number of salient features. The LRC's involvement as facilitator was intensive and protracted and the parties addressed complex and multifaceted restructuring challenges, often in circumstances involving radical commercial or regulatory changes. With the exception of Waterford Crystal, LRC facilitation occurred in the absence of disputes. The process of facilitation sometimes included quasi-adjudication, taking the form of reports and recommendations issued to the parties. Some of these early features of assisted bargaining were to remain integral to the LRC's subsequent work in this area.

For some of those interviewed the dominant mode of dispute resolution provided by the LRC is 'directive conciliation', involving an 'assertive approach', where the third party presses for a settlement and 'heads are banged together' to that end. This view is epitomized by the maxim of a former Director of Conciliation regarding dispute resolution in the LRC: 'just get them fixed and out' (McGee 2013:55). In the view of LRC officers experienced in assisted bargaining and other modes of facilitation, the default skills and processes involved are very similar to those that are applied in conventional dispute-based conciliation.

The process of facilitation in assisted bargaining is, however, understood to be distinctive in significant respects. As outlined in Box 11.1, assisted bargaining is characterized by a significant degree of process flexibility. Assisted bargaining is portrayed by some facilitators as 'more informal' than classical conciliation. It is also seen to be more intensive and often, but not always, more prolonged than conventional conciliation and facilitation activity. The parties presenting for facilitation also tend to be 'less confrontational' in their dealings with each other. Facilitators themselves tend to be 'less assertive' in their dealings with the parties than when involved in conventional conciliation because the process may be 'less about fire-fighting than about prevention':

> Quite often we're less assertive because in a dispute situation you really do have to press people very hard to face reality and to get a conclusion because we don't have the luxury of not getting to a conclusion. Whereas in a facilitative exercise, over a more extended time-frame,... you can actually allow time for parties to come together and go apart, to facilitate a lot more extended dialogue. If the parties wanted facilitation, a clinical facilitation, you may just be acting as chairman throughout a full process, where the parties are talking [and] have a set agenda.

Notwithstanding the less directive role of the facilitator in assisted bargaining as compared with classical conciliation, it was clear that more directive interludes could arise in which the facilitator sought to focus the parties and inject urgency into the process. The facilitator could advocate the benefits of proposals on the table to one or other of the parties, feeling less constrained by the impartiality that needs to be maintained more strictly in conciliation. An example was provided of a management proposal in assisted bargaining talks in a pharmaceutical firm (see Box 11.3) where the facilitator sought to 'focus' the unions by highlighting that management's proposal meant 'offering money rather than taking money away'.

Directive interludes could also be aimed at altering the pace of engagement or the urgency attaching to reaching settlement. In the case of disputes or impending disputes, short-time horizons established parameters for conciliation that needed to be conducted 'against the clock'. Assisted bargaining outside the context of a dispute was conducted 'over a longer time frame, without as much urgency about it'. So to prevent the often intensive and prolonged nature of assisted bargaining becoming an obstacle in itself to a successful outcome, facilitators sometimes chose to become more directive by setting time limits on their involvement or by insisting on making progress a pre-condition for their continuing involvement. As one colleague advised another: 'tell them at the next meeting, they do business or you're finished with them.'

The parties, particularly unions, sometimes undertook assisted bargaining by making it explicit at the outset that their involvement was 'without prejudice' to options they could exercise under 'normal' dispute resolution procedures. The implication was that, if the process failed to deliver the outcomes expected, other options might be exercised down the road.

Agendas and time frames in assisted bargaining tended to be strongly influenced by employers' objectives and time horizons:

> I've never had to agree terms of reference as such.... Usually what happens is that a company will say "look we've got to save €50 million or €100 million and here's a plan".... They might say "we need agreement on this by the end of March or June", whatever it might be. "Can we come in and see you?" ... 'Will you facilitate us with it?'

At the outset of the process of assisted bargaining the facilitator agreed objectives and ground rules with the parties. These included the principle that the process involved a 'standalone' initiative, outside of normal industrial relations procedure. Facilitators emphasized the need to maintain flexibility in the assisted bargaining process as matters evolved and snags or blockages arose:

> Our skill set is solution-focused. So if you're suggesting, for example, that a working group may help and it's shot down straight away that can then evolve into a joint training initiative, where the principals on both sides are brought together off-site and we draw up an agenda and we work through that agenda to the same end as a working group; but we're just taking a more circuitous route.

Agendas in assisted bargaining range from multiple items connected with complex restructuring programmes to challenging single issues. An example of an assisted bargaining cycle involving a complex restructuring programme is provided by the reconfiguration of acute medical services for a population of one million people in the Dublin North-East region of the Health Service Executive (HSE) – the body responsible for delivering healthcare in Ireland. This is outlined in Box 11.2. An example of assisted bargaining focused around a significant single issue is provided by the multinational pharmaceutical firm, Wyeth/Nestlé Nutritionals, where management presented unions with a new framework for determining pay on a multi-annual basis linked with productivity. This case is outlined in Box 11.3.

Box 11.2 The Reconfiguration of Hospital Services in the HSE Dublin North-East Region

The Health Service Executive (HSE) is responsible for delivering healthcare in Ireland.

In 2007 the HSE began reconfiguring healthcare delivery in the counties of Louth, Meath, Cavan, Monaghan and North Dublin. The region serves a population of around one million people.

Work began on a plan to reconfigure acute hospital services in the Cavan-Monaghan area. Central to this was the transfer of services from Monaghan hospital, which employed about 180 people, to Cavan. About 80 people would move to Cavan.

Managers engaged intensively with staff at all levels within the services and work sites affected and with unions representing different categories of healthcare workers. Negotiations were difficult and highly adversarial and were affected by community opposition and political controversy surrounding the redesignation of the local hospital in Monaghan. With the sides entrenched and little movement in prospect, the principals on the union and management sides agreed to seek the involvement of the LRC in a facilitation capacity.

The LRC chaired intensive day-long negotiations based on agenda items that unions and management had been invited to submit. Agreement was reached on some areas. Industrial relations difficulties arose around the issues of staff redeployment and allowances and matters in dispute were referred immediately to the conciliation service of the LRC. This 'parallel process', combining facilitated agreement on some issues and conciliation on matters that remained in dispute, allowed the parties to proceed with redeployment without

(continued)

Box 11.2 (continued)

becoming bogged down in industrial relations issues. Conciliation was subsequently conducted at the LRC to resolve disputes involving radiographers and laboratory scientists. A dispute about loss of earnings, disturbance and a diminution of promotion opportunities for laboratory scientists transferring from Monaghan to Cavan Hospitals, was referred to the Labour Court. A dispute over staffing levels in Monaghan for non-nursing grades was referred to the LRC and then to the Labour Court, which nominated a private facilitator to work with the parties to find a solution. In July 2009 acute on-call medical services were transferred from Monaghan General Hospital to Cavan General Hospital.

The LRC next became involved in facilitating the reconfiguration of services and redeployment of staff between hospitals in the Louth and Meath area. The plan was for acute general medicine and critical care to be concentrated at Drogheda and day and outpatient services to be expanded at Dundalk and Navan hospitals. Agreement was reached that management would hold immediate direct meetings with the unions impacted by the opening of the emergency department and also engage on the handling of the transfer of acute medical services from Dundalk to Drogheda. Management also committed to a recruitment process for vacant posts. During 2010 a new accident and emergency department, three times the size of the original A and E unit, opened at Drogheda Hospital. A new coronary care unit was also established at the hospital.

The LRC's involvement in the HSE Dublin North East reconfiguration process was intensive, involving around one meeting each month. Facilitation involved a combination of plenary meetings, conferences with the principals and nominated representatives on both sides and standard conciliation meetings with the parties in separate rooms. The facilitation process rendered engagement between the parties less adversarial and more productive. Facilitation provided what was described as a mode of 'governance' for the talks process. Vetoes, the issuing of threats, refusals to engage around issues or the leaking of information to the media were no longer

Box 11.2 (continued)

acceptable within the framework guiding the talks. The 'badge of the LRC' brought credibility and earnestness to the facilitated negotiations. Despite difficult negotiations and spill-over from local protest activities in Monaghan, industrial action was never threatened during the reconfiguration process.

Sources: LRC, HSE and various media reports

Box 11.3 Assisted Bargaining at Wyeth/Nestlé Nutritionals

Wyeth Nutritionals, now part of Nestlé, has manufactured infant and child nutritional products at its plant in Askeaton, Co. Limerick, since 1974. The plant employs about 500 people and prior to its acquisition by Nestlé in 2012 was acquired by Pfizer in 2009.

The plant is strongly unionized and the workforce is represented by different unions. Unite represents administrative, mechanical and electrical grades. The TEEU also represents staff in mechanical and electrical grades. SIPTU represents operative grades at the plant.

In 2012 the company indicated to the LRC that they were considering appointing a facilitator to assist in talks with their unions on pay. The LRC offered to provide facilitation and an experienced industrial relations officer, familiar with industrial relations at the plant, commenced the facilitation process in early July 2012 with the intention of concluding the process later that month when the plant closed for holidays. The process began with joint sessions with the administrative and the mechanical and electrical grades at which management outlined their proposed new framework for pay. The intention was that pay awards in future would be linked to improvements in productivity arising from changes in work practices. Pay increases were not to be discussed until the parties had agreed to changes required by management. The facilitator chaired sessions at which clarification of management proposals was provided and sought to move the process forward with the groups involved.

(continued)

Box 11.3 (continued)

SIPTU were not a party to the facilitation process, as they were pursuing an outstanding pay claim that had been the subject of a Labour Court recommendation. The Labour Court had recommended that the union and the firm should return to talks under the aegis of the LRC and the parties entered conciliation provided by the LRC's industrial relations officer for the region.

During the facilitation process, the administrative grades and the firm came to an understanding in principle on a new pay framework, contingent on the other groups involved also agreeing.

All grades involved in the facilitation process expressed concern that SIPTU was not involved and it became clear that agreement would not be secured until SIPTU's ongoing pay dispute with the firm had been resolved. Amid these concerns, progress was delayed and the original deadline for facilitation expired without the process being brought to a conclusion. Following conciliation, the SIPTU pay claim was referred back to the Labour Court. Prior to the scheduled hearing by the court, the parties held direct talks that resulted in an agreement providing for an 8 % pay increase over the period to the end of March 2016, plus an additional day of annual leave.

Following on from the agreement with SIPTU, the company had consented to extend the terms agreed to grades represented by the TEEU and Unite. The groups can opt for this to be done through local talks or via the facilitation process.

Opinion on the part of management on the facilitation process was positive. In particular, the process was seen to have been designed and owned by the parties, and as having been flexible, as distinct from the conventional dispute resolution process, where the procedure is prescribed and proceeds to being owned and controlled by the LRC. Facilitation provided by the LRC was also seen to have enjoyed credibility by being independent in a way that private facilitation, paid for by the firm, could not have been.

Sources: *Industrial Relations News* and LRC

Assisted bargaining sometimes involves the use of a parallel conciliation process. The parties may resort to conciliation and adjudication around proposed changes to terms and conditions of employment. This parallel approach can prevent the mainstream facilitation process from becoming stalled by issues that can only or better be addressed and resolved through conciliation. An example is provided by the reconfiguration of health services in HSE North East, in Box 11.2, where some issues were referred to conciliation to prevent the overall facilitation process from becoming bogged down in differences that were not amenable to resolution in the facilitation process.

Reflecting on the alignment of facilitation and conciliation, a facilitator observed:

> The parties certainly found that advantageous because if you're pursuing an agenda of change, you don't want to get bogged down in the IR issues. You need to be able to progress these.

People who had facilitated in the context of assisted bargaining also highlighted some of the challenges and problems that could arise. While one or both parties might have been willing to embark on the extra-procedural path represented by assisted bargaining, industrial relations legacies inevitably influence the process.

A case in point is that of the pharmaceutical manufacturing firm, summarized in Box 11.3. The union representing operatives at Wyeth/Nestle Nutritionals, the largest category at the plant, pursued a claim for a pay rise on the grounds that this had been conceded by other plants within the firm. The firm sought to defend its refusal to concede the claim on the basis that a major cost saving and competitiveness programme at the plant had 'absorbed' the claim. Following conciliation the dispute was referred to the Labour Court. Management sought to respond to the claim on the basis of discussions on pay and productivity. The Court recommended that the parties enter joint discussions facilitated by the LRC. With a view to escaping a legacy of difficult industrial relations, the firm opted to seek agreement on a new multiannual framework for pay based on productivity by means of facilitation rather than conventional collective bargaining and the associated disputes procedure.

They became frustrated with the length of time it takes for an issue to proceed from local discussions through to the Labour Court because, inevitably, everything, no matter how big or small, ends up as a row. So they were looking for a mechanism to bypass the frustration.

The industrial relations legacy was compounded by a complex bargaining structure in which separate unions represented general operatives, electrical crafts and combined mechanical, technical, engineering and administrative grades. Notwithstanding the Court's recommendation, operatives at the plant sought to address the claim on its merits within conventional conciliation, opting to remain outside the facilitation process that had been engaged in by other categories at the plant. The result was a dual-track approach where the largest category remained within conciliation while other categories agreed to proceed on the basis of facilitation.

Legacy issues could also surface in other ways in an assisted bargaining process. An instance was given in which unions distrusted each other and remained as reluctant to work together within the facilitation process as they had been in conventional collective bargaining. Gaining agreement from the large group of shop stewards also made progress difficult. In an instance involving a manufacturing firm, significant but varying progress had been made in facilitation with a number of categories involved. The facilitator sensed that management would have been prepared to allow them to arbitrate on unresolved matters – in effect adopting mediation–arbitration ('med-arb'). The unions, on the other hand, had engaged in facilitation 'without prejudice' and expected to revert to normal industrial relations procedure (involving conciliation) if agreement could not be reached. Any other means of dispute resolution would have involved shop stewards relinquishing power, which they were not prepared to do.

While the adoption of a dual-track process, in which some categories engaged in facilitation but others sought to proceed through conventional collective bargaining, could allow facilitation to progress, the fact that a large category opted to proceed through conventional collective bargaining and conciliation meant that they might 'hold the cards' with respect to the eventual success of the process. The case of Wyeth/Nestlé, outlined in

Box 11.3, exemplifies this issue. Here the new pay determination framework was obviously predicated on all categories being willing to settle. When management and the plant's operatives failed to resolve the long-running pay dispute in conciliation, the dispute was referred back to the Labour Court. The facilitation process was then suspended pending the outcome of the Labour Court investigation. The facilitator was asked by the company to return at that point to bring the process to a conclusion.

Facilitation and conciliation operating as parallel processes *within* assisted bargaining appears to present few problems, with each process reinforcing the other. An example is provided by the reconfiguration of hospital services in the HSE Dublin North East Region (see Box 11.2). Here the LRC facilitator made provision for conciliation by another officer on the contentious issue of loss of earnings for staff transferring between hospitals. What the parties referred to as the 'parallel process' allowed them to proceed with the handling of staff transfers and other aspects of service reconfiguration without these being bogged down by spin-off industrial relations disputes. The LRC's facilitation of collective bargaining in this case helped the parties to resolve highly contentious issues surrounding staffing levels, new facilities and services, staff transfers between work sites and compensation for loss of earnings in an environment that became financially increasingly difficult and constrained over the period during which the changes were introduced. Hospital services were eventually reconfigured across five work sites without industrial action occurring in a process that was logistically complex and involved an equally complex set of negotiating issues.

Some facilitators contrasted the manner in which they assisted the parties to collective bargaining and the manner in which they understood that facilitation was conducted in formal interest-based bargaining. This comment, however, needs to be seen in the light of the view conveyed by another facilitator that conciliation was now commonly conducted in contexts marked by some of the features of interest-based bargaining, in particular, parties seeking 'win–win' solutions and exchanging their understandings and aspirations in that context.

The key features of assisted bargaining, as facilitated by the LRC, are summarized in Box 11.4.

Box 11.4 Features of Assisted Bargaining with Facilitation Provided by the LRC

- No current dispute between the parties involved.
- Proactive in addressing significant issues or multiple issues.
- Proactive in seeking to forestall disputes.
- Process applies core skills of classical conciliation, adjusted to facilitating engagement in non-dispute circumstances.
- Longer time horizons by parties than in other forms of facilitation or conciliation and process conducted without the urgency engendered by a dispute.
- Parties opt to step outside conventional dispute resolution procedures.
- One or both parties seek to depart from conventional adversarial engagement.
- Less directive style of facilitation.
- Conciliation may be provided and proposals may sometimes be presented to the parties.
- Deeper engagement than would be possible with conventional collective bargaining, facilitation or conciliation.
- Facilitation process can encompass conciliation and possibly adjudication/arbitration.

Objectives and Outcomes of Assisted Bargaining

Facilitators emphasized that the parties to assisted bargaining were concerned in the main with avoiding disputes or industrial conflict by reaching agreement on substantive or concrete issues. Process or relational outcomes, like changes in underlying relationships between the parties, were not common objectives. Sometimes assisted bargaining was seen to have deepened levels of engagement between the parties involved and, in this way, to have resulted in improvements in the underlying quality of employment relations. This was seen to have arisen as an offshoot of a process where more immediate and pragmatic objectives dominated. Even in instances where facilitation had occurred against a background of a legacy of difficult or fractious industrial relations, the focus of the parties, as of the facilitator, was on substantive outcomes. Those providing facilitation highlighted that the process was generally 'non-transformative in the sense of relationships'.

Overall assisted bargaining was judged as having often worked successfully. But it was not seen as a panacea. The process had sometimes collapsed and disputes had resulted, especially where complex restructuring programmes had been at issue. In such circumstances unresolved issues could be dealt with through conventional dispute resolution procedures, including conventional conciliation. So, even where unsuccessful the process might still provide an 'orderly path to an industrial dispute that is then amenable to resolution through conventional dispute resolution mechanisms'. The process could also educate the parties involved, giving them a deeper understanding of the issues being addressed and a better appreciation of the concerns of their interlocutors. Where the process terminated in a dispute, it might narrow down the issues requiring conciliation or adjudication.

Conclusion

It is a long-standing axiom of conflict resolution that third parties ought to assist in the search for agreement only after the parties directly involved became deadlocked and registered a failure to agree. Third-party involvement in assisted bargaining stands this principle on its head by bringing third parties in at the outset, or early on, with a view to helping employers and unions to avoid deadlock and potential conflict, to achieve deeper engagement and to reach agreement without becoming involved in a formal dispute.

The recent availability of assisted bargaining in Ireland reflects international experience in Anglo-American countries. This chapter has provided an empirical portrayal for the first time of the processes involved and of how these differ from more conventional collective mediation, known as conciliation in the Irish case. The chapter has also examined the circumstances in which employers and unions opt for assisted bargaining, their objectives in engaging the process and the outcomes with which it is associated.

Assisted bargaining was triggered by a series of influences. Complex change and restructuring programmes were commonly identified as important influences. Intrinsically difficult issues, like changes in payment systems and working-time arrangements, or proposals for the use of outsourcing, also triggered assisted bargaining. The resolve of parties to step outside established disputes procedures to explore ways forward could also be an influence. The predominant view of these interviewed was that the use of facilitation to assist employers and unions engaged in collective bargaining had grown and would continue to grow over the medium to long term.

While the LRC's work in assisting the parties to collective bargaining outside of dispute situations draws heavily on classical conciliation skills and techniques, these skills are nevertheless transposed in important ways. Third parties work in a less directive manner and facilitation has a longer-term focus than commonly arises in conciliation. Facilitation can involve informal and formal conciliation initiatives. In the LRC, facilitation cases have sometimes included formal conciliation conferences, conducted by different officers to those involved in assisting the parties to collective bargaining. The complex and blurred relationships between the processes of facilitation, conciliation and adjudication in assisted bargaining extend to the complex sequences in which these processes may progress. In some instances, facilitation triggers conciliation and proceeds onward to adjudication. In other instances, requests for conciliation may trigger facilitation, possibly combining formal conciliation efforts and leading onwards to adjudication.

The primary purpose of those facilitating assisted bargaining is to prevent conflict and deepen engagement by making the process of collective bargaining more effective than when conducted directly between employers and unions, supported by conventional dispute resolution procedures. While assisted bargaining initiatives sometimes end in failure and even in disputes and work stoppages, the general view of facilitators is that the process was generally effective in helping employers and unions to gain a deeper understanding of both their interlocutors' and their own interests and thereby to reach agreement. The primary objective of employers and unions in undertaking facilitation was to reach agreement on concrete issues that often arose in the context of complex change programmes. Relational outcomes, such as ongoing improvements in industrial relations, where they arose, were seen as beneficial but usually unintended consequences of a process with more immediate and prosaic objectives.

The predominant view of those involved in assisted bargaining was that demand for the process had grown and would continue to grow over the medium to long term. This view chimed with a regular observation by the LRC regarding developments in collective bargaining since the 1990s. While the volume of requests for collective conciliation was declining, the LRC noted that the complexity and challenges posed by the cases in which the agency intervened had risen significantly. The provision of assisted bargaining is one major response to change in the external environment and seems destined to remain a significant feature of collective conflict resolution in Ireland.

References

Acas. (2009). *The alchemy of dispute resolution: The role of collective conciliation.* London: Acas.

Brown, W. (2014). Third-party processes in employment disputes. In W. K. Roche, P. Teague, & A. Colvin (Eds.), *The Oxford handbook of conflict management in organizations.* Oxford: Oxford University Press.

Cohen, G. H. (2010). FMCS as proactive labor–management facilitator. In *Dispute resolution in the workplace: Proceedings of the National Academy of Arbitrators.* New York: National Academy of Arbitrators.

Cohen, G. H. (2011). *A new model for managing labor–management conflicts with early third-party intervention.* Paper presented to the International Agencies Meeting, Cardiff.

Goodman, J. (2000). Building bridges and settling differences: Collective conciliation and arbitration under ACAS. In B. Towers, & W. Brown (Eds.), *Employment relations in Britain: 25 years of the advisory, conciliation and arbitration service.* Oxford: Blackwell.

European Industrial Relations Observatory. (2006). *Collective dispute resolution in an enlarged European Union.* Dublin, Ireland: European Foundation for the Improvement of Living and Working Conditions.

Federal Mediation and Conciliation Service. (2012). *Managing effectively: Conflict resolution and ADR services for government.* Washington, DC: Federal Mediation and Conciliation Service.

Kochan, T. A., & Zack, A. M. (2013). The potential roadmap towards work-place fairness in China: With some lessons from the US experience. *The International Journal of Comparative Labour Law and Industrial Relations*, *29*(2), 167–184.

McGee, R. (2013). Conciliation: Art, magic, mystery? In B. Sheehan (Ed.), *The labour relations commission: Recalling 21 years, 1991–2012*. Dublin, Ireland: Labour Relations Commission.

Steadman, F. (2003). *Handbook on alternative dispute resolution*. Geneva, Switzerland: International Labour Organization.

Thompson, C. (2010). *Dispute prevention and resolution in public service labour relations: Good policy and practice*. Geneva, Switzerland: International Labour Organization.

Valdes Dal-Re, F. (2003). Synthesis reports on conciliation, mediation and arbitration in the European Union Countries. In F. Valdes Dal-Re (Ed.), *Labour conciliation, mediation and arbitration in European Union countries*. Madrid, Spain: Ministero de Trabajo y Asuntos Sociales.

Welz, C., & Kauppinen, T. (2005). Industrial action and conflict resolution in the new member states. *European Journal of Industrial Relations*, *11*(1), 91–106.

12

Reshaping the Role of the Tribunal as Third Party in Australian Workplace Conflict Resolution

Bernadine Van Gramberg, Julian Teicher and Greg Bamber

Introduction

In common with courts and tribunals in other developed countries, Australia has experienced the rise of the self-represented litigant. This chapter examines innovations in the approaches taken by the Australian Fair Work Commission (FWC), the national employment relations tribunal, in responding to the growing number of self-represented employers and employees appearing before it or seeking redress. In particular, the chapter explores and discusses the shift towards alternative dispute resolution (ADR) and an increasing number of self-help initiatives in the context of the growing individualization

B.V. Gramberg
Swinburne University of Technology, Melbourne, Victoria, Australia
e-mail: bvangramberg@swin.edu.au

J. Teicher • G. Bamber (✉)
Department of Management, Monash Business School,
Melbourne, Victoria, Australia
e-mail: julian.teicher@!monash.edu; Greg.Bamber@monash.edu

© The Editor(s) (if applicable) and The Author(s) 2016
R. Saundry et al. (eds.), *Reframing Resolution*,
DOI 10.1057/978-1-137-51560-5_12

of the Australian labour market and the consequent rise of self-represented litigants before the tribunal. These changes are reshaping the role of the tribunal as a third party in Australian workplace conflict resolution.

In order to explore these developments, the chapter commences with a brief overview of the rise of the self-represented litigant in Australian employment relations before providing an overview of the changes introduced by the Fair Work Commission to facilitate effective participation by those who are unfamiliar with the system. We next consider the difficulties and challenges faced by both litigants and tribunal members in the hearing of their cases. The final section reconsiders the Australian experience in the light of international developments, largely in the United Kingdom. The chapter draws on interviews with members of FWC to explore the range of innovations and approaches introduced by that body to increase access and fairness to individuals.

The Role of the Fair Work Commission

Australia has had a national employment relations tribunal in one form or another since 1904. The present incarnation, the Fair Work Commission, was established under the *Fair Work Act 2009*, and among other things its functions include supervising and assisting in the making and implementation of workplace agreements and modern awards which cover the terms and conditions of work for most Australian workers. It also performs a supervisory role over workplace negotiations, which may culminate in the making of an enterprise agreement. In its dispute resolution role the FWC has responsibility for determining unfair dismissals, resolving industrial disputes that give rise to industrial conflict in a limited set of circumstances and settling disputes arising from the operation of workplace agreements and modern awards. Most recently, the FWC has been given resolution responsibility for resolving complaints of workplace bullying (Schedule 3 of the *Fair Work Amendment Act 2013*). This new anti-bullying jurisdiction commenced on 1 January 2014 and forms part of a set of 'general protections' for workers, which protect a specified list of workplace rights including freedom of association and protection against various forms of workplace discrimination.

In dealing with all types of disputes the FWC has the power to use a variety of ADR techniques including mediation, conciliation and arbitration.

It is not without significance that the work of the Fair Work Commission is mostly directed toward the protection of individual rights. The predecessors to the FWC – at least until 2005 – had largely been charged with settling or facilitating the settlement of collective disputes, but only those involving registered organizations of employers and employees. Under a conservative government elected in 1996, legislation was enacted, the *Workplace Relations Act 1996* and later the *Workplace Relations (WorkChoices) Amendment Act 2005*, following which the work of the tribunal was reoriented to settlement of individual disputes, and union participation in the system was largely in the capacity of bargaining agents or representatives of aggrieved individuals. Although the *Fair Work Act 2009* partially restored the role of the tribunal, the focus of its work remained with individuals.

More than 70 % of employees are covered by awards or enterprise agreements made pursuant to the *Fair Work Act*. Sections 146 and 186(6) of the Act provide that all awards and agreements must contain a dispute resolution clause. Schedule 6.1 of the *Fair Work Regulations 2009* provides a model dispute resolution clause which the parties to an agreement may choose to adopt instead of writing their own procedure. Typically, dispute resolution clauses provide a step-by-step process for parties to resolve their dispute in the workplace but, where resolution cannot be achieved, the clause provides for any disputant to refer the matter to the FWC for mediation, conciliation, expression of opinion or making a recommendation, and arbitration (*Fair Work Regulations 2009* sch. 6.1).

The Rise of the Self-Represented Party

There is now increasing evidence of the sustained decline in strikes and other overt forms of collective-based conflict in a number of advanced economies, particularly the US, UK and Australia (for the UK, see for example Dix et al. 2009). In Australia, declining levels of industrial action have been accompanied by a rise in individualized forms of conflict and although it is not suggested that these forms of action are direct substitutes, there is a relationship between the two forms of conflict in that the decreasing presence of unions and declining membership may result in disputes only being able to be manifest in an individual form. These forms of conflict include: bullying, interpersonal and individual grievances submitted to industrial or equal opportunity tribunals, and workers compensation claims, including in relation to stress, absenteeism and labour turnover (e.g. Shulruf et al. 2009).

In particular, unfair dismissal claims have risen dramatically in recent years and now comprise the largest component of the dispute resolution workload of the Fair Work Commission, amounting to 40 % of all disputes as can be seen in Fig. 12.1 (Annual Report 2013–2014). In the past many of these conflicts would have been resolved with union involvement but with falling union membership rates in almost all sectors of the economy, individuals increasingly attempt to deal with workplace conflicts on their own (McCallum et al. 2013).

As we have noted above, self-represented litigants are increasingly observed in many other countries and jurisdictions. In the UK, the rise of the unrepresented party has been particularly evident in the work of the Advisory Conciliation and Arbitration Service and also the Employment Tribunal, though this phenomenon seems to be less a matter of personal

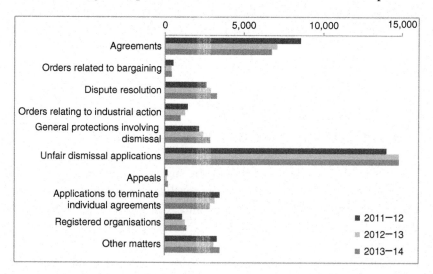

Fig. 12.1 Case load by matter type: Fair Work Commission (Source: Fair Work Commission 2014a)

choice than a response to the unavailability of free or low cost representation (see for example, Aston et al. 2006; Davey and Dix 2011). In the Australian High Court, 41 % of special leave applications (that is, an application to appeal a decision of the Federal Court to the High Court) in 2011–2012 were filed by self-represented litigants (Australian High Court Annual Report 2011–2012). As Deputy Chief Justice Faulks of the Family Court of Australia recently noted:

> Self-representation has reached a level in many courts where it is common for at least one of the parties to be unrepresented for one half of the time. This means that courts are no longer dealing with a minority aberration but are being obliged to contend with change which may require altering the way in which courts operate. (Faulks 2013:2)

Many of these self-represented parties would be 'one-shot' players in these forums with little knowledge or training in how to present a case. The situation is compounded with power and implicitly knowledge imbalances when one party is represented but the other is not. McCallum et al. (2013) Australian report provides evidence that unrepresented litigants are less successful than others in their claims with around 75 % of employees failing to make their unfair dismissal case in the FWC.

In many jurisdictions internationally, courts and tribunals are making changes to accommodate these individuals who may not have any legal knowledge or experience defending an action. Some of these measures have included imposing higher fees in a bid to limit weak or frivolous cases. In the UK, the rising number of claims to the Employment Tribunal culminated in a fee increase imposed on applicants which, since its introduction in 2013, has led to a 70 % reduction in the number of Employment Tribunal applications by March 2015 (Souter 2015). In May 2014, the UK Coalition government made it mandatory for individuals intending to lodge a claim to the Employment Tribunal to first undertake Early Conciliation through the Advisory, Conciliation and Arbitration Service (Acas). This has resulted in a dramatic growth of applications for Early Conciliation; as Souter (2015) notes, between April 2014 and December 2014 Acas received over 60,000 of these requests. An evaluation of the Early Conciliation intervention by Downer et al. (2015) found that the (predominantly) phone-based conciliation service received high satisfaction ratings from both claimants and employers (79 and 86 % respectively) and has contributed to fewer disputes being lodged with the ET.

In their study of the changing role of Labour Boards in Canada, Shilton and Banks (2014) note that with falling union density and fewer industrial campaigns, Labour Boards across Canada have focused largely on individual complaints and human rights complaints. The authors note that 'the presence of self-represented parties changes the dynamic in the hearing room, requiring a cultural shift where adjudicators must deal more directly with affected parties' (op cit. 2014:12). This brief comparative overview of the impact of self-represented litigants defending themselves in workplace dispute in tribunal settings thus demonstrates that the Australian experience is not unique and merits investigation.

Method

This chapter draws on 'elite interviews' conducted with 21 present and former members of the Fair Work Commission between March 2013 and December 2014. These semi-structured interviews were conducted in person and according to a framework of themes. Interviews were typically one hour in duration and were recorded and then transcribed. The advantage of semi-structured interviews with experts is that while consistency is maintained in interview content across a range of interviewees, there is freedom for interviewees to add their own examples and anecdotes which enhances the quality of the findings (Creswell 2005). Transcripts were read through manually as per Creswell (2009) to get a general feel for the data, and themes and codes were then identified and described. Our unit of analysis consisted of sentences and text blocks relating to innovations implemented at the Fair Work Commission to deal with self-represented litigants. We analysed only the data that related to these primary themes of interest in the transcripts, and used content analysis to learn about and understand the participants' viewpoints. We did this through combination of manual and computer aided analysis of coded data using NVivo 10. The results provided us with a pattern of activities which we have labelled innovations and these are presented in the next section of this chapter. These data were also supplemented and interwoven with the large range of materials which have been placed on the FWC website as part of the process of making the tribunal more accessible to potential claimants and in assisting them in preparing and presenting their cases to the best effect; that is, in an effort to ensure that the proceedings of the FWC are efficient, inclusive and fair.

Findings

Our main research question was: What adaptations and initiatives have been introduced by the Australian Fair Work Commission in response to the changing nature of workplace disputes? Our secondary question was: How well do these innovations appear to be working in terms of providing efficient and effective dispute resolution?

Our analysis demonstrated a range of measures implemented by the FWC alone or with the assistance of the Fair Work Ombudsman to deal with individual disputes in which litigants may be self-represented. We categorized these into three broad types. First, we found that the FWC had put in place a number of preventative mechanisms which provide early advice and communications before a formal dispute is lodged. Second, the FWC has made changes to the way disputes are handled which provide for early triaging of disputes and the use of technology and telephone conciliation to deal with matters quickly. Finally, we found a number of strategic initiatives aimed at creating plans for the future, research projects

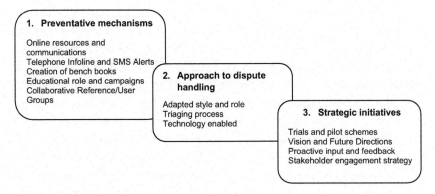

Fig. 12.2 Changes and innovations introduced by the FWC for self-represented litigants

and a stakeholder engagement strategy. These innovations are displayed diagrammatically in Fig. 12.2 and then explained in more detail below.

Preventative Mechanisms

The range of documents, reports and other resources available online at the FWC website has grown tremendously in recent times as a deliberate and strategic response to the increasing number of self-represented litigants and to provide them with sufficient information to decide to lodge an application and then to decide whether to prosecute their own cases. We found six main types of preventative mechanisms comprising online resources and communications; a telephone Infoline and SMS alerts; creation of bench books; education and campaigns; and the formation of collaborative reference and user groups. In addition, it is worth noting that the FWC also offers information to parties either by telephone or in person regarding matters including FWC processes, and can assist in making or responding to an application and in completing application forms. The section below now turns to some of the observations made by Commission members of the preventative measures in place.

Online Resources

Many procedures have been tailored to meet the needs of people who are not familiar with FWC's jurisdiction or its processes. Much of this has been made available online. A feature of these online resources is that they provide detailed guidance on whether a person is eligible to make a claim for unfair dismissal (see https://www.fwc.gov.au/about-us/resources/guide-unfair-dismissal, accessed 23 September 2015). The use of an eligibility resource has been a key way to limit the number of applications which are subsequently heard by the FWC. For example, potential applicants are able to assess their eligibility according to criteria such as: whether a dismissal has occurred; whether the person is in a category of employees who are subject to the unfair dismissal jurisdiction; whether the termination is not subject to review by virtue of being a 'genuine redundancy'; and whether the termination was 'harsh, unjust or unreasonable'. One aim of this process is to discourage applications which are not within the FWC jurisdiction. Finally, completed applications are checked to verify their eligibility before being permitted to proceed.

One FWC member aptly described the impetus for innovations that would make the tribunal and its processes more accessible:

> What did strongly come across was the anxiety and concerns that self-represented parties feel when they're in a tribunal. They're the things that we take for granted. Where do they sit? Do they stand when they speak? How do they address the member? How should they put their material together? We need to do – because we're now – our caseload mix has changed significantly, we need to address these concerns. The virtual tour, the fact sheets, the information we provide, is a way of addressing those issues.

Some members spoke of a strong need to use the website as a 'useful portal' for individuals to consider their own situation through reading case studies, particularly unfair dismissal cases which make up the bulk of individual actions:

> If you look at promoting fairness and improving access, there are new information materials designed to assist parties in understanding the unfair dismissal process. There's a simple eligibility test available on the website.

The online eligibility test is a dynamic form which begins with the words 'I am' and then requires selection from a dropdown list of options including employee, contractor and volunteer. There is also online help to assist those who are unsure of their employment status (see https://www.fwc. gov.au/resolving-issues-disputes-and-dismissals/dismissal-termination-redundancy/eligibility-remedies-0, accessed 23 September 2015).

Another member explained that a 'hot button' has been placed on the FWC website allowing individuals who believe their workplace agreement lies outside of the benchmarks to alert the FWC: '*You can click on it, fill in the details and the email is sent to me. I then investigate the circumstances.*' As with many other private and public organizations there is a growing trend to use social media such as Twitter to spread information about the tribunal and its activities is also now under way:

We're starting to use it in terms of some of own compliance activities, particularly with overseas workers and so forth.

Telephone Information Line and SMS Alerts

A telephone Infoline has been established at the Fair Work Ombudsman, an organization formally separate from the Fair Work Commission and which is responsible for compliance with the Act through education, workplace investigations and ultimately prosecutions. Through a national call centre with 200 operators spread around the country (covering a range of time zones) the Fair Work Ombudsman provides callers with advice and education on aspects of their rights and responsibilities under the *Fair Work Act*. Much of the telephone advice provided is about unfair dismissal:

> Someone's got a problem. There's either a dispute while they're working or they've lost their job. While they're working they've probably got to ring the Infoline and just get some advice.

Provision of education and information is via the Fair Work Commission website, but most of the educational content originates from the Fair Work Ombudsman. At the same time, the FWC members work closely with the Ombudsman's office in providing input into fact sheets and telephone scripts. One interviewee from the Fair Work Ombudsman's office noted:

> We'll work on information and scripts given to us by the Commission or built up with them. So we obviously try and provide the most seamless experience for the public as we can.

The Infoline is supported by a group of around 300 inspectors who provide dispute resolution services initially, and compliance-related services where an issue identified by the Infoline operators (such as an employer breach of the employees terms and conditions) needs to be investigated.

Additionally, a trial of SMS alerts was implemented to advise disputants of hearings and conference times and this is now a permanent feature of the system. The trial commenced in the FWC's large unfair dismissal jurisdiction to avoid delays and cancellations:

> We've had a number of instances where conferences have had to be rescheduled because a party forgets the time, gets caught up in something else. The idea of the SMS alert is that they'll get a message to their mobile phone the day before, reminding them that they've got a telephone conference. We'll evaluate how it works and whether it reduces the number of adjournments that have to be granted.

Creation of Benchbooks

Dealing with self-represented litigants presents a challenge for Commission members and litigants alike, so to standardize the approach taken, the FWC has developed benchbooks which provide detailed procedural guidance:

> We're starting to see in unfair dismissal applications for instance, self-representing parties frame up their positions along the lines of the issues that are raised in the bench book.

Australian courts more generally have developed benchbooks to assist participants in preparing and presenting their cases. The FWC has followed this practice and has now developed detailed benchbooks which include case examples in the areas of workplace bullying, unfair dismissal, general protections and enterprise agreements. There is also a YouTube video which among other things explains where they can be found.

Educational Role and Campaigns

Apart from the educational role provided by the Infoline operators and the range of FWC documents and reports noted above, the FWO offers e-learning opportunities through targeted campaigns. One example is the 'harvest trail' campaign aimed at providing educational support on employment rights to the large body of seasonal workers in Australian farms. Many of these workers are international visitors who are unaware of their rights and vulnerable to exploitation in rural and remote areas. An interviewee from the FWO noted that:

> We run education streams. We run communication. We have a very strong media role, which we see as part of compliance. We see media as a compliance tool.

Collaborative Reference and User Groups

Two user groups have been established by the FWC comprising a Termination of Employment Panel and a Legal Reference Group '*to get their advice and to provide them with an opportunity to comment on any new initiatives that have been taken.*' The Legal Reference group consists of Justice Ross, President of the FWC, and national law firms who frequently appear in matters before the tribunal. The Termination of Employment Panel is headed by the head of the panel of FWC members who handle unfair dismissal cases and representatives from national bodies whose affiliates or members represent applicants and/or respondents in these matters. In addition to these specific user groups, the FWC has been working closely with industry confederations, and specifically the two employer associations – the Australian Industry Group (Ai Group) and the Australian Chamber of Commerce and Industry (ACCI) – along with the Australian Council of Trade Unions (ACTU) in order to develop responses to Federal government industrial relations policy initiatives.

Commission members have also formed a reference group of employers from firms whose employees represent a large proportion of the FWC workload. For example, one member noted he met with these industry representatives:

> … at least quarterly to discuss pro bono issues, issues around access, the tribunal's rules, practice notes and the like. There's not much that we do that doesn't go through an external process. Either it's through that process or in regular meetings with the heads of Ai Group, ACCI and the ACTU.

Approaches to Dispute Handling

The second key area of changes to the FWC's operations in response to the challenges of dealing with self-represented litigants is in its approach to dispute handling. This has largely been in adapting new styles of dispute resolution, first in dealing with the upsurge of unrepresented parties, and more recently in dealing with the new bullying and harassment jurisdiction which commenced in January, 2014. Not only has the approach to hearing matters had to change, but the changes have also encouraged the use of technology in the process of dispute resolution. In this section we explore Commission members' thoughts on the adaptations they have made to their style of dispute resolution, the triaging process used by FWC in managing the vast and varied types of disputes and disputants and the use of communication technologies.

Adapted Style and Role

The majority of the FWC interviewees noted the changing nature of workplace disputes and individual litigants' lack of readiness and training to deal with tribunal processes. For instance, one member observed that this has included making procedures more flexible and easier for self-represented litigants:

> It's an issue everywhere and we have to address it because of fairness, we have to address it because of efficiency. And we have been and we do but now I guess we're formalizing what we've always done. Just try to make sure that people get a fair opportunity to present their cases.

In the context of the work of the Advisory Conciliation and Arbitration Service in the UK, Dix (2011: 6–8) made similar observations regarding the need for a more flexible approach and the greater responsibility of the conciliator where only one party is represented.

The shift to a greater use of mediation has not been straightforward. The FWC's new bullying and harassment jurisdiction represents a set of disputes largely unfamiliar to the tribunal. For instance one member commented that:

We're just not particularly well set up to do it, that's the trouble. We're not trained to do it. We're not selected on the basis that we've got those skills and we've not necessarily resourced to do it.' Another noted that it 'feel[s] like social worker kind of stuff.

Another described it as having '*been teleported to the Family Court, Family Law Court*', while still another was adamant that dealing with bullying and harassment was not novel or unfamiliar as the issues had always arisen in the context of their dispute resolution roles.

Some participants explained in detail what it meant to take a mediation approach. They emphasized their experience in listening, contextualizing and '*helping the unrepresented litigant identify what the nature of their grievance is*.' In the absence of a templated approach to handling disputes, FWC members adopt a variety of approaches based on their training, experience and personal disposition. One participant commented that:

> If you take a more classic mediation approach, you're more open to that kind of active listening, trying to work out what's really going on and trying to suss out what the real problem is and then try and get people to solve the problem rather than get to hung up on what the right or wrong answer is.

For some members this entails a quite structured approach to dispute resolution, while others are more intuitive in the way they approach these matters, particularly in dealing with unrepresented parties who, by their very nature, are less amenable to adhering to the conventions of dispute resolution processes.

The *Fair Work Act 2009* does not define any of the alternative dispute resolution procedures it lists as available to the FWC. However, the (former) Australian National Advisory Council for Alternative Dispute Resolution, which was charged with providing the federal Attorney-General with definitions and policies for ADR, defined mediation as a more passive or facilitative technique and conciliation as active and advisory (Van Gramberg 2006). Indeed as MacDermott and Riley (2012:84) explain: 'From its beginnings, the federal industrial tribunal has adopted an interventionist style of conciliation. This has not apparently changed in any significant respect with the development of a more extensive jurisdiction over individual grievances.'

In our discussions, some members listed the challenges in taking a mediation approach, particularly when both tribunal members and their clients have been accustomed to conciliation. Firstly, there may be confusion in distinguishing the term 'mediation' from some other related concepts such as 'conciliation' and 'arbitration'. One participant commented that people might talk about mediation; however, in most cases they think of it as conciliation. Another member noted that when trying to assist a self-represented litigant *'there's a whole lot of potential objections that can be raised if you're intervening to assist an unrepresented litigant, whether it's an employer or the employee'*. The problem here is that, while a member may wish to assist a party by providing advice on the conduct of their case, if the matter ends with an arbitrated decision, this very informality may provide the basis for an appeal.

Another challenge in taking the mediation approach lies in unrepresented litigants' limited capacity in understanding the nature of their grievance. Members provided examples of how the mediation process was adapted to ensure that individuals were best able to express their case:

> I take the view that whenever there's an unrepresented litigant and someone who is represented [that I generally err] on the side of giving permission to one side even though the other is unrepresented for this reason.

Another observed that even in arbitration, more leniency is accorded to the self-represented litigant:

> I think if you can tease out the issues and also help the unrepresented litigant in cross examination – of course it's tricky for [propositions] that need to be put in a simple series of questions without addressing any of the allegations that 'Dave' made and put into. As I say, where one party is represented and the other isn't, there'll be less likely to be any objection to you engaging in that activity.

Two further issues arise here. First, unrepresented participants may be resistant to assistance. In one case we were told of, an applicant insisted on obtaining a very wide discovery of the company's emails pertaining to him. The Commissioner's advice was ignored with the result that emails that were prejudicial to the applicant were brought into evidence. Second, members were divided on the capacity of individuals to represent themselves on employment matters, with some expressing pleasant surprise at the grasp of the issues that parties were able to gain through the available online resources, and others who were more concerned about the complexity of the legal issues surrounding apparently simple unfair dismissal cases.

Triaging Process

The FWC works with a number of bodies to encourage triaging as a screening process so that *unrepresented litigants can have someone tell them honestly what their prospects look like.* These parties can be a local Legal Aid body such as the Queensland Public Interest Law Clearing House, a non-profit organization providing legal advice in Queensland, or the Royal Melbourne Institute of Technology University's Civil Justice Centre in Victoria. The triaging process also confirms to the litigant if he or she is in the right forum for their dispute:

> That's important because if you're a self-represented applicant, there is nothing worse than getting caught up in the maw of the legal system, only to be spat out at the end with no remedy.

Triaging is also directed at *empowering self-represented parties* and one member noted that for those coming through a triaging process *the level of knowledge and awareness of the tribunal and the functions that it can perform are increasing.*

In undertaking its bullying jurisdiction, the FWC developed a specific process for triaging claims in order to first ensure that the FWC was the appropriate tribunal to hear the matter, and then to provide advice on the prospects of success. Other options that are canvassed in the triaging process include anti-discrimination tribunals, civil and criminal courts and occupational health and safety authorities. A measure of success of the triaging process is that a predicted deluge of claims never materialized

Table 12.1 Anti-bullying claim applications to the Fair Work Commission 2013–2014

Application withdrawn early in case management process[a]	59
Application withdrawn prior to proceedings[b]	34
Application resolved during the course of proceedings[c]	63
Applications withdrawn after a conference or hearing and before decision	20
Application finalized by decision	21
Total	**197**

Source: Fair Work Commission (2014a)
Notes:
[a] Applications withdrawn with case management team or with Panel Head prior to substantive proceedings
[b] Includes matters that are withdrawn prior to a proceeding being listed; before a listed conference, hearing, mention or mediation before a Commission member is conducted; or before a listed mediation by a staff member is conducted. This also includes matters where an applicant considers the response provided by the other parties to satisfactorily deal with the application
[c] Includes matters that are resolved as a result of a listed conference, hearing, mention or mediation before a Commission member or listed mediation by a staff member

in the first full year of the operation of the new jurisdiction (Productivity Commission 2015:278). As demonstrated in Table 12.1, the triaging process successfully reduced 197 claims to 94 before proceedings commenced.

Technology-Enabled

The third initiative in dispute handling is the greater use of technology-based communication. Some members noted that with the aid of information technology there are '*a lot more requests now for doing things by telephone conference, by video conference.*' It is however, a 'double-edged sword' because, on one hand it allows for speedy responses to the lodgement of dispute notifications, but on the other there are disadvantages of communicating online; in particular, bandwidth problems, technical interruptions and difficulties in hearing can make electronically enabled dispute resolution challenging. A particular disadvantage of telephone-based mediation was described as the lack of body language that members rely on when mediating:

> You're not looking at people in the eyes, you're not getting that reaction of saying this person is absolutely dead against what I'm talking about. Or alternatively that person might be, but this person on their side might not seem as indisposed to what I'm saying and, maybe if I talk to them separately, I can try and work out what's happening on this side.

One member described technology-based mediation as being more focused on settlement of a dispute:

> It's a lot more settlement focused. Whereas, when you do it face-to-face, you've got the time and the ability, because you've actually got them there to do more of the story telling and for that to have a lot more weight in the moving towards a possible resolution.

This focus on settlement may have implications for participant assessments of justice, depending on the nature and the complexity of the issues at stake.

Strategic Initiatives

A number of strategic initiatives have been put in place by the FWC, including pilot schemes; a vision for future directions for dispute resolution; proactive input and feedback; research and strategic partnerships; and a stakeholder engagement strategy.

Experimenting and Trialling Pilot Schemes

The first strategic initiative we introduce here involves trials and pilot schemes. This has given rise to a number of programmes: the General Protections pilot programme; a work allocation pilot, the Unfair Dismissal pro-bono pilot programme; and implementing a 'cooling-off period' for phone conciliations.

The General Protections pilot programme was launched in Western Australia to provide legal advice to self-represented applicants. Reflecting the focus of the FWC's jurisdiction on individual claims, General Protections is the term given to a series of delineated workplace rights (such as protection from discrimination based on personal attributes or union membership or non-membership) for which employees may not be treated adversely (for instance, being dismissed).

Another pilot scheme was launched in South Australia dealing with the allocation of disputes to members of the tribunal. Traditionally, tribunal members operate on industry panels and disputes relating to an industry are forwarded centrally to the panel for allocation to one of its members. The new pilot allocates applications to members based in the State where the application was lodged. One member commented that 'initial results have been very positive, both in terms of performance and in terms of party feedback'. The pilot will be evaluated at the end of 2015.

The Unfair Dismissal pro-bono programme was trialled in Victoria in 2013 and, following an evaluation, was implemented throughout the state in 2014. There were 14 major law firms participating in this scheme on a roster system. The purpose of the scheme is to provide legal advice to unrepresented applicants who are unable to get assistance elsewhere in relation to their dispute. Sessions are limited to an hour and focus on the issues likely to be raised at hearing, and advice may be given on drafting submissions, witness statements and providing relevant documents. In this way, the scheme contributes to access to justice and is particularly aimed at 'one time' users of the tribunal. One member commented that:

> The provision of appropriate and timely legal advice can assist a party in the presentation of their case at the tribunal, and can promote efficiency by focusing the proceedings on the real issues in dispute.

In relation to unfair dismissal conciliations, the FWC is also trialling a cooling-off period to deal with agreements made by phone conciliation. As one member described it:

> Where a party is unrepresented and at an unfair dismissal telephone conciliation they reach an agreement, they have a period of time – three

days – in which to decide whether or not they wish to maintain the agreement. It's a self-executing system inasmuch as if they don't let us know within the period, it's assumed the agreement will go forward.

Future Directions

'Future Directions' is the name which the FWC has given to its ongoing and overarching change programme which presently enumerates 30 initiatives, many of which are directed toward making the organization and its processes more accessible (Fair Work Commission 2015). These initiatives can be grouped under four broad themes: promoting fairness and improving access; efficiency and innovation; accountability; and productivity and engagement. One member commented that:

> The sort of information that we have to provide as an organization, put on our website, our approach to parties, is very different when you're dealing with a 'one-shotter' as opposed to a repeat player. It's that transition phase that we're in at the moment.

Alongside implementing these initiatives, the Commission seeks feedback from its users in developing new initiatives. For instance, a feedback form is now sent through to disputants lodging unfair dismissal with a view to improving processes and information. One member observed that:

> We've had a number of changes and suggestions that have come both from within the organization and externally, and we're very keen to get the views of participants in the system as to how we can improve how we go about our task.

Another member commented that:

> We get a lot of feedback from advocates like employer associations or ACTU or unions. We seek out that feedback as well. It's certainly shaped our dispute resolution pathway.

As a result of the feedback thus far, the Commission has developed an appeal procedures practice note with a draft placed on their website (https://www.fwc.gov.au/at-the-commission/how-the-commission-works/practice-notes/appeal-proceedings, accessed 25 September 2015):

> That's been developed in consultation with members and the legal profession reference group. It's designed to give some broad level of consistency in relation to directions that are issued in appeals.

The Commission also engages regularly with its major stakeholders:

> I think it's important for our members to engage with their constituents within those organizations, to attend conferences, to explain what we're doing. We've done that more broadly by putting draft rules on our website and inviting comment.

Stakeholder Engagement Strategy

Engagement with stakeholders emerged as an important strategy encompassing initiatives aimed at the public including providing fact sheets, online jurisdictional tests, and organizing meetings at which people could share their experience with the tribunal. Workplace engagement was another avenue of engagement typically aimed at conference sponsorship with key industry stakeholders such as the Australian Chamber of Commerce and Industry, the Australian Council of Trade Unions and the Australian Industry Group. As one member noted: *'The intent of the conference was, if you like, to lift the tone of the conversation around workplace relations issues and some of the challenges facing us collectively'*.

Discussion

From a system based on conciliating and arbitrating collective disputes over wages and conditions, the work of the FWC has moved predominantly to facilitating the settlement of individual disputes over alleged unfair dismissals and other breaches of employee rights. Faced with an increasing clientele of self-represented, usually once-off parties, the FWC has introduced initiatives broadly aimed at increasing access and ensuring fairness to individuals. In our interviews these initiatives fell into three broad themes: preventative measures; changes to dispute resolution; and strategic and future planning. This chapter has detailed these innovations through the eyes of FWC members who have contributed to their implementation. In this section, we briefly discuss each of the three themes in relation to their contribution to innovation but also the challenges they pose for the future of the tribunal's dispute resolution role.

In both the UK and in Australia, a key preventative measure implemented to deal with the increasing numbers of applications lodged by individuals, particularly for unfair dismissal, is the use of restraints and disincentives to lodge. In Australia, this has taken the form of an online, self-managed eligibility checklist which provides feedback to applicants on whether they are permitted to apply or not. Applicants must complete the online checklist before they submit their claim. While lodgement fees apply to FWC processes, these are modest and there is scope for exemption in cases of hardship. A second check is made by the FWC itself once an application is lodged. In this way, some control is placed on those applicants who do not conform to the parameters of the jurisdiction. In the UK, the introduction of fees for lodgement with the Employment Tribunal provided a significant disincentive for applicants. This has greatly reduced the working time of the tribunal on individual grievances but it has been highly controversial. As Dickens (2014:245) warns in the UK, case disposal should not be the prevailing objective of a good dispute resolution system:

Constraints on resources affect the way in which conciliation is conducted lessening the likelihood of any beneficial impact beyond the individual case. Such constraints, for example, have reduced the opportunities for conciliators to deal directly with parties in person. Conciliation conducted by telephone makes any underlying employment relations issues that might give rise to further disputes less likely to be detected, explored or resolved.

Prevention has also included education and online campaigns conducted by FWC. This has meant that the tribunal now makes considerable and increasing use of social media, SMS texting and provision of online resources to the public than ever before. This activity has increased the awareness of members of the importance of participating in social media and this has given them a higher profile in the Australian community than hitherto. For instance, the FWC YouTube 'Virtual Tour' video series consists of the President's Introduction, explanations of FWC's jurisdiction, case studies and mock trials. The FWC video entitled: 'What happens at a Conciliation' which was launched in 2014, has attracted 4,215 views (Fair Work Commission 2014b). The implications of this new role for members and FWC administration includes new training, as well as a raft of policies and practices around the use of the communication technologies by FWC.

The second main area for innovation has been in the way dispute resolution itself is handled. The FWC, like Acas, has now introduced an early conciliation stage. In the FWC this is conducted by professional, ADR-trained civil servants who are not members of the tribunal but who provide the first attempt of settlement. In unfair dismissal cases, first attempts at ADR through telephone conferences may precede a hearing before a tribunal member but this is not mandatory. According to a survey undertaken for the FWC, more than 90 of unfair dismissal mediations and conciliations are undertaken by telephone (TNS Social Research 2010). The FWC members also utilize phone, Skype and video-conference mediation and conciliation meetings to deal with disputes, but this is confined to cases where it is requested by the parties or necessitated by problems of access or the need for an expeditious attempt at settlement. Overall the FWC exhibits a high degree of flexibility in the manner of conducting hearings, albeit not without complications.

While the benefit of technology has been in its ability to bring the parties together quickly, more cheaply and avoiding the delays associated with face-to-face meetings, it is sometimes riddled with complexities including problems with bandwidth and other technological problems, particularly given the vast geographical size of Australia and the inconsistency in standards of telecommunications technology available to different regions. The inability of phone conciliators and FWC members to detect body language emerged as an important human issue related to settlement by ADR. The same observation was made by MacDermott and Riley (2012:94) who noted that:

This can affect the rapport that develops between the parties, which in turn may affect the parties' capacity to engage in a genuine problem solving and interests based negotiation that is the foundation of the mediation model on which conciliation is based.

Members are highly experienced and trained in ADR, and this includes the ability to read body language and the capacity to judge when to call for a private caucus or to pose some careful questions. In this way they may be able to bring the parties to an agreement which they can both accept. While the settlement rate in phone conciliation appeared to be tracking well at the FWC, and an early evaluation by independent consultancy firm TNS Social Research (2010) reported that some 86 % of applicants and 88 % of respondents indicated that phone conciliation was both convenient and cost effective, this was not conclusive. FWC members noted concerns that some parties perceived pressure to settle, and the FWC introduced a three-day 'cooling off' period so unrepresented litigants had time to reconsider what they had agreed by phone (for a review of this see Centre for Innovative Justice 2013). Alternatively it can be argued that in some situations, telephone conferencing can alleviate power imbalances and remove the discomfort associated with face to face interactions. More generally, where the case is simple, telephone conferencing may be the most effective means of resolution (Macdermott and Riley 2012:95).

The third area for innovation in the FWC has been in the area of future planning and strategic initiatives. The FWC sees itself in transition from its traditional role in the settlement of collective disputes to one where its focus is on individual, and in particular, once-off self-represented litigants. As part of this transition, FWC now plays a greater role in stakeholder engagement, and participating in industry conferences and in research partnerships. This is perceived as a part of a process of proactive engagement in which the services of the FWC will develop organically; it also aligns with the ethos of client centred delivery of public services. These sentiments and the underlying risks are captured in the speakers notes attached to a presentation by the President of the Fair Work Commission:

> Justice institutions rely ultimately on public confidence and the consent of the governed. There was an urgent need to repair the reputational damage to the Commission. We had to become more efficient and accountable. We

sought to address these challenges through a new change program – called Future Directions. (Ross 2014:3–4)

While such an approach to the development of processes and procedures is superficially attractive, in the final analysis the tribunal may be called on to conduct an arbitral function. At this point, considerations of 'public value' defined in terms of measures including efficiency, accessibility and informality may come to erode the legitimacy of organization among its potential users.

Conclusions

The future of workplace dispute resolution in Australia, as in countries such as Canada and the UK, lies in its ability to meet a jurisdiction dominated by individual disputes. In Australia, there are two main features in the response. First there is greater reliance on information and communication technologies both to provide ADR and also in the processes of information, education and support. Second, there has been a major shift to more flexible and informal processes to accommodate the needs of individual and unrepresented parties appearing before the tribunal. As the literature canvassed above demonstrates, these responses are not unique to Australia, although the extent of such responses is distinctive.

With the greater use of communication technologies comes a raft of new issues which pose challenges to tribunal members, such as emerging requirements for training in social media and training in therapeutic mediation to deal with emotionally charged litigants. For the FWC itself it has meant compensating for the absence of body language when mediating by phone or Internet by introducing a cooling-off period, and providing considerable investment into a growing pool of resources to deal with the difficulties self-represented litigants face in making their case.

Acknowledgment We wish to thank Dr. Robyn Cochrane for her assistance in coding and analysing the interviews and her help in managing the wider project on workplace dispute resolution in Australia.

References

Aston, J., Hill, D., & Djan Tackey, N. (2006). The experience of claimants in race discrimination Employment Tribunal cases. *Department for Trade & Industry Employment Relations Research Series*, No. 55.

Centre for Innovative Justice. (2013). *Report for Fair Work Commission assessment of cooling off period pilot in unfair dismissals conciliation process*. https://www.fwc.gov.au/documents/documents/dismissals/cooling-off-period-assessment.pdf. Accessed 24 Sept 2015.

Creswell, J.W. (2005). *Educational research: Planning, conducting, and evaluating quantitative and qualitative research*. Upper Saddle River, NJ: Merrill.

Creswell, J. W. (2009). *Research design: Qualitative, quantitative, and mixed methods approaches*. Thousand Oaks, CA: SAGE Publications, Inc.

Davey, B., & Dix, G. (2011). The dispute resolution regulations two years on: The Acas experience. *Acas Research Paper*, 07/11.

Dickens, L. (2014). The coalition government's reforms to employment tribunals and statutory employment rights – Echoes of the past. *Industrial Relations Journal*, 45(3), 234–249.

Dix, G., Sisson, K., & Forth, J. (2009). Conflict at work: The changing pattern of disputes. In W. Brown, A. Bryson, J. Forth, & K. Whitfield (Eds.), *The evolution of the modern workplace*. Cambridge: Cambridge University Press.

Downer, M., Harding, C., Ghezelayagh, S., Fu, E., & Gkiza, M. (2015). Evaluation of Acas early conciliation 2015. *Acas Research Paper*, 04/15.

Fair Work Commission. (2014a). *Annual Report 2013–2014: Australia's national workplace relations tribunal*. Melbourne, VIC: Fair Work Commission.

Fair Work Commission. (2014b). What happens at a Conciliation?. *Virtual Video Tour Series*. https://www.youtube.com/watch?v=rHX6zFcvX3M. Accessed 24 Sept 2015.

Fair Work Commission. (2015). *Continuing the change program: Future directions 2014–15 progress report*. Available from: https://www.fwc.gov.au/documents/documents/media/fd2-continuing-change-program.pdf. Accessed 25 Sept 2015.

Faulks, J. (2013). *Self-represented litigants: Tackling the challenge*. Managing People in Court Conference, National Judicial College of Australia and the Australian National University. http://njca.com.au/wp-content/uploads/2013/07/Justice-Faulks.pdf. Accessed 26 Sept 2015.

High Court of Australia. (2012). *Annual report 2011–2012*. Kingston, ON: ACT.

MacDermott, T., & Riley, J. (2012). ADR and industrial tribunals: Innovations and challenges in resolving individual workplace grievances. *Monash University Law Review, 38*(2), 82–102.

McCallum, R., Riley, J., & Stewart, A. (2013). Resolving disputes over employment rights in Australia. *Comparative Labor Law & Policy Journal, 34*(4), 843–876.

Productivity Commission. (2015). *Workplace relations framework: Draft report.* http://www.pc.gov.au/inquiries/current/workplace-relations/draft. Accessed 25 Sept 2015.

Ross, J. I. (2014). *Future directions – Improving institutional performance and the concept of 'Public Value'.* https://www.fwc.gov.au/documents/speeches/IRSNSW-notes-24-May-2014.pdf. Accessed 25 Sept 2015.

Shilton, E., & Banks, K. (2014). *The changing role of Labor Relations Board in Canada: Key research questions for the 21st century.* Kingston, ON: Centre for Law in the Contemporary Workplace, Queen's University.

Shulruf, B., Woodhams, B., Howard, C., Johri, R., & Yee, B. (2009). Grievance gravy train picking up speed: Myths and reality around employment disputes in New Zealand. *Journal of Industrial Relations, 51*(2), 245–261.

Souter, C. (2015, March). The future of Employment Tribunals. *CAS Employment Newsletter,* 1–10.

TNS Social Research. (2010). *Fair Work Australia Unfair Dismissal Conciliation Research.* Fyshwick, South Canberra: ACT.

Van Gramberg, G. (2006). *Managing workplace conflict: ADR in Australian workplaces.* Sydney, NSW: Federation Press.

13

Workplace Mediation Schemes: Antagonism and Articulation in the Discursive Process of Organizational Conflict and Disputes

Louise McArdle and Pete Thomas

Introduction

In recent years the role of mediation in workplace dispute resolution has increased and has been lauded as a means of efficiently handling conflicts and resolving, and even avoiding, antagonistic employment relationships. Empirical research has highlighted the positive impact of workplace mediation, with studies finding high rates of resolution and satisfaction amongst the parties to the process (for example: Bingham and Pitts 2002; Latreille and Saundry 2014). Some contributions to the literature on mediation, such as Bush and Folger (2005) and also recent UK Government evaluations (Department of Business, Innovation and Skills 2011), even

L. McArdle
School of Management, University of Central Lancashire, Preston, UK
e-mail: LMC-ardle@uclan.ac.uk

P. Thomas
Lancaster University Management School, Lancaster University, Lancaster, UK
e-mail: p.thomas2@lancaster.ac.uk

© The Editor(s) (if applicable) and The Author(s) 2016
R. Saundry et al. (eds.), *Reframing Resolution*,
DOI 10.1057/978-1-137-51560-5_13

265

suggest that it offers the potential to trigger broader transformations in workplace relations and culture, and mediation can sometimes invoke a somewhat evangelical fervour amongst its proponents. However, despite there being good empirical accounts of the process and impact of mediation there is very little written that offers a more conceptual or theoretical perspective on mediation in the workplace. Within the industrial relations literature, where most accounts of workplace mediation are to be found, theoretical aspects of work are rarely made explicit (Edwards 2011).

In this chapter we attempt to correct this by providing a more theory-informed account of mediation, conceptualizing how and why mediation schemes are developed in organizations, beyond the impetus that the standard promised 'benefits' offer to organizational actors. We offer a more 'politically' nuanced account of mediation that considers the interests and power of various 'stakeholders' in the mediation process and can provide an understating of how mediation schemes can unfold in organizations. To do this, we explore the introduction of in-house mediation into an NHS Primary Care Trust (PCT) in the North of England, using a Critical Discourse Analysis (CDA) approach (Chouliaraki and Fairclough 1999). Specifically, we use an adapted version of Laclau and Mouffes's (1985) analytical framework to explore the discursive processes involved in this development, and to understand the ways in which antagonistic articulations on the part of various individuals and groups shaped what mediation came to mean in that context, and helped shape broader workplace relations.

We begin the chapter by briefly reviewing the literature on the contested nature of mediation, and the roles and responses of different 'stakeholders' in its establishment as a dispute resolution process. There is a notable gap in the research to date, and a need for work which explores and conceptualizes the social processes around the implementation of mediation schemes. The paper then introduces the CDA perspective and specifically Laclau and Mouffe's (1985) work on discourse and social practice, which we propose as an appropriate way to understand the processes through which the 'discourse' of mediation develops and meanings are shared or contested. We then introduce our case material beginning with the methodological underpinnings of the research. The findings define the research 'conjuncture,' and explore the development of the grievance and partnership discourses and analyse the trade union role in the development of mediation. We then conclude by briefly evaluating the contribution of the framework.

Workplace Mediation, Conflict and Discourse

Workplace mediation is a growing area of activity in contemporary organizations (Latreille 2011), and was given added impetus in the UK by the publication of the Gibbons Review (2007), which saw mediation as a means of speedy dispute resolution and reducing the burdens placed on employers, employees and the state. A good deal of the literature supports this positive evaluation of the idea and, as Gaynier (2005) and Ridley-Duff and Bennett (2011) describe, mediation has been promoted with some stridency. Mediation is said to exhibit clear advantages over more traditional grievance and disciplinary processes (Anderson and Bingham 1997; Fox 2005; Sergeant 2005; Goldberg 2005; CIPD 2007), and there may be indirect benefits from mediation such as the improvement of management skills and problem solving capacity (Bingham 2004; Kressel 2006; Saundry et al. 2013). In summarizing the supposed benefits of mediation, Latreille (2011), following Lynch (2001), identifies five basic motives for using mediation: compliance, cost, crisis, competition and culture. However, such a summary rather underplays the potentially contested nature of mediation and the differential impact the process can have on different groups and individuals within an organization.

In short, the literature generally tends to frame mediation in a managerialist or functionalist way, situated within a unitaristic discourse where it is essentially conceptualized as a managerial solution to the 'problem' of conflict without acknowledging the variable effects such schemes might have on different interest groups. For example, the cost advantage of mediation (Lipsky and Seeber 1998; Lynch 2001) to an organization will be of little interest to a trade union which feels its role is being diminished by the individualized nature of mediation (Colling 2004; Gospel and Edwards 2011), and which encourages the co-option of employees and masks a coercive form of employee relations (Hyman 1987). The traditional managerialist view of mediation serves to decontextualize and depoliticize workplace problems (Seaman 2010), whilst potentially becoming an object of dispute itself. For this reason there is a need to develop an analytical framework that conceptualizes the socio-political processes involved in implementing and operating mediation in the workplace, so as to develop a richer understanding of contemporary practices. In order to do this we propose a discourse-based theorization using the

CDA approach of Chouliariki and Fairclough (1999), and their development of Laclau and Mouffe's (1985) discourse theory.

Discourse Analysis has emerged as a popular approach to organizational research in the last 10 years (Grant et al. 2004), though not without controversy, debate and dispute (Alvesson and Kärreman 2011; Iedema 2011; Mumby 2011; Bargiela-Chiappini 2011). Discourse analysis is diverse in nature, both conceptually and methodologically (Alvesson and Kärreman 2000), so it is necessary to spell out the conception of discourse that underpins our ideas. We share Chouliariki and Fairclough's CDA (1999) view of discourse, as an important aspect of social practice, inasmuch as discourse is a significant mode of representation of social practices, and plays a significant role in constituting those practices. Like Chouliaraki and Fairclough (1999), however, we prefer to consider discourse as significant alongside other moments of social practice (Harvey 1996), such as: values and emotions; institutions and rituals; power relations and materiality. No social practice is reducible to one moment, nor is any individual moment wholly explainable by any other. Instead we must consider discourse as one of several interrelated moments, and acknowledge that in taking a discourse focus we cannot allow ourselves to lose sight of the others. CDA provides an opportunity to consider the ways in which discourse shapes power and knowledge relations within which subjects are positioned, subjectivities constructed and bodies disciplined or, put another way, how identities, social relations and knowledge systems are constructed (Fairclough 2003; Ainsworth and Hardy 2004). All of these issues are relevant to our consideration of mediation which is itself a knowledge (and belief) system and which involves specific types of social relation and identity.

In developing the link between discourse and social practice Chouliaraki and Fairclough (1999) have drawn on the work of Laclau and Mouffe (1985), which is of particular relevance to this paper because, whilst their framework is quite general in focus, Laclau and Mouffe do make specific reference to the labour process as one of the features of capitalist society that might be better understood through its use. In their brief examination of the labour process in capitalist society, they argue that 'workers' abilities to resist domination in the workplace depend upon their position within an *ensemble of social relations*, and not just the relations of production. In contrast to the then orthodox Marxist view they reject the idea of a homogenous working class, and similarly reject the notion of a singular form of managerial control. Foregoing a structural determinism for a more contingent process of struggle and antagonism, they present a view of the labour process similar to that of Edwards (1990). As he states:

> Structured antagonism is a basic feature of any exploitative mode of production and...consent, tacit skills, the negotiation of order and so forth have to be understood as shaping how this antagonism is developed and not as principles which can totally counteract it. (Edwards 1990:147).

As Phillips and Jørgensen (2002, 25–26) suggest, Laclau and Mouffe's take on discourse analysis is a means by which we can 'map out the processes in which we struggle about the way in which the meaning of signs is to be fixed, and the processes by which some fixations of meaning become so conventionalized that we think of them as natural,' and also understand the discursive struggles that characterize social practices. In any social field actors strive to fix the meaning of signs, by relating them to other signs in ways which they find socially or politically beneficial. For example, the meaning of 'mediation' depends upon the signs to which it is related by social actors. From a managerial point of view it might be related to the signs of efficiency or economy and thus becomes meaningful in these terms. Alternatively, a trade unionist might relate it to a discourse of individualization in the work-place, thus imbuing it with meaning that is associated with a challenge to collective representation. However, the meaning of any sign is never fixed, as it is constantly brought into relation with other signs that might disrupt its meaning, thus the social field is characterized by struggle and antagonism. Laclau and Mouffe (1985) describe signs as *elements*, which when related together can become *moments*, with a (temporary) fixation of meaning. Meaning becomes fixed around what they term *nodal points*, that is, privileged signs around which other signs are ordered. In an organizational context an example of a nodal point might be 'strategy,' a discourse around which many moments of organizing are ordered. Meaning emerges as possible alternatives are excluded in the *field of discursivity*, creating a unified system of meaning or discourse (Phillips and Jørgensen 2002). In more straightforward terms, social practices involve a constant struggle to fix the meanings of concepts through *articulation*, a political process which is inherent in the social.

Chouliaraki and Fairclough (1999) argue that Laclau and Mouffe (1985) overplay the degree of contingency evident in social practices, and suggest that some social forces will have more influence over articulatory practices than others, evidenced by patterns in meaning across different practices and contexts. It is abundantly clear that in many contexts social actors do not have equal opportunities to make articulations or equal capacity to fix meanings through that process. To avoid seeing meaning within these practices as permanently provisional and endlessly open to new meaning, whilst also avoiding structural determinism, Chouliariki and Fairclough (1999) develop the idea of conjunctures, that is, relatively durable assemblies of people and practices that come together around specific social projects. Conjunctures exhibit relative stability, but also hold the possibility of change, though the range of possible changes is limited, thus avoiding the excessive contingency of Laclau and Mouffe's (1985) ideas.

Phillips and Jørgensen (2002) argue that the primacy of politics is a feature of Laclau and Mouffe's thinking. This politicized view of social organization sits well with the antagonism that Edwards (1990) sees as characteristic of workplace relations, and allows an understanding that goes beyond the usual class or relations of production explanations of conflict. The process of antagonism is played out in struggles over articulation within organizations; for example, Thomas and Hewitt (2011) recently used Laclau and Mouffe's work to examine the ways in which managers and clinicians articulated their ideas of professionalism in the context of Clinical Governance initiatives in a Primary Care Trust (PCT) in the NHS. A framework that acknowledges struggle and uses the idea of articulation might be useful in the context of the employment relations that surround mediation, being an appropriate way of conceptualizing the social relations that take place between those involved in the development and practice of mediation in the workplace. It would seem to counter the simplistic view of mediation as simply a means of managerial control, as it represents a rejection of the unilateral managerial authority implicit within conventional procedures, and also involves recognition of the validity of the conflicting views inherent in organizations. To explore its value further, we will now apply the framework to the development of a mediation scheme in a specific organization.

Methodology

The research upon which this chapter is based took a multiple method approach which was used to construct a case study of mediation in the respondent organization, a Primary Care Trust (PCT) in the NHS. The research explicitly sought to examine the effects of the development and implementation of mediation on relationships between key groups in the employment relations process, most notably senior trust managers, HR professionals and trade union officials representing several employee groups. The research strategy comprised two main elements: archival research and a programme of semi-structured interviews with key respondents in the PCT. Several archival sources were used in the research, beginning with the examination of policies and procedures relating to various aspects of employment relations in the Trust, including grievance, discipline and performance management. In addition, several sources of statistical data were accessed: firstly, statistics relating to the frequency (and outcomes) of grievance and disciplinary cases, mediations and tribunal applications, secondly, data from three consecutive years of the staff attitude survey, and thirdly, published figures on absenteeism and staff turnover.

The second element of the research strategy involved a programme of nineteen semi-structured interviews with key organizational actors. This did not include individuals who had been through mediation but focused on those involved in its development; that is, individuals who were pivotal to the introduction of mediation at PCT. Overall, five members of HR staff (broadly defined) were interviewed, drawn from advisor, manager and director level, three of whom were also trained mediators. One HR manager, who was primarily responsible for the introduction of the scheme, was interviewed twice. Six operational managers were interviewed, drawn from different areas of the organization, of which three were trained mediators. Six trade union representatives were interviewed, five from UNISON, the largest recognized trade union, and one from Unite, though one of the UNISON respondents had been the Royal College of Nursing (RCN) representative until recently. Three of the union respondents were trained mediators, and the other three had no direct involvement with the mediation scheme. Finally, the external consultant who had provided the initial mediation training was also interviewed. The majority of the interviews were conducted face-to-face, but three were conducted by telephone for logistical reasons and in total just under 20 hours of interview data were recorded.

Transcripts of the interviews were used as the basis of the qualitative analysis, the data being coded around several themes. Firstly, conjunctural characteristics prior to the development of mediation were examined in relation to data from documentary sources. Respondent views on the relations between HR, union representatives and operational managers were examined in the context of broader developments in and around the PCT. Secondly, the data was analysed for evidence of new opportunities and forms of articulation being evident in the relations between the three groups. In particular we looked for evidence of nodal points in the case, that is, discourses that had particular influence on the way in which the meaning of mediation became fixed in the PCT. Finally, we considered the position of individuals in this discursive process and the impact it had on the identity of key people.

Findings

In our analysis of mediation in the PCT we focus on a number of aspects of Laclau and Mouffe's (1985) discourse theory. We begin by defining the boundaries of the *conjuncture*, before showing how the development of mediation was shaped by two *nodal points*, 'grievance culture' and 'partnership,' two discursive features against which a range of *elements* were defined, helping to shape a shared understanding or temporarily *fixed meaning* for mediation. We also consider the opportunities that arose for articulation by groups and individuals involved in the development of mediation, and the ways in which the discursive resources available to them changed.

Defining the Conjuncture

Our first task must be to define the appropriate conjuncture for this piece of research. Theoretically, the conjuncture could be the entire NHS project, or at the other end of the scale, an instance of local service provision within the PCT. For the purposes of this research we have framed the PCT itself as the conjuncture, though it was made up of several different services and functions, and was geographically dispersed. The logic for this will become clear through the following analysis, but this definition would also be recognized by the respondents interviewed, who despite working within separate services did tend to identify with the PCT as the appropriate umbrella organization for their work.

Within the case, three groups emerge as significant in relation to the development of mediation: the HR function, the trade union representatives (often referred to by respondents as 'staff side'), and operational management, heading up specific services within the PCT. The interplay of relations between the three groups (and between significant individuals within each group) is very evident in the account of how mediation was developed and run, and our analysis focuses on the political processes the groups engaged in, especially on attempts to fix discursive meaning through articulation. It would be inaccurate to present the groups as homogenous, as some significant differences of opinion were evident in the data collected and we also found that the role of key individuals was very influential on the way in which mediation developed. In the ensemble of social relations, these individuals did not always adhere to the expected collective views and responses, and articulations within the local 'field of discursivity' were not wholly determined by broader structural or sociopolitical factors, such as the policy positions of the various groups, but were sometimes locally determined by the social practices of individual actors.

At the time of the research[1] the PCT was responsible for commissioning primary care in an area of the North West of England serving 386,000 people, and covering services such as general practitioners, dentists, pharmacists, opticians and other community provision. PCTs were substantial organizations, responsible for around 80 % of the total NHS spend in the UK and providing the majority of services that are most used by the population. The PCT employed more than 2,700 employees (April 2010), a fairly stable figure, though influenced by the transfer of some staff to other agencies. At the time of the research the PCT was facing external pressure regarding service provision and it was thought that some services would be lost to other providers, making for an uncertain environment for all members of the organization.

---

[1] PCTs were abolished in 2013, following the passing of the Health and Social Care Bill 2011 in March 2012. The responsibilities of the PCT largely passed to General Practitioner-led Commissioning Consortia.

Employee relations within the PCT were conducted in the context of far reaching changes in NHS management, including the formation of the PCT itself from the reorganization of a number of separate bodies, and more specifically were shaped by the NHS *Agenda for Change* grading and pay system, agreed in 2004, which is claimed to improve flexibility and fairness in terms and conditions (NHS Employers Organization 2011). The formal structure of employment relations in the Trust reflected patterns in the NHS as a whole. Several trade unions and employee organizations were recognized, including UNISON, UNITE, the Royal College of Nursing (RCN) and the British Medical Association (BMA), with trust-level collective bargaining and consultation taking place through the Joint Consultative and Negotiating Committee. In 2006/2007 a Partnership Framework agreement was made within the newly formed PCT with the stated aim of 'fostering long-term good relations between unions, staff and managers, based on common interest which promote the PCT's performance, the quality of working life for staff and enhanced patient care.' A revised 'Workforce Partnership Agreement Framework' was introduced in 2009, which set out the role played by trade union representatives within PCT. A designated 'partnership lead' would oversee and coordinate staff side representatives, with a specific responsibility to 'analyse and monitor grievances, disciplinary cases and fair treatment complaints.' Thus the management and resolution of individual conflict was explicitly seen as within the overall scope of partnership.

The Grievance Culture Discourse

Employee relations in the PCT prior to the introduction of mediation were heavily characterized by conflict, a view shared by both management and unions. A discourse of conflict permeated relations between management and unions at this time. As one of the operational managers reported there was 'a really typical confrontational conflict management style if you like, where there was an "us and them," *management versus staff side situation.*' Generally, respondents identified that there was a lack of trust between union representatives and management (both operational and HR), coupled with insecurity associated with numerous organizational changes within the NHS. In simple terms this antagonism could be attributed to union militancy, and indeed, union representatives freely admitted that their style was confrontational:

> We went in always with a big hammer, trying to get a bigger hammer than they had. It was all of that – banging on the table; a lot of, this is what policies are. 'You'll do this or we'll do that and if you don't do that, we're going to grievance.' (Union Representative)

However, the situation was rather more complex. As several respondents suggested, the antagonism, which was largely centred in one service area but with a corrosive influence further afield, stemmed from an operational management style that drew confrontation from staff side. According to one senior HR manager operational managers did not treat union reps with much respect and there was a lack of openness in management, which meant that unions had little voice in the organization other than that exerted through formal processes. Indeed the HR lead on mediation described some operational managers as feeling themselves as having an 'absolute divine right' to manage, introducing changes with little or no consultation or discussion with staff side at all. As one union representative said, 'You couldn't sit down with management. Management never wanted to sit down with you.' Combined with the relative inexperience of some operational managers, some of whom seemed to relish the opportunity to adopt a heavy-handed 'business' approach, this provoked an aggressive response from union representatives, who felt formal procedures were the only means of asserting their voice in the PCT.

In terms of conflict resolution, the result, as described by several respondents, was a 'grievance culture,' which became a dominant discourse or nodal point in the conjuncture. Actions and communications were invariably interpreted and understood in relation to this grievance discourse, the conflict being so intense as to be seen as a culture in its own right. For example, management respondents claimed that trade unions would immediately formalize employee grievances and encourage the submission of formal complaints on a wide range of issues. At the same time, management also tended to apply and enforce procedures very rigidly, 'sticking to policy' (union representative) with a degree of inflexibility that provoked a similarly stubborn response from union representatives.

In the absence of opportunities to articulate the interests of their members, unions were using the procedures to provide a platform for their collective voice, and reinforce their collective identity as a counter to management. One particular union representative, nicknamed the 'Grievance King,' a sobriquet he came to relish, was especially willing to use the grievance procedure as a means of resisting management. He commented,

> Sometimes I'd say I've got to go back and have a go at these people…. We'd go after certain managers but, equally, they would go after certain ones of us…. It was just a game of who's going to get each other.

Typically the outcome from this would be a protracted formal grievance process that, more often than not, would be found in the employee's favour.

In terms of our framework the development of the grievance culture discourse arose primarily from operational managers marginalizing staff in decision-making, and creating a context within which the only opportunity for staff and unions to articulate their interests was through formal procedures. This then became a nodal point around which individuals and groups developed meaning for processes of conflict resolution, and more generally the '(ill) health' of the employment relationship in the PCT. Managerially, the culture became a 'problematic' discourse, as the costs of formal processes were high, whilst from a union perspective the culture initially meant 'winning' and 'getting one over' on management, thereby simply reinforcing the distance between the groups. However, the situation would change, and a new nodal point would emerge within the conjuncture.

The Partnership Discourse

Attempts to remedy the climate of mistrust at the PCT began with the development of partnership working. While the Agenda for Change initiative had involved partnership working, this was largely construed by unions as a management tool to facilitate change in grading and pay systems. Thus they claimed that there was little 'real' partnership evident in management and staff relations. A key event that changed this was the appointment of an Acting Director of Human Resources who placed significant emphasis on building personal and direct relationships of trust with trade union representatives, changing the meaning of partnership in the trust and creating a different mode of partnership working.

The Director made a number of material changes to the partnership approach, including two significant developments: firstly, union representatives were given substantial facility time and access to resources, which allowed them to play a much more active role, but was also a clear sign that they were respected and valued by management. Secondly, trade unions were consulted to a greater extent and invited to meetings where key decisions were being discussed:

> They gave us the access to meetings; they gave us access to information. They were more open. And they were honest as well. You know, they acknowledged the fact that we do have issues and it was that open dialogue, and I think there was a development of trust. (Union representative)

Even the 'Grievance King' union representative recognized the positive changes. The new HR Director, who had brought partnership working to the organization, 'was very quick…getting parties round the table, which I always wanted and the union reps wanted.'

The 'investment' in partnership working brought about a new meaning for the process, with the unions now seeing it as a possible opportunity for constructive dialogue in the organization. For some operational managers the developments were seen as a threat, undermining their 'right to manage,' but others recognized that the staff side brought something positive to the organization:

> It puts them in a position where perhaps they feel they've got a greater voice in the outcome of something … And certainly I think it's been a positive move from a staff side point of view as well, because they have a big involvement. (Operational manager)

Some senior managers also believed that while these early attempts to develop partnership were positive they were fairly fragile and that actors could 'very, very quickly…revert to type' (Senior Manager).

The development of the partnership approach by the HR Director, seems to have had a significant impact on workplace relations within the PCT. Crucially, however, this was largely based on building high trust social relations between key individuals. Therefore, while there was still antagonism between management and unions at the level of specific disputes, there was now a better shared understanding of the corrosive culture that had prevailed and a broader view that it could and should be changed. In terms of our framework the development of this new nodal point was not simply born out of discursive actions. The new meaning of partnership was rooted in the material changes initiated by the HR Director that gave union representatives real opportunities and resources to participate in partnership activities. This also represented a symbolic change in the PCT, shaping new understandings of what partnership meant. Although some operational managers saw the changes as indicative of a decline in their right to manage, most respondents viewed them positively and partnership became the new nodal point around which the meaning of mediation would be created.

Developing Mediation and the Union Role

The mediation scheme in the PCT was developed at the point at which the 'grievance culture' discourse began to give way to the 'partnership' discourse. As Laclau and Mouffe's (1985) theory suggests, we cannot easily disentangle events and meanings, nor see them in simplistic sequences of actions and articulations; within the field of discursivity signs are continually brought into meaning against other signs. In this case the meaning of mediation emerges alongside the transformation of 'partnership' from a meaningless label to 'real' partnership between management and staff side.

Like the new partnership approach, the impetus for the introduction of the mediation scheme came from the Acting Director of HR, who had previously been responsible for introducing a similar scheme in another NHS organization. Often seen as a way of reducing the costs of grievance and dispute handling she also felt mediation would contribute to a different culture in the PCT. Recounting an early meeting with two union representatives (including the 'Grievance King'), she felt the situation they described was:

> ...clearly claim and counter claim, claim and counter claim, but all really relationship issues that, if we could just bring these people into the room and start talking, it was so obvious to me as a trained mediator, that 90 % of the issues they had would go away.

She got support and funding from the HR directors to develop the scheme, even though there was some suspicion of mediation within the HR function, which was 'out of the HR comfort zone' as it potentially threatened 'their professionalism' (Acting HR Director) and their adherence to 'safe' formal procedures.

The idea was strongly supported by senior management who saw the introduction of the scheme as reflective of a shift towards:

> ...a collaborative approach to managing employment relationship issues. This type of cultural development, aimed at minimizing the use of formal resolution processes is very effective in reducing costs and time for the organization and also has a more positive outcome for the individual. (PCT Annual Report and Accounts, 2008/2009).

However, trade unions were initially hostile to the proposal for similar reasons to the HR function; mediation threatened to take the central task of dispute resolution out of their hands, and some operational managers also saw the scheme as a further threat to their right to manage.

In order to begin to develop support for mediation, the HR Director encouraged one of the HR managers to be trained as a mediator by Acas. Importantly, the manager in question was well-respected by colleagues, and this established the credibility of mediation amongst the HR department. An awareness event was then held, involving about fifty people, including HR managers, operational managers and trade union representatives, and those interested in becoming mediators were identified. However, key union representatives were still extremely negative. In particular, they saw mediation as a deliberate strategy to blunt their ability to fully represent members:

At the time it was regarded with great suspicion because some union representatives felt it was a way for management to pull the union's teeth.... No, this is to get rid of the only way we have a voice. (Union representative)

Initially, the mediation scheme was interpreted by unions as a deliberate attempt at incorporation and identity regulation. Even the awareness event represented an opportunity for resistance to managerial control and an opportunity to bolster the union line on conflict resolution. The HR Director had identified the 'Grievance King' as one of a number of key individuals who were targeted to take part in the event, for three reasons. Firstly, as the lead representative he would deal with the largest number of individual cases. Secondly, he came from a part of the organization that had a high number of disputes. Thirdly, and most significantly, he was well respected by union representatives and by staff and therefore his validation of mediation would help to reduce opposition, suspicion and resistance. His initial reaction at the event was perhaps predictably negative but after some discussion with other union officials and a period of reflection, however, he decided to participate in the mediation training programme, though he still thought he would 'kibosh' it if necessary.

At this stage it was clear that the Acting HR Director recognized the importance of changing the meaning of mediation in the organization and focused her attention on key opinion formers in the HR function and the union. However, the process cannot really be seen as one of simple manipulation and co-option, as she seems to have been intent on letting groups and individuals arrive at their view of mediation without too much direct influence on her part. For example, the way in which the mediation training was designed and conducted did not seek to sidestep or underplay the pervasive adversarial employee relations in PCT. Instead it used existing employer–union conflicts as a focus. There was time to discuss existing issues of mistrust and conflict; role-play exercises dealt with real situations facing the organization; and individuals had to take roles that would challenge existing assumptions, union representatives taking on management roles and vice versa.

Existing divisions between unions and management were very clear, even physically, 'you had staff side people sat over here and you had managers sat over there' (Operational Manager). Participants were encouraged to air grievances and explain how they felt about the roles played by managers, employees and unions; a critical area of discussion being 'the right to manage.' Despite difficult discussions all those respondents (HR, operational management and union representatives) who had attended the training believed that this approach was necessary in order to shift entrenched attitudes and establish trust between the mediators. In the language of our framework, this was a process within which different positions and views could be openly articulated, perhaps for the first time, with groups that were usually seen as opponents. From this process there was a clear sense of a transformative impact on those that involved, and in particular on those participants who had previously adopted a confrontational approach to disputes:

> During the training, it was like these eureka moments. You could see people having these, like, oh you know, really enlightening, you know, light bulbs switching on and things like this that they could see the value of, you know, using mediation. (Operational Manager)

The 'Grievance King,' who had been very sceptical of the entire concept and process, explained that the mediation training had helped him to understand (for the first time) the perspective of managers: 'Mediation gets people to sit in the other person's shoes…until you can understand what pressure somebody's under, or how they think, you know, don't judge them.' Not only did he now recognize the perspective of managers but he also began to see that an approach based on dispute resolution as opposed to adversarial resistance would deliver improved outcomes for trade union members. However, it would be inaccurate to see the developments as involving the co-option of union officials. Their involvement was a very self-conscious and calculated move. As the 'Grievance King' said,

> Some [union representatives] were a bit sceptical thinking, 'Hang on a minute, have we been sucked in here?' but the vast majority would say, 'If **you** like it, [knowing what my previous was, which is grievance king and everything else] you've either been brainwashed within six, seven days or you genuinely think it is a better way'…. And I said, 'But if we don't stop all

these grievances we're going to end up in a mine full of problems.... So let's give it a go, give it a little while, give it a year or so and see what happens.'

During the training the shared meaning of dispute resolution was changed from one of a conflict to be won at the expense of opponents, to one more focused on understanding the 'other side' and arriving at resolutions that would benefit union members and employees, as well as the organization. Given their success with grievances there was no necessity for union officials to give ground to management, but as more common ground on the meaning of conflict and appropriate forms of resolution was found the hostile antagonism seems to have given way to a more 'cooperative' struggle, with renewed dialogue and better mutual understanding.

Despite the expectation that union officials would feel mediation undermined their role and risked atomizing the collective role of the union, the most significant discomfort was found amongst operational managers. Line managers had to agree to mediation being used, and the mediation agreement stated that if parties were unable to resolve their dispute, 'normal' management process may be implemented. Even so, managers were concerned that the mediation process could undermine their authority and their ability to manage. As one mediator commented,

> They couldn't see why it was taken out of their hands. It was a control issue for managers you know. They regarded themselves as not managing if they were not actually doing the thing that fixed the problem. So it was trying to convince managers to relinquish control in order to gain more control.

Such managerial concerns were made more acute by the appointment of the 'Grievance King' as one of the scheme co-coordinators. His previous militant and confrontational style increased the threat that managers felt, heightening their sense of the risk of losing control and their 'right to manage' disputes, '...you can imagine that gave lots of scepticisms, because of this person who was now coming and saying mediation, mediation, mediation. So that I think was quite a big barrier for a lot of managers across a lot of levels.' (Operational Manager).

Most union representatives initially had mixed feelings about the scheme. Those uninvolved in the training were concerned that the mediation discourse and the associated discursive and social practices were a deliberate attempt to reduce union influence, and that opting for mediation was in some way conceding defeat. However, the 'Grievance King's' assurances were listened to and some got involved in the scheme as mediators or through making referrals:

> And the more people got involved and members were going back to their staff rep saying, 'Hi, we've got it resolved, a lot better than I thought. You know, a bit frightened when I went but I think a better outcome.'

Indeed, as the scheme progressed, clear benefits for the union emerged. Firstly, it was suggested that the introduction of mediation had facilitated informal processes of resolution which in turn generated improved outcomes for members, 'You've got the member back to work; you've got the situation where there's a better working environment for the member.' (Union representative) Secondly, union respondents claimed that this had also led to increased membership and a strengthened union organization. A clear demarcation was kept between individual disputes, appropriate for mediation and the collective representation process. There was also always the option to revert to the formal process if mediation did not work, so the union representatives did not feel that the mediation scheme had undermined their position. The position from which they articulated their views had changed and the grievance culture had been dismantled, but to be replaced by what the officials thought was a more positive, co-operative, and no less strong position.

Conclusion

The developments at the PCT would seem to fit into the theoretical framework we have proposed, which provides an appropriate way to conceptualize the changes that took place. The role of managers and trade union officials in the development of the scheme has to be placed in context; that is, the conjuncture of social and power relations and institutional structures that were found in the Trust at the time. The data shows that meaning played a central part in the development of the mediation scheme, and the move from the 'grievance culture' (nodal point) to 'partnership' was of great significance in the process. Partnership provided union representatives with greater opportunities to articulate their views and interests and also built trust and confidence in the motives of the Acting Director of HR, who was championing the introduction of mediation.

Whilst the mediation scheme was initiated by HR, there was no evidence that there was any co-option of the unions into the scheme. The union representatives became involved in the developments with a high degree of scepticism, if not hostility, and fully aware that such schemes could undermine their role in representing members. Equally there was no evidence to suggest the scheme was developed with a view to challenging or undermining the unions. Acknowledging the antagonism between operational managers and unions, the HR managers seemed to see the scheme as a means to develop a new, less antagonistic discourse in the case of individual conflicts, in short replacing the discourse of grievance with that of resolution.

For Laclau and Mouffe (1985) political processes are at play in social organization through struggles between discourses. In our case these processes are evident at several levels. Firstly, there is an underlying discourse of industrial relations shaping the ways in which union officials and managers relate to each other; the basic antagonism that Edwards (1990) identifies. In the PCT this antagonism was sedimented and intensified by local circumstances into a second discourse, that of the 'grievance culture,' which then shaped the discursive and political activities of social agents in the conjuncture. However, such discourses, though dominant, remained fluid, and the revitalized 'partnership' discourse evolved to provide a different political environment, within which new articulations and positions could be developed. What is also evident in our case is the role of individuals in the ensemble of social relations. The Acting HR Director and the 'Grievance King,' both played significant roles in shaping the meaning of mediation and in fixing that meaning with other social actors in the conjuncture. The implication of this is that we cannot simply look at structural influences on discourse, or even the collective 'views' of groups as the defining elements in shaping meaning, we must also acknowledge the contingent influence of specific people at specific times. Although this makes for uncomfortable 'theorizing,' as it limits generalizing about particular phenomena, it seems more realistic and still allows us to identify political processes that may be evident in other contexts. In addition, it provides one way of developing an alternative to the binary distinction between managerialist approaches that sees dispute resolution processes as means of correcting the problem of workplace conflict, and perspectives which locate such initiatives within managerial attempts to restrict the influence of labour within the relations of production. Instead by focusing on the way in which the interests of workers and managers are constituted and reconstituted through an ensemble of social relations, including the personal relations between individual actors, we are able to develop a more nuanced understanding of the changing nature of workplace employment relations.

References

Acas/TUC. (2010). *Mediation: A guide for trade union representatives*. London: Acas/TUC. http://www.Acas.org.uk/index.aspx?articleid=1680. Accessed 14 Sept 2015.

Ainsworth, S., & Hardy, C. (2004). Discourse and identities. In D. Grant, C. Hardy, C. Oswick, & L. Putnam (Eds.), *Handbook of organizational discourse*. London: Sage.

Alvesson, M., & Kärreman, D. (2000). Varieties of discourse: On the study of organizations through discourse analysis. *Human Relations, 53*(9), 1125–1149.

Alvesson, M., & Kärreman, D. (2011). Decolonializing discourse: Critical reflections on organizational discourse analysis. *Human Relations, 64*(9), 1121–1146.

Anderson, L., & Bingham, L. (1997). Upstream effects from mediation of workplace disputes: Some preliminary evidence from the USPS. *Labor Law Journal, 48*(October), 601–615.

Bargiela-Chiappini, F. (2011). Discourse(s), social construction and language practices: In conversation with Alvesson and Kärreman. *Human Relations, 64*(9), 1177–1191.

Bingham, L. (2004). Employment dispute resolution. *Conflict Resolution Quarterly, 22*(1–2), 145–174.

Bingham, L., & Pitts, D. (2002). Highlights of mediation at work: Studies of the national REDRESS evaluation project. *Negotiation Journal, 18*(2), 149–160.

BIS. (2011). *Resolving workplace disputes: Government response to the consultation*. London: BIS.

Bush, R., & Folger, J. (2005). *The promise of mediation: The transformative approach to conflict* (Revised ed.). San Francisco: Jossey-Bass.

Chouliaraki, L., & Fairclough, N. (1999). *Discourse in late modernity*. Edinburgh, Scotland: Edinburgh University Press.

Colling, T. (2004). No claim, no pain? The privatization of dispute resolution in Britain. *Economic and Industrial Democracy, 25*(4), 555–579.

Edwards, P. (1990). Understanding conflict in the labour process: The logic and autonomy of struggle. In D. Knights, & H. Willmott (Eds.), *Labour process theory* (pp. 125–152). London: Macmillan.

Edwards, P. (2011). Message from the Editor-in-Chief. *Human Relations, 65*(1), 3–4.

Fairclough, N. (2003). *Analysing discourse: Textual analysis for social research*. London: Routledge.

Fox, M. (2005). *Evaluation of the Acas pilot of mediation and employment law visits to small companies*. London: Acas.

Gaynier, L. (2005). Transformative mediation: In search of a theory of practice. *Conflict Resolution Quarterly, 22*(3), 397–408.

Gibbons, M. (2007). *A review of employment dispute resolution in Great Britain*. London: DTI.

Goldberg, S. (2005). How interest based grievance mediation performs in the long term. *Dispute Resolution Journal, 60*(4), 8–15.

Gospel, H., & Edwards, P. (2011). Transformation and muddling through: Industrial relations and industrial training in the UK. *SKOPE Research Paper No. 106*. Cardiff: SKOPE.

Grant, D., Hardy, C., Oswick, C., & Putnam, L. (2004). *Handbook of organizational discourse*. London: Sage.

Harvey, D. (1996). *Justice, nature and the geography of difference*. Oxford: Blackwell.

Hyman, R. (1987). Strategy of structure: Capital, labour and control. *Work, Employment and Society, 1*(1), 25–55.

Iedema, R. (2011). Discourse studies in the 21st century: A response to Mats Alvesson and Dan Kärreman's "Decolonializing discourse". *Human Relations, 64*(9), 1163–1176.

Kressel, K. (2006). Mediation revisited. In M. Deutsch, & P. Coleman (Eds.), *The handbook of constructive conflict resolution: Theory and practice*. San Francisco: Jossey-Bass

Laclau, E., & Mouffe, C. (1985). *Hegemony and socialist strategy*. London: Verso.

Latreille, P. (2011). Mediation: A thematic review of the Acas/CIPD evidence. Acas Research Papers, 13/11.

Latreille, P., & Saundry, R. (2014). Mediation. In W. Roche, P. Teague, & A. Colvin (Eds.), *The Oxford handbook on conflict management in organizations*. Oxford: Oxford University Press.

Lipsky, D. B., & Seeber, R. L. (1998). In search of control: Corporate embrace of ADR University of Pennsylvania. *Journal of Labor and Employment Law*, *1*(1), 133–157.

Lynch, J. F. (2001). Beyond ADR: A systems approach to conflict management. *Negotiation Journal*, *17*(3), 207–216.

Mumby, D. K. (2011). What's cooking in organizational discourse studies? A response to Alvesson and Kärreman. *Human Relations*, *64*(9), 1147–1161.

NHS Employers Organization. (2011). *How Agenda for Change Works*. http://www.nhsemployers.org/PayAndContracts/AgendaForChange/Pages/Afc-AtAGlanceRP.aspx. Accessed 15 Sept 2015.

Phillips, L., & Jørgensen, W. (2002). *Discourse analysis as theory and method*. London: Sage.

Ridley-Duff, R., & Bennett, A. (2011). Towards mediation: Developing a theoretical framework to understand alternative dispute resolution. *Industrial Relations Journal*, *42*(2), 106–123.

Saundry, R., McArdle, L., & Thomas, P. (2013). Reframing workplace relations? Conflict resolution and mediation in a primary care trust. *Work, Employment and Society*, *27*(2), 212–231.

Seaman, R. (2010). Locating the mediator within workplace discourse: Supporter of the status quo or humble 'midwife' of dialogue? Developing an alternative workplace mediation practice. *Unpublished PhD thesis*, Bournemouth University.

Sergeant, J. (2005). *The Acas small firms mediation pilot: Research to explore parties' experiences and views on the value of mediation*. London: Acas.

Thomas, P., & Hewitt, J. (2011). Managerial organization and professional autonomy: A discourse-based conceptualization. *Organization Studies*, *32*(10), 1373–1393.

Part IV

New Perspectives on Conflict Management

14

The Evolution of Conflict Management Policies in US Corporations: From Reactive to Strategic

David B. Lipsky, Ariel C. Avgar, and J. Ryan Lamare

Introduction

Over the last four decades, the policies and practices used in the US to resolve workplace conflict have undergone a historic transformation. Beginning in the 1970s, a growing number of non-union employers, responding to a series of workplace statutes that had been passed by the US Congress, began to use alternative dispute resolution (ADR)

D.B. Lipsky (✉)
Scheinman Institute, ILR School/Cornell University, Ithaca, USA
e-mail: DBL4@cornell.edu

A.C. Avgar • J.R. Lamare
School of Labor and Employment Relations, University of Illinois,
Urbana-Champaign, USA
e-mail: avgar@illinois.edu; rlamare@illinois.edu

© The Editor(s) (if applicable) and The Author(s) 2016
R. Saundry et al. (eds.), *Reframing Resolution*,
DOI 10.1057/978-1-137-51560-5_14

to resolve disputes with their employees. At first, employers principally used arbitration and mediation on an *ad hoc* basis to handle their employees' statutory complaints. Over time, however, the case-by-case use of ADR evolved into the institutionalization of ADR policies by employers, especially in large US corporations. Employer-promulgated ADR policies began to be used to handle not only statutory complaints but also an expanding range of non-statutory workplace issues as well. Although arbitration and mediation have continued to be the principal techniques used by US employers to manage workplace conflict, the portfolio of ADR techniques available to employers expanded to include, for example, fact finding, peer review, conflict coaching, facilitation, early neutral evaluation, and other innovative methods. As the so-called 'ADR revolution' took root in American employment relations, an increasing number of employers used ADR not merely as a response to the threat of litigation and unionization but also as a proactive strategy designed to help achieve the organization's larger goals. The use of ADR evolved from a reaction to the legal environment to a strategy for managing workplace conflict.

This chapter examines this evolution of conflict management policies, focusing particularly on the use of ADR and conflict management in large US corporations. It discusses the factors that drove these corporations in the direction of a more strategic use of ADR, and it relies on three surveys of Fortune 1000 corporations in the US to document changes in the use of ADR and the adoption of conflict management policies in these corporations. We begin with a brief review of the historical evolution of dispute resolution policies and practices in the union and non-union sectors of the US economy. We then turn to an examination of the external and internal factors that have affected organizations' adoption of conflict management policies. Next, we move from reactive explanations for the rise of organizational conflict management to a discussion of the strategic motivations guiding choices, especially by large US corporations. As part of this discussion, we review conceptual arguments and empirical evidence supporting the strategic shift in the organizational adoption of conflict management policies and practices.

Factors Affecting Organizational Choices in Conflict Management

Over the past twenty years, empirical evidence demonstrates that corporate choices in workplace dispute resolution policies and practices have grown more varied, rather than less. The corporate surveys conducted in 2011 and 2013, described in more detail below, revealed considerable variation in the use of ADR and conflict management systems by Fortune 1000 corporations (a list of the 1,000 largest US-based corporations, as measured by their annual revenues). On the one hand, we estimated that as many as one-third of these companies used a form of a conflict management system. On the other hand, we also found that as many as 40 % of these corporations rarely used any ADR techniques and continued to rely on litigation to resolve workplace disputes. 'Our findings also show that major US corporations that rely on ADR have adopted a wider array of ADR techniques…including so-called hotlines, open door policies, early neutral evaluation, early case assessment, conflict mentoring, and conflict coaching.' (Lipsky 2014b:36). The diversity of ADR techniques and conflict management strategies used by US corporations has apparently grown. Most corporations that use ADR, our research reveals, no longer confine their choice of techniques merely to mediation and arbitration but select from a full range of options that include both internal and external dispute resolution methods along with both interest-based and rights-based options. As one of us wrote recently,

> [T]he evolution of ADR policies and practices in U.S. corporations has not been a story of convergence around a common set of techniques and systems. Instead, it has been a story of experimentation, variation, and attempts by companies to tailor the ADR policies and practices they use to their perceptions of the needs and interests of their organizations. (Lipsky 2014a:22)

What factors explain the variation in the corporate choice of ADR techniques and systems? Scholars have maintained that the factors that affect a corporation's choice of conflict management practices and processes can be divided into two categories: external or environmental factors, and internal or organizational factors. In addition, the factors that affect an organization's decision to use various ADR techniques (such as mediation and arbitration) to resolve workplace disputes may not be identical to the factors that affect an organization's decision to adopt a more proactive, systems approach to managing and resolving conflict. On the one hand, theoretically one might view an organization's decision to move from relying on mediation and arbitration to an organization's decision to adopt a conflict management system (CMS) as steps along a continuum – an incremental organizational change motivated largely by the same set of factors. On the other hand, the decision by an organization to adopt a conflict management system might be more than an incremental change and could very well represent a major re-orientation in how the organization regards the management of workplace conflict. Accordingly, in our judgement, the first task in conducting empirical testing of the adoption of corporate conflict management is to determine whether the dependent variable in the model is (a) ADR techniques such as mediation and arbitration; or (b) a measure of the use of a conflict management system by the organization. The empirical tests we have conducted in recent years strongly suggest that, although some of the factors that predict the former also predict the latter, one has to consider the influence of additional organizational factors to understand why corporations adopt conflict management systems (see, for example, Lipsky et al. 2014). It is important to note that alongside the increased adoption of ADR in large US firms, there is still a substantial proportion of organizations that are reluctant to embrace a proactive conflict management approach. It is also important to note that adoption patterns observed in the United States may not hold in other countries (for evidence on this reluctance in non-union MNCs in Ireland to acknowledge conflict or the need for conflict management practices, see Chap. 16).

External/Environmental and Internal Factors Affecting Strategy

It has usually been assumed that market factors strongly influence a corporation's adoption of conflict management practices. '*Our field research strongly suggests that one important environmental shift that has changed the approach of business to dispute resolution is the competitive pressure brought about by the glo-*

balization of the economy.' (Lipsky et al. 2003:128) The empirical results we have obtained to date, however, suggest that the relationship between competitive factors and conflict management strategies is more nuanced than we initially imagined. US data reveal that larger corporations, particularly those with more than 5,000 employees, are more likely than smaller corporations to adopt both particular ADR practices and conflict management systems. The largest corporations operate in highly concentrated industries, so one might surmise that the *lack* of competition is associated with ADR practices and systems. Moreover, larger corporations have the resources to invest money and staff in the operation of an ADR programme. For many smaller employers, a major investment in ADR and conflict management systems is not warranted by the minimal cost of litigation or by other factors driving the organization's conflict management strategy.

We have not found, however, that statistically testing for the industry in which the corporation operates has a significant influence on the incidence of ADR practices and systems. The absence of a statistically significant industry effect per se might very well be explained by the widespread adoption of ADR practices and systems across all major industries in the US. Earlier we noted the apparent growth in the variation of the types of ADR practices adopted by US corporations. But this variation does not appear to be linked to the industry in which the corporation operates.

Whether a US industry has been deregulated, however, does appear to be linked to a corporation's adoption of ADR practices and systems. Prior to the 1970s, many industries in the US were heavily regulated by the federal government.

> Deregulation had begun in earnest during the Carter presidency, starting with the passage of the Airline Deregulation Act in 1978, which virtually eliminated federal controls of the airline industry. During the Reagan years, it spread rapidly to telephone, telecommunications, trucking, and other heavily regulated industries... (Lipsky et al. 2003:57).

The empirical testing we have conducted reveals that industry deregulation is closely associated with the corporate use of ADR practices and systems. The adoption of ADR practices is particularly noteworthy in the telephone and telecommunications industry, as documented by Batt et al. (2002) (see also Colvin 2003). Deregulation increased competition in the industries in which it occurred, and competition motivated employers in these industries to adopt cost-saving practices, such as ADR.

Another external factor affecting the adoption of ADR practices and systems is unionism. Union density in the US reached a peak of 35 % of wage and salary workers in 1954, but steadily declined thereafter. By 2014 union density had fallen to 6.5 % in the private sector and 35.8 % in the public sector (US Department of Labor 2015). The simultaneous decline of unionization in the US and the rise of ADR suggest, to many observers, that the two phenomena are causally linked. Indeed, case studies suggest that some US employers have adopted ADR practices and systems in an effort to deter the unionization of their facilities (Avgar et al. 2013). These employers believe that providing their employees with fair (or at least adequate) procedures for resolving their complaints reduces the employees' incentive to form a union. But the fact remains that for most large US corporations unionization, at least in the short term, is no longer a major threat. The list of Fortune 1000 corporations contains a growing number of finance, banking, insurance, and service corporations, as well as high-tech companies (such as Facebook, Twitter, and Netflix), which have been formed in the last decade or so. There is a virtual absence of unionized employees in all of these firms. Union avoidance may be a factor motivating some large corporations to adopt ADR, but for the vast majority of US corporations it is no longer a major force. Statistical tests that we have conducted confirm the view that the level of unionization of the corporation's workforce does not significantly influence the firm's adoption of ADR practices and systems (Lipsky et al. 2014).

Arguably other external or environmental factors can be identified that theoretically might influence the adoption of ADR practices and systems. For example, the level of competition in the labour markets from which the corporation recruits and hires its employees may influence the organization's use of ADR: if a firm depends on finding its employees in highly competitive labour markets, packaging ADR as a benefit that helps ensure the fair treatment of employees could conceivably help the firm in its recruitment efforts (i.e. to become an 'employer of choice' (Latreille 2011)). On the whole, however, we have found that external and environmental factors are not sufficient to explain a corporation's adoption of ADR practices and systems. Our research confirms the view that one must turn to factors that are internal to the organization to provide a more complete explanation of why organizations adopt ADR practices and systems.

What are the internal factors that drive a corporation's conflict management strategies? We have concluded that it is top management's attitudes about conflict that almost always shape the corporation's strategy. In their 2003 book, Lipsky et al. reported on their field interviews with top managers in nearly 50 large US corporations. They wrote: 'Many decision makers view conflict as being either zero sum or variable sum', and these deep-seated dispositions about conflict often drove the organization's conflict management policies (Lipsky et al. 2003:119–120). Top managers who believed that organizational conflict was fundamentally a zero-sum game favoured the use of litigation and rights-based techniques to resolve conflict, whereas top managers who believed that organizational conflict was fundamentally a variable-sum game favoured the use of interest-based techniques and conflict management systems. As Lipsky recently wrote, 'We have never encountered a top corporate attorney or manager who had a zero sum, 'I win–you lose' attitude about conflict who supported the adoption of [an integrated conflict management system]' (Lipsky 2014b:39). Precisely why top managers differ in their dispositions about conflict is a matter that may require a psychologist or psychoanalyst to answer. Nevertheless, we discovered that managerial attitudes almost always align with the conflict management policies the corporation adopts.

If managerial attitudes are at the root of corporate conflict management strategies, there remain other internal factors that correlate with those strategies. For example, in the US over the last three decades many employers have moved from hierarchical authority structures to team-based work. A so-called 'high-performance work system' is an approach to structuring work in organizations that features not only the use of teams but also other design elements that promote participation and engagement by employees (see, for example, Applebaum and Batt 1994). We have discovered that there is a strong correlation between a corporation's use of a high-performance work system and its use of a conflict management system: 'A growing number of managers have come to realize that delegating responsibility for controlling work to teams is consistent with delegating authority for preventing or resolving conflict to members of those teams' (Lipsky et al. 2003:68).

A Strategic Approach to the Study of Organizational Conflict Management

In our research we have discovered that the decision to use ADR techniques to resolve workplace disputes is generally in the hands of inside attorneys, outside counsel, and human resource managers in the organization. Key decision makers usually include the general counsel and the employment counsel but do not necessarily involve the CEO or members of the board of directors. By contrast, the adoption of a conflict management system is almost always a decision made by the CEO, the corporate counsel, and other members of the top management team. The difference in the way corporations make decisions about handling workplace conflict reflects the difference between operational decisions and strategic decisions. For most corporations, using ADR techniques is no longer considered truly strategic, but adopting a conflict management system requires the involvement of top managers and often members of the board of directors.

We contend that a corporation's conflict management policies can give it a 'unique value proposition' compared to its competitors. We have observed this phenomenon in many industries in the US over the last two decades. For example, Prudential adopted an innovative conflict management system in the 1990s not only because it believed doing so would deter lawsuits (especially class action suits) but also because the corporation believed a CMS would give it a competitive advantage over other corporations in the financial services and insurance industry (Lipsky et al. 2003:147–150). In industries like financial services and insurance, the recruitment and retention of highly trained and talented human resources is so critical to the success of a corporation that human resource policies (including conflict management) converts those policies into genuine strategic decisions (see, for example, Millard 2004:181–184, for a discussion of the adoption of employment dispute resolution policies at Credit Suisse First Boston). But even in more traditional blue-collar industries, such as electrical appliances and nonferrous metals, we have found that top management regards the adoption of conflict management policies to be a key strategic matter (see, for example, Nordstrom 2004:197–226 for a discussion of the adoption of ADR policies at GE; and Perdue 2004:233–234 concerning the adoption of a conflict management system at Alcoa).

Organizational Conflict Management as a Strategic Choice

Workplace conflict can have devastating effects on a host of organizational, group, and individual-level outcomes. The management of conflict is, therefore, viewed by many academics and practitioners as an essential organizational activity that can have transformational effects on firms, their employees, and other stakeholders. Over the past three decades, scholars have documented the potential organizational benefits associated with the planned and deliberate management of workplace conflict (Avgar 2010; Lipsky et al. 2003; Lipsky and Avgar 2008). Nevertheless, although all organizations deal with conflict in one way or another, not all organizations deal with conflict in a proactive manner (Lipsky et al. 2003). On the one hand, some organizations deal with conflict by ignoring its presence, while on the other hand, other firms set up elaborate and sophisticated systems designed to manage and resolve conflicts and disputes (Avgar 2008; Lipsky et al. 2003). One of the key questions motivating our recent research is the extent to which organizations address conflict in a deliberate and strategic manner. Do organizations have clear and defined strategic orientations toward conflict and its management? Do organizations adopt specific ADR and conflict management policies in an effort to advance a defined set of goals and objectives?

On the one hand, quantitative and qualitative research has indicated that a growing proportion of large firms have adopted a variety of different conflict management practices (Colvin 2013; Lipsky et al. 2003, 2014; Teague et al. 2012). This evidence suggests that an increasing number of firms have recognized the need for and the potential of practices tailored for the resolution of conflict, such as mediation, arbitration, or an ombuds office. Furthermore, a growing proportion of firms have integrated a number of different practices into what is referred to as a conflict management system (CMS) designed to provide multiple options and access points for the resolution of conflict (Constantino and Merchant 1996; Lipsky et al. 2003; Rowe and Bendersky 2003).

On the other hand, much of the existing research on workplace ADR and conflict management has explained this rise in new methods for dealing with workplace conflict as a *reactive* response to a set of external and internal pressures (see, for example, Colvin 2003). According to this research, firms are primarily reacting and responding to changing legal and competitive environments alongside dramatically restructured work practices and arrangements (Colvin 2004). As such, firms are being *pushed* to adopt new conflict management practices. This explanation acknowledges firms' agency in responding to environmental and internal pressures, but leaves relatively little room for the concept of choice. The argument that we have advanced in our conflict management research is that alongside the role that external and internal pressures play in explaining the adoption and implementation of ADR and conflict management practices, firms' strategic choices also play an important role. The adoption of specific ADR and conflict management practices is not merely a defensive manoeuvre designed to buffer the organization from threats and pressures but is also a means of delivering on broader, forward-looking strategic goals and objectives.

In the 1980s, industrial relations scholars argued that firms make a series of strategic choices about the way in which they manage their workforce and engage with different stakeholders (Kochan et al. 1984, 1986). According to this approach, firms have the discretion and flexibility to make decisions about the practices they adopt and the managerial choices they make among a number of possible options. This stream of research has been extremely influential in helping to document widespread and consequential labour-management developments over the past thirty years (Avgar and Kuruvilla 2011). Applying a strategic choice lens, industrial relations scholars have been able to better understand variation in the adoption and implementation of workplace practices such as the spread of high performance work systems (Katz and Darbishire 2000).

Interestingly, there has been relatively little application of these seminal strategic frameworks in the study of conflict management (for a similar argument, see Lipsky et al. 2014; see also Lipsky and Avgar 2008). This is surprising given that, like the management of employees, managing conflict effectively can have positive effects on a host of employee- and employer-related outcomes. In our research we have built on and extended this strategic choice perspective applying it to the study of organizational conflict management (Lipsky and Avgar 2008; Avgar et al. 2013; Lipsky et al. 2014). At the heart of this research stream is the argument that just as firms make strategic decisions about the work practices and arrangements they adopt, they are also likely to apply a strategic approach to the way in which they resolve and manage conflict. In fact, the array of potential conflict management practices that firms can make use of, ranging from interest-based practices such as mediation to rights-based options like arbitration, provides a clear incentive for firms to be deliberate about the set of practices they adopt. Different conflict management practices vary greatly in terms of the outcomes they are associated with and the benefits they provide organizations and their employees (Avgar 2015; Lipsky and Avgar 2008). Thus, for example, interest-based practices such as mediation are uniquely suited to firms seeking to advance problem-solving capabilities, while rights-based options, such as arbitration, are better suited for firms seeking dispute resolution certainty and finality.

Aligning an Organization's Broad Strategy with Its Conflict Management Strategy and Practices

To what extent do strategic orientations influence choices made on conflict management policies? Do organizations view their conflict management decisions as a vehicle they can use to deliver on broader strategic objectives? We argue that the answer to both of these questions is 'yes'. As organizations have shifted from the use of a single dispute resolution practice, common in the ADR era of the 1980s and 1990s, to the adoption of integrated conflict management systems, increasingly common in the late 1990s and 2000s, there has also been an increase in the use of different configurations or bundles of practices (Lipsky et al. 2014). The proliferation of different bundles or systems of practices strongly suggests that even among firms that have adopted a proactive and systemic approach to the management of conflict, different choices guide actual adoption patterns.

Specifically, in Lipsky and Avgar (2008) we conceptualize three overarching motivations or objectives guiding the adoption of conflict management practices and systems: (1) resolving individual disputes; (2) providing employees with institutionalized mechanisms for voice; and (3) enhancing broader organizational coordination. Some organizations are seeking to make use of conflict management practices as a way to deal with everyday disputes, while others see these practices as a means they can use to elicit greater levels of employee voice beyond the resolution of ad hoc individual disputes. Finally, some organizations, we maintain, see a broader potential in the adoption of conflict management practices, namely, the ability to better coordinate and communicate across organizational boundaries.

Each of these different objectives, we argue, drives very different patterns of ADR practices. For example, firms that view conflict management practices as a means of resolving individual disputes are likely to adopt a relatively limited number of practices with a relatively constrained mandate. Firms that see their conflict management approach as linked to broader organizational coordination are, on the other hand, more likely to make use of a varied and sophisticated set of practices that go beyond the mere resolution of ad hoc individual disputes. Thus, for example, a firm subscribing to a traditional model of authoritative employment relations is likely to rely on a conflict management policy that provides the most basic deliverable, namely, the resolution of individual disputes. By contrast, firms adopting team-based employment relations are more likely to have broader coordination and communication objectives that go beyond conflict resolution and provide a broader voice for their employees.

Our research has also provided empirical support for the view that organizational strategies guide the deployment of conflict management practices. In the 2011 survey of Fortune 1000 firms, respondents were asked (among other questions) about their motivations for adopting conflict management policies (Lipsky et al. 2014). In particular, we asked respondents about the benefits they expected to attain by making use of ADR and conflict management practices. We found that some firms were motivated by their view that conflict management was principally a tool they could use to enhance their position in employment litigation. More specifically, these firms viewed ADR as a vehicle they could use to buffer themselves from the external legal environment and promote the private resolution of workplace conflicts. Other firms, by contrast, focused on the efficiency benefits they could attain through the management of conflict. These firms were primarily interested in the logistical and administrative cost savings that would accrue as a result of the proactive management of conflict. Finally, a third category of corporations viewed conflict management as a means they could use to enhance their managerial and problem-solving capabilities. Firms in this category seek to advance their ability to create an infrastructure for a more durable and satisfying resolution of conflicts. Also, these firms saw broader managerial potential in the management of conflict (for a similar discussion, see Avgar 2008; Lipsky and Avgar 2008; Lipsky et al. 2014).

This empirical evidence provides additional support for our central thesis that firms vary in their strategic approach to conflict management. Nevertheless, merely demonstrating that firms vary in this way does not get at the broader question of whether different strategic orientations or motivations actually drive different conflict management choices. If the industrial relations and strategic human resource management insights reviewed above apply to the study of conflict management, we would expect each of these different strategic orientations to be associated with different patterns in the organizational adoption of ADR policies.

In Lipsky et al. (2014), we tested this proposition by examining the extent to which a firm's strategic orientation is associated with both the number of conflict management practices the firm adopted and the actual type of practices the firm made available to its employees. Our regression analysis, based on responses from the corporation's general counsel or his/her deputy in 368 Fortune 1000 firms, provides strong support for the link between strategic orientation and conflict management choices. First, we found that firms that emphasized the managerial and problem-solving benefits associated with conflict management practices were more likely to provide their workforce with a more extensive portfolio of practices. Second, our analyses also support the relationship between a firm's strategic orientation and the specific ADR practices the firm adopted. For example, we found that firms that reported a managerial-centred strategic orientation were more likely to adopt interest-based practices, such as early case assessment. Firms reporting a litigation-focused strategy, on the other hand, were more likely to adopt rights-based practices, such as arbitration and peer review panels. These findings suggest that firms have a great deal of agency in shaping their conflict management portfolio and, in making strategic choices about which practices to put in place, they are guided by defined objectives and clear rationales about the expected link between the resolution of conflict and organizational benefits. Nevertheless, this stream of research is still in its infancy and there is much more work to be done in examining the relationship between strategy and conflict management in organizations.

Mapping the Landscape of Corporate Policies: Three Surveys of the Use of ADR by Major US Corporations

In 1997, Cornell University's Scheinman Institute on Conflict Resolution set out to profile and document the use of ADR among large US corporations listed on the Fortune 1000 (Lipsky et al. 2003). Although the 'ADR revolution' had transformed US conflict resolution during the final quarter of the twentieth century, scholars knew very little empirically about the types of ADR mechanisms companies favoured, the strategies they employed to handle conflict, or the systems of dispute resolution that were emerging within these organizations (Shavell 1995; Stipanowich 2004). The 1997 Cornell survey was designed to shed light on each of these facets of conflict resolution, and in so doing this survey painted the first comprehensive picture – the landscape – of ADR policies and practices in large US corporations.

In the years that passed after the initial Fortune 1000 survey was conducted, the conversation regarding the role ADR plays in resolving conflict within the corporation has continued and in many ways intensified. For example, after the US Supreme Court decided two seminal cases, one in 1991 and the other in 2001, it became crystal clear that employers could require their employees to sign agreements waiving their right to sue their employer in court and requiring them instead to use arbitration to resolve their complaint. The appropriateness of employers requiring their employees to sign waivers and use mandatory arbitration continues to be one of the most controversial topics in US employment relations (see, for example, Colvin 2011, for a critique of mandatory arbitration, and Estreicher 2001, for a defence).

In 2011, we returned to the Fortune 1000 to conduct a new survey of their ADR practices. The survey was co-sponsored by Cornell's Scheinman Institute on Conflict Resolution, the Straus Institute for Dispute Resolution at Pepperdine University School of Law, and the International Institute for Conflict Prevention and Resolution (CPR). The aim of this new survey was to not only garner a sense of the then-current state of ADR at major US corporations, but also to explore the extent to which ADR practices had either remained stable or undergone change in the fifteen years between the two surveys (Stipanowich and Lamare 2014). Were corporations still optimistic that ADR would represent a better method of handling conflict than traditional litigation? Did these companies continue to favour interest-based approaches like mediation, or were they moving to more rights-based practices, such as arbitration? Were firms becoming more sophisticated in their conflict management systems than they might have been fifteen years earlier?

The results of the 2011 survey offered answers to each of these questions, many of which might be considered surprising. For instance, the findings provided evidence that there had been a significant *decline* in the corporate use of arbitration, in most types of dispute arenas, compared to the findings in the 1997 survey. On the one hand, in the consumer arena the use of arbitration remained roughly unchanged over the 1997–2011 period. In 1997, 17.4 % of Fortune 1000 companies indicated that they had used arbitration to resolve conflicts with consumers, whereas in 2011, 20.6 % reported using consumer arbitration. This suggests a degree of stability in the use of consumer arbitration among the Fortune 1000, though these companies used this method of dispute resolution infrequently on the whole.

On the other hand, employment arbitration had undergone a sizeable shift over the period 1997–2011. When surveyed in 1997, nearly two-thirds of the companies (62.2 %) indicated that they had used arbitration to resolve at least one employment conflict over the past three years. When asked again in 2011, however, slightly more than one-third of the firms (37.8 %) affirmed that they used employment arbitration. These results were not unique to the employment arena. A similar result was found when looking at commercial disputes, where

62.3 % of companies used arbitration in 2011, a substantially lower proportion than the 85 % that had reported using arbitration to resolve commercial disputes in 1997.

Are there dispute resolution methods that have replaced the use of arbitration in the commercial and employment arenas? The answers, according to the 2011 survey of Fortune 1000 firms, are mediation and other interest-based options. Virtually every company surveyed in 2011 reported that it had used mediation at least once in the prior three years. This represents an overall increase in the use of mediation of about 11 % when compared to the 1997 findings. The use of mediation in commercial disputes rose from 77.7 % of Fortune 1000 companies in 1997 to 83.5 % in 2011, and from 78.6 % to 85.5 % in employment cases.

In fact, the 1997 and 2011 corporate surveys revealed that the use of mediation by large US corporations grew across almost all categories of disputes. Even in the consumer arena, where the use of arbitration held steady over the 1997–2011 period, the use of mediation grew substantially, from 24.1 % of Fortune 1000 firms in 1997 to 43.9 % in 2011. Firms were also asked about their use of mediation in corporate finance, environmental, intellectual property, personal injury, product liability, real estate, and construction disputes. Uniformly, mediation was used more frequently in 2011 than in 1997.

Corporate respondents were asked not only whether their firm had used mediation 'at least once' over the previous three years, but also to estimate how many times (on a five-point scale, ranging from 'always' to 'never') the firm had used it during that period for each type (employment, consumer, etc.) of dispute. The results were similar: the majority of companies indicated that they had either 'always' or 'frequently' used mediation in commercial, consumer, and employment disputes. By contrast, a minority of these firms indicated that arbitration was 'always' or 'frequently' used to resolve commercial and employment disputes. Consumer cases, however, were again an exception – though even in consumer disputes the majority of survey respondents told us that their firm had 'never' used it.

Why did the use of arbitration by major US corporations decline over the period 1997–2011? Why were these companies less interested in using arbitration to resolve their disputes, relative to other ADR options, in 2011? Many of the corporate attorneys who participated in our surveys believed that over time arbitration had become similar to litigation, particularly with regard to the time and cost of pursuing a case. They also suggested that 'external' law (the law on arbitration that grew out of court decisions) had made arbitration increasingly complex, as well as more costly and time-consuming. Respondents further expressed concerns about the quality of available arbitrators, the difficulty of appealing arbitration awards, and the possibility that arbitrators might not follow the law. Many of the concerns associated with arbitration in 2011 were similar to those found in the 1997 survey, only fears regarding the arbitration process more generally and especially the growing cost of arbitration had grown considerably between 1997 and 2011. Some senior attorneys recalled that when they had begun their careers arbitration had been an informal, problem-solving exercise, but over time it had become a more formal, adversarial process.

It may therefore be the case that Fortune 1000 companies adopted arbitration in the 1990s as a favoured approach to conflict management because they believed it would be a faster, cheaper option than litigation. Upon discovering that arbitration in fact sometimes proved quite costly and time-consuming, these same companies appeared by 2011 to rely increasingly on interest-based options to resolve disputes at the earliest possible stage. Not only was mediation on the rise when firms were surveyed in 2011, so too were options like fact-finding and the use of an in-house grievance procedure. Other less traditional, generally interest-based ADR practices like early neutral evaluation and early case assessment have also proven popular amongst the Fortune 1000.

Companies were also asked, in both 1997 and 2011, about their future plans for using mediation and arbitration. The results confirm what might be expected: irrespective of the dispute arena (commercial, consumer, or employment), about 80 % of firms reported that they were either 'very likely' or 'likely' to use mediation to resolve disputes in the future. Over half of the corporations, however, regardless of the category of dispute indicated that they were either 'unlikely' or 'very unlikely' to use arbitration in the future. This finding stands in stark contrast not only to the results for mediation in 2011 but also to the findings for arbitration in 1997. When asked the same question fifteen years earlier, fully 71 % of the corporate respondents indicated that they were 'very likely' or 'likely' to use arbitration in the future.

In 2013 Cornell and CPR drew a subsample of companies from the 2011 survey and added companies from CPR's membership list to construct a sample of companies that were known to have particularly innovative or cutting edge approaches to managing workplace conflict (Waks et al. 2014; Erickson 2015). Of the 99 firms included in this new sample, ultimately 57 were contacted and surveyed about their ADR operations and practices. For this survey, the principal manager of the firm's ADR programme (rather than the general counsel) was the target respondent because the objective of the survey was to obtain a deeper understanding of how large corporations managed their ADR programmes.

In this sample of organizations, just over three-fourths had used employment arbitration at least once during the previous three years. Perhaps a surprising result, however, was the fact that the vast majority of these firms used voluntary, not mandatory, arbitration. Less than one-fourth of these firms used mandatory pre-dispute arbitration. These findings are consistent with other findings in the 2011 survey that show that firms with conflict management systems prefer voluntary approaches to managing and resolving conflict (Lipsky 2014a:13–15).

These innovative companies did not limit the scope of their dispute resolution practices to only one subset of employees, such as managers or key performers. Almost 60 % of the firms surveyed in 2013 included *all* of their employees in their ADR programmes. In regard to other characteristics of their ADR programmes and policies, however, there was substantial variation across these cutting edge firms. Rather than converging around a common set of 'best practices,' these innovative companies had adopted ADR programmes that they had tailored to meet their own needs.

The cutting edge companies surveyed in 2013 echoed those contacted in 2011 in their desire for voluntary, interest-based conflict management policies as opposed to mandatory, rights-based ones. Nearly half of the innovative firms had entirely voluntary programmes, while a quarter implemented mandatory options alongside voluntary ones (for instance, shifting from a voluntary system to a mandatory one if an employee opted to go to arbitration). Less than a fifth of companies used fully mandatory ADR programmes.

In the 2011 survey, just under 60 % of the respondents indicated they used ADR to resolve statutory claims, including employee allegations of discrimination, violations of wage and hour statutes, or other violations of state and federal laws. Among the cutting edge companies surveyed in 2013, however, the scope of their ADR programmes extended well beyond complaints dealing with statutory infractions. Almost 70 % of these companies used their ADR programmes to handle non-statutory complaints, including employee concerns about the quality of work in their organizations. Over a quarter of these companies relied on their conflict management programmes to handle disputes between units or departments within the corporation.

Conclusion

This chapter has reviewed a number of key themes central to a comprehensive understanding of the deployment of ADR and conflict management systems in US firms. First, in the US, there is a clear distinction between conflict management in the union and non-union settings. As noted, unionized firms have made use of internal mechanisms designed to resolve workplace conflict (individual and collective) for the past 70 years. In the non-union setting, however, the use of internal and private methods is a much more recent development. Despite the use of overlapping practices, the institutional logic of and support for these practices varies greatly across these settings. After many decades in which unionized establishments served as the primary conflict management innovators, the past three decades have seen innovation in workplace conflict resolution shift into the non-union arena. In the US, in which union density has declined dramatically over the same period of time, this shift suggests that a growing proportion of the workforce will have access to the non-union manifestation of these practices, particularly mediation and arbitration, which have been unilaterally promulgated by their employer.

Second, the chapter also highlights the major factors that have likely influenced the rise of non-union ADR and CMS in the US. Early research that attempted to explain this workplace phenomenon focused on external factors such as the threat of litigation and unionization as key determinants. Although there is no doubt that such factors played a central role in the diffusion of these practices in the early stages of institutionalization, it seems clear that the range of factors, both external and internal, has expanded considerably over the past two decades. For example, the competitive environment and state of deregulation in a firm's industry also appear to influence the adoption of conflict management policies.

Third, our chapter points to the likely role that management strategy plays in the adoption and implementation of new conflict management practices. Our research has provided conceptual and empirical support for the argument that firms make strategic choices about the manner in which they address workplace conflict, and these choices are a function of different management motivations and orientations. Firms are not simply pressured by environmental factors into adopting new conflict management practices. Rather, they seek to leverage conflict management as a vehicle they can use to advance their broader goals and objectives. In addition, the chapter reviewed evidence regarding a link between a firm's strategic conflict management orientation and the adoption of specific practices.

Finally, our review of findings based on three corporate surveys conducted by Cornell's Scheinman Institute on Conflict Resolution paints a portrait of the evolving use of ADR and CMS in US firms. Evidence from these surveys points to a decrease in the use of arbitration by Fortune 1000 firms and an increase in interest-based practices. These findings provide additional support for the broadening of the function that conflict management plays within American organizations. This conclusion is also supported by evidence from a subset of Fortune 1000 firms that appear to rely on innovative conflict management policies for the resolution of workplace disputes. Taken together, this survey evidence strongly suggests that many American firms have moved beyond viewing ADR and CMS as merely a means of addressing litigation threats and challenges and have come to appreciate the range of organizational benefits associated with the internal management of conflict.

References

Applebaum, E., & Batt, R. (1994). *The new American workplace: Transforming work systems in the United States*. ithaca: Cornell University Press.

Avgar, A.C. (2008). *Treating conflict: Conflict and its resolution in healthcare* (Ph.D. dissertation). Ithaca: Cornell University.

Avgar, A. C. (2010). Negotiated capital: Conflict, its management, and workplace social capital. *International Journal of Conflict Management, 21*(3), 236–259.

Avgar, A. C., & Kuruvilla, S. (2011). Dual alignment of industrial relations activity: From strategic choice to mutual gains. *Advances in Industrial and Labor Relations, 18*, 1–39.

Avgar, A. C., Lamare, J. R., Lipsky, D. B., & Gupta, A. (2013). Unions and ADR: The relationship between labor unions and workplace dispute resolution in U.S. corporations. *Ohio State Journal on Dispute Resolution, 28*, 63–106.

Avgar, A. C. (2015). Internal resolution of employment disputes. In A. G. Felieu (Ed.), *ADR in Employment Law* (pp. 45–85). Arlington, VA: Bloomberg BNA.

Batt, R., Colvin, A. J. S., & Keefe, J. (2002). Employee voice, human resource practices, and quit rates: Evidence from the telecommunications industry. *Industrial and Labor Relations Review, 55*(4), 573–594.

Colvin, A. J. S. (2003). Institutional pressures, human resource strategies, and the rise of nonunion dispute resolution procedures. *Industrial and Labor Relations Review, 56*(3), 375–392.

Colvin, A. J. S. (2004). The relationship between employee involvement and workplace dispute resolution. *Relations Industrielles/Industrial Relations, 59*(4), 681–704.

Colvin, A. J. S. (2011). An empirical study of employment arbitration: Case outcomes and processes. *Journal of Empirical Legal Studies, 8*(1), 1–23.

Colvin, A. J. (2013). Participation versus procedures in non-union dispute resolution. *Industrial Relations: A Journal of Economy and Society, 52*(s1), 259–283.

Constantino, C. A., & Merchant, C. S. (1996). *Designing conflict management systems: A guide to creating productive and healthy organizations*. San Fransisco: Jossey-Bass.

Erickson, H.T. (2015, April 21). Cutting edge companies use dispute resolution techniques to address workplace conflict. *Inside Counsel*. Found at| http://www.insidecounsel.com/2015/04/21/cutting-edge-companies-use-dispute-resolution-tech. Accessed 17 July 2015.

Estreicher, S. (2001). Saturns for rickshaws: The stakes in the debate over predispute employment arbitration agreements. *Ohio State Journal for Dispute Resolution*, *16*(3), 559.

Katz, H. C., & Darbishire, O. R. (2000). *Converging divergences: Worldwide changes in employment Systems*. ithaca: Cornell University Press.

Kochan, T. A., McKersie, R. B., & Cappelli, P. (1984). Strategic choice and industrial relations theory. *Industrial Relations: A Journal of Economy and Society*, *23*(1), 16–39.

Kochan, T. A., Katz, H. C., & McKersie, R. B. (1986). *The transformation of American industrial relations*. New York: Basic Books.

Latreille, P.L. (2011). Workplace mediation: a thematic review of the Acas/CIPD evidence. *Acas Research Paper*, 13/11.

Lipsky, D. B. (2014a). How leading corporations use ADR to handle employment complaints. In J. W. Waks, N. L. Vanderlip, & D. B. Lipsky (Eds.), *Cutting edge advances in resolving workplace disputes* (pp. 5–25). New York: International Institute for Conflict Prevention and Resolution.

Lipsky, D. B. (2014b). The evolution of integrated conflict management systems. In J. W. Waks, N. L. Vanderlip, & D. B. Lipsky (Eds.), *Cutting edge advances in resolving workplace disputes* (pp. 25–43). New York: International Institute for Conflict Prevention and Resolution.

Lipsky, D. B., & Avgar, A. C. (2008). Toward a strategic theory of workplace conflict management. *Ohio State Journal on Dispute Resolution*, *24*(1), 143–190.

Lipsky, D. B., Seeber, R., & Fincher, R. D. (2003). *Emerging systems for managing workplace conflict*. San Francisco: Jossey-Bass.

Lipsky, D.B., Avgar, A.C., & Lamare, J.R. (2014). *The strategic underpinnings of conflict management practices in U.S. corporations: Evidence from a new survey of Fortune 1000 companies*. Working Paper.

Millard, E. W. (2004). Credit Suisse First Boson employment dispute resolution program. In S. Estreicher, & D. Sherwyn (Eds.), *Alternative dispute resolution in the employment arena: Proceedings of New York University 53rd annual conference on labor*. Kluwer Law International: The Hague.

Nordstrom, M. (2004). General electric's experience with ADR. In S. Estreicher, & D. Sherwyn (Eds.), *Alternative dispute resolution in the employment arena: Proceedings of New York University 53rd annual conference on labor*. Kluwer Law International: The Hague.

Perdue, D. C. (2004). Employment dispute: Resolve it! Alcoa at the forefront of alternative dispute resolution. In S. Estreicher, & D. Sherwyn (Eds.), *Alternative dispute resolution in the employment arena: Proceedings of New York*

University 53rd annual conference on labor. Kluwer Law International: The Hague.

Rowe, M., & Bendersky, C. (2003). Workplace justice, zero tolerance, and zero barriers. In T. A. Kochan, & D. B. Lipsky (Eds.), *Negotiations and change: From the workplace to society.* Ithaca: ILR Press.

Shavell, S. (1995). Alternative dispute resolution: An economic analysis. *The Journal of Legal Studies, 24*(1), 1–28.

Stipanowich, T. J. (2004). ADR and 'the vanishing trial': The growth and impact of 'alternative dispute resolution. *Journal of Empirical Legal Studies, 1*(3), 843–912.

Stipanowich, T. J., & Lamare, J. R. (2014). Living with ADR: evolving perceptions and use of mediation, arbitration and conflict management in Fortune 1,000 Corporations. *Harvard Negotiation Law Review, 19*, 1–68.

Teague, P., Roche, B., & Hann, D. (2012). The diffusion of alternative dispute resolution practices in Ireland. *Economic and Industrial Democracy, 33*(4), 581–604.

U.S. Department of Labor, Bureau of Labor Statistics. (2015). Economic news release: union members summary. Available from http://www.bls.gov/news.release/union2.nr0.htm. Accessed 16 July 2015.

Waks, J. W., Vanderlip, N. L., & Lipsky, D. B. (Eds.) (2014). *Cutting edge advances in resolving workplace disputes.* New York: International Institute for Conflict Prevention and Resolution.

15

Transforming the Culture of Conflict Management: Lessons from In-House Mediation

Paul Latreille and Richard Saundry

Introduction

The promotion of mediation and other alternative forms of employment dispute resolution have largely been driven by a business case revolving around efficiency benefits compared with conventional rights-based processes and the potential of costly litigation. In both the USA and the UK, the spectre of legal action and consequent costs has seen organizations turn towards mediation, viewed as offering a greater likelihood of resolution and savings in terms of staff time relative to grievance and disciplinary procedures (see Latreille and Saundry 2014). However, it has also been argued that mediation can have positive 'upstream' effects, acting as a catalyst for wider changes in the way organizations manage individual conflict. For example, there is evidence

Sheffield University Management School, Sheffield, UK
e-mail: p.latreille@sheffield.ac.uk

R. Saundry
Plymouth Business School, Plymouth University Plymouth, UK
e-mail: richard.saundry@plymouth.ac.uk

© The Editor(s) (if applicable) and The Author(s) 2016   **315**
R. Saundry et al. (eds.), *Reframing Resolution*,
DOI 10.1057/978-1-137-51560-5_15

that it fosters conflict-handling skills (Anderson and Bingham 1997; Kressel 2006) and can enhance employer–employee relationships (Seargeant 2005). In the UK, the government has promoted mediation on the grounds that it can help transform 'employer–employee relationships, the development of organizational culture and the development of "high-trust" relationships' (BIS 2011: 3).

This chapter explores the extent to which mediation can effect such transformation and the conditions under which these broader organizational benefits can be delivered. It does so through a detailed case study of the introduction and operation of an internal mediation service set within Northumbria Healthcare NHS Foundation Trust (NHCT), located in the North East of England. NHCT manages hospital, community health and adult social care services and is one of the region's largest employers, with over 8,500 staff delivering care to over half a million people.

This case provides an ideal opportunity to explore both the potential and limitation of workplace mediation as source of innovation in conflict management due to the extent to which mediators are involved in broader conflict management activities and the development of conflict competence in the organization. The chapter therefore poses three key questions: Can mediation transform the culture of conflict management in an organization? What are the necessary and sufficient conditions under which this will take place? What are the key barriers to this taking place?

Mediation and the Potential of Systems of Conflict Management

Growing concerns over the cost and impact of workplace conflict have seen increased attention being given to alternative systems of dispute resolution. In the UK, this has largely been focused on the promotion of workplace mediation. A wide-ranging government-commissioned review (Gibbons 2007) concluded that mediation offered one antidote to the problem caused by the growing formality of workplace processes designed to manage conflict. The review recommended mediation as 'a pragmatic, flexible and informal way of providing both parties with positive outcomes' (p. 38) and urged the government to 'challenge all employer and employee organisations to commit to implementing and promoting early dispute resolution' (p. 30).

Evidence suggests that mediation (in some form) is an increasingly important part of the toolkit of contemporary organizations. In the UK, the Workplace Employment Relations Study 2011 found that mediation by an impartial third party was used in 17 % of workplaces that experienced a formal individual grievance (in the 12 months preceding the survey), while mediation by an impartial third party was provided for within written disputes procedures in around two-thirds of those workplaces that had disciplinary and grievance procedures (Wood et al. 2014). There is also evidence that mediation is much more likely to be used by larger organizations (Wood et al. 2014). While there is evidence of enthusiasm for mediation amongst small and medium sized enterprises (SMEs), the personal nature of their employment relations and the cost of mediation are barriers to its use (Harris et al. 2008; Johnston 2008; Rahim et al. 2011; Latreille et al. 2012).

The basic case for mediation has largely been driven by its capacity to resolve disputes quickly and efficiently when compared with slow, complex and adversarial grievance and disciplinary procedures which focus on rights as opposed to interests (Reynolds 2000; Pope 1996). Mediation not only requires less managerial input but is argued to be relatively quick and to require much less staff time. But perhaps most importantly, it is more likely to restore the employment relationship, therefore avoiding long-term absence and minimizing the likelihood of legal action (Corby 1999; Kressel 2006). In the UK, data suggest resolution rates (full or partial) of around 90% (or more) (CIPD 2008; Latreille 2011; Saundry et al. 2013; Saundry and Wibberley 2012).

It is also argued that mediation provides opportunities for greater employee voice by offering a less confrontational way of dealing with problems and for employees to express their feelings in a relatively safe and secure environment. As a consequence, workers are more likely to try and resolve problems rather than exiting the organization (Seargeant 2005; Singletary et al. 1995; Sulzner 2003). Evidence for the USA, suggests that participant satisfaction is extremely high, both in terms of process and outcome (Bingham et al. 2009; Kochan et al. 2000).

However, while the potential savings from the resolution of specific disputes should not be discounted, if mediation is to be more than just 'another tool in the box', it must have a broader and deeper impact on the way organizations deal with conflict. There is certainly evidence that involvement in mediation – either as a mediator or a participant – can shape attitudes to conflict and enhance conflict-handling skills (Bingham 2004; Saundry and Wibberley 2014). A longitudinal study of the Resolve Employment Disputes, Reach Equitable Solutions Swiftly (REDRESS) mediation programme in the US Postal Service found that supervisors who were trained as mediators or took part in mediation 'listen more, are more open to expressing emotion, and take a less hierarchical top-down approach to managing conflict' (Bingham et al. 2009: 43). Furthermore, it has been argued that the use of mediation can lead to improved employer–employee relationships and underpin more positive organizational cultures and high-trust relationships (BIS 2011). Saundry et al.'s (2013) case study of the introduction of mediation at a public health organization in the UK found that highly adversarial employment relations were turned around by the introduction of a mediation service in which key union leaders were not only trained as mediators but involved in the management of the service. Their involvement provided a basis on which high-trust relationships with HR practitioners and senior managers were built. Importantly, this also fed through to the way in which problems that did not reach mediation were handled, restoring informal social processes which facilitated the early identification and joint resolution of conflict.

It is also argued that wider cultural transformation cannot be delivered by mediation alone but is more likely where mediation is an element of a strategic and systematic approach. The potential for integrated conflict management systems (ICMS) has gained widespread support in the US (Lipsky et al. 2003; Lynch 2001, 2003). Here, mediation and other interest-based processes may sit alongside conventional rights-based approaches. Furthermore, they operate within a framework where managerial skills and competences in conflict handling are emphasized. Consequently, there is a focus on managing conflict rather than simply resolving disputes after they have escalated. Importantly, research to date in the UK suggests that mediation tends to be used as a dispute resolution mechanism of last resort (Wood et al. 2014; Saundry and Wibberley 2014).

There are also more fundamental criticisms of the transformative power of mediation. Some commentators point out that while there may be an approximation of equity within the conduct of a mediation, the asymmetrical nature of the employment relationship remains (Sherman 2003). Mediation is ultimately a managerial process, instigated and motivated to reduce costs and increase efficiency. In this context, mediation is a means of controlling dissent and asserting control; parties are not only pressured into agreeing to mediation but also settlement. Furthermore, there is a danger that mediation provides a way of masking managerial mistreatment and inequity. For example, bullying and harassment can be reframed as an interpersonal clash or relationship breakdown. Accordingly some commentators argue mediation should not be used in cases of overt mistreatment where the enforcement of rights through grievance processes and disciplinary sanctions may be more appropriate (Bellman 1998; La Rue 2000).

Some authors have also contended that the use of mediation is a means of privatizing dispute resolution and eroding socialized and unionized processes of negotiation and accommodation. There is no doubt that in the USA, the adoption of ADR has been associated with union avoidance and substitution (Colvin 2003; Olson-Buchanan and Boswell 2008; Lipsky and Seeber 2000). It is perhaps not surprising that some unions are sceptical about mediation, which they see as 'a way of undermining the role of the union in representing members with individual problems at work' (Bleiman 2008: 15). Against this, there is some evidence that public sector unions in the USA have extended their influence by embracing alternative forms of dispute resolution (Robinson et al. 2005). Lipsky and Seeber (2000: 45) contend that for some unions this 'can extend the authority and influence of a union into areas normally considered management prerogatives'. Similarly, Saundry et al. (2013) have argued that active involvement in mediation potentially offers trade unions and their members an ability to shape the resolutions of individual employment disputes as opposed to relying almost exclusively on the enforcement of individual employment rights to challenge managerial control. The potential of improved relationships with management, combined with a focus on resolution as opposed to procedure, also offer unions the chance to re-establish important informal processes of resolution in relation to a wide range of issues, including disciplinary cases.

Methodology

A mixed methods approach was adopted in this research in order to provide both a broad overview of the management of workplace conflict and also a deeper examination of the way in which managers and employees interact within different processes of dispute resolution. The first stage of the research involved examining existing documentation regarding individual dispute resolution. This included policies and procedures relating to grievance, discipline, capability, and bullying and harassment. In addition, we had access to statistical data regarding disciplinary and grievance cases between 2008 and 2014 and staff survey data between 2005 and 2013. Records in relation to mediation were also examined, including details of case types, durations and outcomes, together with anonymized evaluations completed by mediation participants between 2006 and 2014.

The second stage of the research was to conduct interviews with a sample of mediators, HR practitioners and trade union representatives. These interviews were designed to provide an overview of the key issues and explore the nature of conflict resolution in NHCT; the introduction and operation of the mediation service; and the extent to which this had shaped the way in which conflict was, and is, managed. In total, 16 interviews were conducted which lasted between 35 and 90 minutes.

The third stage was a survey that sought to explore line managers' and supervisors' experiences of, attitudes to, and approaches for dealing with work conflict, and the effects of such conflict on them and their team. Crucially, the study was also designed to evaluate the two innovative training sessions provided by NHCT for managers and supervisors on handling difficult conversations and dealing with conflict, bullying and harassment.

The survey instrument was developed with reference to the existing literature on workplace mediation and conflict management, drawing on themes emerging from the initial in-depth interviews. This process was undertaken iteratively and with feedback from NHCT in the form of the mediation coordinator and a colleague in Occupational Health, who also piloted the final draft of the survey, administered online, for timing and final sense-checking.

At the advice of NHCT, invitations and the survey link were initially provided to top layers of management in each of the business units to be cascaded down. This approach reflected internal resource and data protection constraints, as well as the need to recruit participants who had undertaken the training identified above and a corresponding sample of those who had not. It was also felt this approach would secure higher response rates, which were further incentivized by a prize draw.

The survey questions examined: basic demographics of the individual and job (sex, age, tenure, length of time as a manager/supervisor, number of staff managed/supervised, occupational group and pay band); training receipt in relation to conflict handling and views about its impact; experience of conflict at work and its handling; awareness of mediation and views towards this and wider approaches to conflict; and final thoughts. Participants were also invited to take part in follow-up interviews; 54 offered to do so. The survey went live in April 2014, and after reminders, 237 completed responses were achieved – a response rate approaching 50%.

In relation to management experience, around 30% of respondents had been managers/supervisors for between 5 and 10 years, with more than 40% holding such a position for 10 years or longer. On average, respondents supervised/managed 58 staff (median of 15); seven said they did not in fact manage or supervise anyone else, while at the other extreme, one respondent managed well over 1000 staff. Most respondents were in pay bands 7 or 8 and above (74%), with a further 14% in band 6 and 12% in bands 3–5 combined.

Finally, interviews were conducted with operational managers (of all grades) and mediation participants. A number of interviewees were selected due to the fact that they had been involved in mediation service interventions and/or worked in areas which had faced particular challenges in respect of workplace conflict. This was supplemented by respondents to the questionnaire who indicated a willingness to be interviewed to discuss their views in greater detail. Overall, 35 interviews were conducted, lasting between 20 and 90 minutes.

Findings

Defining the Problem

NHCT runs three district general hospitals and six community hospitals in addition to a wide range of primary care services provided in the community, employing over 8,900 staff. The organization is relatively highly unionized and a number of trade unions are recognized for collective bargaining purposes. The largest union is UNISON, which represents a wide range of workers including nursing and administrative staff.

According to Trust managers, wasted staff and management time was the greatest perceived cost of conflict. However, there was also some evidence that conflict had a more direct impact on both performance and well-being. Over a third of managers felt that conflict reduced motivation and consequently productivity, while 28% reported that it had a negative impact on decision making. In addition, almost a third felt that it led to increased health costs or staff absence. Strikingly, almost one in five respondents mentioned conflict as having compromised the quality of patient care/experience. Critically, this suggests that the management of conflict has wider strategic implications:

> I feel if we get the staff experience right, then do you know what? We'll never have to worry about the patient experience…a few people that have said to me, "You're not here to be social workers". I said "You're right we're not, but you're not going to be productive if you've got an issue, if there's something wrong with your child or you've had an argument with your partner you know or your mum's ill or you're robbing Peter to pay Paul." (Manager)

There were two main challenges facing the organization in relation to managing conflict. First, managers traditionally lacked the confidence to deal with difficult issues. Managers were worried that addressing poor performance or behaviour would escalate and potentially result in grievances from the staff concerned, undermining their authority. Thus, there could be a tendency towards avoidance:

Some of the staff that we've got, they're quite switched on and they're clued in and the managers feel like they lose the upper hand there so they don't do anything about it, either because they might lose the upper hand, or because they know they're potentially going to get into a bit of a conflict situation… So the easiest way to avoid that fight is to avoid the issue. (HR practitioner)

In addition, operational pressures could 'crowd out' time talking to team members to uncover and resolve complex and difficult issues. Training was identified as a key issue in explaining levels of confidence in managing conflict and, in the past, new managers were not necessarily equipped to deal with difficult issues.

Second, while the application of formal procedure was inevitable in some situations, interview respondents also argued that grievance procedures had been complex, time-consuming and stressful for all involved – and rarely led to clear and accepted outcomes satisfactory either to the aggrieved or those to whom the complaint was directed. Moreover, the ambiguity of resolutions for participants could exacerbate workplace conflict.

If you say put in a grievance against someone because you have been bullied…after the investigation they've no feedback, you don't get any feedback in terms of what actually happened to that person. So yes, the process would have been carried out appropriately but the end result might not be satisfying to the victim….They end up with nothing to say this has been addressed….It gets dragged out a lot and it brings in a lot of people and it is quite expensive. (Manager)

These issues should also be viewed in the context of increasing pressure – both in terms of costs and government imposed targets – on all NHS organizations in the early 2000s. At NHCT, senior staff became aware of a significant number of cases involving relationship problems between colleagues, and in the 2005 NHS staff survey, 18 % of employees reported experiencing bullying and harassment from other staff and 42 % suffered from workplace stress. Both of these were above the average level for acute trusts in the NHS.

Addressing the Problem

To begin with, the organization established an internal mediation service. In total, 19 members of staff were trained, drawn from a range of posts including consultants, managers, nurses, HR staff and trade union representatives. This reflected a deliberate attempt to embed the service in different areas of the organization. Critically, the service was coordinated, not by HR practitioners, but by a consultant occupational health psychologist. She argued that mediation was important in providing an alternative to conventional grievance handling:

> We did want [mediation] to be a first port of call, rather than grievances, because…we used to see a lot of people who were heartily sick of the only option for them was to go down a formal route, and often that was what they were advised by their staff side rep who was also feeling pretty hopeless about that, as the only option too, causing stress and inordinate amounts of time off…

In broad terms, trade union representatives welcomed the idea of mediation and saw a need to explore less formal channels of resolution which were less time consuming and arguably obtained more positive results for their members:

> It [mediation] was something that we were keen to look at because we were conscious that there were a number of grievances and disciplinaries that are incredibly time-consuming and incredibly expensive as much as anything else and we just thought that there must have been a way of trying to resolve this without going down the formal route… (Trade union representative)

Locating mediation outside the HR department was argued to be particularly significant as the occupational health psychologists were seen to occupy an impartial role associated with employee well-being, thus helping to encourage buy-in from trade union representatives and staff in general. This stemmed from a belief that conflict and how it was managed were indeed closely related to broader issues of employee well-being, and from the outset the approach reflected priorities that could be seen as strategic rather than transactional, with a clear intention to change the culture of conflict management:

> It was about culture change I think, we thought that really from the outset, that it wasn't just about getting a group of people trained in mediation skills, and providing a service, it was about looking at embedding informal conflict resolution into the whole organization. (Consultant Occupational Health Psychologist)

Therefore, in addition to the mediation service, the conflict management strategy adopted had a number of key elements. First, existing disputes procedures and processes were revised to encourage the use of mediation as an option. In particular, the Dignity at Work Policy, which sought to deal with complaints of bullying and harassment, was redesigned to include not only mediation but to acknowledge the importance of dealing with conflict at work.

Second, a structured and systematic approach to identifying conflict 'hotspots' was introduced by analysing a range of key indicators including: absence rates; turnover; counselling referrals to occupational health; the number of formal disciplinary and grievance cases; the number of violent incidents; conflict; and the existence of organizational change. This information is considered by a Health and Well-being Steering Group which includes representatives from senior management, unions, HR, Occupational Health and the Mediation Service.

Once hotspots are identified, a range of interventions may be considered. These can include a stress risk assessment, potentially followed up by individual mediation(s), targeted training, team facilitation and conflict coaching. Team facilitation involves groups of staff discussing issues that are leading to conflict, facilitated by members of the mediation service and often involving HR and more senior managers. The process is not voluntary and is therefore distinct from individual mediation. In addition, trained mediators can be used to facilitate discussions between two staff members over issues when 'full-blown' mediation may not be deemed necessary. A number of mediators have also been trained as conflict coaches to work closely with individual managers to develop their confidence and capability in handling difficult issues.

Third, training in relation to conflict resolution within teams is offered through the occupational health psychologists, and training in handling difficult conversations is being rolled out to line managers by the HR Department designed and delivered by one of the more experienced workplace mediators (and senior HR managers) in NHCT. Critically, this is a central aspect of the HR strategy and also reflected in the development of key managerial competencies within the organization.

Impact and Outcomes

As with other studies, we found that the direct effects of workplace mediation were largely beneficial. Ninety per cent of mediations were completed with agreement and evaluations from participants were generally positive. A majority of respondents felt that the mediation was effective, and about two-thirds reported that the situation had improved as a result, with 40 % saying that it had improved a lot. This profile was largely supported by qualitative analysis. The interview data certainly suggested that both parties and those who had referred issues to mediation felt it was an effective way of resolving issues without recourse to more complex and lengthy procedures. For some participants, mediation provided a safe environment in which to voice their views and concerns:

> Mediation in my view was very helpful....I felt a lot better solving my issues this way rather than hoping they would solve themselves. I went in nervous, unsure, and came out calm, confident and happy with the results. I felt my issues were solved and it was a great relief for me to be able to talk about these issues and not be judged. (Mediation evaluation)

In some cases, agreements were reached which did not result in a fundamental change in the nature of the relationships. However, mediators accepted that in some instances a pragmatic resolution was both the best outcome that could be attained and a positive step forward:

> [Mediation] can have that kind of resolution that's fantastic and then you get one of those where it's kind of co-operative where you feel like "Yes you're agreeing and probably you're going to stick to it because both of you

want it to work" but from a personal point of view at terms you feel like that's just on the edge of something kicking off again. (Mediator)

As outlined above, other interventions in the form of team facilitations and conflict coaching are used/offered. The former have become quite widely used in response to problems being identified within a particular part of the Trust, and most respondents who had been involved in these felt they had been beneficial to some extent, with senior managers particularly positive about their impact. However, it was also pointed out that facilitations sometimes highlighted deeper issues which then required further action over a longer term via mediation, training or conflict coaching. In this sense team facilitations were commonly one part of a broader intervention.

For example, an HR practitioner explained that a team facilitation had improved relationships but in itself had not dealt with fundamental personality issues that were fuelling conflict:

> I'm aware of a team in my patch who have been through it and I think it did improve overall relationships but then there were specific relationships within that team that were obviously there beforehand and probably influenced the team dynamics generally and they were still there at the end of it....So in that sense it wasn't successful but then it was probably never going to; they probably needed individual mediation. (HR practitioner)

At the time of the study, conflict coaching was relatively new to the organization and it is difficult to provide a detailed evaluation. Nonetheless, the early signs are positive. The same respondent explained that although it was difficult to isolate the impact of the coaching, the individual they had been working with had '*a more open mind*' and '*a much different attitude*', and although they faced similar problems they had '*dealt with them a whole different way*'. Moreover, for one senior manager, conflict coaching had given managers:

> Courage, and actually realizing they are in their right as managers, they have a right to say this, they have a right to expect certain things from staff, rather than always backing down because staff are being aggressive or confrontational. (Manager)

Our research also suggested that involvement in workplace mediation had a positive impact on managers' conflict-handling abilities. Respondents who were trained as mediators believed this had wider benefits for themselves and the organization, and several interviewees believed this had helped them to deal with and manage issues more effectively outside the mediation room:

> I think that helped my management skill a lot and I still rely a lot on the training that I had… I think that's a fundamental skill that should be rolled out to all managers, even in a summary form because it just helped you to think about phrases, sayings, or looking at a particular issue and think…. It just made you think of things differently and made you think about things more carefully; not to jump to assumptions or conclusions, but in terms of dealing with conflict and being calm, rephrasing, I found it an excellent tool. (Mediator)

The evidence from managers suggested that experience of mediation had led most (although not all) to reflect on the way they deal with difficult issues and improve their practice accordingly. For example, one manager who had been involved in an unsuccessful mediation nevertheless had changed their response to conflict:

> I was probably more a person that would reach for the policies and procedures and wait necessarily until someone wanted to make it a formal process, not anymore….I'd spend twenty minutes with someone who's upset or whatever but it doesn't matter, it nips it in the bud, the person has been listened to and we discuss what their options are and what they want to do and what we're going to do going forward. (Manager)

Assessing the Culture of Conflict Management?

As we noted earlier in this chapter, the lack of confidence among line managers can lead to formal and risk-averse approaches to conflict handling. However, there was evidence that a culture of early resolution was embedded within the organization. More than two thirds of survey respondents agreed management generally preferred to deal with problems informally rather than follow formal rules. It was argued that reform to NHCT procedures (outlined above) provides managers with greater scope and encouragement to pursue 'informal' processes of resolution and has reinstalled the 'human element' in conflict handling:

> The policies and procedures gave people...something to hide behind...you didn't have to think, you know it felt like we had a flowchart to work to.... But I think recently I get a sense that people are questioning....Is there something that we can do before we get to the formal process, so it feels as if the human element has come back into it. (Manager)

Furthermore, awareness of the availability of mediation among managers was very high (91% of respondents). Both survey and interview data suggested that while mediation was not embedded everywhere, it had become part of the toolkit for most managers in the Trust:

> [Managers] think, right okay, this is probably a better alternative than going down that...an official path, which takes up such a lot of time. So I think culturally, people now see it as just part of the tool kit they've got as a manager to deal with conflict and difficulty, whereas they didn't before.... So I think there's a change of a...change of cultural acceptance about the way you deal with conflict to some extent. I don't think that's embedded everywhere. (Manager)

It has been found previously that resistance among line managers can be a major barrier to the use and expansion of mediation (Saundry and Wibberley 2014). However, survey responses revealed a positive attitude to mediation. For example, 82% of managers disagreed that 'Mediation is a waste of time' and also that 'Mediation undermines my authority as a manager'. A majority also agreed that mediation improved their ability to manage conflict with just 5% disagreeing (Fig. 15.1).

For the remaining statements, which are broadly positive, the consensus was towards agreement. For example, while many are neutral, the clear balance was in favour of agreement that 'Mediation produces 'win–win' solutions' and, interestingly, that mediation has positively affected workplace culture.

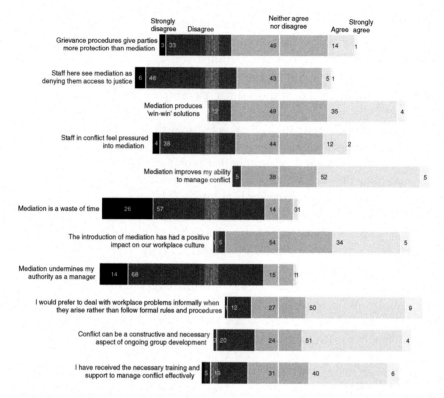

Fig. 15.1 Attitudes towards mediation
Note: N = 199

Respondents were also asked to select from a set of statements the one which they consider most accurately summarized the culture at NHCT in relation to workplace conflict[1] (Table 15.1). While there is some variation, the dominant culture is clearly seen as 'collaborative', that is, involving joint working or problem solving, with a further one in seven saying the culture was 'compromising' (elements of give and take). Few selected more negative cultural descriptors.

---

[1] The statements are adapted from an online conflict audit offered by The Conflict Resolution Centre (http://www.conflictresolutioncentre.co.uk).

Table 15 .1   Perceived workplace conflict culture (ranked by frequency)

Culture	All (per cent)
Collaborative (e.g. joint working/problem solving)	58
Compromising (e.g. demonstrating elements of give and take)	14
Accommodating (e.g. agreement with some element of sacrifice)	9
Resigned (e.g. 'that's the way it is')	8
Ignoring (e.g. paying lip service)	7
Avoidant (e.g. walking away)	3
Aggressive (e.g. shouting or threatening)	1

Note: N = 233

This culture was also reflected in the relationships between key organizational actors and the roles they played in responding to and attempting to resolve workplace conflict. There were very close working relationships between HR, the mediation service and the occupational health team (including psychologists and counsellors). Indeed, the mediation coordinator stressed strong partnership working with the wider occupational health team who use, for example, case conferencing approaches (including managers, HR, staff side) to move cases forward that are stuck because of relationship breakdown at work.

HR practitioners saw early (and where appropriate, informal) resolution as a key objective. This was also informed by mediation principles:

We would always encourage fact find[ing] and meet with the other person to try and unpick all of that and determine an appropriate way forward.... If we had concerns there we would approach an independent person and in other words start off on a kind of facilitative approach. So the mediation principles are often applied in the workplace between the manager, employee, HR, trade union. (HR practitioner)

In general, the relationship between HR and operational and line managers in the UK is often more complicated, with managers sometimes feeling that they are restrained, directed and even policed by the HR function (see Saundry and Wibberley 2014). Within NHCT however, while this was the view of one or two managers, the majority view was that HR played a supportive and constructive role within which managers retained autonomy and authority for decision making:

> You tend to work with different people at different time points, but I have to say I've always found them incredibly supportive. My strategy tends to be that I'd go to them with what I think is a plan and I'll talk them through what's happened, what I'd like their advice on and only then if necessary they'll be the policy and procedure…[but] that's not their starting point you know it's always well have you spoken to that person, it's always the informal approach that's recommended first. (Manager)

Most senior managers and HR business partners enjoyed close and trusting working relationships. One HR manager explained that relationships had improved significantly in recent years:

> There was a very strong sort of push towards partnership working and actually making that meaningful, rather than just "well, we'll talk to staff side". We do genuinely want a good relationship with them and want to involve them in issues and that I think has made a difference, so that I suppose they have confidence that we're going to listen to them and try and resolve things. But they take some responsibility as well and don't necessarily take the entrenched view anymore. (HR practitioner)

Staff side union representatives were also considered to play a positive role in managing conflict. While managers reported that this could again depend on the individual approach taken by the representative, most felt that union presence, particularly in formal situations, was constructive. It was common for managers and union representatives to be able to discuss issues off the record, and this could help managers get to the bottom of an issue or convey clear messages to the employee involved regarding the potential implications of their actions:

> We meet with them [trade unions] on a monthly basis to have a bit of an informal: what's the issues from our perspective, what's the issues from their perspective, are they aligned, are they at loggerheads and what kind of solutions can we explore. (HR practitioner)

Challenges and Barriers

Despite the positive developments outlined above, our findings also pointed to resistance from both employees and managers to the emphasis on informal channels of resolution in general and mediation in particular. From an employee perspective there were concerns that mediation and similar interventions were not necessarily appropriate for serious cases of bullying and could simply cover up mistreatment:

> I found the whole thing traumatic, neither of the other two parties would apologize and once again they have both got away with bullying....I think mediation is a poor substitute for management's handling of bullying in the workplace....What do bullies have to do before they are called to account for their actions? (Mediation evaluation)

This echoes arguments in the literature that the use of mediation in cases where there may be a breach of rights is problematic (Bellman 1998; La Rue 2000; Mareschal 2002) and can simply obscure unacceptable behaviours (Saundry et al. 2013). Employees thus had concerns about entering into mediation. As for the manager survey, this was particularly the case where there is an apparent power relationship; critically, even if mediators are able to create a degree of balance within the mediation room, it does not change the fundamental power balance outside:

> Although it's a facilitated environment, I've had a lot that have come out and said, "Well, I didn't dare say what I wanted to say because I've got to go back and work and this is my line manager". Or, "This is a colleague and I still don't feel it's resolved." So I feel like I've let people down when we haven't been able to find a resolution because they haven't felt confident enough to bring it up. (Mediator)

However, while the majority of managers we interviewed were positive about mediation, some concern was expressed that it had become a default option. Here there were two issues: first, some respondents felt undermined when more senior managers suggested they should attend mediation with staff whose performance they were attempting to address.

This was seen as reflecting a lack of senior support; while being asked to manage performance more pro-actively and deal with misconduct in a more assertive way, if the matter escalated, they felt their judgement would be questioned.

Second, there was a view that while mediation might resolve any personality differences, the performance or conduct issue would remain and would ultimately have to be dealt with. These concerns were encapsulated by the following comment from a line manager who had been asked to attend a mediation session:

> I don't think that I'll get anything out of it, I don't want to go to mediation, I don't even know what the issues are so I don't know what I am going to hear. Which I think is hard because I think if it's going to be something personal then, about you know, that I'd like to prepare myself for it. I think that the performance issues are still there and have to be dealt with so I am not sure if that is going to resolve anything in that way…but I'll go and do it and I think that the member of staff will find it beneficial.' (Manager)

Perhaps not surprisingly, managers often felt that they were expected to attend – that they had 'agreed' rather than volunteered. In fact, a number of managers talked of being 'taken to mediation'. According to one:

> It was clear that it was a voluntary process, I was given the option to step out of it or not get involved in it, absolutely. But it was hurriedly suggested at the time that it wouldn't have been helpful to do that. (Manager)

However, the consultant occupational health psychologist who championed the development of the system of conflict management at NHCT argued that in some circumstances an intervention such as mediation is needed as a way of getting managers to reflect on their practice and to improve the way they communicate with their staff.

Discussion and Conclusion

The findings outlined in this chapter provide further evidence pointing to the efficacy of mediation compared with more conventional rights-based disputes procedures (see also Latreille 2011; Saundry and Wibberley 2014).

Rates of settlement are relatively high, as is participant satisfaction. Mediation also represents a low cost and comparatively speedy way of addressing and resolving conflict.

In the UK, government and the proponents of workplace mediation have suggested it can transform the culture of conflict management. In this case there is evidence that the introduction of workplace mediation provided the basis for a significant change in the way conflict is addressed and managed. Informal and early resolution appears to be embedded within the organization. Furthermore, the survey of managers found that the overriding approach to conflict is one of collaboration. In addition, most managers feel well equipped to deal with conflict, and training both in conflict resolution and handling difficult conversations appears to be making significant inroads, at least within more senior managerial ranks. Critically, there is a view that conflict-handling skills are valued and that conflict management is seen as linked to strategic imperatives in terms of both staff well-being and the delivery of effective patient care.

However, it is equally clear that these advances cannot simply be attributed to the adoption of mediation, but instead to the development of a systemic approach to conflict management and critically to an acceptance by senior management that conflict was a strategic issue inextricably linked to the well-being of both staff and patients. This approach had a number of key features. First, the introduction of mediation was accompanied by the development of the grievance and dignity at work procedures which not only encouraged the use of mediation but underlined a commitment to using informal and alternative methods of resolution. Second, key indicators of workplace stress and conflict are examined systematically by organizational stakeholders, with a range of interventions considered and deployed. Third, conflict management was clearly seen as a strategic issue by senior management, reflected by the importance placed on management training around conflict. Furthermore, people management competencies and core values are increasingly central to recruitment and development within the Trust (Saundry et al. 2014). Taken together, this arguably represents an integrated system of conflict management (Ury et al. 1988; Lipsky et al. 2003).

Of course, challenges remain. The study identifies a number of barriers to effective conflict resolution, the most significant being the role played by front-line and operational managers. Despite, the increased emphasis on training and development, a lack of confidence in addressing difficult issues at an early stage is still an issue, particularly for newer and more junior managers. Furthermore, a context characterized by increasing pressures on managers to increase efficiency and improve performance creates an environment in which conflict is inevitable. In particular, the data suggest that although they are generally positive about early resolution, lower level managers are less convinced than their more senior colleagues as to the use of mediation and other conflict management initiatives. This reflects a tension between the operational pressures they face and the emphasis on less formal and more collaborative approaches to conflict.

Nonetheless, we would argue that this case study has important implications for both policy and practice, and suggests that the impact of mediation can be maximized when used as part of a broader approach that sees workplace conflict as a central issue in staff well-being and engagement. Furthermore, it provides yet more evidence that the involvement of key stakeholders in the design, implementation and delivery of workplace mediation can underpin the development of more constructive and collaborative approaches to conflict resolution.

References

Anderson, J., & Bingham, L. (1997). Upstream effects from mediation of workplace disputes: Some preliminary evidence from the USPS. *Labor Law Journal, 48,* 601–615.

Bellman, H. (1998). Some reflections on the practice of mediation. *Negotiation Journal, 14,* 205–210.

Bingham, L. B. (2004). Employment dispute resolution: The case for mediation. *Conflict Resolution Quarterly, 22*(1–2), 145–174.

Bingham, L. B., Hallberlin, C., Walker, D., & Chung, W. (2009). Dispute system design and justice in employment dispute resolution: Mediation at the workplace. *Harvard Negotiation Law Review, 14,* 1–50.

BIS (Department of Business, Innovation and Skills) (2011). *Resolving workplace disputes: A consultation.* London: BIS.

Bleiman, D. (2008). 'Should I try mediation?' A discussion paper for trade union members. Available from: http://www.scottishmediation.org.uk/downloads/Mediationunionmemberdiscussion.pdf. Accessed 22 August 2008.

CIPD (2008). *Workplace mediation – How employers do it?* London: CIPD.

Colvin, A. J. S. (2003). Institutional pressures, human resource strategies, and the rise of non-union dispute resolution procedures. *Industrial and Labor Relations Review*, 56(3), 375–392.

Corby, S. (1999). *Resolving employment rights disputes through mediation: The New Zealand experience.* London: Institute of Employment Rights.

Gibbons, M. (2007). *A review of employment dispute resolution in Great Britain.* London: DTI.

Harris, L., Tuckman, A. and Snook, J. (2008). Small firms and workplace disputes resolution. *Acas Research Paper*, 01/08.

Johnston, T. (2008). Knowledge and use of mediation in SMEs. *Acas Research Paper*, 02/08.

Kochan, T., Lautsch, B., & Bendersky, C. (2000). An evaluation of the Massachusetts commission against discrimination alternative dispute resolution program. *Harvard Negotiation Law Review*, 5, 233–274.

Kressel, K. (2006). Mediation revisited. In M. Deutsch, & P. Coleman (Eds.), *The handbook of constructive conflict resolution: Theory and practice.* San Francisco: Jossey-Bass.

La Rue, H. (2000). The changing workplace environment in the new millennium: ADR is a dominant trend in the workplace. *Columbia Business Law Review*, 2000(3), 453–498.

Latreille, P. L. (2011). Workplace mediation: A thematic review of the Acas/CIPD evidence. *Acas Research Paper*, 13/11.

Latreille, P., & Saundry, R. (2014). Workplace mediation. In W. K. Roche, P. Teague, & A. Colvin (Eds.), *Oxford handbook of conflict management in organizations.* Oxford: Oxford University Press.

Latreille, P., Buscha, F., & Conte, A. (2012). Are you experienced? SME use of and attitudes towards workplace mediation. *International Journal of Human Resource Management*, 23(3), 590–606.

Lipsky, D., & Seeber, R. (2000). 'Resolving workplace disputes in the United States: The growth of alternative dispute resolution in employment relations' [Electronic version]. *Journal of Alternative Dispute Resolution*, 2, 37–49.

Lipsky, D., Seeber, R., & Fincher, R. (2003). *Emerging systems for managing workplace conflict: Lessons from American Corporations for managers and dispute resolution professionals.* San Francisco: Jossey-Bass.

Lynch, J. F. (2001). Beyond ADR: A systems approach to conflict management. *Negotiation Journal*, 17(3), 207–216.

Lynch, J. (2003). *Are your organization's conflict management practices and integrated conflict management system?*. Available from: http://www.mediate.com//articles/systemsedit3.cfm. Accessed 15 April 2013.

Mareschal, P. (2002). Mastering the art of dispute resolution: Best practices from the FMCS. *International Journal of Public Administration*, *25*, 1351–1377.

Olson-Buchanan, J., & Boswell, W. (2008). An integrative model of experiencing and responding to mistreatment at work. *Academy of Management Review*, *33*(1), 76–96.

Pope, S. (1996). Inviting fortuitous events in mediation: The role of empowerment and recognition. *Mediation Quarterly*, *13*(4), 287–295.

Rahim, N., Brown, A., & Graham, J. (2011). Evaluation of the Acas code of practice on disciplinary and grievance procedures. *Acas Research Paper*, 06/11.

Reynolds, C. (2000). Workplace mediation. In M. Liebmann (Ed.), *Mediation in context*. London: Jessica Kingsley.

Robinson, P., Pearlstein, A., & Mayer, B. (2005). DyADS: Encouraging 'dynamic adaptive dispute systems' in the organized workplace. *Harvard Negotiation Law Review*, *10*, 339–382.

Saundry, R., McArdle, L., & Thomas, P. (2013). Reframing workplace relations? Conflict resolution and mediation in a primary care trust. *Work, Employment and Society*, *27*(2), 221–239.

Saundry, R., & Wibberley, G. (2012). Mediation and informal resolution – A case study in conflict management. *Acas Research Paper*, 12/12.

Saundry, R., & Wibberley, G. (2014). Workplace dispute resolution and the management of individual conflict – A thematic analysis of 5 case studies. *Acas Research Paper*, 06/14.

Seargeant, J. (2005). The Acas small firms mediation pilot: Research to explore parties' experiences and views on the value of mediation. *Acas Research Paper*, 04/05.

Sherman, M. (2003). Mediation, hype and hyperbole: How much should we believe? *Dispute Resolution Journal*, *58*(3), 43–51.

Singletary, C., Shearer, R., & Kuligokski, E. (1995). Securing a durable mediation agreement to settle complex employment disputes. *Labor Law Journal*, *46*, 223–227.

Sulzner, G. (2003). Adjudicators (arbitrators) acting as mediators: An experiment in dispute resolution at the Public Service Staff Relations Board of Canada. *Journal of Collective Negotiations in the Public Sector*, *30*, 59–75.

Ury, W., Brett, J. M., & Goldberg, S. B. (1988). *Getting disputes resolved: Designing systems to cut the costs of conflict*. San Francisco: Jossey-Bass.

Wood, S., Saundry, R., & Latreille, P. (2014). Analysis of the nature, extent and impact of grievance and disciplinary procedures and workplace mediation using WERS2011. *Acas Research Paper*, 10/14.

16

HRM, Organizational Citizenship Behaviour and Conflict Management: The Case of Non-union MNC Subsidiaries in Ireland

Liam Doherty and Paul Teague

Introduction

Over the years, an evergreen in the literature on the management of the employment relationship is the observation that organizations will pay a high price if workplace conflict is not addressed quickly and effectively. Days may be lost to some form of industrial action, sickness and absenteeism rates can be high, and management–employee relations can become strained if not embittered. Just what constitutes an effective approach to managing workplace conflict has always been the subject of debate. But there has been a fair amount of agreement that it involves HR managers establishing a range of formal procedures to address disputes and grievances (Turnbull 2008). At the moment, a popular theme in the relevant literature is that many organizations

P. Teague
Queens Management School, Queens University Belfast, Belfast, UK
e-mail: P.Teague@qub.ac.uk

L. Doherty
Resolve Ireland, Dubline, Republic of Ireland
e-mail: Liam@resolveireland.ie

© The Editor(s) (if applicable) and The Author(s) 2016   **339**
R. Saundry et al. (eds.), *Reframing Resolution*,
DOI 10.1057/978-1-137-51560-5_16

are seeking to upgrade these traditional formal procedures by diffusing new ADR practices and processes (Lewin 2008). The argument is that workplace conflict has become more small-scale and individual in character, which needs to be addressed by new conflict management strategies.

A healthy debate has emerged about the extent to which, and in what ways, organizations are diffusing innovative conflict management practices. Although important, we should not get transfixed about these discussions as equally significant other developments are emerging in relation to workplace conflict management. This paper suggests that one important new development that has yet to receive the attention it deserves, is attempts by HR managers in some organizations to delegitimize workplace conflict. Instead of modernizing conflict management practices to take account of new forms of disputes and grievances at work, the purpose of this HR strategy is to socialize conflict out of the organization by promoting a form of organizational citizenship behaviour that seeks to create a socio-psychological community consisting of common internal organizational beliefs, values, attitudes and even loyalties: employees and management work together, hand-in-hand, to realize shared objectives; employment relations are harmonious and consensual. The corollary of creating this type of 'unitarist' organization, which Alan Fox (1966) talked about so long ago, is that conflict at the workplace is frowned on as it undermines efforts at creating collaboration inside the firm. As a result, a key feature of the organizational citizenship behaviour promulgated by this form of HR strategy is that negative consequences await employees who use formal dispute resolution procedures.

The chapter is organized as follows. The first section explains why the creation of organizational citizenship behaviour is an important, yet underexplored, goal of the HR function in organizations. The following section explores the relationship between organizational citizenship behaviour and conflict management, with a particular focus on the implications for the former if organizations adopt workplace ADR practices to address conflict. The subsequent section presents details of the research methodology employed to gather data on the extent to which subsidiaries of non-union multinationals are diffusing innovative conflict management practices. The fourth section sets out the main descriptive statistics that emerge from the survey and discusses the import of the findings. The next section explains why it was considered important to interview senior HRM managers in some of the surveyed subsidiaries and presents the findings of these interviews. The conclusions discuss the significance of the findings and bring together the arguments of the chapter.

HRM and Organizational Citizenship Behaviour

Discussions about the nature of HRM in organizations over the past decade or so have been dominated by two interrelated themes. One is the organizational design of the HRM function (see Ulrich et al. 2009). Issues that figure prominently in this part of the literature include the need to create shared services or centres of excellence; develop more integrated ties between HR and line managers; and revamp organizational architectures to create differentiated workforces. The other is the type of employment practices that need to be adopted to create high performing organizations and employees. The literature is now brimming with studies of how HR managers need to combine employment practices that fit together, horizontally and vertically, to create high performance organizations (see Wall and Wood 2005).

Some of this literature – though by no means all – provides rich insights into the activities of modern HR managers. However, a matter that does not receive the attention that perhaps is merited concerns the role of the HR function in developing the social structure of the organization so that employee attitudes and behaviours are aligned with the objectives of the enterprise. It has long been understood that to function properly organizations need social systems that shape internal hierarchies (particularly in terms of power and status), define the boundaries between permissible and non-permissible behaviour, develop cognitive frames to allow organizational members to understand the demands placed upon them, and promote certain values to give rise to a particular organizational culture (see Stinchcomb 1965).

Relatively little has been written about how and in what ways the HRM function contributes to the shaping of the social system of an organization. One notable exception is an interesting paper by Bowen and Ostroff (2004), who argue that a key responsibility of HR managers is to use the HR system to cultivate an organizational climate that aligns the collective behaviour of employees with the core business objectives of the organization. They suggest this is done by organizations developing HR systems that are customized to meet their distinctive needs, encouraging managers to behave consistently and even-handedly, and promoting consensus decision-making that empowers employees. Although in general agreement with Bowen and Ostroff, we wish to develop a slightly different argument by suggesting that a core function of HRM is to mould the social system of the organization in a manner that promotes organizational citizenship behaviour.

The concept of organizational citizenship behaviour has been around the organizational studies literature for some time now. Although defined in different ways, studies on the topic tend to focus on broadly similar issues. Thus, Podsakoff et al. (2000) identify seven recurring themes in the related literature: helping behaviour; sportsmanship; organizational loyalty; organizational compliance; individual initiative; civic virtue; and self-development. As can be gleaned from these themes, organizational citizenship behaviour is about employees coming to view their own career advancement being intertwined with the success of their employing organization. Thus, it is about employees who willingly help each other, tolerate the day-to-day hassles at the workplace, support (and even occasionally defend) the mission of the organization, internalize positively organizational rules and procedures, 'go above and beyond the call of duty' to advance organizational performance, and strive to develop their own attributes and abilities.

Thus, organizational citizenship behaviour manifests itself in employees having a positive commitment to the organization and displaying ongoing discretionary effort to help the organization achieve its goals. A key goal of HRM is to elicit this behaviour (Ulrich 1997). It seeks to do so by creating a belief system in the organization that orients employees towards the mission of the organization by defining it for them and by identifying its salient features. A set of cognitive lenses are created by a battery of interlinked organizational practices and processes through which employees come to understand what organizational values and behaviour they are expected to uphold.

Organizations seem to focus on a number of broadly similar policies to build organizational citizenship behaviour. Thus, for example, the entire thrust of the highly fashionable policy of employee engagement is to engender organizational loyalty among employees and to encourage them 'to go the extra mile' for the organization (see MacLeod Review 2009). Other policies that have recently come to the fore can also be viewed as primarily about promoting organizational citizenship behaviour.

The strong emphasis currently placed on coaching and mentoring at the workplace is about nothing if it is not about managers interacting with employees to encourage them to improve their own capabilities and work efforts so that continuous improvements can be realized in the organization (Anderson et al. 2009). Similarly, the shift towards competency models in human resource development is motivated to provide employees not simply with narrow technical or cognitive skills, but also with a set of behavioural capabilities that are aligned with organizational objectives (Wright and McMahan 2011). Thus, there is evidence of HRM professionals pursuing policies that seek to create a symbiosis between employee behaviour and organizational performance.

At the same time, it would be misleading to suggest that HRM managers have a neatly prescribed set of policies which they follow to cultivate organizational citizenship behaviour. There are healthy, ongoing debates about the extent to which particular HR people policies will engender positive employee behaviour (Caldwell 2003). Thus, considerable disagreement exists in the profession about the extent to which performance-related pay schemes foster employee commitment and loyalty (see Kochan 2007).

Workplace conflict is another area where different views exist about what needs to be done to advance organizational citizenship behaviour. One view that has gained popularity, mostly in the USA, is that firms are forging a 'new social contract' at work by diffusing alternative dispute resolution (ADR) practices to solve workplace conflict (Lipsky and Seeber 2003). In relation to organizational citizenship behaviour, this development suggests that the best way to gain employee commitment and loyalty is by HR managers recognizing that workplace conflict will be part and parcel of organizational life and thus establishing formal arrangements for it to be resolved properly (Bendersky 2003). This view tends to stand apart from the more orthodox view that workplace conflict can prevent organizations – particularly those that are non-union – from developing a unitarist culture which manifests itself in high levels of cooperation between managers and employers (see Lewin 1987).

Thus, there appears to be some uncertainty about the strategies HR managers should employ in the area of workplace conflict in order to forge organizational citizenship behaviour. The purpose of this chapter is to investigate this matter in detail. It does so examining the manner in which workplace conflict has been addressed by the subsidiaries of non-union multinationals in Ireland. These organizations were selected for two reasons. On the one hand, multinationals are widely considered to be carriers of state-of-the-art HR policies and thus a good weathervane of the nature of HR innovations in particular areas (see Festing and Eidems 2011). On the other hand, non-union organizations are widely considered to be open vessels for the diffusion of ADR-type conflict management strategies (see Rowe 1997). Before this assessment can begin, however, it is necessary to provide some commentary on how workplace conflict is managed in non-union organizations.

Conflict Management in Non-union Organizations

One argument is that many non-union organizations, particularly those following state-of-the-art strategic HRM policies, are developing innovative conflict management practices and procedures that provide employees with a range of formal avenues to pursue grievances (Lipsky and Seeber 2003). Non-union firms are seen to be motivated by a number of factors when creating these formal arrangements: (1) to stave off a perceived trade union organizing threat; (2) to diffuse a battery of soft HRM strategies, including conflict management procedures; (3) to create conflict management procedures to accommodate the growing preference on the part of employees for conflict management practices that are more individual in focus and confidential; and (4) to improve internal conflict management procedures in order to avoid disputes going to public dispute resolution bodies. Thus, there is a line of argument in the HRM literature that suggests non-union firms are at the forefront of innovative action to create formal conflict management policies (see Dundon and Rollinson 2004).

A fair amount of consensus exists that the innovative activity occurring involves the diffusion of innovative ADR practices (Colvin 2003). Table 16.1 sets out the practices most associated with the ADR approach to workplace conflict management. As can be seen, ADR practices for workplace

Table **16.1**   ADR workplace resolution procedures

Ombudsman	A designated 'neutral' third party inside an organization assigned the role of assisting the resolution of a grievance or conflict situation. The activities of an ombudsman include fact-finding, providing counselling and conciliation between disputing parties. High grade persuasion skills are the key asset of a good ombudsman
Mediation	A process under the stewardship of a third party designed to help those involved in a dispute reach a mutually acceptable settlement. The third party has no direct authority in the process and is limited to proposing or suggesting options that may open a pathway to a mutually agreeable resolution
Peer Review	A panel composed of appropriate employees or employees and managers which listens to the competing arguments in a dispute, reflects upon the available evidence and proposes a resolution. Whether or not the decision of the panel is binding varies across organizations
Management Review Boards	Sometimes called dispute resolution boards, these panels are solely composed of managers and have more or less the same remit as peer reviews. Again the decision of the panel may or may not be final
Arbitration	A neutral third party is empowered to adjudicate in a dispute and set out a resolution to the conflict. This may or may not be binding depending upon the prevailing labour legislation and the design of the arbitration process

conflict do not throw overboard tried and tested methods of resolving disputes. Established methods of reaching settlements to workplace grievances – mediation, conciliation, arbitration and so on – are at the centre of many ADR procedures used to address workplace conflict, but these are designed and packaged in new ways. Thus, ADR is probably best seen as an umbrella term to capture new initiatives that are being introduced by organizations – mostly non-union organizations – to modernize workplace conflict management arrangements (Teague and Thomas 2008). It is these arrangements that are seen to be at the centre of innovative workplace conflict management by non-union firms.

Establishing formal workplace ADR practices to resolve problems and disputes quickly and fairly is likely to impinge on the model of organizational citizenship behaviour that takes shape in an organization. By creating workplace ADR structures, HR managers are effectively recognizing that conflict will emerge in the workplace. Accepting that managers and employees will not always see eye to eye cuts against a model of organizational citizenship behaviour predicated on the idea that managers and employees will have common beliefs, values, attitudes. It is at least tacit recognition that the best way to secure employee commitment and loyalty is to create workplace institutions predicated on procedural and substantive fairness. In non-union firms, these institutions are unlikely to be heavily collectivist in orientation, but to be credible they cannot be seen as organs of managerial interests. A variant of this argument is pursued by Lipsky and Avgar (2008). They suggest that the dominant trend in USA is for large organizations to adopt a strategic approach to workplace conflict by diffusing various combinations of ADR practices. The effect of these innovations, they argue, has been to rewrite the rules of organizational citizenship behaviour that involves some form of institutionalized conflict management strategies.

The Survey and Data

We decided to investigate this line of argument outside the United States (US) context through a survey of 83 subsidiaries of non-union foreign-owned multinationals located in Ireland. Selecting the sample for the survey was complicated and time-consuming. As a number of other researchers have also noted, there is no one comprehensive database that lists the number of foreign-owned multinationals in the country (McDonnell et al. 2007). As a result, the second best alternative was employed and a list was compiled drawing from a range of sources, including IDA Ireland, Enterprise Ireland, Irish Times List of Top One Thousand Companies, IBEC, The American Chamber of Commerce and Dun & Bradstreet. This exercise yielded a population of 472 multinational companies. The next task was to separate out unionized multinationals and non-unionized multinationals.

Advice was sought from officials of trade unions and employer organizations, HR consultants and staff from public dispute resolution bodies on whether or not particular multinationals were unionized or non-unionized. At the end of this process we obtained a population of 143 non-union multinationals. Then a sample of 90 multinationals was randomly selected weighted by sector, country of origin and size. Getting access to non-unionized firms to discuss their human resource management regimes is notoriously difficult. Through the use of contacts, persistence and good fortune we were able to gain access to 83 multinationals; seven companies simply did not want to participate in the survey. Given the nature of the topic, securing a sample of 83 non-unionized multinationals is considered to be a significant achievement.

It was decided to administer the survey through face-to-face interviews due to the length of the survey and the nature of the topic. The survey sought to obtain information on a range of topics, including: the characteristics of the multinationals; the formal and informal dimensions to the conflict management systems; the motivation behind setting up their particular form of conflict management system; the type of issues that can be raised under the conflict management system; the extent to which innovative conflict management practices have been diffused; the nature of the representation afforded to employees involved in workplace problems; training provided for managers and employees on problem-solving and conflict management; the extent to which workplace conflict inside the multinational reaches the public dispute resolution agencies; and the systems used to evaluate the effectiveness of the system. Initially, the survey contained questions about the incidence of conflict in multinationals and how these were resolved, but a pilot survey found that companies were not willing to answer these questions and to try and obtain such information might jeopardize access. Thus, it was decided to omit these questions. As a result, the survey relates mostly to the architecture of the conflict management systems in non-union multinationals.

Conflict Management Systems in Non-union Multinationals

This section sets out the findings relating to the core characteristics of conflict management systems in non-union multinationals in Ireland. Six features of these systems are worthy of note. First of all, over 90 % of organizations surveyed had a formal HR department and, as Table 16.2 shows, the overwhelming majority had formal policies to address workplace

Table 16.2 The formality of conflict management systems in non-union multinationals

Does your company have a formal policy to resolve employment related problems or disputes that arise with staff?	98 %
Is your company's problem solving process provided for in	
Employment contracts	47 %
Company handbook	86 %
Management policy	28 %
Other	11 %
Does your organization have a formal bully & harassment policy	96 %
if yes, is a problem solving procedure specified?	94 %
Does your organization have a formal grievance procedure?	100 %
if yes, is a problem solving/appeals procedure specified?	98 %
Does your organization have a formal disciplinary procedure?	100 %
if yes, is an appeals procedure specified?	94 %

disputes and grievances in their organizations. This result is not surprising: putting in place formalized procedures relating to workplace conflict is now seen as standard human resource practice to comply properly with various aspects of employment law (Dobbin and Kelly 2007) and to meet minimum standards of procedural justice at the workplace. As relatively sophisticated organizations it would be expected that non-unionized multinationals would meet this basic threshold.

A second feature of conflict management systems in non-unionized multinationals that is worthy of comment is the extent to which these organizations use a wide range of techniques or innovatory, ADR-inspired, procedures when seeking to resolve workplace problems. Table 16.3 provides information on these matters. Two important findings emerge from the table. First, only a minority of non-union organizations – roughly about 25 % of those surveyed – use a wide variety of conflict management techniques, ranging from facilitation to arbitration. Second, these organizations cannot be considered adopters of ADR-inspired approaches to conflict resolution. Almost all surveyed firms say that they operate an open door policy, which is minimally in line with ADR workplace conflict resolution practices. But only about a quarter say they use peer

Table 16.3 Conflict management techniques
and procedures in non-union multinationals

	Frequency (%)
Mediation	39.5
Facilitation	43.2
Arbitration	18.5
Employee hotline	25.9
Open door policy	97.5
Management review	65.4
Peer review	16.0
Ombudsperson	6.2

review methods to solve disputes. A very small number – four all told – of multinationals make use of an ombudsperson to help solve employment disputes and grievances, despite this procedure being touted in the literature as a highly effective mechanism to solve workplace problems (Rowe and Simon 2001). Thus, the main message from this table is that non-union multinationals are not operating what are widely considered to be innovative conflict management strategies. The table also suggests that management is eager to remain in control of the conflict management process: progressive forms of management review appear to be the norm, and few organizations engage external people to help solve problems.

A third feature that needs highlighting is the motivations behind non-union multinationals creating their particular conflict management system. Probably the main view in the literature is that these systems are devised as part of a wider strategy to keep out unions (Stone 1999). But other literature suggests non-union organizations are also motivated by additional factors such as complying with the requirements of legislation and wanting to create arrangements that strengthen employee morale and confidence in the organization (Rowe 1997). Table 16.4 provides information on the motivations for non-union multinationals in creating their distinctive conflict management system. The striking fact that emerges from this table is that union avoidance is not identified by managers as a big consideration: seeking to create a system in which employees have confidence and which is capable of solving disputes internally are the two most important factors. A cynical view would be that HR managers are unlikely to admit to wanting to keep trade unions

Table 16.4   Primary motivations for introducing a particular form of conflict management system

What were the primary motivations for introducing the particular form of conflict management system in your company? (rank top 1, 2, 3 in order of importance)

	Rank 1	Rank 2	Rank 3	No	Missing
Comply with employment legislation	22	14	13	29	5
To avoid employees using the state machinery	0	5	6	67	5
As part of union avoidance	6	4	10	58	5
Corporate initiative	5	3	7	63	5
To enhance employee satisfaction and morale	28	18	8	24	5
To resolve matters in house if possible	18	26	16	18	5
Precipitation event	2	2	6	68	5
Local HR/management champion	3	4	6	65	5
Other	0	0	0	78	5

at bay. There is no way of verifying this claim and the reported views of management suggest that they are motivated to establish what they perceive as a fair and efficient conflict management system.

A fourth aspect of the conflict management systems of non-union multinationals that can be gleaned from the survey is the extent to which employees involved in a conflict are permitted to have representation during the process, a core feature of procedural justice at work. Table 16.5 shows that the overwhelming number of organizations in the survey possesses conflict management procedures which all employees can access and which allow parties to use representation. However, less than a quarter of non-union multinationals permit employees to use trade unions during the process; more firms allow employees to use solicitors than trade unions. The norm appears to be for employees to use a work colleague during the conflict resolution process, while just over half of companies allow human resource managers to represent employees. Overall, the table shows that non-union multinationals constrain the option of independent representation in the management of disputes by employees.

A fifth feature of the survey that is worth commentary upon is the extent to which there is an informal dimension to conflict management systems in non-union multinationals. Table 16.6 sets out information on this matter. A number of interesting points emerge from the table.

Table 16.5 Employees, representation and conflict management systems in organizations

Can all employees access the company's problem solving process?	91.6 %
Is there a service requirement before employees who can access the company's problem solving process?	3.6 %
Can an employee have a representative at the company's problem solving process?	94 %
if Yes, who can potentially represent the employee?	
Work colleague	90.4 %
HR representative	48.2 %
Solicitor	34.9 %
Trade union official	22.9 %
Any person of their choosing acting in a personal capacity	44.6 %
Other	6 %

Table 16.6 Informal problem solving and dispute resolution in processes

Does your organization have 'informal' problem solving mechanisms to detect employee grievances?	96.4 %
If yes, does this involve any of the following:	
Conducting regular employment audits with employees	32.5 %
The organization of focus groups	35 %
HR personnel interacting with employees on an informal basis	87.5 %
Line managers responsible for interacting with employees on an informal basis	86.3 %
Other	20 %
Does the organization follow an informal problem solving procedure to obtain a speedy resolution to an employment grievance?	95.2 %
If yes, does this involve any of the following:	
The immediate manager/supervisor meeting the involved parties	94.9 %
HR personnel meeting the involved parties	80.8 %
Other	10.3 %
Are all employment related matters covered by the informal problem solving procedures?	
Yes, all covered	72.3 %
Yes, some covered	21.7 %
No	2.4 %
How are the informal problem solving procedures monitored and evaluated?	
Through an organized HR policy	15.7 %
Informal feedback between HR and employees	62.7 %
Informal feedback between line managers and HR	78.3 %
Other	10.8 %

Nearly all the surveyed multinationals suggest that they have an informal dimension to their conflict management system, which the vast majority say covers nearly all issues. In almost all cases, middle managers appear to be the lynchpin of informal arrangements, which is in line with a core tenet of HRM thinking that argues middle managers should be at the front end of managing the employment relationship. Only in a minority of multinationals does there appear to be an organized connection between the formal and informal dimensions to conflict management. In addition, the majority of organizations do not monitor the informal process in any systematic manner: the emphasis is very much on word-of-mouth interactions between different tiers of management. Moreover, only about a third of organizations seek to evaluate the informal process systematically through the use of audits or focus groups. Thus, although the informal dimension is a large aspect of conflict management systems, it does not appear to be organized to any great extent.

A number of important conclusions emerge from these descriptive statistics. Probably the most notable finding is that non-union subsidiaries of multinationals located in Ireland are not using ADR practices to address workplace conflict, at least not in any substantial way. Nor is there evidence of the subsidiaries following any type of sophisticated or innovative conflict management practices: these organizations are not big HRM innovators in the area of conflict management. For the most part, the subsidiaries use relatively standard, unexceptional formal and informal conflict management practices. The common pattern that emerges is of multinational subsidiaries possessing traditional formal grievance and disciplinary procedures while at the same time expecting line managers to try and settle disputes informally. These findings are at odds not only with a lot of literature on employment relations in Ireland that portrays multinational subsidiaries as the carriers of leading edge HR strategies including conflict management, but also with the important strand of the international literature which suggests organizations are using ADR practices as part of a HR wider strategy. Such strategies are simply not being used by non-union MNC subsidiaries in Ireland, at least not to any significant extent.

Getting a View from the Inside

These findings are illuminating, but they also beg a number of questions. Why are non-union subsidiaries not adopting ADR or other innovative conflict management practices in any systematic manner? Does the overwhelming use of fairly mainstream approaches to disputes and grievances reflect a 'satisficing' strategy on the part of HR managers in these organizations – persisting with tried-and-tested practices that are broadly effective even though more state-of-the-art practices are available? If this were the case, then it would suggest that HR managers do not conceive conflict management as part of the repertoire of policies needed to create some form of organizational citizenship behaviour or a high performance organization more generally. Or does the use of relatively standard conflict management practices mask a different type of interaction or dynamic between conflict management and organizational citizenship behaviour not fully captured by the survey?

Thus, to gain fuller insight into the meaning of the survey findings, it was considered prudent to examine further why non-union multinationals subsidiaries located in Ireland are not engaging in workplace conflict management innovation. To this end, it was decided to conduct a series of in-depth interviews with senior HR managers in some of the subsidiaries that took part in the original survey to find out more about their approach to workplace conflict management. A preliminary target list of 22 organizations was identified. Following consultations with employer organizations, CIPD and experienced HR consultants, the list was reduced to a target group of 10 organizations, all of which had been located in Ireland for more than five years. Contact was made with the organizations and all agreed to be interviewed. The interviewees were in all cases the most senior site HR representative in Ireland (HR Director or HR Manager) as these people were considered best placed to comment on the organization's conflict management system.

The interviews sought to obtain information on a number of important matters. The first point that became evident was that organizational context had a big influence on the views of the HR managers on workplace conflict. The fact that the HR managers worked for non-union MNC subsidiaries had an important influence on the lack of innovation on conflict management. To be successful, MNC subsidiaries increasingly have to engage in a form of subsidiary entrepreneurship to maintain their business mandate. In this context, HR managers were reluctant to make the business case for innovative conflict management policies as it might be construed by the MNC headquarters as the subsidiary not being able to deal effectively with organizational problems. Most HR managers were of the view that developing a business case for innovative conflict management policies could work against the subsidiary when competing in the future for investment with other sister sites; as one manager put it: '*Why would we give them the ammunition to shoot us with?*'

A second organizational context that needs recognizing is the non-union status of the organizations. Virtually all the HR managers considered non-union organizations as operating in a fundamentally different way to unionized organizations. In particular, non-union organizations were considered to be less bureaucratic, allowing for pro-active HR practices to be enacted systematically. One manager put it like this:

> HRM in unionized companies expect to be challenged by Trade Unions. HRMs in non-union companies will generally work to drive innovation in their people strategy to match their culture. Therefore different skill sets and mindsets are required. We hire bright people and we need to create an environment in which they can be free to comment.

To set the scene, the HR managers were asked to rank on a scale of 1–10 whether their organization adopted a strategic approach to the management of people. This question was considered appropriate, for if organizations did not consider themselves as following a strategic HR approach, then it would hardly be surprising that they did not pursue innovative conflict management policies. Nine HR managers ranked their organizations either 8 or 9 in terms of pursuing strategic HR policies and practices. Only one HR manager rated their organization as a 7. Thus the HR managers were firmly of the view that their organizations adopted a strategic approach to HRM matters.

The HR managers were then asked whether innovative conflict management was a priority area for strategic HR action. Only 2 out of the 10 HR managers interviewed were of the view that conflict management was a very important matter for HR strategy. None of the HR managers considered conflict management more important than other aspects of their HR strategy, including recruitment and selection, performance, employee communication and engagement. Only two companies viewed it as being of equal importance, both of which were manufacturing facilities with a perceived exposure to union organizing efforts. Eight HR managers stated that they regarded conflict management as less important than other areas of HR management, which is a clear indication that most non-union subsidiaries do not see any significant role for the problem solving/dispute resolution system in their organization.

HR managers were also asked if conflict management was the least important HR function. Overwhelmingly, the managers stated that no other HR practice was less important than conflict management. The typical attitude is captured by one HR manager who said:

> None – I would not invest resources in it compared to recruitment, development or reward.

Only one organization was anxious to position their problem solving/ dispute resolution system as equivalent to other HR processes. These findings strongly suggest that when it comes to allocating scarce HR resources or considering innovative HR action, problem solving and dispute resolution is way down the pecking order if not at the bottom. One fairly blunt representative view was that '*It does not merit a line in our HR strategy.*'

All the HR managers were clear as to why their organizations did not consider conflict management a priority area for HR action. A strong consensus emerged on this matter, and all 10 managers pointed to two factors. One was that the language of dispute resolution and conflict management did not fit with the culture that their organization was seeking to promulgate. The aversion displayed to using the language associated with workplace conflict was vividly captured by the comment of one HR manager when he suggested that discussing disputes and grievances was analogous to '*culture contamination*'.

Thus, workplace conflict was seen in a wholly negative light; a symptom of management failure that had the potential to corrode good working relationships in the organization and in the process damage business performance. Because HR managers wanted to avoid using the language of conflict, they had no appetite to develop innovative workplace conflict practices, which would signal to employees that conflict management was a strategic priority for the HRM function. For most, using language associated with conflict was seen as creating a more permissive organizational environment for its emergence, which would cut against efforts aimed at building an integrated, harmonious organizational culture where the interests of employees and employers are overlapping. For the most part, the language of conflict management was considered the preserve of the unionized sector. Thus, the interviewed HR managers regarded workplace conflict as deviant and did not want to do much to institutionalize its acceptability.

The second factor highlighted by the HR managers to explain why conflict management innovations were so thin on the ground was the absence of a 'compelling business case' for such initiatives. Most were of the view that no innovation was occurring on conflict management simply because there was no persuasive case for it; as one respondent put it: '*We simply do not feel the need at this stage.*'

Another argument made was that the focus on conflict management was *passé*: if anything, HR managers interviewed were of the view that their goal was to squeeze conflict out of the organization by stressing the virtues of common purpose and working together. Thus, some HR managers stated that they would prefer to use any available resources to drive an employee engagement agenda to foster mutual cooperation between employees and managers. For example, one HR manager said that he would prefer to build positive and healthy working relationships:

> I would focus on creating a work environment in which people can feel free to raise any issues without fear or concern for their future.

But, the flipside of cultivating a positive working environment where employees felt engaged was a fairly negative, hard-line attitude towards employees using the formal grievance procedure. One HR manager was fairly representative when he stated that:

The grievance procedure is for people that do not have a future in our organization.

In other words, although all the organizations interviewed had a formal grievance policy, the near unanimous view was that it very much represented the default position. Employees were not only expected to exhaust all other methods before invoking the procedure, but also to realize that once they had done so they had crossed a rubicon. For the HR managers, an employee pursuing a grievance was in violation of organizational citizenship behaviour and even if the problem was resolved, would be unlikely to display the required trust and loyalty to the organization in the future.

All in all, there was little appetite to introduce any new or innovative workplace conflict management practices. Certainly none of the HRM managers were engaging in any way with workplace ADR. As one dismissively suggested:

In my opinion...the literature is too aspirational and is certainly not grounded in the organization I work in.

The emphasis was very much on resolving conflict internally within the organization and in a manner consistent with organizational culture. HR managers said strenuous efforts would be made to avoid an employment grievance or dispute ending up in front of an employment tribunal or any other public dispute resolution agency. There was even reluctance to use external experts that might assist in the resolution of a dispute or grievance. Thus one HR manager said:

It would be counter-cultural to have a structured external role formalized within our procedures. People choose to buy into our culture – we do not give them the formal option of an external person.

The views emerging from the interviews were consistent with the main findings of the larger questionnaire that innovative conflict management practices – particularly those inspired by ADR thinking – are not being diffused in the subsidiaries of non-union multinationals in Ireland.

On the surface, it appears that the main reason why no concerted innovative action was taking place was because of the low incidence of workplace conflict or problems: HR managers did not consider workplace problems and disputes as a problem area requiring strategic interventions. But this is only part of the story, as nearly all the interviewed HR managers were very much focused on building a belief system in their organization in which conflict and disputes were considered deviant. The emphasis was very much on building a culture that promoted key elements of organizational citizenship behaviour, employee loyalty, mutual support and reciprocity. HR managers wanted disputes to be resolved informally and quickly, for employees to see dealing with hassles and problems as a day-to-day organizational routine. The use of formal processes to solve grievances was cultivated as an organizational taboo. Certainly the HR managers were eager to keep the use of formal processes as low as possible to prevent these acquiring any level of legitimacy as a way to address problems. There was even a level of professional contempt for conflict management policies, generally viewed as part of the HR toolbox from a bygone era, ill-suited to modern organizations and the challenges they face.

Conclusions

A number of important conclusions arise from this study. Perhaps the most revealing conclusion is that, for the most part, subsidiaries of non-union multinationals based in Ireland do not systematically use innovative workplace conflict management practices. Certainly there has been no widespread diffusion of ADR-type practices to resolve problems and disputes at work. Why have subsidiaries of non-union MNCs' abstained from adopting innovative conflict management practices? At first blush, the evidence from the survey and the interviews seems to suggest that that there is no need for such innovative practices as the incidence of workplace problems and disputes was low: in other words, there was no 'business case' for innovative workplace conflict management practices. However, this assessment was viewed as unpersuasive.

During the interviews with HR managers a different picture started to emerge. First of all, it was evident that the HR managers had a deep antipathy to the 'conflict management' paradigm, seen as a throwback to the old days of personnel management, strong unions and widespread industrial action. None of the HR managers viewed conflict management as part of the package of policies needed for the HR function to be strategic in character. For these HR managers, conflict management has become the poor cousin of HRM; there is a family association, but it is not talked about if at all possible. As a result, most of the HR managers did not want the language of conflict or conflict management to be used in the organization as they considered nothing positive could come from it. Thus a common endeavour was to expunge conflict from the vocabulary of the organization.

In nearly all organizations, the HR managers sought to socialize conflict out of the organization by trying to create organic communities where all members shared common beliefs, values, attitudes and even loyalties. Through policies like employee engagement, the HR managers wanted to create organizational citizenship behaviour that fostered among employees a sense of belonging to the organization, a feeling of duty to other employees, an obligation to contribute something to the core mission of the organization. This form of organizational citizenship behaviour does not recognize the inevitably of conflict or the need for formal, easily accessible, procedures to manage conflict management, which is the main thrust of the argument for ADR at the workplace, and evident in other contributions in this volume. Instead, it is a form of organizational citizenship behaviour that seeks to push conflict to the margins, framing it almost as dissident behaviour. The expectation is that employees will shake off any problems, perhaps occasionally with the help of line managers, quickly and informally, treating it as one of the hassles that may be encountered in the hurly-burly of everyday working life.

From this perspective, the HR managers are far from 'satisficing' on workplace conflict, prepared to go along with bog standard dispute resolution practices. They are being highly innovative on the matter of conflict management, but not in the way suggested by the dominant themes in the literature. It is not about turning their organizations into bleak houses where a form of authoritarian management prevails. At the same time, it is not accepting of the view that one of the best methods of signalling to employees that the organization is serious about fairness and justice is to create credible procedures for the resolution of conflict at work. It is about focusing HR efforts on promoting organizational citizenship behaviour which puts at a premium employee compliance with the core goals of the organization. Conflict management procedures are not abandoned in this approach, but are kept dormant in the HR cupboard only to be used in exceptional circumstances. Thus the innovative activity by HR management on workplace conflict in these organizations is almost exclusively concerned with downgrading its importance, if not to de-legitimatize its incidence.

References

Anderson, V., Rayner, C., & Schyns, B. (2009). *Coaching at the sharp end: The role of line managers in coaching at work*. London: CIPD.

Bendersky, C. (2003). Organizational dispute resolution systems: A complementarities model. *Academy of Management Review, 28*(3), 643–656.

Bowen, D., & Ostroff, C. (2004). Understanding the HRM-firm performance linkages: The role of the strength of the HRM system. *Academy of Management Review, 29*(2), 203–221.

Caldwell, R. (2003). The changing roles of personnel: Old ambiguities, new uncertainties. *Journal of Management Studies, 40*(4), 983–1004.

Colvin, A. (2003). Institutional pressures, human resource management and the rise of non-union dispute resolution procedures. *Industrial and Labor Relations Review, 56*(3), 375–392.

Dobbin, F., & Kelly, E. (2007). How to stop harassment: The professional construction of legal compliance in organizations. *American Journal of Sociology, 112*(7), 1203–1243.

Dundon, T., & Rollinson, D. (2004). *Employment relations in non-union firms*. London: Routledge.

Festing, M., & Eidems, J. (2011). A process perspective on transnational HRM systems – A dynamic capability-based analysis. *Human Resource Management Review, 21*(1), 162–173.

Fox, A. (1966). *Industrial sociology and industrial relations*. London: HMSO.

Kochan, T. A. (2007). Social legitimacy of the HRM profession: A US perspective. In P. Boxall, J. Purcell, & P. Wright (Eds.), *The Oxford handbook of human resource management*. Oxford: Oxford University Press.

Lewin, D. (1987). Dispute resolution in the non-union firm. *Journal of Conflict Resolution, 31*(3), 465–501.

Lewin, D. (2008). Workplace ADR: What's new and what matters? In S. E. Befort, & P. Halter (Eds.), *Workplace justice for a changing environment, Proceedings of the 60th Annual Meeting, National Academy of Arbitrators.* Washington, DC: Bureau of National Affairs.

Lipsky, D., & Seeber, R. (2003). The social contract and dispute management: The transformation of the social contract in the US workplace and the emergence of new strategies of dispute management. *International Employment Relations Review, 9*(2), 87–109.

Lipsky, D. B., & Avgar, A. C. (2008). Toward a strategic theory of workplace conflict management. *Ohio State Journal on Dispute Resolution, 24*(1), 143–190.

McDonnell, A., Lavelle, J., Collings, D. , & Gunningle, P. (2007) Management research on multinational companies: A methodological critique and blueprint for the future. Paper to the *10th Annual Conference of the Irish Academy of Management,* Queen's University Belfast.

MacLeod Review (2009). *Engaging for success.* London: HMSO.

Podsakoff, P. M., MacKenzie, S. B., Paine, J. B., & Bachrach, D. G. (2000). Organizational citizenship behaviors: A critical review of the theoretical and empirical literature and suggestions for future research. *Journal of Management, 26*(3), 513–563.

Rowe, M. (1997). Dispute resolution in the non-union environment: An evolution toward integrated systems for conflict management? In S. Gleason (Ed.), *Frontiers in dispute resolution in labor relations and human resources.* Michigan: Michigan State University Press.

Rowe, M., & Simon, M. (2001). Effectiveness of organizational ombudsmen. In *Handbook of the Ombudsman Association.* Hillsborough: Ombudsman Association.

Stinchcomb, A. (1965). Social structure and organization. In J. March (Ed.), *Handbook of industrial organization.* Chicago: Rand McNally.

Stone, K. (1999). Employment arbitration under the Federal Arbitration Act. In A. E. Eaton, & J. H. Keefe (Eds.), *Employment dispute resolution and worker rights in the changing workplace.* Industrial Relations Research Association: Madison.

Teague, P., & Thomas, D. (2008). *Employment standard-setting and dispute resolution.* Dublin: Oak Tree Press.

Turnbull, P. (2008). Industrial conflict. In N. Bacon, P. Blyton, J. Fiorito, & E. Heery (Eds.), *Handbook of industrial and employment relations*. London: Sage.

Ulrich, D. (1997). *Human resource champions: The next agenda for delivering value and delivering results*. Boston: Harvard Business School Press.

Ulrich, D., Allen, J., Brockbank, W., Younger, J., & Nyman, M. (2009). *HR transformation: Building human resources from the outside in*. New York: McGraw Hill.

Wall, T., & Wood, S. (2005). The romance of HRM and business performance and the case for Big Science. *Human Relations, 58*(1), 29–62.

Wright, P., & McMahan, G. (2011). Exploring human capital: Putting human back into strategic human resource management. *Human Resource Management Journal, 21*(2), 93–104.

Erratum to: Reframing Resolution

Richard Saundry • Paul Latreille • Ian Ashman

DOI 10.1057/978-1-137-51560-5

The foreword which is missing in the book is given below:

FOREWORD

In the public and policy imagination, conflict at work has perhaps tended to be pigeon-holed as synonymous with industrial action. It is true that strikes—threatened and actual—were important markers in the manifestation of conflict across the lion's share of the last century and this remains the case albeit with reduced incidence. But workplace conflict is a more complex phenomenon than this. Conflict can be a response to

---

The updated original online version for this book can be found at
DOI 10.1057/978-1-137-51560-5

---

a very varied set of influences. These include the economic and policy environment in which organisations operate through to a response to a perceived imbalance in power relations, or simply a difference of opinion between individuals.

It follows that the question of how to manage conflict, and resolve disputes, is central to organisational effectiveness, and requires the kind of strategic approach currently followed for other business and operational questions. And beyond the workplace itself, conflict management remains an important area for research and empirical investigation. Acas recognises the value of both best practice inside the workplace and the significant role that research and analysis can play in shaping the future of this agenda. Indeed, the knowledge gained from practical experience and research has always been crucial to informing Acas' approach to fulfilling its statutory responsibilities. These duties, set out 40 years ago in the Employment Protection Acas of 1975, are the promotion of good industrial relations and providing assistance to support parties in resolving differences through conciliation, mediation and arbitration services.

Our commitment to excellence in these areas, promoting productive workplaces and a high quality of working life, remains our central concern. We learn about what works best through our daily exposure to workplaces, but also through research and analysis of trends and behaviours. And I am delighted to see much of the Acas commissioned research featured in this publication.

There are some aspects of the conflict at work that we are well sighted on. For instance, the Office for National Statistics manages an important data source on the incidence of strikes in the UK, and the Employment Tribunal statistics alongside Acas data provide a record of aspects of collective and individualised workplace conflict. The internationally recognised Workplace Employment Relations Studies, dating back to 1980, provides a supplementary evidence base on the incidence of conflict via the prism of the workplace. All these sources are reviewed in this volume and presented alongside informed commentary and analysis. This evidence is supplemented by data from overseas, and by evidence from surveys and qualitative data from a multitude of projects. Collectively they provide a rich picture of trends in conflict, and the evolving nature of dispute resolution. There are also some longstanding gaps in what we know about conflict at work. These include the availability of systematic data on the incidence of less visible forms of conflict, and disputes that remain unaddressed but which nonetheless have a potentially damaging impact on workplace relations. This volume is particularly important for identifying gaps in our knowledge and helping to shape the future research agenda.

The depth and breadth of the book, its rigour and insight, are commendable. In our fortieth year, the volume offers a timely contribution in assisting Acas to reflect on the structural, policy and practical influences that have shaped the way conflict is handled in the modern workplace. This will provide a vital resource as we look to the future and to development of conflict management strategies that fit with organisations and reflect the changing world of work. Crucially, the book makes important observations about the diffusion of new practices. We are particularly attracted to those practical solutions that offer expedient and non-adversarial routes to addressing disputes. The further embedding of such practices, and the value of identifying new approaches, offers a challenge for Acas, and others with an interest in workplace relations. And this volume will provide a starting point for stimulating debate and improving practice.

I believe that the value of this important publication will soon be recognised by all those with an interest in this vital field of enquiry. I am grateful to all the contributors for their work, and particularly to the editors for their individual contributions to this field of enquiry over a protracted period.

Sir Brendan Barber, Chair of Acas

Conclusion: The Future of Conflict Management and Resolution

In some respects, the evidence presented in the early part of this book confirms long-standing trends in the pattern of workplace conflict. As John Forth and Gill Dix explain clearly in Chap. 3, there has been a rapid and fundamental decline in the incidence of collective expressions of conflict both in the UK and other developed economies. While the explanations for this decline are complex, it undoubtedly reflects the erosion of trade union organization and bargaining power. In its place there has been increasing attention paid to the incidence and nature of individual employment disputes. In the UK, for example, the declining prevalence of strike action has been accompanied by a rapid expansion in the volume of legal claims to employment tribunals, but we would argue that this does not reflect simply the individualization of employment relations, rather, as John Forth and Gill Dix suggest, it is a manifestation of the likelihood that many individual workplace issues and disputes are essentially collective in character. Ultimately it is the channels through which conflict develops, is handled and eventually resolved that have been individualized.

© The Editor(s) (if applicable) and The Author(s) 2016   **363**
R. Saundry et al. (eds.), *Reframing Resolution*,
DOI 10.1057/978-1-137-51560-5

This is important because, whereas conflict has been traditionally resolved through collective and social processes of negotiation, accommodation and resolution, it is now generally either subject to individual manager–subordinate relations or individualized rights-based grievance and disciplinary procedures. Either way, it is fundamentally dependent upon managerial discretion and prerogative, such that the possibility of informal resolution hangs on the existence of high-trust relationships between managers and other stakeholders. In this sense, the findings in Chap. 4 from Jonny Gifford, Matthew Gould, Paul Latreille and Peter Urwin, which suggest that smaller organizations are less likely to experience conflict are not surprising – here the strong and close networks of relationships among employees, or the social capital that Ariel Avgar, Eric Neuman and Wonjoon Chung highlight in Chap. 5, may be seen to be crucial in preventing conflict and facilitating resolution where it does become manifest. As organizations grow and such social ties begin to become stretched, weaken and even break, so the likelihood of conflict increases.

The dilution of these 'social structures' poses significant challenges for larger organizations where, conventionally, working relationships have been constituted in workplace institutions through which conflict is regulated collectively and whereby relationships between trade union representatives and senior managers and/or HR practitioners are developed. It is true that, even accounting for the gradual decline of collective bargaining, there still exist relatively high-trust relationships in many workplaces through which conflict can be resolved. Nevertheless, as Gemma Wibberley and Richard Saundry contend in Chap. 7, effective structures of representation, and not just voice, play a critical role in sustaining informal social processes of resolution. Employee representatives provide an early warning system of conflict allowing intervention at the earliest opportunity. They can also manage the expectations of members and they can unfreeze defensive attitudes by providing an objective and legitimate perspective. Importantly, Wibberley and Saundry's research finds that managers overwhelmingly see employee representation as a help rather than a hindrance.

There is a clear conclusion from the research presented in this book that the web of relationships underpinning the potential for early and informal resolution is progressively unravelling. The erosion of union organization means that fewer workplaces recognize trade unions and, even in those that do, workplace representatives are less likely to be found 'on the ground.' At the same time significant changes to the nature of the HR function have weakened their role in conflict resolution. The devolution of people management responsibilities has exposed a lack of confidence and competence among front line managers now expected to handle such issues. Carol Jones and Richard Saundry point out in Chap. 6 that this means that managers are less likely to pursue creative and informal routes to resolution and instead seek protection from HR and/or the rigid application of procedure. Furthermore, the rationalization and centralization of HR management, sometimes under a banner of becoming more 'strategic,' has in effect increased the distance between HR support, operational managers and (where they are present) employee representatives. Among the uncertainty and challenge of downsizing initiatives, Ian Ashman (Chap. 8) identifies a similar pattern in the relationship between HR professionals and line managers in public sector organizations. In short, the social capital and associated trust and mutuality identified by Ariel Avgar and his colleagues, and so vital for effective resolution, is less likely to be created under such circumstances. Isolated managers will inevitably, it seems, become increasingly conservative and risk averse, with relations between them, unions and more 'remote' HR functions likely to be undermined by distrust and the consequent danger that HR advice will become generic and lack context; ingredients for a vicious circle that may incubate rather than prevent and resolve conflict.

It is in this setting that workplace mediation and other forms of ADR have developed. It is notable, as David Lipsky, Ariel Avgar and Ryan Lamare point out in Chap. 14, that various ADR practices have penetrated and developed quickly in non-unionized workplaces in the USA where, perhaps, the collective frame and relationships discussed above have been less prevalent and remain so. In non-union settings, mediation, ADR and systemic approaches to conflict management may have been introduced to provide mechanisms not only to resolve disputes but also to ward off the threat of union organization by providing a channel for employee voice and access to equity and workplace justice. The contributions in this book from Tony Bennett and Virginia Branney

(Chaps. 9 and 10) question the extent to which mediation delivers 'justice' for disputants and certainly it would seem that union representatives are reluctant to countenance the idea of mediation replacing existing formal and legalistic protocols through which they believe employees' rights can be enforced more robustly. Nonetheless, the case for mediation extends beyond an immediate and narrow cost saving agenda, although there is some evidence that mediation does deliver pragmatic and timely resolutions that 'get people back to work,' and that it can also provide enhanced employee voice, better outcomes for all disputants than might otherwise be achieved in its absence and can, in some circumstances, be used to challenge managerial behaviours.

The wider potential benefits of mediation processes are also examined in Bill Roche's study of the use of 'assisted bargaining' in Ireland (Chap. 12) to intervene in emerging disputes between employers and trade unions. While conventionally, mediation has been used in collective disputes as a last resort, here the intervention of a third party at an early stage in the process helped to develop concrete solutions to conflict but also cement engagement between the parties. Critically, alternative dispute resolution in this context was not a way of warding off collective regulation or organization but was aimed at increasing the effectiveness of collective bargaining. In Australia too, there is evidence of innovation in the management of disputes, with the public Fair Work Commission implementing a range of initiatives, notably in response to the growing numbers of unrepresented tribunal claimants. These include measures grouped under the headings of prevention mechanisms, approaches to dispute handling, and strategic developments. While sharing the imperative in the UK towards reducing the number of (unwarranted) claims and enhancing the efficacy of the processes with which these are handled, the discourse appears altogether different, with clear evidence in the Australian context that these have been designed with the aim of supporting parties in making effective and appropriate decisions.

On the other hand, as Louise McArdle and Pete Thomas argue in Chap. 13, mediation is certainly not a panacea, and generalizable evidence of its transformative powers remain elusive. That said, where mediation and ADR is used as a foundation for a more systematic and strategic approach to conflict management, it has been shown to have the potential to shape both corporate and managerial attitudes. Certainly, this is the conclusion reached by Paul Latreille and Richard Saundry in Chap. 15. In the specific case that they examine, mediation and mediation skills were used flexibly and in a targeted way to intervene in situations in which conflict was developing. So, rather than being deployed to resolve disputes, it was part of a broader effort to increase the conflict management capacity of the organization. However, the case also shows that simply introducing an integrated 'conflict management system' was not enough on its own because its impact was dependent on context and, critically, a belief among managers and key stakeholders that it was a fundamental part of achieving wider organizational objectives, such as improved patient care. In some respects their case study reflects the conclusion of David Lipsky, Ariel Avgar and Ryan Lamare (Chap. 14) who explain the apparent growth of integrated conflict management systems in the USA, not in terms of risk minimization, but strategic choice.

The future of conflict management is in some ways shaped by its past in two main respects. First, in many organizations, the traditional institutions of negotiation and accommodation no longer function or are under significant strain. Second, the networks of relationships that foster informal social processes of resolution have become increasingly stretched. These institutions and social structures developed because conflict was acknowledged as an inevitable part of organizational life. However, as Liam Doherty and Paul Teague contend in Chap. 16, in some workplaces conflict is simply not part of the organizational discourse. Not only is the management of conflict not seen as central in achieving wider goals of efficiency, engagement and well-being, but it is viewed as an admission of failure and inadequacy. Therefore, the prognosis for the diffusion of innovative approaches to conflict management is likely to rest on senior managerial leaders accepting not only the inevitability of conflict as a part of organizational life, but that the way it is managed shapes employee well-being, engagement and consequently performance.

Index[1]

---

[1] Note: Figures are show in *italics*; tables in **bold**.

© The Editor(s) (if applicable) and The Author(s) 2016
R. Saundry et al. (eds.), *Reframing Resolution*,
DOI 10.1057/978-1-137-51560-5

Printed by Printforce, the Netherlands